The Afterlife of Ottoman Europe

Stanford Studies on Central and Eastern Europe
Edited by Norman Naimark and Larry Wolff

The Afterlife of Ottoman Europe
Muslims in Habsburg Bosnia Herzegovina

Leyla Amzi-Erdoğdular

Stanford University Press
Stanford, California

Stanford University Press
Stanford, California

© 2024 by Leyla Amzi-Erdoğdular. All rights reserved.

No part of this book may be reproduced or transmitted in any form or by any means, electronic or mechanical, including photocopying and recording, or in any information storage or retrieval system, without the prior written permission of Stanford University Press.

ISBN 9781503645899

First paperback printing, 2026

The Library of Congress has cataloged the hardcover edition as follows:
Names: Amzi-Erdoğdular, Leyla, author.
Title: The Afterlife of Ottoman Europe: Muslims in Habsburg Bosnia Herzegovina / Leyla Amzi-Erdoğdular.
Other titles: Stanford studies on Central and Eastern Europe.
Description: Stanford, California : Stanford University Press, [2024] | Series: Stanford studies on Central and Eastern Europe | Includes bibliographical references and index.
Identifiers: LCCN 2023003009 (print) | LCCN 2023003010 (ebook) | ISBN 9781503636705 (cloth) | ISBN 9781503637245 (ebook)
Subjects: LCSH: Muslims—Bosnia and Herzegovina—History. | Bosnia and Herzegovina—History—1878-1918. | Bosnia and Herzegovina—Relations—Turkey. | Turkey—Relations—Bosnia and Herzegovina. | Austria—History—1867-1918.
Classification: LCC DR1674.M87 A49 2024 (print) | LCC DR1674.M87 (ebook) | DDC 305.6/97094974209034—dc23/eng/20230124
LC record available at https://lccn.loc.gov/2023003009
LC ebook record available at https://lccn.loc.gov/2023003010

Cover photograph: Interior of Kiraethana, 1901

The authorized representative in the EU for product safety and compliance is: Mare Nostrum Group B.V. | Mauritskade 21D | 1091 GC Amsterdam | The Netherlands | Email address: gpsr@mare-nostrum.co.uk | KVK chamber of commerce number: 96249943

Contents

Note on Transliteration and Names		vii
Acknowledgments		ix
Map 1. Habsburg Bosnia Herzegovina		xi
Map 2. Ottoman and Habsburg Empires, 1909		xii
	Introduction	1
1	Diplomacies of Separation	19
2	Migration: Those Who Left	49
3	Hijra: Views and Debates on Migration	81
4	Competing Empires	108
5	Negotiating Imperial Ties: Mobilization and Politics	140
6	Allegiances and Final Separation	169
	Epilogue: Alternative Muslim Modernities	200
	Notes	231
	Bibliography	279
	Index	307

Note on Transliteration and Names

Ottoman Turkish, Turkish, Bosnian/Croatian/Serbian, and Arabic transliteration systems are used throughout the book. For Ottoman Turkish and Bosnian written in Arabic script, modern Turkish and Bosnian transliteration is used whenever possible. Exceptions are words commonly used in English in their original form, such as pasha, and not *paşa* (Turkish) or *paša* (Bosnian). For terms that are commonly known in English in their Arabic form, I used the IJMES standard transliteration guide, so it is shari'a and not *şeriat* (Turkish) or *šerijat* (Bosnian). I used language-specific transliteration when it referred to the context of the region and language: it is *vakuf* and *medresa* (Bosnian), *vakıf* and *medrese* (Turkish), and *waqf* and *madrasa* (Arabic).

Proper names are kept in the form that would have been used in the individuals' cultural and linguistic circles, so it is Šerif in Bosnian and Cemal in Turkish. For place names, I used modern-day names, so it is Skopje instead of the Ottoman and Turkish Üsküp, and Dubrovnik instead of Ragusa. I also used English versions and transliterations if they are commonly known (such as Mecca and not Mekke, and Salonica instead of modern-day Thessaloniki and Ottoman Selanik). Bosnia and Bosnia Herzegovina are used interchangeably, but Herzegovina used alone refers to the actual region. Ottoman calendar dates have been converted to Gregorian.

Transliterations that might appear unusual should be considered in their context. For simplicity, Cyrillic script is transliterated in Latin. Unless noted otherwise, I have done the translations for all text that is not published in English.

Acknowledgments

The Afterlife of Ottoman Europe would not have been possible without the support of family, friends, mentors, and scholars who were vital on this journey. My mentors—Mark Mazower, Nader Sohrabi, Christine Philliou, Rashid Khalidi, and Timothy Mitchell—shaped my thinking about empire and encouraged the early development of this project. In New York, Istanbul, and Sarajevo, friends and colleagues offered encouragement, helped me develop my ideas, and provided support in research and writing of this book. I am thankful for Faiz Ahmed, Cemil Aydın, Zeinab Azarbadegan, Isa Blumi, Lale Can, Šeila Domljanović, Damir Imamović, Adnan Kadrić, Elektra Kostopoulou, Milena Methodieva, Mostafa Minawi, Tsolin Nalbantian, Piro Rexhepi, and Amina Šiljak-Jesenković. Discussions with Harun Buljina, Edin Hajdarpašić, David Henig, Dženita Karić, and Ana Sekulić expanded my understanding of Bosnian studies. I am grateful for their support, their insightful commentary, and their humor.

I would like to acknowledge my colleagues in the Department of History at Rutgers University–Newark who created a nurturing environment and Christina Strasburger for her ingenuity and exuberance. I am thankful to my colleagues in Middle Eastern and Islamic Studies, especially Nükhet Varlık and Mayte Green-Mercado for their friendship and support every step of the way. Zeynep Çelik encouraged and supported me in crucial ways. Her intellectual rigor and impact on Ottoman studies served as an inspiration over the years, and I am grateful for her friendship and the opportunity to work with her.

Research for this book was conducted in the archives and libraries in Bosnia Herzegovina and Turkey. In Bosnia Herzegovina I would like to thank the staff at Archives of Bosnia-Herzegovina; Sarajevo Historical Archives; Gazi Husrev-beg Library; and the Bosniak Institute in Sarajevo. In Istanbul, my thanks go to Ayten Ardel, Fuat Recep, Yıldırım Ağanoğlu, Seyit Ali Kahraman, at the Ottoman Archives and the staff of Beyazit Library and ISAM Centre for Islamic Studies.

Material from the Epilogue originally appeared in my "Alternative Muslim Modernities: Bosnian Intellectuals in Two Empires" in *Comparative Studies in Society and History* 59:4 (2017). The research and writing of this book were made possible by grants from the Fulbright-Hays Program, the Institute of Turkish Studies, the American Council of Learned Societies, and the Middle East Institute at Columbia University. I would like to express my appreciation to the Rutgers University Research Council for their help with publication. I thank Margo Irvin and the team at Stanford University Press, who are wonderful to work with. I was pleased that editors Larry Wolff and Norman Naimark appreciated my project and included it in the series.

My deep gratitude is to my family—Ferida, Alush, Selma, and Adem—for their unconditional love and encouragement, and to Kamile, Ömer, Aslı, and Ali for always being there for me.

This book exists because of Ahmet's infinite love and support that carried me through the tribulations of this journey along with Zeynep, Zehra, and Mehmet Ali, who are as old as this project. *The Afterlife of Ottoman Europe* is dedicated to them.

MAP 1. Habsburg Bosnia Herzegovina.

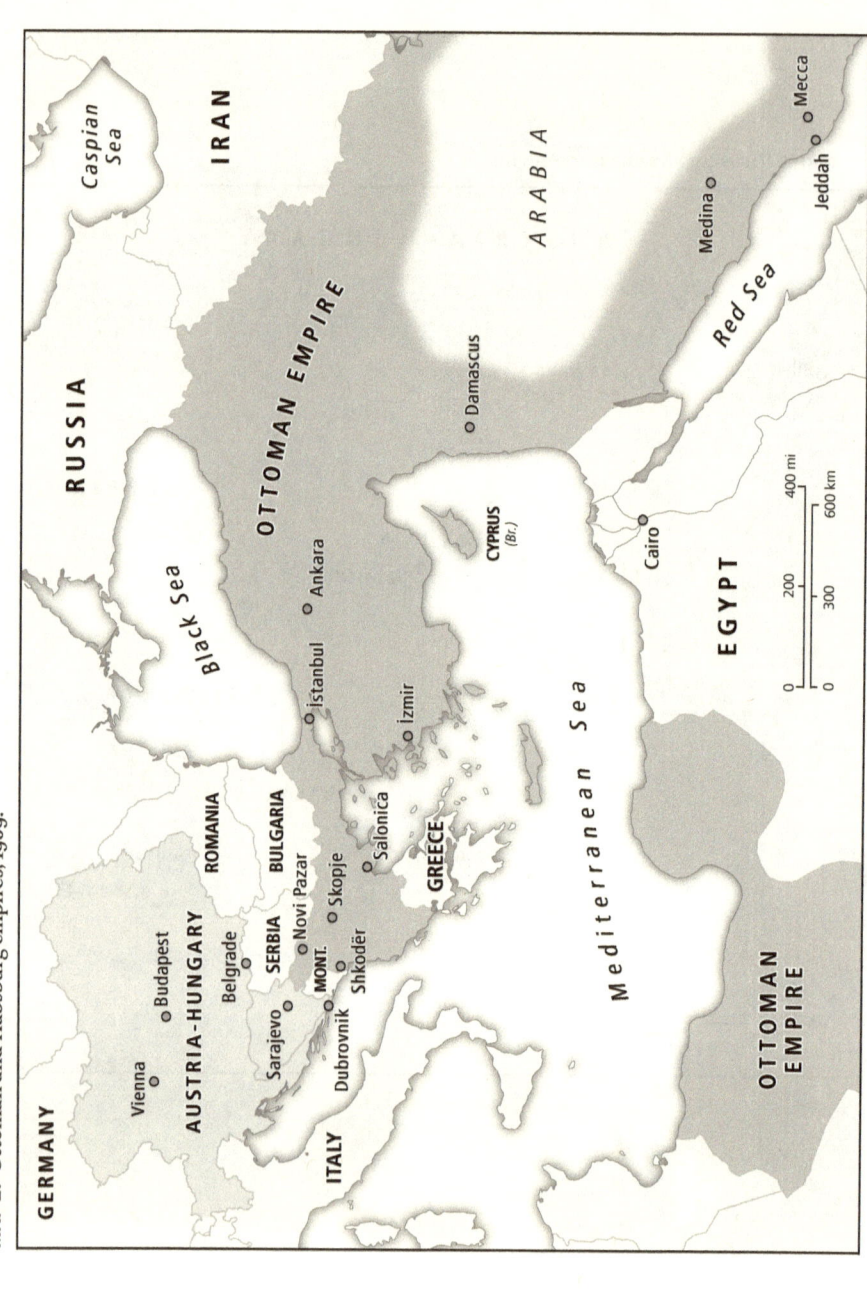

MAP 2. Ottoman and Habsburg empires, 1909.

The Afterlife of Ottoman Europe

Introduction

WHEN THE FORMER TURKISH foreign minister Ahmet Davutoğlu spent the Muslim holiday of Eid al-Fitr in Bosnia Herzegovina in 2011—symbolizing the new Turkish foreign policy approach that has since been labeled "neo-Ottomanism"—he evoked emotional reactions from officials and the general public. He attended the congregational prayer on the occasion of Bajram, as Eid is known in Bosnian and Turkish, held in the early sixteenth-century Gazi Husrev-beg Mosque, restored to its glory after it was targeted during the siege of Sarajevo in the Serbian aggression war of 1992–1995. The historic mosque is situated in the Baščaršija district, Ottoman Sarajevo's bazaar and core of the city, built in the fifteenth century. With Davutoğlu in attendance, the Reis ul-ulema Mustafa Cerić (the highest Muslim religious authority in Bosnia Herzegovina) stated in his sermon, "Today was a day for which we have waited for centuries." According to accounts, after the Eid prayer, an elderly man approached the foreign minister. After shaking his hand, he asked: "Where have you been? You are 150 years late!"

Less than 150 years earlier, in 1878, the Ottoman Empire had reluctantly accepted the stipulations of the Berlin Treaty that relinquished its province of Bosnia Herzegovina to Austria-Hungary without any specifics on extent or duration of the mandate. This understanding achieved at the Congress of Berlin created a number of gray areas in which the Habsburg and

Ottoman empires attempted to assert claims and maintain their spheres of interest. Because the occupation and administration were new and legally vague concepts, both empires and their shared subjects had an opportunity to exploit the ambiguities. Milestones in the Habsburg takeover of the province—the initial military occupation (1878), conscription (1882), and annexation (1908)—were also causes of international controversy that led the two empires to throw around their diplomatic weight. Subjects reacted by inciting further diplomatic action to secure their positions within both empires. As a result of the ambiguities of the Berlin Treaty, the province remained nominally under the sovereign authority of the Ottoman sultan until 1908. Taking advantage of the turmoil during the Young Turk Revolution, Austria-Hungary annexed the province and fully incorporated it into their domains, remaining so until the monarchy's dissolution in 1918.

The Habsburg occupation of Bosnia Herzegovina was markedly different from other territorial losses in Ottoman Europe. Ottoman withdrawal from Eastern Europe since the late seventeenth century was concurrent with the process of de-Islamization of the lost peoples and regions, making this consistent method so common that it is still overlooked by contemporary scholars who discount the practice as expected without considering its concrete consequences. Upon Habsburg occupation of Bosnia Herzegovina however, the Muslim population was protected by the incoming administration and was considered vital for the Habsburg plans in the province. This is in contrast to the experiences of Muslims in post-Ottoman Greece, Serbia, Romania, and Bulgaria. In those regions, even after wartime violence targeting them, the remaining Muslims continued to be victims of policies meant to exclude and ultimately expel them in order to make the new nation-states ethnically and religiously uniform, which would, in turn, solidify the new nations' claims to land.

Bosnia's diversity fascinated European travelers, although the rest of the Ottoman Balkans were just as diverse, if not more so, in terms of religious and linguistic variety. While nation-states carved out of Ottoman Europe worked to homogenize their populations after separating from the Ottoman Empire, Bosnia Herzegovina was able to preserve its diversity—and specifically its Muslim population—precisely because of Habsburg rule. The Habsburg administration hoped for Muslim cooperation in disengaging the province from the Ottoman Empire and incorporating it into Habsburg domains. The policies focused on attracting and persuading Bosnian Muslims to seek patronage from the Habsburg emperor in order to view him, not the sultan, as protector of Bosnian Muslim interests. This unique situation in the former Ottoman Balkans, where Muslims continued to command political presence, allowed Bosnian Muslims to actively strengthen their place and to reinvent their ties to the Ottomans; they were in a relatively comfortable position compared to that of Muslims in other post-Ottoman nation-states.

The Afterlife of Ottoman Europe: Muslims in Habsburg Bosnia Herzegovina explores the Ottoman continuities—cultural, social, and political—during the Habsburg administration, and the enduring influence of the Ottoman Empire, an influence perpetuated by the imperial state from afar and supported by the empire's former subjects in Bosnia Herzegovina. In particular, this book focuses on the ways that Bosnia's Muslims responded to new sociopolitical circumstances and navigated their Habsburg and Ottoman loyalties. In concentrating on Bosnia Herzegovina after the Berlin Congress, the chapters that follow analyze the Ottomans' efforts to maintain their sphere of influence in the region through a deep reliance on Muslim loyalties. They show how the Ottoman experience transformed in reaction to the strategic and political circumstances that overlapped with the context of the Habsburg Monarchy.

The aim of the 1878 Berlin Congress was to resolve what European states had come to call the Eastern Question of Turkey in Europe, which they situated in the discourse of "liberation of a people from the spiritual domination of the Ottomans" and "progress of the West toward the East."[1] Ottoman efforts to implement reforms, centralize their administration, and suppress peasant uprisings were all grouped together to form a new European understanding that the Ottomans were unable to rule their Balkan provinces, and specifically their Christian subjects. In the words of Karl Marx, the Balkans were a "splendid territory [that] has the misfortune to be inhabited by a conglomerate of different races and nationalities, of which it is hard to say which is the least fit for progress and civilization," and where the "attempts at civilization by Turkish authority" have failed due to the "fanaticism of Islam."[2] Similarly, the rise of the Eastern Question was to be found in the presence of an "alien substance," that is, the "Ottoman Turk," in the "living flesh of Europe."[3] Although explicit Orientalism that juxtaposed the civilized West to the barbaric East, with overtures of Islamic "fanaticism," have faded from scholarly literature, the historical paradigm set at this time continues to burden Balkan historiography into the twenty-first century.[4] Maria Todorova observed this "remarkable similarity" and "amazing continuity" in rendering the Ottoman Empire backward and any problematic phenomena to be a consequence of its legacies.[5] Historians, then, to appeal to nineteenth-century European intellectual sensibilities, constructed a record of nationalist struggle impeded by a foreign "Asiatic" empire.[6]

The constant equating of Ottoman with Islamic and Turkish in historical and political discourses not only rendered established Muslim communities across the Balkans as alien but also stigmatized religion, architecture, language, arts, and other regional aspects of Ottoman heritage as backward—leading to policies of "de-Ottomanization" and "de-Islamization," and justifying ethnic cleansing and genocide.[7] Denying the role of the Ottoman past in the Balkans' historical and cultural legacy continues in nation-state historiographies serving to repudiate the imperial hybridity and communal experience of the region.[8] For much of the twentieth century, scholars treated Muslims in southeastern Europe as an anomalous remnant of Ottoman rule and the site of the East–West encounter—as a symbolic bridge and occasionally the physical location of a clash of civilizations. Others concentrated on nationalist narratives, developmentalism, and models of state rule over ethnic and religious minorities. None, however, addressed Muslims' own endeavors to grapple with the changing circumstances and their reconfigured ties with the former imperial center. That is the focus of this book.

Muslims in Ottoman and Habsburg Bosnia Herzegovina
The geographic boundaries of Bosnia Herzegovina that were established after the Berlin Congress roughly corresponded to the province's Ottoman borders, with the exceptions of border areas of Herzegovina awarded to Montenegro in 1878 and Novi Pazar Sandžak (Ottoman Turkish *sancak*, meaning district), which remained Ottoman. The parameters of Habsburg Bosnia Herzegovina continue today as the borders of independent Bosnia Herzegovina.[9] The Ottoman and Habsburg administrations both surveyed the population of the province in confessional terms: they distinguished Muslims, Orthodox Christians, Catholics, Jews, and Roma.[10] These classifi-

cations stemmed from what is broadly considered as the Ottoman *"millet system,"* yet the Habsburg administration continued to group the Bosnian population according to religion, and not language, as it did in its other domains. Bosnia's population approximations in the mid-nineteenth century range from 900,000 to 1,050,000, and these doubled by the second decade of the twentieth century.[11] Despite overall population growth, the size of the Muslim population declined to less than 40 percent of the total population (measured in Habsburg censuses) as a result of uprisings, war, and migrations in the volatile period of 1875–1878.[12]

Over a period of four decades, Bosnian Muslims transformed from prominent members of the Ottoman imperial polity, governed by a Muslim ruler, to minority subjects of the Habsburgs' Christian empire, with which they had a history of conflict. The period analyzed here reflects a gradual separation from the Ottoman Empire, the reassessment of new loyalties and ties with both states, and changes in organization and relationships within the community. This period saw two major Muslim responses to the Habsburg occupation: first, the migration of Slav Bosnian Muslims to the Ottoman territories; and second, among those who stayed, an attempt to sustain relations with the Ottoman Empire in the realms of religion, politics, culture, and socioeconomic involvement. Migration was justified with religious rhetoric, including discussions of whether it was acceptable for Muslims to live under a non-Muslim ruler and the extent of religious freedoms under such a sovereign. The reality, however, was that most migrants had underlying political and socioeconomic motives. For those who stayed amid an ethnoreligious local politics in which emerging national groups relied on the support of powerful European states with regional interests, Bosnian Muslims, too, learned to use their religious and political clout. Ottoman imperial allegiances and sentiment played an important role for Muslims' strengthening and restructuring of ties with the Ottoman Empire, which they considered their Great Power protector.

In this study, I show how imperial continuities evolved to respond to the diplomatic initiatives of both empires: questions of sovereignty, occupation, migration, and minorities, as well as the activities of Muslims who negotiated their place both within the two empires and in Europe, informed by the realities of new geopolitical inevitability. In addition to questioning the definitiveness of the break with the Ottoman Empire for its subjects,

I analyze Ottoman efforts to maintain a sphere of influence in the region through reliance on Muslim loyalties. My research shows that Ottoman policies did not always follow a singular direction or strategy. While the sultan might have implied one message to encompass Muslims worldwide representing the Pan-Islamic rhetoric of the caliphate, the workings of consuls, diplomats, administrators, and officials of the Migrants Commission reveal a different logic and interests based on concrete local and regional considerations that ultimately affected policy implementation and outcomes. The Ottoman cabinet and consuls, for instance, continuously advised the sultan against encouraging migration—not necessarily out of lack of sympathy for the Muslim cause in Bosnia Herzegovina, but precisely for the purpose of maintaining a strong Muslim presence in the legally ambiguous former Ottoman territory. They assumed that those Muslims who stayed would, in turn, promote Ottoman interests in the region. The Ottoman Imperial Treasury and the Migrants Commission found migration equally problematic, but from a financial and logistical perspective, given the costs and feasibility of such large-scale transportation and settlement. Ambiguities in the Ottoman attitudes regarding the position of Balkan Muslims reflected their practical considerations and the changing perceptions of the Ottomans about themselves.[13] These oscillations likewise affected the understanding of the various actors about what was at stake in transforming the patterns of Ottoman association and the dynamics of these connections.

In Bosnia Herzegovina, the Muslim reading public was aware of nationalist movements and Pan-Slavism in Eastern Europe. In addition to their established ties with the sultan, they held out hope that the Young Turk movement would bolster Ottoman power. Islamic reform and revivalist movements in the Ottoman Empire, India, and Egypt, as well as conditions of institutional and educational reorganization among Russian Muslims and those in post-Ottoman Bulgaria, provided comparative reference for Muslims' existence in Habsburg Bosnia Herzegovina. What has been variously termed "Pan-Islam(s)," "interislamic networks," and "Muslim cosmopolis" incorporated Bosnia Herzegovina in its intellectual spheres and geographic reach.[14] *The Afterlife of Ottoman Europe* contributes the Bosnian outlook to the robust revisionist literature on transimperial Islamic networks and the impact of their exchanges at the turn of the twentieth century. Travel for education and work, migration and return, and the continuation of family and commercial relations all played a role in enduring ties with the Ottoman Empire. Proliferation of print and the availability of steam and rail travel further enhanced the reading public's access to global information about developments and major debates worldwide. Muslim intellectuals in Bosnia, not least for their polyglot education, navigated the diverse Islamic intellectual domains in the Ottoman Empire and beyond. Such comparative references helped them rationalize and come up with solutions expressed in Islamic idiom for their own particular circumstance in Bosnia Herzegovina. Bosnian Muslims' efforts at shaping their own Islamic modernity—advanced within the Habsburg system—in turn became a model in the Muslim world. Remarkably, Hamidian attempts to harness Pan-Islam as a policy that could benefit the Ottoman Empire vis-à-vis the imperial powers in the international arena had a modest effect on these developments, despite colonial empires' disquiet as they ruled over much of the world's Muslims at the time.

Public opinion, too, came to have an increasingly important role in both empires. The Ottoman establishment became concerned with the resonance of its policies among subjects, in the Muslim world, and in Europe. Austria-Hungary sought to show the success of its inclusive imperial model in the midst of nationalist and pan-nationalist movements afflicting the domains of the Dual Monarchy. Muslims in Bosnia used the prospect of migration to Ottoman lands as leverage in their negotiations with Habsburg and Ottoman authorities, as well as local political allies and foes, counting on the potential complications Muslim migration would cause for all parties involved. Dual Monarchy investigated how other empires—Russia in Central Asia, France in North Africa, and Great Britain in India—dealt with their respective Muslim populations and acted to incorporate Islamic institutions into their state system. They were tapping into the "imperial cloud"—the shared, collective imperial knowledge, pointing to yet another transimperial perspective.[15] In an attempt to attract the allegiance of their Muslim subjects, Austria-Hungary encouraged and revitalized several features of the Ottoman administration. Most significant was the Habsburg modification of provincial Islamic institutions, working to diffuse the role of the sultan-caliph at the height of Ottoman Pan-Islamic efforts, and in effect creating their own Habsburg Muslim *millet*.

For both empires, Bosnia Herzegovina was indicative of the dilemma in the long nineteenth century over how to resolve the contradictions of maintaining the supremacy of a territorially vast, multireligious empire along with modern principles of sovereignty and legitimacy that were increasingly based on ethno-linguistically homogeneous nation-states.[16] The afterlife of the Ottoman Empire in Habsburg Bosnia exposes legacies of an empire that no longer held effective control in the province, but was still actively trying to find ways of remaining relevant in its lost territories in the Balkans. All the while, the former subjects and other regional actors engaged with the Ottomans in order to fortify their interests, thus exposing and acknowledging the Ottoman presence and endurance of its authority, albeit transformed and diminished. These were individuals and groups who allied around common causes; some diverged at different times and disagreed about whether to oppose or support the Habsburg administration and what their role should be in these endeavors. They were political activists, bureaucrats, intellectuals, clergy, teachers, landlords, peasants, and nationalist activists of various persuasions, who had a choice of venues and coalitions through which they worked to advance their interests. The relationship of the Ottoman Empire with Austria-Hungary was further enhanced due to their common interests in containing the nationalist movements that worked to undermine imperial legitimacy and rule in southeastern Europe as supported by other European powers and, in particular, Russia.

Transimperial Loyalty and Local Agency
Bosnian Muslims were Slavs (and Slavic speakers), imperial subjects of the Habsburg and Ottoman empires, and adherents to Islam associated with the rest of the Muslim world. Seeing themselves as members in these different categories provided Muslims with social environments and imagined communities, allowing for a distinctive trajectory of Muslim life in Bosnia Herzegovina.[17] In this period, characterized by both rupture and continuity, different aspects of provincial social and political circumstance, imperial competition, and the changing international order shaped Muslims' responses and affected their allegiances. With that recognition, this book necessarily shifts away from the fixation on national histories and scholarly works on "late" and "incomplete" Muslim nationalization to investigations of imperial ties.

Focus on imperial continuities and the imperial connections maintained and restructured does not deny the existence of various ways of nationalization, but shows that these developments were not singular, linear advances as they are often presented in national historiographies and particularly in approaches to studying Bosnia Herzegovina. Furthermore, they are not unique to Bosnia Herzegovina, as scholarly studies show "national indifference" along other hybrid identities in systems of fierce nationalist competition in other regions of Eastern and Central Europe.[18] Acknowledging and investigating this diversity and range also helps put nationalization and its effects in perspective. Long-term processes of nationalization in Bosnia date back to the Ottoman period and to the endeavors of Serbia and Croatia and their nationalist activists in Bosnia Herzegovina, who equated liberation from empire with the conquest of land and people they imagined as part of their respective nations. Confessional differentiation became key to understanding the national dimension of the Bosnian population: Catholics were equated with Croats, Orthodox Christians with Serbs, and Muslims with Bosnians or Bosniaks (Bošnjaks). Much of Bosnian history in the long nineteenth century was written through the lens of nationalism and Bosnian Muslim nationalization, focusing on the province's peripheral yet exceptional status for having a considerable Muslim population.

From this perspective, Muslims were in a liminal position, having been appropriated into the Serbian or Croatian national body, while simultaneously being the "terrible Turk" and the "other" of stock nationalist narrative. Edin Hajdarpasic showed that nationalists viewed native Bosnian Muslims as (br)other: a figure that is neither "us" nor entirely "other." Serbian and Croatian nationalists perceived Bosnian Muslims as their brothers ("our Turks"), since they shared language, customs, and ancestry, and as potential participants in the triumph of South Slavic unity, conditioned by their emergence from the backwardness their Muslimness epitomized. As an interpretive device exposing the reversibility of processes of national identification, the (br)other concept reveals that "us" and "them" binaries are challenged and continuously redefined by the nationalists themselves.[19] Nationalism and the nationalizing processes to stake claims on Bosnia Herzegovina were unfinished and multidirectional, engaging nationalists as well as the Habsburg and Ottoman empires.[20]

Exploring the shifting realities that characterized the late imperial period contributes to an understanding of subjecthood and citizenship at the turn of the twentieth century that was based not on political allegiance, as is assumed today—almost exclusively tied to nation-states and ethnicities—but on parallel, overlapping, and composite loyalties. Recognizing it as an interactional relation, loyalty implies the possibility of alternatives.[21] The notion of belonging to the Ottoman polity and holding loyalty to the Ottoman state and sultan existed alongside local, regional, religious, occupational, linguistic, ethnic, and other identities, and it was often influenced by pragmatic considerations. These social agents' expressions of loyalty were affected by their existence in intersecting networks with connections of varying intensity at different times.[22] Loyalty, in this sense, presents as a more nuanced device than sole focus on nationalism.

Contrary to common historiographical assumptions that post-Ottoman Muslims in southeastern Europe lingered on as indolent recipients of imperial and national policies, or even as zealous Muslims who were "stuck" living in the past and unable to adjust to modernity, *The Afterlife of Ottoman Europe* shows that these imperial subjects understood the limits of their predicament and sought ways to remain relevant in the developments pertaining to the future of the province and their place within it. Bosnian Muslims insisted on religious, human, and civil rights in their petitions to both empires, each of which claimed to champion these privileges in order to legitimize its right over the province and to build allegiance among the population. They similarly employed their potential to migrate in negotiations counting on its undesirability for both states. Taking up this perspective allows for focus on agents' "subjective capacities" to engage in both sociohistorical processes and its narrative constructions.[23]

The emphasis in this book on Muslim agency, that is, their "capacity for action" within the Habsburg and Ottoman "organizational terrain," demonstrates the role of Muslims' own endeavors to shape their self-perceptions, community organization, and institutions.[24] What is more, their efforts influenced imperial considerations and policies by "pulling in" the empires to advance their own interests.[25] Inspired by Pierre Bourdieu's reflexive sociology and emphasis on the strategies that social agents employ, *The Afterlife of Ottoman Europe* offers an understanding of how Bosnians made sense of their world and actions they undertook to navigate the boundaries and leverage the potential of their environments. Bourdieu considered these strategies a product of agents' experiences of social space—their "practical sense." These practices, more than structures such as societal rules, inform social actions within the limits and possibilities of their social environment. When analyzed in this way, individuals are revealed to be agents who actively negotiate their social environment rather than passively follow predetermined societal structures.[26]

Evaluating Bosnian Muslim activity in the Habsburg provincial system, I distinguish between levels of integration into the new sociopolitical structures of the Habsburg and Ottoman empires, as well as emerging notions of alternative Muslim modernity. Muslim political parties, religious institutions, and educational organizations all functioned within the Habsburg provincial system, yet they incorporated Ottoman laws, practices, and symbolic ties to Istanbul. In publications Bosnian Muslims portray themselves as part of overlapping global communities of Muslims, Slavs, and citizens of the "civilized" world. These actors' environment was located at the intersection of imperial and national, as well as European, Ottoman, Balkan, and Muslim intellectual trajectories—which are often considered separate and even contradictory. Yet, the overlap of these affiliations shaped the ways people in the province mediated and experienced modernity.

The Afterlife of Ottoman Europe evaluates the distinct features of the empire that continued to structure the lives of subjects and their understanding of place, identity, and future prospects. Challenging the view that Ottoman provinces stopped being Ottoman in a meaningful sense after their formal separation from the empire, this book addresses the chief historiographical issue regarding Muslims in Bosnia Herzegovina after 1878: how Bosnia's Muslims maintained and transformed relations with Istanbul specifically and the rest of the Muslim world generally, while at the same time substantiating accommodations with the new authorities in Vienna. Bosnian Muslims' watershed moment did not come about with the separation from the Ottoman Empire; instead, the empire continued to live on in the imperial institutions, administrative and state practices, traditions, and loyalties that were reproduced and repurposed in the post-Ottoman context.

My emphasis in *The Afterlife of Ottoman Europe* is on the loyalties that were possible in the imperial milieu, to assess fluid notions of sovereignty and legitimacy, defined through interactions between empires and their subjects.[27] The question of loyalty has been observed in the Hungarian Habsburg national experience based on language and ethnicity and as supranational, defined by allegiance to the Habsburg dynasty and empire.[28] Comparable questions were raised with regard to Jewish loyalties and communal transformations in the post-Habsburg Austrian Republic and Weimar Germany.[29] While scholars wrote extensively on citizenship and political allegiances in instances of fragmented and mixed sovereignty,[30] and analyzed the causes and consequences of imperial collapse for multiethnic societies triumphed over by national discourses,[31] little has been written on loyalties of former Muslim and non-Muslim Ottoman subjects, as in Bosnia Herzegovina.[32] Analyzing allegiances as parallel and overlapping in the imperial framework further reveals the role of empire and its continuities in the postimperial state formations.

Tracing Imperial Continuities: Studies and Sources

Focus on Muslims in my analysis of Habsburg Bosnia Herzegovina allows for a perspective that takes ruptures as well as continuities into consideration and elucidates the ways in which imperial projects overlapped in the province. Set in a transregional framework, this study engages with the theoretical discourses that consider imperial legacies and their imprint on the present.[33] Structured as such, it focuses on transimperial subjects as actors in interimperial and postimperial histories to contribute to the developing historical reassessment globally.[34] *Afterlives of Empire* as an analytical heuristic then, offers a view into Ottoman imperial continuities as perpetuated by the Habsburg and Ottoman empires and their subjects. It informs a novel perspective about the complexity and nonlinearity of historical processes, as expressed in the strategies of imperial states and their subjects' intersecting interests and compound loyalties. This approach underscores the role of historical actors who maintained imperial continuities in diverse settings and for different reasons, while revealing the open-endedness of such processes. As a method, it led to an understanding of "Ottoman half-lives," in the case of post-Ottoman displaced persons and the constructions of their pasts that were dependent not only on their own understanding of it but also its political attention and recognition;[35] and it was explored in theoretical approaches to post-Ottoman topologies—the existence and experiences of multiple pasts in different times.[36]

In this book, I introduce Ottoman sources to the study of the Habsburg period in Bosnia Herzegovina for the first time. Centering Ottoman material allows me to trace the many ways in which the Ottoman Empire continued to exist in institutional, community, and individual lives in the province. I contextualized a variety of previously untapped Ottoman archival materials from the Turkish State Archives, from library and archival sources in Turkey and Bosnia Herzegovina, and from print papers, periodicals, pamphlets, and literature—all of which allowed me to conceptualize this new take on the ways that former Ottoman subjects continued and restructured ties with their previous center. Primary materials provided insights into the logic of Ottoman imperial policies in their lost territories and contemporaneous ideas of sovereignty, extraterritoriality, allegiance, and nationalism. Individual and group petitions, policy proposals, local and regional administrative reports, and publications exposed an array of strategies and solutions that these actors had proposed and employed. The sources provide not only the view from the Yıldız Palace and the diverging views of Ottoman administrators, but also how they transect with the interests of former subjects in Bosnia Herzegovina, Muslim and Orthodox Christian clergy, Ottoman and Balkan intellectuals, and merchant elites. Diverse multilingual source material presents us with change over the Habsburg decades and the political transformations in the province, regionally, and internationally.

As perhaps the most studied period of Bosnian history, the Habsburg era has long attracted scholarly attention in German and South Slavic languages, setting 1878 as a point of rupture when the enlightened European government replaced the despotic Ottoman regime, but ended with the assassination of Archduke Franz Ferdinand in Sarajevo in 1914, which ushered in World War I.[37] Several important studies had been published in English until the war in the 1990s attracted wider scholarly interest in Bosnia Herzegovina and its immediate post-Ottoman period.[38] Major works in English that explore the dynamics of the Habsburg Bosnian administration, the movement for Islamic religious and educational autonomy, the Habsburg "civilizing mission," and the province as the site of convergence of multiple political movements and external nationalization processes extensively use Bosnian Habsburg source material. Building on this existing rigorous research, *The Afterlife of Ottoman Europe* contributes an Ottoman perspective, expanding the historical conceptualization of the period by investigating the lasting Ottoman impact through previously unexplored source material.

Emphasizing multiple Ottoman perspectives through new sources also intervenes to contribute an outlook across area studies. This book departs from the historiographical and disciplinary convention that locates the end of the Ottoman period in 1878 and views the Habsburg arrival and its rule as a historical rupture, introducing the province to Europe and into the modern world. In fact, the very switch from Ottoman studies of Bosnia Herzegovina to (East and/or Southeast) European studies is projected back to this juncture. Such a perspective creates an absurd situation wherein Southeast Europe belongs to East European studies, whereas its Ottoman period is studied as part of Ottoman and Middle East studies. Following geopolitical demarcations relevant to the Cold War, nation-state borders of the mid-twentieth century outlined each area's boundaries.[39] Such boundaries are not only inadequate for contemporary study of regional diversities and their borderlands, exposing "geographies of ignorance,"[40] but they are even less appropriate when projected back in time. The Balkans are not the only region of the world afflicted with what scholars call "cartographic violence" and "cartographic surgery."[41] To develop a transregional and interimperial perspective in the analysis of Habsburg Bosnia, I built upon strategies employed to transform the spatial limitation of area studies and illustrate a more sophisticated texture of transregional interactions and networks: "scaling" regional space to imagine configurations that include borderlands and transnational flows; examining areas as intersecting arenas formed around social geographies that change through historical processes; and focusing attention on connections in historically durable patterns across Muslim Asia and its interregional dynamics concealed by area divisions into South and Central Asia, Eastern Europe, and the Middle East.[42]

Moving away from the conventional area studies approach to the Muslim question in Southeastern Europe, *The Afterlife of Ottoman Europe* addresses these shortcomings head-on by considering the Ottoman context of Bosnia Herzegovina even after the Ottomans' withdrawal from the region, as well as the significance of Islamic intellectual history to the history of Bosnia Herzegovina and Eastern Europe. Turning to primary materials in multiple languages and scattered across the former imperial domains, I have constructed a comprehensive picture of Bosnia Herzegovina's history outside the typical geographic and disciplinary confines. My assessment shows that Ottoman European regions such as Bosnia Herzegovina must be integrated into the scholarly study of Islam and of Muslim modernity, which are usually examined in Middle Eastern and South Asian contexts. In this vein, the book contributes to revisionist studies that tap multilingual sources to promote new ways of envisioning Muslim modernity. This is not a one-sided (or two-sided, for that matter) account of European influences and Muslim reactions, as we have seen so often. Instead, it is a larger story of an interconnected, transimperial world that demonstrates the importance of taking into account European imperial connections and continuities with the Middle East.

Book Structure and Scope

The narrative presented in the following pages underscores the lasting impact of empire on contemporary perceptions of political allegiance, international law, and extraterritoriality, showing that it was concrete conditions and actions at the turn of the twentieth century that shaped the modern understanding of categories such as citizens, minorities, and migrants, which are habitually assumed to be fixed abstractions. Because of their status as Muslims, and because religion separated Muslims from other subjects and, later, from other citizens, various dimensions of Islam assumed political relevance in the post-Ottoman period. Islamic legal norms and discourses were interpreted by imperial administrators and nationalist activists, whereas the ulema was called upon to articulate Muslims' rights and assumed a vocal political presence influencing communal and political organization. It is in this context that the confessional dimension mediated the social, political, and legal aspects of Muslims in the post-Ottoman Balkans at the turn of the twentieth century. Modern notions—such as laws of occupation, sovereignty, and citizenship, have developed out of practices from this period, as have state–subject negotiations at regional and transimperial sites. The activities of Bosnian Muslims in responding to societal challenges show their concern for concrete solutions to questions of migration; political activity in the Habsburg and Balkan nationalist environments; preservation of the autonomy of Islamic religious institutions in the state apparatus; and reassessment of Bosnia's place and ties in Eastern and Central Europe, with the Ottoman Empire, the caliphate, and the Muslim world.

The effort to transform and modernize, as articulated in the Bosnian Muslim discourse, was equally situated in European and Islamic intellectual traditions. By considering the role of Muslims and Islam in Habsburg Bosnia Herzegovina, we can see that a nuanced understanding of southeastern Europe is possible only by looking beyond geohistorical and disciplinary divisions. The history of Muslims is essential to the story of Europe, and the European Muslim experience is indispensable to the scholarly study of Muslims and Islam.

Chapter 1 analyzes the Habsburg occupation of Bosnia Herzegovina and its negotiations with the Ottoman Empire to define the unwritten implications of the Berlin Treaty. In contrast with the struggles of Bosnian notables to sidetrack Ottoman efforts at centralization in the early nineteenth century, the eventual occupation prompted them to seek support in asserting Ottoman sovereignty over Bosnia Herzegovina. They hoped that under the circumstances of a legally ambiguous occupational regime, the Ottoman Empire would limit Habsburg plans in the province that now threatened the status of Muslim notables, religious institutions, and rights to land, all tied to the Ottoman legal order and sociopolitical structures. The Habsburg Empire, on the other hand, interpreted the treaty as expanding its reach and established itself in Bosnia Herzegovina and the Balkans.

Chapters 2 and 3 investigate Bosnian Muslims' migration to the Ottoman Empire and the debates generated in response to the broader population movements that characterized the last Ottoman century. In Chapter 2, I evaluate the petitions for migration and related Ottoman consular and administrative reports to contextualize reasons for migration and diplomatic consequences. Migrants hoped to return, which drove many to settle in regions closest to Bosnia Herzegovina, seeing their relocation as temporary. As a political act, migration was a response to different aspects of the Habsburg administration and a show of loyalty to the Ottoman Empire. Chapter 2 discusses the significance of Muslim demographic presence in Europe and what that meant for the Ottoman and Habsburg empires.

Chapter 3 examines the desirability of migration from Ottoman, Habsburg, Bosnian and Serbian vantage points. Whether a Bosnian madrasa student seeking a fatwa on migration from the renowned Egyptian Islamist reformer Rashid Rida; itinerant preachers advising that Muslims can only be subjects of a Muslim ruler; conflicting Ottoman positions; and the worries of administrators, intellectuals, and nationalists about demographic dominance in the province—migration debates permeated Habsburg Bosnia.

Debates on whether and where Muslims should migrate occurred in similar fashion in Bulgaria, Crimea, Bosnia, Egypt, and across the Ottoman empire, reflecting the religious and political implications for migrants. These Bosnian migrations were part of large population movements at the turn of the twentieth century that would critically transform the demographics of Southeastern Europe and the Middle East. The motivation behind these debates and emerging views on minorities as problematic have had an important role in shaping the aftermath of world wars, population transfers, and the current understanding of population politics in the region.

Chapter 4 analyzes imperial competition over Bosnia Herzegovina. With the legally ambiguous occupation of Bosnia after the Berlin Congress, the sultan was still sovereign, but the population was expected to show allegiance to the new ruler—the emperor. The Ottoman Empire competed with Austria-Hungary to uphold its presence in Bosnia Herzegovina, and this resonated in the province and influenced public opinion in Europe and globally. Whereas the Habsburg Monarchy occupied and administered the province, the sultan extended his caliphal protections over Bosnian Muslims and Orthodox Christians.

Chapter 5 analyzes the petitioning practice and emphasizes the activity of Muslims in asserting their role within the state by appealing to both empires. It considers Bosnian Muslim organization and political mobilization. Muslim endeavors to maintain ties with the caliphate in Istanbul, and the Habsburg efforts to sever them, produced the Islamic Community—an official, semiautonomous religious organization rooted in the Ottoman system that still functions as an independent institution today, having outlived the Habsburg Empire, the Kingdom of Yugoslavia, and the Republic of Yugoslavia.

Chapter 6 focuses on the transformation of Muslim ties to the Ottoman Empire in light of the new political situation in the period after 1908, when the Habsburg Monarchy annexed Bosnia Herzegovina. Claims of Ottoman sovereignty in Bosnia became obsolete, and the Young Turks shifted the Ottoman focus to the territories remaining under their control. This period in Bosnia was characterized by social and civic organization, the proliferation of the press, and national movements. The first elections and engagement with representative government in the Bosnian provincial assembly began in 1910. The Muslim experience of political participation and mobilization in the Habsburg period became instrumental in safeguarding their rights and religious institutions in the postimperial period.

Finally, the Epilogue considers Bosnian Muslim intellectuals and cultural reformers: a former member of the Ottoman parliament and a Habsburg mayor; Pan-Islamist graduates of the University of Vienna; and writers, publishers, and ulema. These individuals developed a particular European Islamic modernist discourse rooted in the Ottoman concepts of modernity that were transformed within the Habsburg framework. The Epilogue argues for incorporation of Islamic intellectual discourse and cross-regional exchanges as integral to the history of Southeastern Europe.

1 Diplomacies of Separation

On Thursday around the time of the afternoon prayer, on Rajab 3, 1295 Hijri, and July 4, 1878, a la franga, and Haziran 22, 1294, of the Ottoman fiscal calendar, the residing Austro-Hungarian consul general in Sarajevo, Monsieur Vasić, went over to the mansion of the Ottoman governor of Bosnia, Ahmed Mazhar Pasha to inform him that Austria-Hungary would soon enter Bosnia Herzegovina and take control of the military and civilian authority in the province. Hearing this, Ahmed Mazhar Pasha sent a coded message by telegraph to Istanbul.[1]

So began the description of the implementation of the Berlin Treaty by Muhamed Enveri Kadić, a contemporary Bosnian chronicler whose career spanned two empires and a kingdom as an administrator in the local Ottoman, Habsburg, and Yugoslav administrations in Sarajevo. Kadić went on to note that the news was a leak, most likely from the consulate, that instantly spread around the city. In reaction, Muslims met in the central Gazi Husrevbeg Mosque at the time of the congregational night prayer, and they invited several prominent Orthodox Christian Sarajevans to discuss their course of action. The decision was made not to open shops the following day.

As anxiety over the looming occupation spread among the population in the coming days, crowds gathered in the streets of Sarajevo, and they compelled the Ottoman military commander Ferik Veliuddin Pasha to resign, over concerns that he would not represent their interests.[2] The governor feared that the armed crowd, which the chronicler Kadić likened to a rabble (*hazele*), would storm the city armory. The diary of a Franciscan friar from Fojnica likewise described those who were recruiting the poor peasants (who were armed only with hoes and clubs) into resistance units as "rejects" (*odbijenici, anarhia*).[3] Locals who wanted to prepare for defense killed the county chief administrator and military commander in Mostar, in spite of Ottoman orders not to organize any resistance to the Austro-Hungarian military.[4] A contemporary account from Mostar described a "mob of crooks, a frightening crowd," who broke into the meeting room of the main government building and dragged out the mufti and the judge, who had called for calm, killing them on the porch. The chronicler remarked that the incident distressed the dignified Muslims in the city as much as the events of Karbala.[5] In response, "representatives of all classes" were summoned to a meeting at the governor's mansion in Sarajevo, the culmination of which was an agreement to get in touch with other districts of Bosnia Herzegovina by telegraph and designate representatives among the Muslim, Jewish, and Orthodox Christian inhabitants.[6]

A week after the news of the Habsburg takeover, a telegram finally arrived from the Ministry of Internal Affairs in Istanbul, softening the nature of the potential Habsburg occupation, describing it not as a conquest but as a joint endeavor with the Ottoman Empire that would be beneficial for Bosnia Herzegovina by securing it from possible Serbian and Montenegrin attacks.[7] The Ottoman Ministry of War informed the Ottoman forces in Bosnia to stay put and send a protest note only in the case of Habsburg military assault.[8] The Ottoman attitude corresponded to Emperor Franz Joseph's proclamation that was circulating in Bosnia as the Habsburg troops entered the province. It emphasized that the troops were coming to restore "peace and welfare," and that the sultan, desiring the safety of his subjects, had entrusted them to the protection of "his friend," the Habsburg emperor-king.[9] The details and nature of the Habsburg occupation decided at the Berlin Congress were yet to be negotiated between the two empires. The news of Habsburg military preparations to cross the river Sava—the northern border with Austria-Hungary—stoked fears among the populace and motivated some to action despite Ottoman orders. Subsequently, the People's Council and People's Government were formed in Sarajevo and several other towns. By the end of July, locals who had taken over administrative, military, and telegraph command posts replaced the Ottoman authorities in several regional centers.[10]

Ottoman officials who joined the preparations to oppose the oncoming army donned "Bosnian clothing" in place of their Ottoman attire and uniforms.[11]

The anticipation and uncertainty elicited a number of responses. Some advocated for inaction, while others joined excited mobs or organizations in various stages of development to protect against and resist the impending occupation. Locals organized and led armed resistance. Among the more serious challenges to the invading army was the resistance led by the mufti of Pljevlja (Taşlıca), Mehmed Vehbi Šemsekadić, who recruited volunteers from as far as Kosovo and attempted to forge anti-Habsburg alliances across the region.[12] For a brief period in the summer of 1878, when neither the Habsburgs nor the Ottomans had full control of Bosnia Herzegovina, those Bosnian inhabitants who engaged in opposition to the advancing Habsburg forces became rebels in the eyes of both empires.[13] This, however, was not the first time they had caused headaches to the Ottoman administrators in Istanbul and had been at odds with both the Ottomans and the Habsburgs.

FIGURE 1. Resistance at the time of occupation, as depicted in Battle for Sarajevo, by G. Durand.

Source: *The Graphic* (London), no. 462 (5 October 1878): 8–9.

This chapter discusses circumstances surrounding the occupation and the unique aspects of the Habsburg mandate that allowed for Ottoman imperial continuities. As one of the core provinces of the early westward expanding Ottoman Empire and later as the westernmost Ottoman border, Bosnia's position at the time of the Berlin Congress was not that of an immaterial periphery, as the post-1878 studies often dismiss it to be. The province became the focal point for Habsburg efforts at extending its own spheres of influence while containing Russian expansion in the Balkans. At the same time Bosnian occupation and administration played an important role in defining the Dual Monarchy's own image as an imperial power internally, and in Europe.

Critical to the inhabitants in the province, as well as to the Ottoman administrators, was that for the first time Ottoman territorial loss did not also mean the loss of Muslim populations, as was the case elsewhere in the Ottoman Europe where local Muslims were consistently dispossessed and expelled after the Ottoman withdrawal. Bosnia was caught at the intersection of evolving mechanisms of international politics, imperial competition, and local and regional political aspirations. The Berlin Congress and the novelty of an international (interimperial) mandate to occupy Bosnia Herzegovina awarded to Austria-Hungary created a range of gray areas for all actors to exploit. Nominal Ottoman sovereignty and the vaguely defined Habsburg direction in the province prompted each empire to negotiate and advance their own understanding of the treaties. The ambivalence also allowed leeway for the subjects to interpret and negotiate the meaning of these new terms with both empires in order to promote their existence and interests. Whereas Bosnian notables in the first half of the nineteenth century worked to deflect Ottoman centralization efforts and preserve their relative independence in local affairs, by the end of the century, they asserted Ottoman sovereignty and jurisdiction in order to preserve their status, rights to land, and socioeconomic standing legitimized by the Ottoman structures.

Ottoman Bosnia and Its Muslims

In a westward expanding Ottoman Empire, Bosnia had an important constitutive place while its inhabitants became some of the foremost Ottomans.[14] That they forged the province's imperial role on their own terms characterized centuries of flexible Ottoman rule and effective statecraft across its diverse domains. By the turn of the fifteenth century, even before they took Constantinople in 1453, the Ottoman presence in Bosnia had been established through their trade links with Venice, political and geostrategic campaigns across the region, and itinerant Sufi preachers. Sultan Mehmed Fatih II, the conqueror of Constantinople, led the Ottoman forces himself in 1463 in the occupation of the *sancak* of Bosnia, the Ottoman military-administrative unit that later expanded to Herzegovina. Tursun Bey, the chronicler of Mehmed II's conquests, highlighted Bosnia's natural and human resources and described the region as a strategically relevant, yet mountainous and inaccessible land.[15] First cities were established by imperially decreed Islamic pious endowments (*vakuf*) and expanded by formidable endowments of governors and other high officials. Novi Pazar and Sarajevo emerged in the fifteenth century, with their growth driven by imperial and other pious endowments for mosques, markets, public baths, schools, public kitchens, water fountains, inns, dervish lodges, aqueducts, roads, bridges, mills, and guesthouses. Across all of Bosnia Herzegovina, Islamic pious endowments played a central role in infrastructural, urban, and institutional development, leading to its growth into a relevant trading, educational, and cultural center in the Balkans. Considering their widespread significance, it is no surprise that such endowments would later become the focal points for forging sovereignty and identity in the post-Ottoman period.

Under the Ottomans, networks of cities and the infrastructure connecting them facilitated the uninterrupted flow of goods, peoples, and ideas. The growth of cities, and their economies, was also enhanced by imperial grants of exemptions from various taxes and obligations; these in turn encouraged local industry, natural resource management, and the establishment of enduring trade links from the Ottoman Empire to the north and west. Education in the elementary *mekteb* and higher *medresa* schools did not differ much from the system and curriculum in the rest of the empire. Schools in Sarajevo, Mostar, and Prusac became renowned for the quality of education they offered. Graduates went on to Istanbul, Edirne, and Bursa in pursuit of higher degrees. Arabic, Turkish, and Persian were taught in Bosnian *medresas* until the twentieth century. Scholars wrote in these languages as well as in Bosnian Aljamiado and Cyrillic scripts, but the language of the province remained Bosnian.

Dervish lodges were established in almost all the early urban settlements, attesting to the role of Sufi brotherhoods in the spread of Islam.¹⁶ The Sufi brotherhoods' organization, which extended beyond the empire, integrated adherents into its networks across the Muslim world. Conversions to Islam in Bosnia Herzegovina were gradual and became most intensive in the first two centuries after the establishment of Ottoman rule.¹⁷ Ottoman records show the connections between Ottoman urbanization and Islamization throughout the Ottoman Balkans, where cities were predominantly inhabited by Muslims and rural areas by Christians.¹⁸ Until the twentieth century, however, the majority of all Bosnians were peasants.

Franciscans defined much of Bosnian Catholicism until the arrival of the Habsburgs.¹⁹ Orthodox Christians, whose Patriarch was the subject of the Ottoman sultan, were encouraged to settle across Bosnia in the early modern Ottoman period. Sephardic Jews, expelled from the Iberian Peninsula toward the end of the fifteenth century, were welcomed by the Ottoman Empire. Some found a new home in Bosnian cities, especially Sarajevo, where a sizable Jewish community existed until the Nazi occupation in World War II.

The Ottoman *devşirme* was the practice of collecting mostly Christian boys, predominantly from the Ottoman Balkan provinces, and educating them for military and administrative service. Diverging from the Ottoman custom of enlisting non-Muslims only, in Bosnia Muslims were recruited as well.²⁰ The *devşirme* opened up avenues for upward mobility, and Bosnians attained some of the highest positions in the Ottoman Empire within a generation of conquest. Rising through the ranks, men from Bosnia Herzegovina served in the imperial military and administrative apparatus, and they were integrated into the scholarly and intellectual elite of the Ottoman Empire.²¹ The sixteenth-century Ottoman statesman and intellectual Mustafa Ali, who served in Bosnia, attributed Bosnians' physical, ethical, and spiritual qualities to divine intervention in his description of the peoples of the empire and their contribution to Ottoman glory.²² Becoming one of the core provinces of the empire, Bosnia was included in the Ottoman land tenure system known as *timar*. The sultan granted nonhereditary rights to land tied to military service by the cavalrymen of the Ottoman *sipahi* corps, which in its early stages included Muslims and Christians. The Ottoman legal, administrative, and military system was typically flexible enough to be adjusted to various provinces and their existing socioeconomic arrangements while also accounting for political and strategic conditions. The exceptions to the structures introduced in Bosnia had long-lasting consequences. *Timar* landholders in Bosnia worked out a privilege to inherit *timar* lands in the sixteenth century and to have them assigned among locals.[23] The *ocaklık timar* was inherited by male progeny and, over time, by females and extended family.

By the turn of the eighteenth century, Ottomans had been forced out of Hungary, Slavonia, Lika, and Dalmatia. Participation in frequent Ottoman wars, banditry, decimation caused by several bouts of plague, and Austrian incursions—including Prince Eugene of Savoy's torching of Sarajevo—had already worn down the Bosnian population. Bosnia's economy suffered as a result of territorial contraction, loss of population and revenues, and disruption of trade. Muslims in the lands that were lost to the Habsburgs were expelled, and some settled in Bosnia. Those who stayed had to convert to Christianity, and even the toponyms in the lost territories were changed to erase any Ottoman vestiges. The inhabitants of Bosnia knew they were the first line of defense against further Habsburg expansion and knew their province was the most at risk.

Bosnia Herzegovina underwent administrative and military reorganization as the Ottomans' westernmost border region (*serhat*). Communication and infrastructure were strengthened to create a succession of border and inland military zones led by local notables who were expected to mobilize their own forces. *Kapetanije*, a system of captaincies led by hereditary nobles that functioned as administrative-military units, proliferated in this borderlands reorganization.[24] Readying for war became the main task of Bosnian governors. They relied on local manpower as well as leadership from Bosnian district notables, with whom the governors began to hold regular council.[25] One incursion by the Habsburg forces into Serbia in 1737 cut Bosnia off from Istanbul to the east and was followed by a military attack in the northwest. The governor Hekimoğlu Ali Pasha led the Bosnian notables and their local armies to defeat a coordinated Austrian attack on the northwestern city of Banja Luka.[26] The Habsburgs correspondingly created their Military Frontier across the border, extending it to southern Hungary and Transylvania, and populated it mostly with Orthodox Christians who had received tax exemptions to settle there. Although the three-way borderland between the Venetian Republic, the Habsburg Monarchy, and the Ottoman Empire is often regarded as *the* fault line in European modern historiography, it also led to the creation of a particular frontier ethos that contradicts the understanding of the "clash of civilizations" between Islam and Christianity as well as that of the East and West, that is still current in political discourses about Bosnia Herzegovina.[27]

The Habsburg interest in Bosnia Herzegovina, and Ottoman territories generally, never ended. Just like Russia and other European powers, the Habsburgs began cultivating relationships with the non-Muslim Ottoman groups in hopes of an all-out rebellion against Ottoman authorities that would allow them to attain the territories as liberators rather than conquerors. The 1788 Habsburg attack on Bosnia, known as the Dubica War or the last Austro-Turkish War, was a consequence of another such attempt at conquest. Its aim was to further weaken the Ottomans, who were already at war with Russia, by opening a western front. Both empires sent instigators to Montenegro to encourage Montenegrin attacks and a rebellion in Herzegovina, thereby introducing yet an additional front.[28] Although the war drew to a close with the Sistova Treaty in 1791, it did not significantly change the Habsburg-Ottoman border; instead, the Austrian emperor confirmed the Habsburgs' status of "protector" of Christians under Ottoman rule, similar to the 1774 Treaty of Küçük Kaynarca that had granted such status to the Russian tsar in relation to Orthodox Christian subjects of the Ottoman Empire.[29] Novel interpretations of these protections played an important role in justifying Ottoman territorial losses and diplomacy throughout the nineteenth century.

That the notables in northwestern Bosnia refused to accept the provisions of the Sistova Treaty, causing an international crisis, is illustrative of regional conditions and their relationship with the Sublime Porte. According to the treaty, Austria was to return several fortified towns to the Ottomans, keeping for itself Cetingrad and Drežnik. The Porte sent the text of the treaty with a map and even a fatwa to appease the regional notables, who refused to surrender their fortresses. The Sublime Porte then sent a special envoy with orders for the governor to personally complete the marking of the border, giving him the power to punish and exile insubordinate notables.[30]

It took four years just to mark the Ottoman–Habsburg border, but the notables remained irritated that the sultan "gave away *their* land so easily."[31] Not relenting, the notables took advantage of the Napoleonic engagement with the Habsburgs in Dalmatia and seized Cetingrad in 1809, proudly informing the governor that they had recovered the lost territory. The Habsburgs accused the Ottomans of breaking the treaty provisions, as the notables had not heeded the orders of the Bosnian governor and the Sublime Porte to return the besieged territory. The French tactically supported the disobedient notables, a signal of Napoleon's support for Bosnian ownership of the disputed territories. However, Bosnians became anxious when the French surrounded and turned their cannons toward the occupied fort, claiming it for themselves.[32] The notables petitioned the Porte for help, seeing French insistence on a sliver of Bosnian territory as part of a plan for an all-out takeover of Bosnia. They predicted that, since Bosnia was also engaged in fighting back Serbian and Montenegrin attacks, without the Sublime Porte's support Bosnia's fate would go the way of Crimea, which had been annexed by the Russian Empire.[33] The fortress was ultimately returned, but some notables from the northwestern border region continued to make incursions into Austrian territory. The irritated Porte sent a succession of governors who could not achieve full control over the provincial notables, as they persisted in their attempts to occupy the disputed fortress in the years to follow.

In addition to its experiences close to home, Bosnia Herzegovina was also afflicted by political and socioeconomic transformations in the rest of the Ottoman Empire.[34] With the decline of the *timar* system—and following the expansion of tax farming (*iltizam*) and its life lease variation, *malikane*—the commercial estates (*çiftlik*) increasingly became vehicles of economic and political power in the provinces, linked to the rise of provincial potentates, the *ayans*.[35] The *ayans* successfully exploited their positions as landowners, tax farmers, local tax assessors, and military recruiters in their regions. Capitalizing on their status, some prominent *ayans* presided over local and regional councils and proceeded autonomously from the central government, which had little recourse when they challenged it. At the same time, they drew their legitimacy within the Ottoman framework. Their autonomy also opened up the way to rampant abuses of power, excessive taxation, nepotism, and the freedom to interpret and evade imperial orders. The circumstances became more restrictive for peasants, as *ayans* increased their dues and labor obligations and limited their rights, to which peasants reacted with rebellion and flight. Muslim peasants had more avenues for avoiding the mounting pressures brought about by the same changes that emboldened local Muslim notables, including increased taxation, displacement, and anxieties about further territorial losses. Muslims could join the military and claim various exemptions, opening the way for conflation of religion and class in Bosnia Herzegovina.[36]

The notables viewed themselves as critical defenders of the empire and the province, fighting off enemies on the province's northern, western, and southern borders. They did so through locally sourced manpower, enlisting mostly the Muslim population into the military class. Doing so came with salaries, as well as tax and legal exemptions. This led to a situation where salaried Janissary positions could be bought, so much so that a contemporary complained that the population of Sarajevo consisted of Janissaries, craftsmen, and merchants and no one else—the wood sellers, bread makers, and even Christians converts to Islam had bought their membership in the military.[37] Writing in the early years of the nineteenth century in a tell-all tract to the sultan, Muhamed Emin Isević detailed how intertwined the administrative, military, judicial, and religious posts had become in Bosnia Herzegovina through bribes and blatant abuse of power with little central oversight.[38] Given the range of exemptions Bosnia enjoyed, it is no surprise that the notables in particular would oppose further centralization measures beginning in the nineteenth century.

Ottoman reforms entailed the abolition of the Janissary corps in 1826 and a comprehensive set of policies known as the Tanzimat, the Ottoman administrative and political "reordering." Tanzimat's two relevant decrees, the Rescript of the Rose Chamber (1839) and the Reform Edict (1856), defined the state centralization measures and confirmed equality of Ottoman subjects before the law as Ottomans, abandoning the legal distinctions between Muslims and non-Muslims of centuries past. In Bosnia these measures included redistricting, restructured land regimes and tenure, and military reforms. Anticipating resistance, the Ottoman central administration attempted to fill the newly reconfigured provincial positions from among the notables, but they unanimously refused, united in safeguarding their independence.[39] Moreover, the independent notables and numerous Janissaries rejected reforms that would curtail their political power and legal and economic privileges. Merchants, too, feared that greater central oversight would change their existing transborder arrangements and so opposed change.

Bosnian notables insisted that no Tanzimat measures be implemented in Bosnia and resorted to declaring the reform measures "un-Islamic" in order to justify their opposition to imperial orders. They demanded that their existing properties, rights, and immunities be protected and that future governors be appointed from their number. Bosnian *ayans* were in communication with other likeminded Balkan *ayans*-turned-warlords, such as Işkodralı Mustafa Pasha Bushatli, who similarly resisted the centralization reforms.[40] The Sublime Porte found that some *ayans* received monetary aid from the Serbian leader Miloš Obrenović and the khedive of Egypt, Kavalalı Mehmed Ali,[41] the latter hoping Istanbul would be preoccupied in the Balkans so that he could expand into Syria without disturbance. Led by Husein Kapetan Gradaščević (1802–1834), Bosnian notables challenged and defeated Ottoman forces in 1831. The residing governor was forced to flee, and Gradaščević declared himself governor.

Forces led by Gradaščević were soon defeated, though. He fled to the Habsburg territories and was eventually exiled to Istanbul. The most powerful Bosnian *ayans* were politically and physically eliminated in 1850 by the punitive actions of Governor Omer Pasha Latas. Notables' actions and demands were meant to protect their power and privileges but did not step out of the Ottoman framework, on which they based their legitimacy. The empire's center continued to reintegrate the notables into new state structures. The state had reasserted itself, but it still relied on the notables to complete the reordering. Ahmed Cevdet Pasha, who came to Bosnia Herzegovina in the mid-1860s as imperial inspector general, arranged for volunteer Bosnian troops for the first year.[42] The notables accepted participation in the new military, but not before they negotiated that soldiers would serve within Bosnia only, have local commanders, and a limit on years of service.[43] Even while participating in the implementation of the Tanzimat measures, wary notables insistently tried to preserve their autonomy.

The Tanzimat period in Bosnia Herzegovina was cut short by the Habsburg occupation. However, it introduced a variety of measures and set the foundation for modernization in all aspects of society. The changes were especially discernable in cities, including legal and administrative organization, economy, infrastructure, modern education, notions of civil rights, constitutional government, and the power of public opinion. The provinces of Bosnia and Danube were the first to experience the new *vilayet* form of regional organization, the most important feature of which was the introduction of representative councils at different administrative levels that included both elected and appointed members. Governor Topal Şerif Osman Pasha (1861–1869) left a vital mark on the province of Bosnia Herzegovina in a rather short time.[44] Among his important legacies were an interconfessional provincial assembly and executive council, several modern roads, a stretch of railway, new schools and libraries, a modern hospital, and a printing press in Sarajevo. In response to anti-Ottoman nationalist propaganda from Croatia and Serbia, as well as Christian missionary organizations and schools proliferating in Bosnia Herzegovina, Topal Osman Pasha, just like his Habsburg Bosnian counterpart Benjamin von Kállay (1882–1903) some decades later, encouraged the idea of Bosnianism as a form of regional identity to counter the nationalistic propaganda threatening the province and endangering imperial rule in the Balkans.

Ottoman reform measures also introduced equal citizenship and a uniform agricultural tax rate, among other things, but were, paradoxically, received with displeasure, since the state was viewed as encroaching on the life of its subjects as never before. This aggravated Muslims who had lost their privileges, and the Christian populations resented the new obligations and state intrusion into matters over which they formerly had autonomy. The state became ever present through extensive administrative oversight, telegraph communication, conscription, and the building of new roads. The central government encountered the overwhelmingly agricultural Ottoman domains through its land surveys, recording of deeds, and taxation of landlords and peasants. The fact that the majority of landlords in Bosnia Herzegovina were Muslim and peasants were Christian set the struggle along confessional lines that were in retrospect interpreted in national terms. Abuses of position and power, however, were rooted in class rather than religious difference.

Excessive burdens on peasants and exploitation by landlords led to several rebellions throughout the nineteenth century. The Ottoman Land Law of 1858 and the 1859 Law of Sefer were intended to address these abuses directly. The land law introduced greater oversight of agricultural land distribution and usage, and it promoted stable tenure and taxation, building on the Tanzimat reforms. Centralization and classification of the pious endowment properties and their greater oversight were also initiated. Later adopted by the Habsburg administration in Bosnia, these regulations became the basis of land claims in the first decades of the twentieth century in Austria-Hungary and even in the Kingdom of Yugoslavia. Yet the initial implementation was slow, partial, and difficult, as the notables worked to increase their land and tithe rights and their power over Christian and Muslim peasants.

One such peasant rebellion started in Herzegovina in 1875, in response to persistent tax collection efforts after a bad harvest. The Habsburg emperor's visit to Dalmatia in 1875, in which he announced the invasion of Bosnia Herzegovina, is also regarded to have contributed to the outbreak of the rebellion.[45] It developed into an international incident that became fused with the Eastern Question. Local revolt spread to other regions in Bosnia, where it was met with harsh responses from the governor's forces and irregulars who had been assembled by landlords.[46] Exploiting the unrest, Serbia and Montenegro agreed to take over Bosnia and Herzegovina, respectively, and declared war on the Ottoman Empire in 1876. Russia declared war in 1877 with a focus on Bulgaria, and promising Bosnia Herzegovina to the Habsburgs if they did not interfere, in an agreement known as the Budapest Convention. Volunteers, funds, and arms from Croatia, Serbia, Montenegro, and Russia helped perpetuate the crisis, preventing normalization and shaping the conflict in confessional terms.[47] National histories have portrayed this moment as a failure of three decades of nationalist insurrectionary work in Bosnia Herzegovina and a considerable investment of Serbian human and financial resources in agents, organizations, weapons, clothing, and monetary compensation to "awaken" a certain kind of "national consciousness."[48] The aim was to replicate the Greek and Serbian rebellions earlier in the century that had succeeded in establishing national principalities. The San Stefano and Berlin treaties ending the 1875–1878 conflicts, however, propelled what began as local agrarian issues into an interimperial competition for influence in the Balkans. The crisis in Bosnia Herzegovina became part of a series of crises in the Balkans that the Great Powers exploited to limit Ottoman presence in southeastern Europe by redrawing maps at the Berlin Congress in 1878.[49]

Negotiating Mandates

Nineteenth-century reports and travelogues that proliferated after the opening of foreign consulates in Bosnia Herzegovina were characteristic of European accounts of the East: it was an Oriental backwoods but also a land of resources that could become "paradise" in "civilized hands."[50] The Habsburgs had historically coveted Bosnia, and by the mid-nineteenth century, there were at least three distinct plans worked out for its annexation.

One of those plans was formulated with the aid of Benjamin Kállay—a Hungarian aristocrat, diplomat, scholar, and a Slavic specialist, then a consul in Belgrade and the future Habsburg joint finance minister and administrator of Bosnia Herzegovina from 1882 to 1903.[51] Habsburg experts and informants freely traversing Ottoman Bosnia Herzegovina compiled surveys of roads, resources, mineral riches, and infrastructure that made it into the plans and aided in eventual occupation. Military and strategic motivations were the most prominent reasons for incorporating Bosnia into the Habsburg lands. Bosnia was the hinterland of the Dalmatian coast and would serve to further Habsburg influence down the Ottoman Adriatic coast and against Italy, vying for the same. Also important was trade, which in Bosnia developed in the direction of the monarchy's center, as trade routes and Adriatic ports were the main nodes for Bosnian exports, local products, and goods from other Ottoman domains.[52] Commercial networks were important especially for the Dalmatian, Croatian, and Slovenian traders, and they, more so than the politicians, advocated for the Habsburg annexation of Bosnia when the uprising in 1875 disturbed and then halted trade.[53] Even the river Sava, the natural Habsburg–Ottoman border, was used to make a case for occupation of Bosnia on hydrological grounds. Like the Orient Bosnia Herzegovina represented, Sava was unregulated: it destroyed fertile land, disturbed shipping and trade, and brought disease, threatening the survival of Habsburg inhabitants on its northern shore; therefore it warranted the introduction of an orderly administration in Bosnia.[54]

However, it was not until fears of Serbian expansion into Bosnia and the prospect of Russian backing for a large southern Slav state that the Habsburgs decided to act. Not only would such proximity of a Russian client state be undesirable; it would also threaten the balancing act of the monarchy's large Slav populations that had been established only a decade earlier through the dualist system that coupled Austria and Hungary into a Dual Monarchy. These strategic and political reasons were juxtaposed with the costs of such an occupation, as well as the consequences of adding a large Slav population to the monarchy, swaying the Habsburg parliament and the public opinion against the occupation. Debates developed around the question of the position of Bosnia Herzegovina within the monarchy, which had strictly delineated ministerial allocations and budgets for Austria and Hungary respectively, both of which guarded their prerogatives.[55] The Habsburg joint foreign minister, Count Gyula Andrássy (1823–1890), had to consider public opinion at home as he negotiated the expansion of Habsburg influence at the Berlin Congress, weighing the tangible expenses, the threat of nationalism, and possible Russian sphere of influence in Bosnia Herzegovina.[56] In his proclamation to the inhabitants of Bosnia Herzegovina, Emperor Franz Joseph I presented the occupation as an effort to put an end to the troubles that the province had been experiencing for several years. He could no longer bear to see "how hardship and misery knocked on the borders of his states," so he brought the situation to the attention of the council of nations (*Rathe der Völker*), which had decided that "Austria-Hungary should give you back the peace and welfare that you have been lacking for so long."[57]

At deliberations in Berlin, the Ottoman representatives resisted the otherwise unanimous plan to allow a Habsburg mandate in Bosnia Herzegovina. But they did not base their argument on the fact that Bosnia Herzegovina had been Ottoman for hundreds of years or that Muslims were a majority in the province. Instead, they claimed that the Bosnian people *desired* to stay under the Ottoman administration, which reflected a novel consideration in international politics and was readily employed by Ottoman diplomats. When pressured to accept the decision, the Ottoman negotiators insisted on a written confirmation that sovereign rights of the sultan in Bosnia Herzegovina would be maintained and that the occupation was temporary. The fate of Bosnia Herzegovina was defined in Article 25 of the Berlin Treaty, giving Bosnia Herzegovina to Austria-Hungary to occupy and administer, while the Novi Pazar district was to have limited Habsburg military presence. A separate convention between the Habsburg and Ottoman empires outlined the details of the occupation.

The Ottoman military had orders not to oppose the Habsburg forces occupying Bosnia in 1878, but the news that the soldiers had abandoned military barracks and joined the oppositional groups compelled the Porte to advise its envoy at the negotiations, the Ottoman foreign minister Aleksandros Karatodori Pasha (1833–1906), to quickly come to an agreement.[58] Disapproving public opinion at home was another reason for the Ottoman administration to conclude the question of Bosnia Herzegovina.[59] Frustrated with the other congress participants' united stance in their plans for the Ottoman Empire, Karatodori Pasha wondered whether the outcome of the resistance in Bosnia Herzegovina would influence negotiations.[60] There was also the hope that public opinion in the Habsburg Monarchy had tilted toward opposing the occupation. The Ottoman consul in Pest informed the Porte that "half of the Habsburg soldiers" who were about to enter Bosnia were Hungarian and "sympathetic to the Ottoman Empire," as they expressed their opposition to the Hungarian role in acquisition of Bosnia Herzegovina.[61] Although it looked like Bosnia Herzegovina was to be lost to the Ottomans in a way similar to the ongoing crumbling of Ottoman territories, it also seemed to the negotiators that other outcomes might be possible. Considering various diplomatic strategies was the only approach the Ottomans were left with, especially after Ottoman officials lost effective control in the province. Telegrams were sent to several European monarchs, including the British queen, expressing hope that the events in Bosnia Herzegovina would impel the Great Powers to stop Habsburg advancement and limit the occupation—but with little success.[62]

On his return to Istanbul from Bosnia, General Seyyid Ahmed Hafız submitted an eyewitness report on the entry of Austrian forces. In addition to having entered Bosnia without an official agreement between the two states—itself a great insult to Ottoman integrity—he criticized the Austrians for behaving as if Bosnia were their own property: "they invited people to live under the same banner" and promised collective clemency. When the intent of permanent military occupation became obvious, he continued, the people "who had been accustomed to Ottoman just rule for nearly 450 years" chose death over living under Austrian rule. According to his report, the Austrian response to the opposition was intense violence: "as if the Bosnians were their own subjects who continuously rebelled," they were treated like bandits with unusual cruelty. "The houses from which shots were fired on the Austrian army were set on fire," and those inside were shot, including women and children.[63] Another official's account also emphasized that

Habsburg forces entered Bosnia Herzegovina without waiting for the conclusion of the bilateral agreement, seeing it as an attempt to disregard and marginalize the Ottoman Empire, which needed to stand up for its honor and glory.[64] Reports of other Ottoman officials and military personnel, as well as telegrams from locals about Habsburg military actions, citing murder of women and children and the capture of Ottoman soldiers, were presented to the highest officials in Istanbul.[65] The harsh Habsburg approach was part of the occupation strategy to show the might of the Habsburg Empire and deter any resistance. The northeastern town of Brčko, for example, was bombarded for several days, and its Muslim quarter destroyed, as part of a plan to cause "panic and fear" among the population.[66] Indeed, the first Habsburg institution in Bosnia established in August 1878 was the court-martial.

In response to these reports, the sultan called a special cabinet meeting.[67] It was decided to send a note of protest to the Habsburg Monarchy, and to describe Austrian violence in detail to other European powers, since it was in complete opposition to the purpose of their mission in Bosnia Herzegovina as outlined in the Berlin Treaty. Ottoman protests were mostly ignored. The responses, or the lack thereof, summed up European ambivalence toward Ottoman grievances: the Russian Ministry of Foreign Affairs did not bother to respond; the London chargé d'affaires reported that Lord Salisbury related England's concern and had contacted Count Andrássy about the events; France's minister of foreign affairs justified Habsburg actions as a reasonable response to opposition but underlined that the Habsburg forces would not go against their interest, which was to attract the Muslims; and the Italian foreign minister expressed regret for the events, saying that Italy was in no position to take up the Ottoman cause with the Habsburgs.[68] The Habsburg officials were annoyed: the Ottoman ambassador in Vienna was asked why this had to become a public matter, as the two states could have resolved "false assumptions" had they been contacted directly. They also expressed that it was unnecessary to spread this news across Europe, as the Ottomans could never win public opinion anyway.[69] He was right. Despite actively dispatching reports of Habsburg "cruel actions" (*harekat-i gadarane*), the Ottomans were not able to muster the desired public opinion in Europe; the situation was not even close to similar campaigns that polarized the European public against the Ottoman Empire, of which Gladstone's "Bulgarian Horrors" was the most prominent.

As the decisions of the Berlin Congress were rather vague and the situation on the ground in Bosnia Herzegovina was fluctuating, members of the Ottoman cabinet discussed different options for Bosnia Herzegovina that would enable Ottoman administration of the province. Autonomy frequently resurfaced as a solution for Bosnia Herzegovina, anticipated by both Ottoman statesmen and Bosnian Muslims. The cabinet members also deliberated a collective transfer of the Muslim population south toward the provinces of Işkodra (Shkodër) and Kosovo as a last resort, to save them from anticipated persecution.[70] From the experiences of the Ottoman Empire up to that point—each loss of territory resulted in Muslim refugees fleeing post-Ottoman regimes—it was expected that the Habsburg takeover would not be much different from the Russian, Greek, Serbian, Bulgarian, or Montenegrin occupations.

The Habsburg military completely controlled Bosnia Herzegovina by late 1878. One district, the Novi Pazar Sandžak, Bosnia's corridor to the Ottoman Empire, which was tucked between then-independent Serbia and Montenegro, was to have a limited Habsburg and Ottoman military presence. Sultan Abdülhamid II (1876–1909) approved negotiations with the Habsburg Monarchy regarding Bosnia and Novi Pazar, as he was concerned that the region could also be fully occupied like Bosnia Herzegovina, which would give the Austrians more of an opportunity to engage in "harmful activity" in the Ottoman Empire.[71] Furthermore, the Ottomans had only a written note from the Habsburg Foreign Minister Count Andrássy, regarding Ottoman sovereignty promised in Berlin, and the sultan thought it would be beneficial to make the claim official by way of a bilateral convention. The sultan's approval was conditioned by four main requirements: Ottoman sovereignty in the province, temporary nature of the occupation, observance of Ottoman laws for Bosnian subjects, and determination of the number and location of Habsburg soldiers to be stationed in Novi Pazar.[72]

The Ottoman cabinet met in the sultan's private quarters on the evening of April 19, 1879, to discuss the bilateral agreement. According to informal news and intelligence presented at the meeting, armed resistance by locals in the Novi Pazar district was expected. It was also acknowledged that they would not obey Austrian or Ottoman orders—after what had happened in Bosnia Herzegovina—but would instead fight "to the death." The fact that Austria insisted on sharing military presence with the Ottomans in Novi

Pazar was understood to be an Austrian ploy to use the Ottoman military to contain any possible upheaval among the locals. Therefore, to avoid "oppressing our own people with our hands," it was concluded by the cabinet that the least that could be done was to secretly encourage and help the population oppose the Habsburgs in the event of occupation.[73] Such resistance to borders drawn in Berlin was locally organized in regions given to Serbia and Montenegro and populated by Slavic- and Albanian-speaking Muslims and Catholics. In one instance, the locals from a cluster of mountainous villages in the Plav-Gusinje region rejected Ottoman orders and repelled Montenegrin forces trying to occupy them, compelling the Ottomans and the European states to seek out another region in exchange.[74]

Sultan Abdülhamid II was also concerned about the intentions of the Habsburg Empire in the Balkans beyond Bosnia. With the memory fresh of Russians at the gates of Istanbul, the fear that Austria would reach Salonica became more tangible with their occupation of Bosnia Herzegovina and their military stationed in Novi Pazar. Also considered were concurrent Habsburg attempts to insert themselves in the Greek expansion plans in order to control parts of Western Rumelia.[75] Habsburg objectives were no secret: a contemporary traveler, Edith Durham, noted a prevalent understanding that consolidation of the Habsburg rule in Bosnia was a stepping-stone to expansion toward Salonica.[76] Assuming that Austria would not stop at Salonica alone, but planned to take over Albania too, the sultan and cabinet members contemplated worst-case scenarios that would press the Ottomans into an unacceptable situation between Russia and Austria-Hungary, in a principality consisting of Istanbul and its surroundings.[77]

The convention between the Habsburg and Ottoman empires was signed in April 1879. Ten articles were prefaced by a statement that the military occupation in no way infringed on the sovereignty of the sultan in the province; however, there was no mention of the temporary nature of the occupation.[78] The emphasis was on upholding religious freedoms for inhabitants of Bosnia Herzegovina, regard for Muslim traditions and religious practices, and confirmation of Muslims' personal and material safety. Guarantees were made that the name of the sultan was to be mentioned in Friday prayers, and the Ottoman flag was to be hoisted on minarets in accordance with the practice at the time. Bosnian income was to be used exclusively within the province, Ottoman money would continue to circulate, and the new administration would continue to employ locals in the provincial government service.

The Habsburg Monarchy violated and invalidated many of the agreement articles, counting on the Ottoman inability to enforce them and the lack of support in European circles if they protested. Free circulation of Ottoman money was prohibited within a year, and Bosnia Herzegovina was included in the Habsburg economic, trade, and customs system. Ottoman assets, goods, and military equipment remaining in the province were to be freely used by the Ottoman Empire as per Article 5, but many Ottoman complaints upon news of their destruction by the Habsburgs met with no response.[79] Because of issues ranging from candidates' loyalty to lack of Habsburg educational and language requirements, the new administration was overwhelmingly staffed by Habsburg citizens. The question of Ottoman representation in the province was avoided in this convention. One foreign observer doubted the survival of even an Ottoman consul.[80] However, the ambiguous situation seemed to have benefited both sides. For instance, the Austrians would not accept an Ottoman governor or a similar representative symbolizing Ottoman sovereignty and Bosnia's autonomy tying the province to the Ottoman Empire, as the Ottomans had hoped. Nor was a consul acceptable to the Ottomans, who would be confirming Bosnia's foreign status and thus negating the sultan's sovereignty if they sent such a representative. With no clear blueprint on the ways in which the occupation was to be carried out, the Habsburg Monarchy was in a position to test the limits in Bosnia Herzegovina and of the Ottoman Empire.

In addition to Bosnia Herzegovina, the Berlin Treaty authorized more territorial losses for the Ottoman Empire: Romania, Serbia, and Montenegro were given independence; Eastern Rumelia and the principality of Bulgaria were created with limited Ottoman authority; Great Britain occupied Cyprus; and the three northeastern Anatolian provinces of Kars, Ardahan, and Batum were given to Russia. Many of these territorial losses were followed by Muslim migrations from these regions into the Ottoman Empire. A million people fled Danube and Edirne provinces as a result of war efforts to achieve a Bulgarian demographic majority and then use the new demographic situation as a basis for claims to territory.[81] Recognition of independence at the congress was conditioned on acknowledging equal rights of all confessional groups, at the insistence of Alliance Israélite Universelle, in reaction to the discrimination of Jewish populations in Romania, Bulgaria, and Serbia. By default, the clause meant equality for Muslims, too. Despite the treaty guarantees, the implementation was slow and inconsistent. Muslims (Slav, Albanian, Roma, Turkish, Tatar, and Circassian) emigrated from Serbia—some by force, some in anticipation of atrocities and dispossession akin to those witnessed during the Russo-Ottoman War. Similarly, Montenegro worked to replace its Muslim and Catholic populations with newly arrived Orthodox Christian refugees from Herzegovina and Dalmatia. Serbia and Montenegro, however, had to balance the nationalist policies of ethnic cleansing with the economic consequences of depopulation.[82] After Ottoman Thessaly was incorporated by treaty into the Greek Kingdom in 1881, it lost almost all of its Muslim population—even the majority in the provincial capital Larissa by 1897, despite official recognition of Muslims as minorities.[83] Aware of the fate of Muslims in the adjacent regions, a contemporary Bosnian author concluded that the Habsburg occupation actually protected Bosnian Muslims from the doom of Muslims in neighboring lands.[84]

Expanding Habsburg Influence

The Congress of Berlin was a manifestation of the late nineteenth-century European understanding of the international system, exposing the inequality of member states qualified along civilizational paradigms: European states were on the civilized end of the spectrum, and semicivilized and uncivilized nations became the object of international law.[85] Treaties between empires were the guiding principle of international interaction for the Ottoman Empire even before the advent of the Concert of Europe, the purpose of which was to maintain the balance of power among European states in the nineteenth century and in which the Ottoman Empire also participated since the Paris Treaty (1856).[86] Although Ottoman sovereignty was legally recognized in these treaties, European empires justified their encroachment upon Ottoman territorial, economic, and political domains in terms of the same international legal framework. In response, the Ottoman Foreign Ministry embraced international law as a defensive strategy, especially when trying to outmaneuver European powers over colonial questions. As a consequence of Ottoman losses at the Berlin Congress, followed by the French occupation of Tunisia (1881) and the British occupation of Egypt

(1882), the Ministry of Foreign Affairs Office of Legal Counsel (Hukuk Müşavirliği Istişare Odası) was created to assert Ottoman equality within the international order.[87] It was to play an important role in interpreting Bosnian subjects' legal relationship in between the Ottoman and Habsburg empires.

The Habsburg takeover of Bosnia Herzegovina was an early case of internationally sanctioned occupation. It was a legally anomalous event even in the skewed understanding of the nascent international law of the nineteenth century. After the 1870s, the autonomy of some Ottoman provinces—until then considered a feature of internal Ottoman statecraft—began to be viewed in terms of diminishing sovereignty of the sultan, and from that perspective, as a steppingstone to autonomous territories' full independence or inclusion into a European state, as the Berlin Treaty confirmed for some.[88] But Bosnia Herzegovina was not an autonomous Ottoman region, and the nature of the Habsburg occupation was akin to annexation. The status of Bosnia Herzegovina also differed from the new autonomies granted at the Berlin Congress to regions such as the Bulgarian Principality and Crete. This ambiguity allowed Austria-Hungary great latitude in the way it planned and conducted the occupation of Bosnia Herzegovina. It also created room for the province's subjects who petitioned both empires to influence the course of diplomatic interimperial trajectories and assert their own interests.

Occupation, the establishment of provincial administration, inclusion in the Habsburg Monarchy's customs system, and the military conscription law established Bosnia Herzegovina's permanency as part of the Habsburg Empire, despite the legal limbo from 1878 to 1908. Habsburg imperial endeavors were rarely defined as colonialism in historiography when compared to European overseas colonies. Bosnia Herzegovina was, after all, a contiguous territory and included Slav population who spoke languages already spoken by some of the empire's other Slav subjects. Robert Donia called this situation a "proximate colony": a contiguous colony with overlapping populations providing the administrators with a better understanding of provincial history and culture, while at the same time allowing the provincial subjects access to policymakers and instruments of public expression. The proximity and interconnectedness of the two polities, however, made the experience more acute and intensified the antagonisms between the colonizer and the colonized.[89]

Recent reassessments rooted in postcolonial theory focus on the Habsburg self-proclaimed cultural and civilizing missions comparable to other European empires, as rationale to rethink the Habsburg colonial role.[90] Following the practices of other colonial powers, the Habsburgs tapped into the discourse of civilization and progress and emphasized the benefits that came with occupation. They borrowed from the repertoire of colonial rule when it came to ruling Muslim populations and subjugating Islamic institutions into the imperial apparatus. In an 1895 interview, Benjamin Kállay confirmed the Habsburg mission in Bosnia as that of an Occidental empire carrying civilization to Oriental peoples.[91] In the imperial system, Bosnia Herzegovina did not belong to either part of the monarchy and was ruled directly by the Joint Ministry of Finance, with great latitude. That there was no Bosnian representation in the parliaments even after the annexation, and that the subjects' personal status was the most restricted, also set Bosnia Herzegovina apart from the rest of the monarchy.

The approach to its southernmost province was similar to the Habsburg redemption and "recasting" of Galicia, its northernmost province a hundred years earlier, where barbarism needed to be reformed and backwardness ameliorated.[92] What is more, the governing of Bosnia Herzegovina was to project the success of a particular Habsburg idea of multiculturalism.[93] Mandate to "civilize" an Oriental province—an effort on behalf of Europe in its borderlands—was to also confirm Austria-Hungary's representative place within Europe. The civilizing project exhibited the ability of the Habsburg state to rule foreign lands at the height of European scramble for colonies. Contemporaries as well as postimperial scholars observed the Habsburg Monarchy as an anomaly for its linguistic, ethnic, and religious diversity, and as a region lagging behind the rest of Europe in economic development, even before the addition of Bosnia Herzegovina. However, scholars have shown that the rest of Europe was as diverse and that it was the state institutions and centralization policies that had a role in standardizing modern national identities.[94] Empire-centered analysis situated Austro-Hungarian uniqueness in the legal and administrative structures it developed to manage cultural differences.[95] As both themes converged in Bosnia Herzegovina, the Habsburgs' success in transforming the eastern province and its diverse inhabitants was to propel the Habsburgs to the European forefront as well versed in matters of uplifting the entirety of the multicultural Balkans that needed to be solved from within the Eastern Question.

Both the Ottomans and the Habsburgs faced nationalist movements in their domains as one of the main challenges to imperial rule. In an effort to contest them, both empires differently engaged with these new forms by using some of the same methods of political activity. The Habsburg Monarchy promoted a sense of imperial allegiance centered on the dynasty.[96] The Ottoman Empire, too, worked to foster a sense of Ottoman imperial identity in response to increasing threats to its integrity.[97] This was particularly evident in Bosnia Herzegovina, which was coveted by Pan-Slavic, Croatian, and Serbian nationalist movements, while its Ottoman and Habsburg administrations worked to provide alternative forms of allegiance. Edin Hajdarpasic showed how in Bosnia Herzegovina these were not separate national and imperial—that is, ethnic and supraethnic politics—but instead can be observed through their intertwined relationships. Namely, in an effort to thwart the emerging forces of nationalism, both Ottoman and Habsburg officials adopted the strategies of nationalist movements, including ethnographic work, rewriting and glorification of particular versions of history, and reliance on print and press in spreading imperial-patriotic sentiment.[98]

This approach was similarly employed in competition among empires vying for the allegiance of the same subjects. While Habsburg administrators justified their presence and countered nationalist propaganda in the province with the civilizing narrative, Bosnian Muslims saw themselves habitually identified with the Ottoman Empire and the trope of the "Turkish yoke," not only by nationalists but also by the Habsburgs and other European observers. Sending petitions to the Ottoman Empire, Muslims complained that Austria had been slandering the Ottomans and Bosnian Muslims by accusing them of tyranny and oppression for hundreds of years, and using that as a pretext for diplomatic action and for inciting Christian vengeance for supposed persecution.[99] Ottoman officials were also informed of a view in a Habsburg report alleging that most of the land in Bosnia Herzegovina was in Muslims' hands because they were pre-Ottoman landowners who converted to Islam just so they could keep the land. The report anticipated that the Muslim landowners would "return to their old faith" in the near future.[100] For the administration of Sultan Abdülhamid II, history and history writing came to have a didactic role, in order to bolster the power of the empire and the Ottoman dynasty and to attain the loyalties of its subjects.[101] Histories diverging from the imperial narrative damaged the Ottoman image and hindered the legitimization of imperial policies at home. Ottoman administrators reported on such narratives of revisionist history when they were used as justification for insurrectionary activities they had to manage with increasing frequency.[102]

Habsburg and other European colonial powers in the Middle East promoted an image of an Ottoman Empire incapable of justly ruling its (Christian) populations and containing its territories, thus warranting European intervention. Linguistic, ethnographic, and cartographic knowledge became important in crafting colonial policies and laying the epistemological foundations of essentialism about Muslims and the "East," as critiqued by Edward Said.[103] Nationalist movements borrowed from the same repertoire, viewing the Ottoman Empire as invaders and exploiters and its subjects as having suffered Ottoman oppression for centuries, in need of European liberation and enlightenment. The narrative became integral to foundational myths of Balkan nation-states, as well as other countries carved out of the Ottoman domains that were colonized by European powers. Before overseas colonies, the European self-knowledge was first shaped in response to its own European East, as observed by Larry Wolff and Maria Todorova.[104] Bosnia Herzegovina and the Ottoman Balkans were the recipients of both layers of otherness.

As the Ottoman Tanzimat instituted legal equality among its subjects, European powers, to the contrary, increasingly insisted on strengthening bureaucratic distinctions between Ottoman Christians and Muslims. Proclaiming themselves the protectors of one or the other Ottoman Christian community, the European powers awarded patronage and endorsed struggles for ascendancy, which often materialized in violence. Such patronage warranted an understanding of the relationship with their Muslim neighbors in terms of rivalry throughout the Ottoman religiously mixed societies, from Western Balkans to Mount Lebanon, effectively undermining Ottoman sovereignty.[105] Once Holy Roman emperors, the Habsburgs tried to establish themselves as protectors of Catholic minorities in the Ottoman Balkans. Istanbul noted the interference in local politics and the bribery of Ottoman officials in the Ottoman provinces neighboring Bosnia, while occasional apprehension of Habsburg spies made Ottoman administrators vigilant about Habsburg activities in Ottoman Albanian provinces (Kosovo, Işkodra, Manastır, and Yanya).[106] Habsburg influence there was projected by way of education and competed with the Russian, Italian, Serbian, Montenegrin, and Greek activists and investments in regional schools. The locals exploited these rivalries to empower themselves and advance their goals, but not necessarily along confessional or ethnic lines as the instigators had hoped.[107] Bosnia Herzegovina provided access to these regions, while Albanian exiles from the newly acquired Serbian territories helped connect the Habsburg Albanology experts to local interests—not unlike the Slav specialists whose expertise played a role in the conquest of Bosnia Herzegovina, in order to formulate policies and cultivate ties.[108] The proximity of Habsburg Bosnia, the Habsburg experience and success in a former Ottoman province, together with the shared subjects, were strategic and diplomatic instruments in asserting a Habsburg sphere of influence in the Balkans.

In 1878, Austria-Hungary settled for occupation rather than direct territorial annexation of Bosnia Herzegovina, the possibility of which was later confirmed by the Three Emperors' League in 1881. Ultimately, Bosnia Herzegovina was ruled by a special joint commission, later the Bosnian Bureau, under the Habsburg Joint Ministry of Finance. Bosnia's status in the Dual Monarchy remained dubious even after annexation in 1908, when it became Reichsland but not Kronland, signifying that it did not belong to either part of the monarchy and could not send representatives to the parliaments in Vienna or Budapest.[109] After the initial military regime, a civilian administration was established in 1880. The number of administrators rose fivefold in the first three years and continued to rise, "yet, only a few good men came."[110] The administration cautiously carried over Ottoman administrative divisions, laws, and practices and only gradually replaced them. This led to further disappointment among the province's peasants, who were expecting the Muslim-owned land to be expropriated and redistributed to them, just like the land grabs that had unfolded in other former Ottoman territories. They so firmly believed that the confiscation of Muslim properties would also take place in Bosnia Herzegovina that they stopped working until the administration warned that it would still enforce the collection of dues and taxes.[111] Habsburg policies and their inherent imperial logic distinguished the takeover of Bosnia Herzegovina from other Ottoman losses in Europe, with consequences for its Muslims that extended beyond the empires' existence.

The Habsburgs never really envisioned the occupation as temporary, but from the start worked on integrating the province into the monarchy, so that ultimately its official annexation would be a natural development. Bosnian Muslims were to play a key role in this absorption by developing allegiance to the emperor and the Habsburg Empire and aspiring to such a union on their own. They comprised the notable class, owned most of the land in the province, and were already a part of the ruling (Ottoman) imperial polity. At the same time, the Habsburg administration was uneasy about enduring Ottoman influence in the province. It tried to unsettle the continuation of relationships and contain the formation of new bonds. Family, business, educational, and trade affiliations continued after the Austro-Hungarian occupation and were significant for recruitment into the Bosnian opposition movements, especially considering the high illiteracy rate, which prevented other forms of communication on the broadest level.[112] To this end, the Habsburg provincial administration tried to limit and control travel to and from the Ottoman Empire. In 1896, Bosnians studying in the Ottoman Empire who wanted to visit during the holidays were not allowed to enter Bosnia Herzegovina. According to the Ottoman consul in Dubrovnik, the Habsburg administration feared that they would rouse the Muslims with anti-Habsburg propaganda.[113] Bosnians in the Ottoman Empire who had attempted to travel to Bosnia Herzegovina with Ottoman passports were treated as foreigners, and sometimes denied visas, of which they complained to the Ottoman authorities. They maintained that Bosnia was still an Ottoman province and cited travel as "a natural right of those belonging to civilized governments," carefully choosing meaningful language that would alert both empires.[114] The ambiguous legal position of Bosnia Herzegovina also affected inhabitants' official nationality, and more practically, issuance of passports, but was left out of the 1879 convention.

Because Bosnia did not belong to either the Austrian or the Hungarian part of the Dual Monarchy, its inhabitants were given a status of provincial subjects (*Landesangehörigkeit*), which remained undefined, but did limit Bosnian subjects in the monarchy and abroad compared to other Austrian and Hungarian subjects.[115] The Habsburg regulations, just like the Ottoman Nationality Law of 1869 and many such laws of the time, focused on the ways of acquisition and loss of membership rather than on rights of subjects.[116] In an effort to disaffect the Ottoman Empire, however, the Habsburg administration was successful in separating Bosnian inhabitants from the Ottoman Empire as far as legal and administrative aspects were concerned. Provincial administration issued three separate kinds of travel documents to Bosnian provincial subjects—still called by their Ottoman name *tezkere*—for travel within the province, to the monarchy, and abroad.

The Ottoman Empire treated Bosnian subjects as Ottoman until proven otherwise when they bought property in the Ottoman domains or traveled for education and work, unless they sought Habsburg consular protections.[117] Archival documents show that legal matters (most commonly cases of inheritance and divorce) were resolved between consulates in Istanbul and Vienna and the legal office of the Ministry of Foreign Affairs, until an Ottoman consulate in Sarajevo was established after the annexation in 1908. Responding to the contraction of Ottoman sovereignty over its lands and subjects, some of whom had a choice of foreign protections, provisions regarding expatriation in the Ottoman Nationality Law did not acknowledge any nationality change by Ottoman subjects without permission.[118] Foreign protections were an extension of extraterritorial rights that European powers, including Austria-Hungary, claimed in the Ottoman Empire. "Capitulations," as they were called, were early modern Ottoman unilateral grants and privileges to Europeans that included tax exemptions, immunity from Ottoman jurisdiction, and consular protection, and they originally functioned as a demonstration of Ottoman power. In the nineteenth century, however, the capitulations began to be enforced as obligatory by European powers who used them as a pretext to interfere in Ottoman affairs. They further extended these rights to their Ottoman protégés. When these privileges were endorsed in the various treaties in the nineteenth century, they assumed the standing of international law.[119]

The Habsburg administration in Bosnia was careful in how they portrayed Bosnian travel to the Ottoman Empire, as migration tainted the image of Habsburg success in the province. It reluctantly allowed and monitored returnees from the Ottoman Empire, as well as those going back and forth and maintaining subjecthood in both empires. Such an approach can be attributed to the legally ambiguous status of the Habsburg-occupied sovereign Ottoman province. It certainly played a role in the Habsburg seizure of the right to enforce jurisdiction over Bosnian subjects, rather than leaving it to the outcome of negotiations with the Ottomans. However, failure of the Habsburg administration to extend its Bosnian subjects' full legal and extraterritorial protections on Ottoman soil, even after any such ambiguity was resolved post-annexation, revealed the Habsburg view of Bosnian subjects as, contrary to propaganda, not full-fledged members of a multicultural state. Namely, in trying to resolve the question of whether consular legal jurisdiction was to be applied to Bosnians according to the Austrian civic code (which was not in effect in Bosnia) or through shari'a courts (operating in Bosnia and comparable to the Ottoman shari'a courts), the administration acted at the expense of its Bosnian subjects. Habsburg Muslim subjects were referred to provincial courts, which was less than the extent of rights of other Habsburg subjects in the Ottoman Empire.[120]

Becoming Habsburg?

From the start of the occupation, the administration encouraged locally sourced efforts at separation from the Ottoman Empire in all matters, most importantly the religious relationships articulated in the bilateral convention with the Ottoman Empire. In addition to working on severing the formal ties facilitated through the Ottoman religious institutions of Muslims and Orthodox Christians (Chapter 4), even symbolic displays of Ottoman-ness were discouraged. Celebration of the sultan's twenty-fifth accession to the throne (*cülus-i humayun*) was not permitted in Bosnia Herzegovina, and in one such public celebration participants were confronted by gendarmes, when "forty-six Muslims and three Orthodox Christians" were fined up to 500 krone.[121] In its place, the celebration of the Habsburg emperor's birthday, accession to the throne, and wedding anniversary were organized and encouraged among all subjects in the province.[122]

The Ottoman consul in Dubrovnik observed the Habsburg policy of playing different groups against each other as "Austria sowing discord among Catholics, Slavs [Orthodox Christians], and Muslims," to prevent the possibility of a provincewide challenge to Habsburg authority. He interpreted the situation in terms of Ottoman interests, noting that Muslims who "seeing their safety and way of life in danger, their wellbeing, honor, and religion threatened, felt the need for strengthening by uniting, for the Sublime State, and even more for maintaining the connection [with the Ottoman Empire]."[123] Indeed, a joint effort among some notables and religious officials produced petitions that were sent to Istanbul with equal regional representation and in collaboration with the Bosnian diaspora in the Ottoman Empire.[124]

The arrival of the Austria-Hungary administration and the provincial policies incited a high level of activity among those who wanted to integrate, engage, and counter them, in a relatively unanimous manner, unseen for much of the nineteenth century. Some reacted by migrating to the Ottoman Empire, seeing it as a safe haven from the policies of the Habsburg administration, and a place to preserve their social status, employment, and wealth, as well as a symbol and expression of their identity. Having built their prominence as defenders of the Ottoman borders fighting in the name of Islam, Bosnian notables had challenged the central administrators and even criticized sultans' actions on the basis of being "un-Islamic." The opposition was grounded in an understanding of their rights to do so as Muslims and as members of Ottoman polity. Centuries-long Ottoman legacy and being Ottoman became features of negotiation, defining interactions with both empires and drawing the Ottomans and the Habsburgs into the process of intervention and competition over allegiances of their shared subjects.

It is important to point out the basic historical irony here: after a troubled relationship in the first half of the nineteenth century, it took a Habsburg occupation for Bosnian notables to affirm their loyalty to the Ottoman Empire. Yet allegiance to the Ottoman Empire was not an exclusive affair. While some migrated in a decisive exit strategy, many maintained ties and saw the Ottoman Empire as their Great Power protector when defining their rights in the province. Others nurtured the Ottoman legacy by maintaining old ties and creating new ones as integral to their Habsburg Bosnian existence.

2   Migration

Those Who Left

WITH THAT REALIZATION that the Habsburgs were to stay in Bosnia Herzegovina, close to a hundred prominent families from Mostar, Trebinje, Čapljina, and Stolac in Herzegovina sent an envoy to Istanbul petitioning for resettlement within the Ottoman domains. Upon receiving permission, they set out on a journey that would take them through Istanbul and Izmir. Those who did not stay there continued on, finally purchasing land and settling in a village outside Damascus. The inhospitable climate and unreceptive neighbors, though, soon pushed them to seek out new settlements. Since they wanted to stay together as a group, the Ottoman government granted them state land in Caesarea (Qaysariyya) and Yanoun near Nablus in Palestine. Some later moved to Anatolia.[1]

About half of those who had set out from Herzegovina made Caesarea their home, building an elementary school, a mosque, an administrative building, and houses in the Herzegovinian style. The fertile lands and harbor provided them opportunities for trade, and soon they had set up a harbor customs office. In Caesarea they maintained their Bosnian language and family names; it was not until later, when immigrants started moving away to larger urban centers, that many assumed the last name Bushnaq (Bosniak) and assimilated to Palestinian culture.[2] Little could they know that their descendants would again be uprooted in 1948, when the Zionist forces expelled the population of Caesarea. Entire families once again went into exile, this time as Palestinians.[3] Today, only the Bosnian Mosque with its minaret (and its name) is still standing, used as a restaurant in the Israeli Caesarea National Park.

For the first time since 1699, withdrawal of the Ottomans from their lost territories in Europe did not entail the elimination of local Muslim populations. The Habsburg civilian administration guaranteed rights related to religion, property, and personal freedoms to its new subjects. Conciliatory attitudes toward the Bosnian Muslims affected their understanding of the prospects in Habsburg Bosnia Herzegovina and modified the meaning of possible advantages of migration. However, to at least a section of the population, the conditions in Habsburg Bosnia Herzegovina were not conducive to staying. Several waves of migration to the Ottoman Empire followed at the turn of the twentieth century. Why did these Slav Muslims, then, decide to leave their homes and insist on settling within Ottoman borders?

Political and diplomatic effects of migration for both the Habsburg and the Ottoman empires were critical, and migratory movements were closely monitored by both. In addition to the destabilizing social and economic consequences of large-scale population movements, Muslim emigration was not beneficial for the Habsburg image at home and in European diplomatic circles. The Habsburg policy toward Muslims was manifold. The monarchy was given Bosnia Herzegovina as part of the European solution to the Eastern Question, so the administration wanted to exhibit its mandate as a successful achievement. Creating an exemplary colony in Bosnia Herzegovina was meant to uphold Habsburg imperial multiculturalism, especially considering that its concept was being challenged even within the Dual Monarchy. This Habsburg sense that imperial unity improved its component cultures was projected outward as well. Administration of a diverse Bosnia Herzegovina would demonstrate the monarchy's approach suitable for bringing stability and development to different groups in the Balkans, further cultivating imperial objectives in southeastern Europe.[4] Finally, Muslim migration would create a demographic imbalance that the administration feared would encourage Russian-sponsored, Serbian nationalist advances in Bosnia Herzegovina; these would not only hinder Austro-

Hungarian plans for the Balkans, but also embolden nationalist activity across Habsburg domains inhabited by Slavs.

For the Ottoman Empire, despite the Pan-Islamic tone of the Hamidian rhetoric, Bosnian Muslim migration was problematic and ultimately disadvantageous as observed from the perspective of Ottoman policies. Ottoman ministers and administrators handling the astonishing flow of millions of refugees to the Ottoman Empire from other parts of the Balkans and Russia advised discouraging the Bosnian Muslim migration until after the funds and locations for their resettlement were secured. Diplomats and consuls likewise desired the Bosnian Muslims to stay put as their presence in the province validated Ottoman reasoning to claim imperial protection of their nominal subjects as well as caliphal jurisdiction of Muslims under non-Muslim rule. Muslim presence in Bosnia Herzegovina sustained, however nominally, claims to sovereignty over the province guaranteed at the Berlin Congress and provided the Ottomans with a diplomatic asset in their eager bid to remain involved in interimperial balancing acts. Bosnian literati, political activists, clergy of all faiths, and even nationalists outside of Bosnia loudly debated the Muslim migration with all of its consequences, making their voice heard through the burgeoning press, activism in the province and abroad, as well as through the growing number of associations. Broader implications of the Bosnian migration were at the center of the question of the Muslim demographic presence in Europe. That is, until the Habsburg occupation of Bosnia as well as afterwards, Ottoman withdrawal habitually meant the withdrawal of all Muslims, so much so that the case of Bosnia Herzegovina became a striking exception. Whether Bosnian Muslims migrated or stayed then became a contested issue involving the Habsburg and Ottoman empires, neighboring nation-states, and an array of provincial actors invested in Muslim existence in the province.

Migration was a response to the Habsburg military occupation and administration, and the social, political, and economic changes it brought. It was the most intense reaction, carrying repercussions for both empires and for those who stayed behind. Former subjects' loyalty to the Ottoman Empire and their distrust and rejection of Austria-Hungary have often been cited as explanations for Muslim migration from Habsburg Bosnia. However, migration was also a tool of negotiation, "forum shopping," and leveraging legal protections. It was not always considered permanent nor unidirectional. For the two empires and the nation-states in the Balkans, migration increasingly meant numbers and demographic dominance tied to territorial control, becoming a new currency in interimperial and national contention.

Migrants did not generally understand their relocation as permanent, especially in the early period of occupation. Many wanted to settle close to Bosnia Herzegovina to make their return easier. Others went back and forth, maintaining residence and sometimes citizenship in both empires. Ottoman legal sovereignty in Bosnia Herzegovina from 1878 to 1908 was an important lever in negotiations with occupying forces, while migration represented an exit option: the fact that Bosnian Muslims had a choice to stay or to migrate distinguished them from most other Balkan migrants to the Ottoman Empire. Consequently, Muslim representatives used migration to bargain with the Habsburg and the Ottoman administrations.

Ever since the Ottomans' withdrawal from Bosnia Herzegovina and the Habsburg takeover, Muslims have migrated—and that migration continued well beyond both empires' existence. Migration to the Ottoman Empire continued throughout the period of the Austro-Hungarian administration in Bosnia Herzegovina, with major waves of population movement at the time of initial occupation in 1878; with the announcement of the conscription law and the rebellion that followed it in 1882–1883, concurrent with the Catholic proselytism and Habsburg colonizing projects, as well as the Bosnian Muslim opposition activity in the following years; and finally after the Habsburg annexation of Bosnia Herzegovina in 1908. Today, the descendants of Bushnaqs and Boşnaks live across the former Ottoman world.

Migration After the Occupation, 1878

Even before the Austrian occupation, the province of Bosnia Herzegovina had already suffered unrest that took a toll on the population. What was termed the Eastern Crisis, began in Herzegovina in 1875, with a peasant rebellion against persistent tax collection measures despite drought and a bad harvest. The rebellion escalated into local insurrection, leading to nearly 250,000 mostly Orthodox Christian peasants fleeing over the borders into the Habsburg and Montenegrin territories.[5] Soon, funds and arms from Serbia, Montenegro, and Russia were supplying local bands to perpetuate the crisis through attacks on Ottoman officials, soldiers, and landlords.

General violence toward the population—as well as destruction of homes, infrastructure, and crops—all posed a threat to returnees.[6] A comparison of the 1870 and 1879 Ottoman population surveys revealed a 7 percent decline of the Orthodox Christian population and a 35 percent decline of the Muslim population.[7] The conclusion of the Eastern Crisis brought Habsburg occupation of the province, which was a new challenge for the already exhausted Bosnian population.

With the arrival of Austria-Hungary, Ottoman officials and the military in the province promptly left for the Ottoman Empire by way of Trieste, Dubrovnik, and Belgrade. A number of those affected by the clashes between the Habsburg forces and the resistance, reported to be mostly women and children, took temporary refuge in Serbia.[8] Fearing repercussions, resistance fighters also sought protection in the neighboring Ottoman regions. Ottoman diplomats protested the harsh treatment of the local population by the occupying Habsburg military, and this changed substantially with the arrival of the new commander, the Duke of Württemberg. The subsequent announcement of amnesty prompted those refugees to return to Bosnia Herzegovina.[9]

Few former Ottoman employees transitioned into the emerging Habsburg administration. Others, who wished to continue their employment or hoped for prospects with the Ottoman government, emigrated to the Ottoman domains. One such man was Ibrahim Bakarević, whom we learn of from preserved correspondence with his family, a rare archival find. Bakarević and his daughter Esma regularly wrote from Istanbul to Ibrahim's brother Mustafa in Sarajevo. Ibrahim, a member of a large landowning and merchant family from Sarajevo, with land and business networks across Bosnia and the Ottoman Empire, was the only one in the family to move to Istanbul after the Habsburg occupation. The Bakarević family continued with their business, and family members traveled between Istanbul and Sarajevo.[10] Despite his wealth and the relatively undisturbed transition between the two imperial administrations, Ibrahim moved to Istanbul with his wife Vasvija, his two daughters Esma and Zehra, and their families. Why did he decide to move? That he was a retired major (*binbaşı*) in the Ottoman army might have influenced his decision.[11] Ibrahim and Vasvija each owned their own properties and businesses in Bosnia, which continued to be managed by Ibrahim's brother Mustafa after their departure, so they regularly received their profits in Istanbul.[12] In addition, Ibrahim received a pension (*tekaüdiye*) as a retired Ottoman officer, which with the profits coming from Bosnia, made their life in Istanbul comfortable.[13] However, the Bakarević family and other well-to-do migrants were the exception. Even when migrants originally set out on the challenging journey with funds, the money quickly ran out, and most had to rely on government aid for housing, land, food, and clothing. When those migrants wrote back to their family and friends in Bosnia, the Habsburg administration publicized their letters in the press in the hopes that the harsh realities of migrant life in the Ottoman Empire would deter further migration.[14]

Within several months of the Habsburg occupation, members of the Ottoman Meclis-i Vukela (Council of Ministers) presented the sultan with their opinions regarding the rise in petitions for migration from Bosnia Herzegovina. A major consideration for the Ottoman government was the transport and settlement of migrants, which would fall on the state, local authorities, and the local population already dealing with the floods of refugees fleeing Bulgaria and Serbia in the aftermath of the 1877–1878 war. It was also brought up that some of the migrants from the Caucasus who had been arriving for over a decade were still awaiting their permanent settlement. Members of the cabinet agreed that Muslim migration from Bosnia Herzegovina, "where 400,000 Muslims and up to 500,000 Christians" of different denominations lived, was certainly not in the interest of the Ottoman state and that there were important reasons for the Muslims to remain in the province.[15]

Primarily, the Ottoman ministers reasoned that the sovereign rights and any territorial claims of the sultan in Bosnia Herzegovina rested with the continuity and size of the Muslim population there. Seriously considering Austria-Hungary's plans for advancement toward Salonica, the ministers predicted that the Muslim population would "naturally" rise to arms, in which case it would be indispensable to have a 400,000-strong Muslim force to counter the Austrian armies. Furthermore, the Habsburg army in Bosnia Herzegovina comprised 60,000 soldiers, who were stationed there "because of the Muslims"; this made any Habsburg military strategy contingent on the Ottoman stance, which provided additional leverage. Finally, the council warned that although the Austrians seemed to oppose Muslim migration, their position was strengthened by the fact that they gave the property of the departing Muslims to Christians. For these reasons, the council recommended that the Muslim presence in Bosnia Herzegovina needed to be supported in order to hinder Habsburg plans in the Balkans and maintain Ottoman spheres of influence.

The Ottoman Council of Ministers also elaborated on the logistics and the feasibility of a possible mass migration. They considered the financial burden on the Ottoman Imperial Treasury, the length of time it would take to organize the transport of 400,000 people, and the difficulties of travel by land and sea to Anatolia. They concluded that the financial capacity of the state could not even partially cover the expenses of a Bosnian Muslim migration and settlement and that the population in Anatolia could not be expected to aid the migrants, especially considering those already present in the Ottoman Empire who were yet to be settled. The Council of Ministers recommended that the Ottomans actively discourage Muslims from migrating by participating in their social, economic, and religious affairs, that is, by becoming their protectors and guardians. However, it was made clear that those who had made a firm decision to migrate should not be turned away. The Ottoman ambassador in Vienna discussing the petitions for migration likewise advised that migration was disadvantageous for both Muslims in Bosnia Herzegovina and for the Ottoman state.[16]

Petitions for immigration to the Ottoman Empire continued and were routinely approved. In 1880, the Ottoman authorities allowed for the immigration of "landless Muslims who lived in remote areas."[17] A number of prominent religious figures and "representatives of the people" (*Bosna ulema ve meşayihiyle mu'teberan-ı ahalisi*) complained to the Porte in 1880 about the ill treatment they experienced at the hands of the Habsburg administration. After listing the various ways in which the Habsburg administration violated the agreements and the guarantees under which it came to occupy Bosnia Herzegovina, the letter explained:

> Our country's intensely difficult circumstances and miserable condition make us envy those who moved onto the other world [passed away]. Although we are of the opinion that it is our duty [*vacibe-i zimmet*] to migrate from here, what has compelled us to stay put until now is the article of the Novi Pazar Convention . . . that confirms the permanence of sultan's legal rule over the land of Bosnia Herzegovina.[18]

Referring to the Novi Pazar Convention, the bilateral agreement detailing the Habsburg occupation and confirming Ottoman territorial sovereignty in Bosnia, the signatories concluded with a plea for justice, noting that they could not bring themselves to interpret the agreement to have meant for more than 400,000 Muslims in Bosnia Herzegovina, "faithful to the Sublime State, to be left to oppression and ruin." Dissatisfaction with the new authorities and the ensuing difficulties in Bosnia Herzegovina seem to have been tolerable as long as the occupation was considered temporary, that is, while there was hope that the Ottoman sultan would exercise his sovereign rights over Bosnian territory. The signatories appealed as Ottoman subjects, based their demands upon relevant international agreements, and referred to their predicament as "against the civilized norms of the nineteenth century" (*ondokuzuncu asrın medeniyyetine karşu*).[19]

Many of those who migrated settled in the areas of the Ottoman Empire closest to Bosnia Herzegovina—Novi Pazar Sandžak, Kosova, Işkodra, and Selanik provinces—hoping to return upon the reestablishment of the Ottoman administration in the near future. Those who went to Istanbul in 1878 joined the 200,000 refugees from Bulgaria, Romania, and Serbia who had already arrived there.[20] Salonica, a major port city, and the broader remaining Ottoman regions in the south of the Balkan peninsula had become a gathering point for numerous Balkan refugees in the aftermath of the Berlin Congress that granted independence to Serbia, Montenegro, Bulgaria, and Romania, all of which worked to homogenize their populations through massacres, intimidation, and expulsion. Bosnians arriving to the Ottoman provinces of Selanik and Kosovo found the area already teeming with refugees:[21] in the winter of 1878, it was estimated that there were 300,000 refugees there.[22] Some Bosnians remained in Macedonia, and others would go on and reach the port of Salonica, wishing to be settled in Anatolia and other destinations in the empire. Migrants found safety in Macedonia but also worked to go back to their hometowns and villages: for example, Bulgarian Muslims petitioned the European Commission of Eastern Rumelia and Serbian Muslims wrote to the British ambassador in Istanbul trying to get back their usurped properties, to no avail.[23] The Ottoman authorities in Macedonia were overwhelmed by waves of refugees and struggled to house and feed them. The British consul general reported a death rate of 40–65 percent in eastern Macedonia among the refugee population, three quarters of whom were widows and orphans.[24] The Ottoman administration rented and bought properties to settle the migrants when there were no imperial lands left for them. New villages formed, as did new neighborhoods on the outskirts of major cities, often simply named "migrant" (*muhacir*) neighborhoods. The name of one newly formed Bosnian village in Macedonia epitomized the dire conditions of many migrants: Bezgaštevo, meaning "without britches."

The Habsburg administration defined the main reason for migration as the inability of some Muslims to adjust to the new economic and administrative circumstances. Bosnia Herzegovina was already a part of the regional trade system, but artisans and merchants were unable to keep up with the competition once they were incorporated into the empire. At the same time, higher taxes affected the peasantry, and the average cost of living almost doubled under the Habsburg administration.[25] Policies of imperial centralization that had begun during the last years of Ottoman rule encroached on subjects' lives through their greater presence and the regulation of daily life. Some saw this as an Austrian imposition and responded by migrating, not realizing that the same processes were underway in the Ottoman Empire.

Considering that the parts of the Ottoman Empire where migrants settled were underdeveloped in comparison to Bosnia Herzegovina at the time, others concluded that "psychological reasons," or a sort of crisis of allegiance, augmented by military defeat and the new administration's initially repressive measures, were the primary motivation for migration.[26] Literature of the period articulated feelings of "being lost," and didactic discussions on migration and its condemnation were pervasive in novels, short stories, plays, and periodicals throughout the Habsburg period and beyond.[27]

With the transition to civil administration, Austrian policies in Bosnia were devised to show the "humanity and efficacy of Habsburg rule," a demonstration of which would make complete Austrian control possible and acceptable by the populace.[28] Austro-Hungarian policymakers and officials made a particular effort to work with the Bosnian Muslims. Wary of Pan-Slavism in its lands and in neighboring Serbia, Austria-Hungary hoped that Muslim imperial loyalty, rather than national loyalty, would contain its spread. Muslim migration disturbed the confessional balance in the province and threatened to embolden Serbian nationalist activity. More importantly, it negatively affected the monarchy's image: after all, the purpose of the Habsburgs' occupation mandate was to improve the situation in the province, not drive its population away. The Habsburg authorities began supporting local efforts to discourage the Muslim exodus and instituted a variety of administrative obstacles to migration without banning it outright. At the same time, they hoped that the departure of hostile oppositionists would make the task of administering the province easier.

Conscription as Motivation for Migration

The introduction of compulsory military service provoked an uprising in Herzegovina in 1882 that quickly spread to other areas.[29] The Bosnian Muslim and Orthodox Christian population protested, claiming that the measure infringed on the sultan's sovereignty and that, as Ottoman subjects, in spite of the occupation, they could not be asked to serve in a foreign imperial army.[30] They also opposed the fact that conscripted soldiers were treated like "any other Habsburg recruits" and sent to other regions of the empire—"even as far as Vienna"—instead of being stationed in the province for local defense, as had been the Ottoman practice that had been worked out during the implementation of the Tanzimat only a few decades earlier.[31]

In addition, Muslims questioned conscription on religious terms—specifically, whether it was permissible to serve in a non-Muslim army. The most incendiary rumors quickly spread among the population, highlighting the ways that Muslims in the Habsburg military would be forced to eat pork and not be allowed to pray, for example. The announcement of the conscription regulations in the newspaper *Sarajevski list*, however, addressed the provincial subjects and confirmed both the freedom of conscripts to fulfill their religious duties and the equality of all subjects in the eyes of their emperor.[32] Furthermore, the mufti of Sarajevo, Mustafa Hilmi Hadžiomerović (1816–1895), issued a fatwa calling on Muslims to serve in the Habsburg military.[33] The administration in Bosnia investigated public reactions to conscription, noting that "the Muslims do not want to grasp that they will no longer serve in the military of the Sultan, but rather in the military of a Christian sovereign."[34] Reports revealed dissatisfaction that translated into an upsurge in migration applications, which the administration read as an act of negotiation—an attempt to pressure the administration to rescind the law.[35]

Herzegovina, the center of the uprising, had a history of resisting conscription and other obligations to the state in the Ottoman period. Some two decades earlier, the Ottoman High Inspector Ahmed Cevdet Pasha visited Herzegovina because of an uprising there and tackled resistance to conscription in the Ottoman reordered military. He was successful in obtaining support of the notables, who pledged allegiance to the sultan and backed conscription in the name of "Islam and the State" (*din ü devlet*).[36] While there had been ways to avoid Ottoman conscription through payments and exemptions, the Habsburg blanket conscription affected all men, and therefore a large segment of the agricultural workforce, further intensifying the opposition's activities. In addition, bandits operating in Herzegovina and the Montenegro region for much of the nineteenth century contributed to the magnitude of the disorder; the border provided shelter for bandits and rebels, as well as for those escaping conscription and migrant families, prolonging the disturbance until the last years of the nineteenth century.

The Ottomans were subsidizing migrants' expenses in Montenegro,[37] while the Montenegrin authorities were inciting their own Muslim populations to migrate to the Ottoman Empire.[38] Shkodër, an administrative center of the Ottoman province of Işkodra on the border with Montenegro, was another arrival point for migrants from Bosnia Herzegovina. Yet another Ottoman region in the vicinity of their homeland, Shkodër was close enough that it was easy to return and to receive news quickly of developments in Bosnia Herzegovina. As such, it provided refuge for participants in the uprising, such as Ismail-aga Šarić of Stolac, labeled by the Habsburg consul there as one of the "fiercest" resistance figures in the uprising against Habsburg occupation of Bosnia Herzegovina.[39] According to the consul, over 2,000 migrants arrived in Shkodër immediately following the uprising.[40] For some, it was a stopover in their eastward migration; others remained and settled (often in groups) in what is today Albania, a few still maintaining the Bosnian language and customs.

The Ottomans did not officially react to the Habsburg conscription act but nevertheless observed the developments with attention. Reports of the time describe rebellious groups in eastern Bosnia engaging in extensive armed fights with the Austrian army.[41] Informants from Shkodër reported that the uprising had spread to Sarajevo and Mostar and that the rebels burned military barracks.[42] Thirty-six families applied to migrate from the small central Bosnian town of Prnjavor in 1882,[43] and around 300 emigrated in 1883 from towns in the northwestern region.[44] The Ottoman administration realized that a massive population shift was about to take place and prepared to take the necessary measures.⁴⁵ They allocated 1 million liras for the transport and settlement of an estimated 10,000–12,000 immigrants in 1882–1883.⁴⁶ The uprising was quelled soon after, and a number of migrants returned to Bosnia.

The failure of the uprising and the onset of conscription in Bosnia Herzegovina initiated more migration. However, in order to receive approval to migrate, individuals had to apply for permission from provincial authorities, who in turn had to verify that those individuals had no outstanding obligations to the state, including debt and military service. A number of applications for immigration were sent to the Ottoman administration and approved in the period immediately following the military conscription law. Families from Čajniče and Foča in southeastern Bosnia Herzegovina petitioned the Ottoman Empire to allow them to migrate because they refused to serve in the Habsburg military and were thus not given passports by the local authorities.⁴⁷

Habsburg Bosnian infantry regiments were established in 1882 and enlarged in subsequent years. The recruits were distinguished by the special uniform of which the most prominent part was the fez, the Ottoman cylindrical red felt hat with a tassel, worn in Bosnia Herzegovina.⁴⁸ The Habsburg administration had hoped that universal military service and imperial allegiance among the conscripts would have integrative effects, dissuading many from migrating, and so made issuance of permissions to migrate mandatory. Avoiding military service, however, was the main reason for illegal migration throughout the period. Archival sources reveal that not only Muslim young men but also Orthodox Christians migrated to Serbia, Montenegro, and even the Americas in order to avoid military service.

Despite the rocky start, service in the Habsburg military was eventually normalized. But identification with the Ottoman Empire prevailed among some recruits for a variety of reasons. For example, having deserted the Austrian military and settled in Adapazarı, Fehim wanted to serve in the Ottoman forces but was given a civilian job within the military.⁴⁹ Originally from Banja Luka, Abdullah Efendi, a student at the Vienna Military Academy, came to Izmir petitioning to be admitted to the military academy there.⁵⁰ Sulejman, son of Salih, a trumpeter sergeant in the Austrian army in Bosnia Herzegovina, arrived in Istanbul with twelve others and was given a rank of sergeant in the gendarmerie of Bursa (Hüdavendigar) province.⁵¹

FIGURE 2. Bosnian Habsburg recruits. Standing second from left is Agan Eminagić, author's great-grandfather. He became a POW in the Battle of Piave (1918) and finally managed to return to Bosnia years after Austria-Hungary ceased to exist.

Source: Private archive.

And Milan Ropović, an officer in the Austrian army, arrived at the Ottoman Empire, converted to Islam, and settled in Ankara and then moved to Eskişehir.[52] Military service became one of the most prominent ways in which the Habsburg Monarchy entered the lives of individual young men of all classes and confessions in the province. Service instilled a common set of practices and a connection to the Habsburg Monarchy, while conscription evasion entailed an active effort to reject the empire and transform the circumstances of entire families who migrated.

Conversions and Colonization

With the arrival of the Habsburg administration, the presence and the activity of the Catholic Church became more intense and visible in Bosnia.[53] The earliest proselytizing activities in Herzegovina in 1881 led local Muslims to immediately petition the Habsburg emperor.[54] Catholic proselytism and agricultural colonization—often realized through church networks—were seen as threatening Islam and Muslims in Bosnia Herzegovina. The Habsburg administration upheld the promise of freedom of confession to gain the trust of Muslims, but cases of conversion and active Catholic proselytism were main grievances to Istanbul and Vienna, providing direct "proof" of Habsburg intentions in Bosnia for those who were promoting Muslim migration to the Ottoman Empire.[55] Instances of conversion that stirred anger among the Orthodox Christian and Muslim populations most often involved young women who were moved out of Bosnia Herzegovina and married off with the help of the Catholic establishment. Already in 1878, two village girls in Herzegovina had converted and married Catholics, later moving away from the vicinity.[56]

The case of young Fata Omanović's conversion in 1899 and the administration's ambivalence to it became a common cause for ulema and notables around the province. Together with the insistence on Muslims' autonomous education, Catholic proselytism became one of the chief motives of the emerging Muslim oppositional bloc, which voiced support for the preservation of Islam and Muslims in Bosnia and later developed into a movement for autonomy in religious affairs. Habsburg administrative reports noted the Muslim offense to the speeches of Bosnia's Archbishop Stadler on the subject of the conversions. The reports warned that such rhetoric could widen the gap between the local Catholics and the Muslims and lead to Muslims' convergence with Orthodox Christians, in no way desirable for the administration.[57] Most troublesome for the Habsburg administrators was that Muslims saw the Habsburg administration acting in unison with the Catholic Church.

Hoping to calm Muslims' fears and stem the tide of migration, laws were devised to prohibit forced conversions. A protocol for conversions was established that required a certificate of departure from clerics of the abandoned religion—these were almost impossible to obtain.[58] In practice, conversions to Catholicism were less cumbersome. Still, the Catholic Church, headed by Archbishop Stadler, expected preferential status in Bosnia Herzegovina. Stadler openly resented the policies he saw as favoring Muslim notables and the provincial laws limiting activities of the Catholic Church. Fearing the spread of Pan-Slavism and Serbian nationalism in the province, the administration sought out Muslim allegiance and hoped Muslims would instead come together with the Catholic population. Stories of forced conversions and church activities created distrust and allowed for the possibilities of cooperation with the oppositionist Orthodox Christians (also struggling for comparable autonomy) and, eventually, the Serbian nationalist cause.[59]

The Habsburg administration did consider the eventual conversion of Muslims desirable, but as an outcome to be achieved in the future, when allegiance to the monarchy would be firmly established among the population.[60] Concerned not to cause public dissatisfaction, the administration bribed local leaders and notables so they would not react to cases of conversion.[61] Archbishop Stadler's proselytizing work diverged from the policies of the administration to such an extent that Minister Benjamin Kállay attempted to remove him from the post several times, unsuccessfully. The archbishop even converted Kállay's wife and daughters, who were Protestant, and engaged in a number of conversions that brought him into personal conflict with Habsburg administrators, Orthodox Christian priests, Muslims, and even some Franciscans and local Catholic representatives who compared his behavior to the likes of an "African missionary."[62] Despite the efforts that were principally directed at Muslims, the number of converts from Islam to Catholicism was slight: official Habsburg data show conversion of fifty individuals between 1878 and 1900.[63]

The Ottoman consul in Dubrovnik reported that Catholic proselytism was one form of Austrian pressure on Bosnian Muslims that forced them to migrate to the Ottoman Empire. He recommended Ottoman involvement by way of sending teachers and religious officials to educate the young, who, in his opinion, were most susceptible to losing their tradition.[64] The Austrian administration in turn blamed Ottoman encouragement and active agitation as the primary reason for Bosnian Muslims' migration. It banned the Istanbul paper *Tercuman-i Hakikat* in 1880 for discussing Catholic proselytism and encouraging Muslims to migrate.[65] Hardly a success, the proselytizing activities of the Catholic Church nonetheless carried weight as a symbol of religious prejudice. Catholic propaganda polarized Muslim public opinion and caused friction in the relationship between the administration and the Catholic establishment in Bosnia Herzegovina. Although conversions affected few people in comparison to other features of the Habsburg occupation, they were often the most prominent in the repertoire of concerns that encouraged Muslim migration.

The Catholic Church and its associations purchased the properties of departing Muslims and settled the Catholic population on those lands in an effort to increase their presence in the province. Muslims likewise observed colonization by farmers from the monarchy as an effort to diminish the Muslim presence and influence in the province. The Habsburg administration settled colonists who had been recruited throughout the monarchy. Colonies such as Windthorst, Rudolfstal, Franzjozefsfeld, and Kenigsfeld were set up in northern Bosnia, where large tracts of fertile land were available.[66] Colonizing opportunities in Bosnia Herzegovina were advertised in publications affiliated with the Catholic Church that presented the endeavor as a modernizing and a civilizing mission.[67] Incentives were provided in the form of tax reductions, interest-free loans, and rent-free land for three years, after which an affordable mortgage was available. In addition to agricultural colonizers, individuals employed in the railroad, forestry, mining, and the government, as well as investors, arrived and settled in Bosnia Herzegovina. They came from across the Habsburg territories and other regions in Europe, including Germany and Netherlands. In addition to agricultural and economic objectives, the Austro-Hungarian political goals of settling loyal peasants from the monarchy were meant to defuse Serbian nationalist and oppositional activities among the Orthodox Christian peasantry.[68] However, the influence colonizers were supposed to project onto their surroundings did not materialize since they lived in isolated colonies, and locals resented the settlers for the concessions they received from the government.[69] Muslims also saw colonization as an attack on their privileges and land access, as well as an attempt to weaken the socioeconomic power of Muslim landowners.

Cases of conversions and colonization, then, galvanized the opposition. Some religious officials and notables saw the demise of Muslim preeminence in the region and ultimate assimilation as implicit in these Habsburg policies. Many opposition activists frequently shuttled between Istanbul and Sarajevo (and Vienna and Budapest), some settled in Ottoman domains, and some were forced to do so. Ali Fehmi Džabić, for example, the leader of the Movement for Pious Endowment and Educational Autonomy, was not allowed to return after a trip to Istanbul in 1902. Mehmed Vehbi Šemsekadić, the mufti of Pljevlja (Taşlıca), who organized an effective resistance to the Habsburg occupation, was likewise "invited" by Sultan Abdülhamid II at the insistence of Austria-Hungary, living in exile in Istanbul for the remainder of his life. Despite their modest impact, Catholic missionary activity and agricultural colonization ended up being the most provocative acts associated with the Habsburg arrival to the province and became reasons for emigration, as well as oppositional organization among those who stayed.

Migration After the Annexation, 1908

By the first decade of the twentieth century, Bosnians had spent almost thirty years under Habsburg rule. Throughout these years the administration attempted to incorporate its new province into the monarchy and projected a cultural mission comparable to those of other European colonies around the world. Inroads had been made to integrate those Bosnian subjects who accepted the Habsburg administration, but when the legal position of Bosnia Herzegovina later changed, it triggered yet another migration to the Ottoman Empire; this time scholars assessed it as a passive expression of political dissatisfaction.[70]

When the Young Turk Revolution took place in July 1908, reestablishing the Ottoman constitution and parliament, the Habsburg administration swiftly annexed Bosnia Herzegovina. It took advantage of the turmoil in the Ottoman Empire, which was unable to respond. The annexation was also aimed at preempting any request by Bosnia Herzegovina for a constitution, which would have reinforced its relationship with the Ottoman Empire. At the same time, it was meant to dismiss Serbian hopes of seizing Bosnia Herzegovina. The Young Turks' opposition and revolution were met by some in Bosnia Herzegovina with anticipation. There was hope that the Young Turks would reinvigorate the Ottoman Empire and that such change would also solve Bosnia's legal ambiguity—even that the province would be reincorporated into the Ottoman Empire. The quick act of annexation, and the even swifter acceptance of it by the Young Turks, was therefore shocking.

Already in October 1908, the Ottoman consul in neighboring Cetinje in Montenegro, requested instructions for the many petitions made by Bosnian Muslims to resettle to the Ottoman Empire. The Ottoman Council of Ministers responded that it was not politically acceptable for Muslims to leave Bosnia Herzegovina and that it was more advantageous for them to stay put.[71] Regardless, the migration started. Migrants who arrived in the Ottoman Empire were not turned away. Revolution in the Ottoman Empire and the Habsburg annexation of Bosnia gave rise to a range of speculation

FIGURE 3. Reading the annexation proclamation, Sarajevo, 1908.

Source: https://commons.wikimedia.org/wiki/File:1908
-10-07_-_Moritz_Schiller's_Delicatessen.jpg

and unsubstantiated rumors on the future of Bosnia Herzegovina, causing panic and flight: that the Habsburg administration would buy out Muslims' properties below value; that religious and cultural restrictions, which the Habsburg administration could not enforce before annexation due to a clause on Ottoman sovereignty, would finally be implemented; and that the authorities would not allow migration after a certain time.

When several prominent Bosnian Muslims returned from the Ottoman Empire after getting caught up in the course of the revolution, it came to the administration's attention that some of them had traveled there to propose a coordinated Bosnian Muslim migration to the Ottoman Migrants Commission. They were close to the administration of Sultan Abdülhamid II, who was deposed in 1909, and so fled "by the skin of their necks."[72] Those who had held positions in the administration of Sultan Abdülhamid II also left, some returning to Bosnia Herzegovina and some fleeing to Egypt. Osman Beg Ajnić Pazarićanin, a confidant of the ousted sultan, was imprisoned, but he escaped and was expected to arrive in Bosnia after reaching out to his brother in Pazarić, near Sarajevo, to cover his travel expenses. Osman Beg Muderizović, an Ottoman army officer, also reached Sarajevo in 1909, warning "each and every Muslim not to migrate to Turkey under any circumstance."[73]

Novi Pazar Sandžak, majority Bosnian Muslim and reinforced by many immigrants from Bosnia Herzegovina, experienced turmoil as a consequence of uncertainty around the annexation as the Habsburg military withdrew from the district leaving it to the Ottomans. Sandžak's inhabitants organized voluntary units claiming readiness for war against the Ottoman enemies to reclaim lost territories—not only Bosnia Herzegovina but also Crete, lost to the Ottoman Empire at the time of the Young Turk Revolution.[74] Worried about the possibility of a Serbian and Montenegrin takeover of Novi Pazar Sandžak after Habsburg withdrawal, some Bosnian migrants who had emigrated earlier and resided there received approval from the Habsburg consulate to return to Bosnia in 1909.[75] Applications for emigration were also submitted from the Gacko region in Herzegovina, after applicants made contact with their relatives, who had emigrated to Sandžak four years prior.[76] Provincial authorities monitored the migration that was particularly vigorous in the Bihać and Banja Luka regions. The regional office in Cazin was overwhelmed: 274 emigration permits were issued in only the first two months of 1911, in comparison to 502 emigrant permits issued in the entire year prior.[77] In Sarajevo, Visoko, and Foča, prospective migrants contacted Bosnian emigrants in the Ottoman Empire to assess the conditions there, while in Travnik preparations for a spring migration were noted.[78]

The agreement between the two empires after the annexation allowed for the migration of Bosnians who had fulfilled legal obligations to the Habsburg state and obtained a migrant passport. Such applicants were documented, along with migrants' "military booklet"—a document certifying completion of Habsburg military service. For example, Rifat Pračić, a laborer from Orahova in northwestern Bosanska Gradiška, was recorded as a forty-one-year-old Muslim who had completed his service. Married, he had a medium build with a round face, blond hair, blue eyes, and a straight nose. He was accompanied by his wife Kadira and three small children: his son Ibrahim and the two young nieces he had adopted, Zahida and Ilda. He had sold all of his belongings and property and had in his possession 200 krone for the trip.[79] One can only imagine what pushed Pračić to take this step after spending all his adult life as a Habsburg subject and the expectations he might have had about opportunities that awaited in the Ottoman Empire.

The Ottoman administration found itself in a difficult position when Bosnian subjects who resided in the Ottoman Empire applied for citizenship but did not possess the necessary migrant passport or had arrived without any documentation. In response to a citizenship application of a certain Mehmed, son of Ali Efendi, who emigrated from Bosnia in this manner, a memorandum by the Foreign Ministry Office of Legal Counsel elaborated: accepting migrants without the migrant passport was in breach of the migration agreement with Austria-Hungary, but there were no practical consequences for the Ottoman state if it naturalized such immigrants. For migrant applicants, however, this meant the loss of legal rights in Bosnia Herzegovina, such as property ownership. The Office of Legal Counsel suggested that the cabinet streamline responses to such applications to include a translation of relevant Habsburg policies and laws so that migrants could make informed decisions before relinquishing their rights in Bosnia Herzegovina.[80] After the Ottoman ambassador in Vienna confirmed that the most necessary and important aspect of said agreement was having completed military service, it was decided that applicants for naturalization who had arrived without the migrant passport be asked to prove that they had completed their military service and maintain residence in the Ottoman Empire for a certain period with the intention to settle.[81] The Office of Legal Counsel was again consulted in the case of Sejid Agić Aga, who had arrived with his family with an "ordinary" passport but settled in Adapazarı and applied for Ottoman citizenship. Cautious of a negative response from the Habsburg authorities, Agić approached the Ottoman administration seeking advice about the best way to handle his property (worth 200 krone) in Bosnia Herzegovina. He was advised to first seek out the emigrant permission from the administration in Bosnia Herzegovina, since, according to the bilateral agreement, he would then be able to dispose of his property as he wished.[82] Many of those who were unfamiliar with such regulations were the most underprivileged; they were encouraged to take the opportunity to sell their properties and bring funds to the Ottoman Empire, which reduced the burden on the state.

This approach became a problem, too, when more and more individuals arrived in the Ottoman Empire and asked for legal protection and citizenship without having complied with the Habsburg emigration requirements. The Office of Legal Counsel once again interjected, recommending that the particular article in the agreement on migration between the empires be amended. The Office of Legal Counsel warned that if these individuals addressed the Habsburg authorities or consulates after becoming Ottoman citizens but without having completed the proper emigration procedure, the Ottoman Empire would be considered to have breached the agreement.[83] Such applicants did contact the Austrian and Hungarian consulates in Mitrovica, Istanbul, Beirut, Alexandria, and Salonica when they desired to return or to handle the sale of their properties in Bosnia Herzegovina. Most who arrived without the migrant passport and were beyond the age of military service turned out to be unfamiliar with the regulations. Some continued to travel back and forth and encountered fines and restrictions when they did so without following the required procedures and obtaining the necessary documents.[84]

While the legal precedent for maintaining ties with the Ottoman Empire vanished with the annexation, the Habsburg administration was frustrated by the plans voiced by the members of the Committee of Union and Progress (CUP) to offset intense nationalist turmoil in Ottoman Macedonia. At a CUP congress in 1910, participants suggested resettling Bosnian Muslims to the Ottoman Empire in order to counter the influence of Christian political factions and provide popular backing for government policies.[85] A report by the provincial government to the Habsburg Joint Ministry of Finance isolated the colonization policies of the Young Turks in Macedonia as the most influential, encouraging primarily poorer Muslims to migrate, since the economic promises of the CUP regime were attractive. It emphasized the need to find a "counterweight to the Young Turk actions in Macedonia that would challenge and contain it."[86] The consul in Skopje likewise reported on colonization efforts in Macedonia, listing Ottoman expenses nearing 19,000 liras in 1909–1910 for properties, house construction, agricultural animals, seed, craftsman tools, and other related expenses. Furthermore, the consul warned that the government intended to settle another 50,000 Bosnian migrants in the eastern regions of the Skopje district to balance the ratio of Christian and Muslim inhabitants.[87]

Many Young Turk officers radicalized their approach to solving the empire's problems after having served in Macedonia, where they observed and experienced the activities of Bulgarian, Greek, and Serbian nationalist organizations and bands, to which the Hamidian administration had no retort.[88] CUP publications such as *Şura-yi Ümmet* had already discussed such ideas in 1903, recommending that Macedonia be settled with Muslim refugees. The committee modeled its policies on the examples of German policies in Poland and Hungarian policies in Slav-populated regions.[89] Once in power, officers affiliated with the CUP assumed analogous nationalist logic regarding population and territory, already widespread in the former Ottoman regions, and projected it as a solution for the remainder of the empire in hopes of retaining the disputed territories.

Instigating Migration

Emigration from Bosnia Herzegovina throughout the Habsburg period was also encouraged by individuals who saw an opportunity to make a profit by participating as agents in property sales.[90] These were both locals and prospectors from other parts of the monarchy in search of easy financial gain. In certain cases recorded in northern and eastern Bosnia Herzegovina, local officials and notables encouraged Muslims to leave for the Ottoman

Empire and then bought their properties below value.[91] In 1884, the Ottoman newspaper *Vatan* discussed Muslim migration and pointed out that in northwestern and western Bosnia, aggressive attacks on Muslims forcing them to sell their property had even led the administration to intervene.[92] A letter published in *Musavat* described one such local merchant, Mustafa Sarajlija, of Kladuša in northwestern Bosnia, who persuaded some locals to migrate and bought their properties. Consequently, as many as 30 families, totaling 150 individuals, started their journey to the Ottoman Empire only to return after they reached a nearby town, as none had passports.[93] Similarly, a mysterious "agent" was reported to the local government in the vicinity of Sarajevo. He was described as a blond-bearded man dressed in a stylish Turkish suit and a long coat, donned with gold jewelry and carrying in his belt "a revolver, a dagger, and a fine Turkish cigarette holder." He was offering young men transportation to the Ottoman Empire for 60 krone.[94]

There was a steady migration of Habsburg Bosnian subjects to the Americas in the first decade of the twentieth century.[95] Most emigrants to the Americas were Orthodox Christian peasants from the karst region of Herzegovina. The rhetoric against their migration was similar to that expressed in the publications that lobbied against Muslim emigration. In several articles, *Srpska Riječ* called for the founding of banks that would provide loans to the impoverished peasants to prevent them from migrating and demanded that the administration tighten the anti-emigration laws.[96] The paper publicized personal accounts of regretful migrants and condemned opportunists who bought emigrants' properties below market value, as well as agents of steamer companies who advertised opportunities in the Americas, helped procure travel documents, and even acquired presentable clothing needed for acceptance overseas. The Ottoman authorities likewise took note of this trend, and reports often specified whether any Muslims were boarding ships to the Americas.[97] Some Bosnian Muslims also migrated to the Americas although in comparatively smaller numbers. Yet, there was enough of a Bosnian Muslim presence in Chicago to warrant creation of *Džemijetul Hajrije* (The Benevolent Society) in 1906, becoming one of the oldest Muslim association in the United States.[98]

Serbian and Croatian nationalist organizations viewed Muslim emigration as advantageous, and both movements thought that a void created by Muslim migration should be filled by settling Serbian and Croatian populations, respectively. They proposed the buyout of Muslims' land in order to populate it with peasants belonging to their own groups, in the hopes of demographically dominating the province and claiming it for imagined national geographies. The Habsburg administration noted that the Orthodox Christians were taking advantage of, and even encouraging, Muslim emigration. Serbian organizations helped them by providing loans to buy out emigrants' properties, targeting the unorganized and uninformed Muslim villager population.[99] The Bosnian provincial administration assumed that with the CUP's plans for Muslim colonization of Macedonia, the Serbian nationalists might not continue to support Muslim emigration from Bosnia Herzegovina. Serbian nationalists laid claims to Macedonia as their national land too, so they reasoned that the encouragement of Muslim emigration from Bosnia would support the CUP's colonization plans for Macedonia, which Belgrade "already recognized as a greater danger to Serbianism."[100]

In an effort to slow and document emigration without an outright ban, the Habsburg administration regulated the status and rights of those who emigrated, accepted foreign citizenship, or lived outside of Bosnia Herzegovina for extended periods; the administration also made the act of encouraging migration punishable by imprisonment.[101] These policies were aimed at limiting the activities of migrants who maintained residence in Bosnia Herzegovina and the Ottoman Empire, especially those in the émigré community, students at the Ottoman universities, and those banished by the Habsburg administration who lobbied the Ottoman government against Habsburg occupation of Bosnia Herzegovina.[102] One of the ways to interrupt ties with the Ottoman Empire was to limit interactions with the diasporic opposition in Istanbul and make the decision to migrate more complicated and precarious: prospects in the Ottoman Empire were unknown, and it was increasingly difficult to return and preserve property in Bosnia Herzegovina.

The 1908 annexation had caused a wave of migration to the Ottoman Empire, but the Balkan Wars that followed in 1912–1913 in the remaining Ottoman European territories prompted the return to Bosnia Herzegovina for those caught up in the conflict. More importantly, the annexation clearly marked Bosnia's legal rupture with the Ottoman Empire. The Balkan Wars physically cut off the Ottoman Empire's territorial continuity with Bosnia

Herzegovina. The annexation and the Balkan Wars had direct consequences on migration and return.

Return

Returns from the Ottoman Empire took place at the same time as the migration, albeit on a lesser scale. Most returnees were affected by the economic situation in the new land. Poverty and the inability to adjust to a new environment—different climate, infertile land, unfamiliar language—were the reasons most often cited. The fact that the Bosnian migrants to the Ottoman Empire had an opportunity and a place to return was significant, putting them at an advantage compared to others arriving in the Ottoman Empire. It allowed migrants to weigh their prospects in Habsburg Bosnia Herzegovina and the Ottoman Empire and to have a choice many other migrants did not. Finally, return was indicative of changes in sentiment and loyalties to an ideal that existed in the minds of Muslims in Bosnia Herzegovina about the Ottoman Empire and a reality they encountered when they moved there. According to the Austro-Hungarian records, the number of returnees was higher than the number of emigrants for several years: in 1902 there were 305 emigrants and 1,031 returnees; in 1903, 194 emigrants and 453 returnees; and in 1904, 155 emigrants and 246 returnees.[103] Considering that in these years the Habsburg administration was relatively settled in Bosnia Herzegovina, it is probable that the migrants who returned were those who had migrated because of uncertainty and volatility in the early years of occupation.

After the annexation, when claims to Ottoman citizenship and sovereignty were clearly delineated and the return procedure standardized, the relevant Ottoman administrative branches were instructed on how to treat those immigrants in the Ottoman Empire who wished to return to Bosnia Herzegovina.[104] Based on the Habsburg–Ottoman agreement, those who came to the Ottoman Empire before the annexation with a Habsburg passport and had not resided in the Ottoman Empire for more than a year would be treated as Habsburg citizens; those who had resided in the Ottoman Empire for more than a year or were not in possession of a passport issued in Bosnia Herzegovina would be considered Ottoman citizens. In peacetime, reasons for return were most often economic. Ottoman authorities actively discouraged return, instructing local administrators to solve the problems that led to migrants' resolve to return.[105] Nineteen-year-old Hamza Brkić, of Bijeljina, applied for repatriation, asking to return to his estate in Bosnia where his mother and brothers lived, saying he was "deluded in his young age" to migrate to the Ottoman Empire.[106]

The Balkan Wars in 1912 and 1913 instigated larger return movements of Bosnian migrants from the Ottoman Empire. The returnees were migrants who had originally settled in parts of the Ottoman Balkans that saw war operations. The Muslim population in Ottoman Europe, local and migrant, was targeted in those war activities. Many migrants were settled in these regions to counter the plans of Greek, Bulgarian, and Serbian nationalists after 1908, but they found themselves under attack by these groups, and many fled. Bosnian immigrants in Macedonia applied for repatriation to Bosnia Herzegovina with the Habsburg consulates, while others fled eastward to the Ottoman Empire, resettling once again, mainly in Anatolia. The Habsburg consul in Salonica recommended repatriation of all those who applied in 1912, pitying their deplorable state and suggesting acceptance of even the most undesirable, since after all the suffering they endured, they were "forever cured" from migrating again.[107]

Returning Bosnians were transported form Salonica to Trieste by sea to pass through quarantine and then sent by train to Bosnia Herzegovina.[108] When the number of those applying for repatriation reached 50,000, the authorities ended free transportation.[109] Some crossed into Bosnia Herzegovina illegally via the eastern border: one report cited several thousand Muslims from Kosovo crossing into Bosnia Herzegovina in 1913.[110] According to the Habsburg consul in Salonica, Ottoman agents worked to persuade the Bosnians in Macedonia not to return to Bosnia Herzegovina and were organizing their transport to Izmir and settling them throughout Anatolia. As a consequence, more than 1,200 migrants withdrew their applications for repatriation from the consulate in January 1913.[111] Thus, the demographic scramble of the Balkan Wars replicated beyond the regions affected by war.

Muslim officials and the public in Bosnia Herzegovina petitioned the Habsburg administration to help their compatriots and even offered *vakuf* (pious endowment) land for settling the returnees. Charitable fundraising events were organized in 1913, and money and clothing were collected for the exhausted returnees in Trieste.[112] Responding to applications for repatriation, the Habsburg administration investigated whether returnees had property in their hometowns and villages to which they could return, so as to not become a burden to authorities. In one such inquiry from Kladuša, the administration was informed of the existence of a local fund for returnees that could be used for those in need.[113] Likewise, Rifat Beg Sulejmanpašić of Gračanica advocated for accepting returnees and providing land for those who had none. He informed authorities that the locals had raised money and collected clothing, and that 100 dunum of state land in the area was available, hoping that the administration would approve all applications for return.[114]

Size of Migration

Insufficient recordkeeping, unofficial migration and return, and the sheer span of years and different circumstances under which migrations took place all contribute to a lack of precise statistical data. Austrian authorities did not keep track of migration from the beginning of the occupation, and their later statistics differ from the Ottoman sources.[115] Ottoman officials recorded arrivals of immigrants who came by sea from Salonica to the ports of Istanbul and Izmir and then settled them throughout the empire. During periods of high flow into the Ottoman Empire, the Ottoman Migrants Commission sent representatives to Kosovo to record and process those crossing from Bosnia Herzegovina to Kosovo and Novi Pazar. Migrants who entered Ottoman domains in smaller groups often did not get recorded unless they themselves reported their arrival to the authorities, which happened when they wanted to be considered for government assistance. Those who settled with family members or had come for educational, trade, and other purposes, including pilgrimage, and then decided to remain in the Ottoman Empire, were seldom recorded in immigrant ledgers.

Emigration to the Ottoman Empire necessitated the completion of Habsburg administrative requirements, which often turned out to be the very reasons for migration: young men wanted to avoid conscription; some were members of the political opposition being investigated by the state; and a few crossed into Ottoman territory illegally to escape debt in Bosnia Herzegovina. In the early period of the occupation, neither the Habsburg nor the Ottoman authorities had a systematic policy toward migrants and issues were resolved on a case-by-case basis. By the time the Habsburg administration was firmly instituted in Bosnia Herzegovina, the records had become more consistent. Likewise, increasing bureaucratization of the Ottoman state's encounters with millions of immigrants arriving alongside Bosnians generated more comprehensive policies and records. Considering all these facts, the actual numbers of migrants and returnees are most likely higher than any records reveal.

The Habsburg official records documented 55,274 emigrants between 1883 and 1910,[116] and up to 60,000 Muslim emigrants in total during Habsburg rule.[117] Ferdinand Schmid, the Habsburg head of the Statistics Office in Sarajevo, estimated 8,000 individuals to have left Bosnia Herzegovina in 1882–1883 to avoid conscription.[118] Based on Ottoman sources, Kemal Karpat calculated about 700 migrants per year, totaling between 80,000 and 100,000 immigrants from Bosnia in the period 1878–1912. He estimated that they accounted for between 3 percent and 10 percent of all annual migrants to the Ottoman Empire.[119] A number of estimates by Bosnian and Yugoslav scholars range from 140,000 to 180,000 migrants in the Habsburg period.[120] It is important to consider that the required application for emigration was not instituted right after the Habsburg occupation, so Habsburg records could not have recorded early emigrants or those who left without notifying authorities, non-migrant travelers, and those migrating illicitly. The legality of travel is also relative: bearing in mind the ambiguous position of the province from 1878 to 1908 as de jure Ottoman territory, the migrants would have traveled, worked, attended school, bought property, and resided within the empire as Ottoman subjects. Recordkeeping from the first decade of the twentieth century revealed a more detailed structure of immigrant populations: of more than 17,000 Muslims who emigrated by 1910, about 86 percent were peasants.[121] Another administrative report broke down a migrant group of 3,098 heads of households and 217 single migrants to 19 landowners, 2,413 free peasants, 25 tenants (*kmet*), 436 agricultural workers, 37 merchants, 120 craftsmen, 192 workers and servants, and 73 individuals of other occupations.[122]

Of all the immigrants to the Ottoman Empire in this period, Bosnian immigrants had the highest rate of return, mostly because return was an option for them. Karpat estimated that 10–15 percent of emigrants returned from the Ottoman Empire, while Habsburg officials registered over 12,000 returnees between 1883 and 1910.[123] The flow of migration from Bosnia Herzegovina to the Ottoman Empire was proportionately smaller than the migration to the empire from other regions of the Balkans and the Caucasus, but it was a high percentage of the population, which demographically affected Bosnia Herzegovina.

Migration and Empires

Imperial administrations understood that migration was often a forewarning and a token of negotiation: a large number of applications for emigration pressured the Bosnian administration to resolve the issues that might cause population flight. In their petitions, Muslims warned of having no choice but to migrate to the Ottoman Empire if their requests were not met. Their petitions to the Ottoman authorities warned of the same possibility. Minister Kállay, in a meeting with the Ottoman ambassador in Vienna, called upon the Ottoman administration to prevent migration harmful to both empires.[124] The Ottoman Council of Ministers continued to stress that Bosnian immigrants should be accepted only after arrangements for their settlement were made and, more importantly, that such decisions be made in light of the political consequences of a complete evacuation of the Muslim population from Bosnia Herzegovina.[125] Throughout its reign, the Austro-Hungarian administration grappled with how to best respond to Muslim migration. It repeatedly rejected calls for government buyout of migrant properties for the purpose of agricultural colonization and development, as it did not want to appear to be expediting Muslim migration. In fact, even after the annexation, the administration observed that the lack of buyers and price declines when only several potential migrants put up their land for sale had a limiting effect on migration.[126]

Migration had been a part of Ottoman state-building from its inception: the early migrations built it, and the latter ones undermined it.[127] Ottoman policy toward immigrants, Muslim or non-Muslim, was liberal: Ottoman society included expelled Iberian Muslims and Jews in the fifteenth and sixteenth centuries; Muslim refugees who fled Russian expansion into the Crimea, the Caucasus, and Central Asia; Hungarian and Polish exiles in the nineteenth century; former Ottoman subjects from its lost lands; and Jews escaping pogroms in Russia and Eastern Europe. Bosnian migrants were part of the larger displacement of Muslims following shrinking Ottoman borders throughout the long nineteenth century.

In the "civilizing process of East Europeans," the Berlin Treaty provided international recognition of national sovereignty for some of the imperial communities, such as Bulgarians in the Ottoman Empire and Jews in Romania.[128] Rights and protections and spheres of new nation-state and imperial influence increasingly took demographic data into consideration. Claims to territory by various Ottoman subject groups proceeded by working toward achieving demographic predominance in the regions they coveted by all means necessary, often under the protection of various European powers and Russia. A comparison of migration within the Eastern Question is a stark example. In this context, Ottoman inability to facilitate the prompt return of Bosnian Orthodox Christian migrants in the 1875–1876 uprising was one reason to deliver the province to the Habsburg administration. The same standard did not apply to the Russian sabotage of Muslim refugee return during their occupation of Eastern Rumelia after the 1877–1878 war, because it was understood that only a significant decrease in Muslim population could provide grounds for creating the "Bulgarian character" of Eastern Rumelia and a basis for an eventual independence under Russian tutelage.[129]

The scale of violence during the Russo-Ottoman War in 1877 and 1878—in Bulgaria over 250,000 Muslims died and approximately 1 million Muslims became refugees (of which about half returned)[130]—was a turning point for the Ottoman government and the reign of Sultan Abdülhamid II, who ascended to the throne only in 1876. The loss of European provinces resulted in a demographic shift for the empire as well: regions inhabited by large numbers of Christian subjects were divided up at the Berlin Congress, and scores of Muslims remaining there migrated and were resettled across the Ottoman Empire. As a consequence of the territorial rearrangement drawn at the Berlin Congress and the related migrations, Muslims came to account for 75–80 percent of the total Ottoman population.[131]

Sultan Abdülhamid II portrayed the European powers as unable to provide for their Muslim subjects, with ample evidence at hand. The Ottoman diplomats claimed the same kind of protections for non-Ottoman Muslims as the Europeans declared for the Ottoman Christian subjects—effectively using European strategies that were weaponized against the Ottoman Empire. They too began to focus on Muslim demographic presence as a tool in diplomatic dealings with European empires and positioned the Ottoman Empire as the Great Power protector of Muslims. The shift in policy was not only a defensive diplomatic undertaking but also a response to the realities of geopolitical and demographic changes in Ottoman domains over the long nineteenth century. Between 5 million and 7 million Muslims immigrated to the Ottoman Empire between 1783 and 1913, mostly from lost territories in the Balkans and from Russia-conquered Crimea and the Caucasus; proportionately fewer came from Central Asia, Tunisia, Algeria, and Libya.[132] To handle such a large influx of refugees, the Ottoman government created the Muhacirin Komisyonu (Migrants Commission) in 1860—perhaps the first of its kind in the world, tasked with regulating transport, housing, feeding, and settlement of immigrant populations within the empire.[133] The Charity Commission (İane Komisyonu) was created in 1877 to collect donations and distribute them to the immigrants.[134]

The incoming migrants arriving in Istanbul and other major ports of empire became more visible as their numbers increased, to the point that authorities were not able to transport or house them upon arrival. Hunger was a real threat, and contemporary sources paint a picture of towns dotted with improvised *muhacir* neighborhoods, streets crowded with beggars, and families lining up to receive aid from charitable endowments.[135] Sometimes the presence of large numbers of immigrants disturbed public safety, and armed units had to be called in to help reestablish order.[136] At one point in 1880, it was suggested that a bank be established to provide loans to immigrants, as a solution to a population of 60,000 immigrants in Istanbul at that time and more than 200,000 already sent to Anatolia—all of them needing housing and jobs.[137] The deplorable conditions of migrants became an illustration of the Ottoman administration's incompetence in safeguarding its subjects. European economic encroachment and territorial and military losses, followed by the influx of destitute Muslim migrants, created dissatisfaction on many levels in the Ottoman society.

Worse was yet to come. During the Balkan Wars (1912–1913), Serbia, Montenegro, Greece, and Bulgaria promptly besieged the remaining Ottoman territories in Europe. Albania declared independence in 1912. Muslims living in Macedonia, many of whom were already refugees from previously lost Ottoman lands, were its major victims. Over 600,000 Muslims were killed in the regions taken over by Bulgaria, Serbia, and Greece, and another 400,000 took refuge in the Ottoman territories.[138] These demographic rearrangements by atrocity continued in the campaigns of World War I. To the remaining Muslims in the Balkans, they were illustrative of the new post-Ottoman order and their position in it, pushing many to migrate.

Bosnian Muslims continued to migrate even after the Habsburg and the Ottoman empires were gone. Muslim migration from Bosnia Herzegovina continued to Turkey into the 1950s, although it was smaller than the size of Muslim displacement from other Muslim-populated regions in the Balkans. Migration was among the most permanent ties that connected Muslims in Bosnia Herzegovina to the Ottoman Empire and later Turkey. When Ahmet Emin Yalman, a prominent Turkish journalist, traveled to Yugoslavia in 1936, he reported that Bosnians viewed Turkey as a "spare" homeland—in case the oppressive policies were to force them to migrate—emphasizing their precarious existence in the postimperial decades.[139]

3 Hijra

Views and Debates on Migration

MUHAMMAD RASHID RIDA, the editor of the popular Egyptian journal *Al-Manar* (The Beacon) and one of the most prominent figures of Islamic reform, published an article titled "On Hijra and Its Rules Regarding the Muslims of Bosnia" in 1909. It was a response to a question sent by Muhamed Tarabar, a student from Travnik in Bosnia Herzegovina.[1] The reader asked Rida to clarify the status of Bosnia Herzegovina after it was annexed by the Habsburg Empire a year earlier. The student explained that a visiting preacher (*vaiz*) from Istanbul alarmed the town's Muslims by claiming that their communal prayers, fast, alms, and legal affairs such as marriage were invalid since Bosnia Herzegovina had become *Dar al-Harb* (Domain of War) after the Habsburg annexation in 1908. The visiting preacher further advised that all Bosnian Muslims needed to migrate (perform hijra) to the Ottoman Empire in order to live righteously under a Muslim ruler, since Bosnia had become a hostile territory for Muslims.

Rida's responses in *Al-Manar* were written and read as fatwas, which are non-binding scholarly opinions. In his response, Rida dismissed the claims and recommendations of the preacher as inaccurate. Reviewing the Qur'an, related hadith (reports of Prophet Muhammad's tradition), and the scholarly opinions on the issue of hijra, Rida cited the circumstances necessitating obligatory hijra. Although scholars differed on the conditions that made migration mandatory for Muslims, Rida explained that they did agree on two conditions: if Muslims, as individuals or a group, are prevented from performing the duties of their faith; and if they needed to participate in the defense of the Muslim community (jihad). Neither were the case for Bosnian Muslims, he concluded, adding that "they [Bosnians] know better themselves."

Rida further elaborated on different migration scenarios relevant for Bosnia Herzegovina, including these two situations: hijra with an aim of acquiring education, where one travels to learn and returns to teach others; and hijra when Muslims would have been bound to leave if they were unable to prevent activities that were forbidden by the religion. However, continued Rida, those would be applicable to individuals. If a group of people were together able to overcome the obstacles that push people to migrate, then overcoming these obstacles would be their primary religious obligation, rather than migration.

Muhamed Zahirudin Tarabar (1882–1957), the author of the letter to Rashid Rida, was born in Habsburg Bosnia and was a student at the Fejzija *medresa* in Travnik at the time. In addition to the Arabic in which he wrote the letter to Rida, Tarabar spoke Persian and Turkish and subscribed to journals in these languages.[2] He likely followed the debates on migration covered in these publications and in the public discussions in Bosnia Herzegovina, testifying to the relevance of the migration question for many Muslims. Articles from *Al-Manar* were translated in the Bosnian press, and Rida's opinion was held in esteem in Bosnia Herzegovina, indicative of the interest and availability of opinions by other Muslims in distant places on issues of local or regional relevance. These phenomena were unique to the turn of the twentieth century, for their intensity of publication activity, travel, and communication. Another contributing factor was the emergent perspective in which the Muslim world was reimagined as a geopolitical and civilizational concept, different from the classical notion of the community of faith, the *umma*.[3] Likewise, classical terms like *Dar al-Islam* and *Dar al-Harb* assumed new interpretations for Muslims worldwide deliberating over their options in Islamic idiom and socio-religious context. Bosnian scholars and intellectuals found themselves enmeshed in these debates taking place regionally in nearby Bulgaria and Greece, but also in Russia, Egypt, and India. Local conditions interpreted through religious and intellectual exchanges set the stage for a global context of Bosnian migration debates. Previously unexplored global Islamic, Ottoman, and transregional intellectual networks, therefore, played an important role in conceptualizing the arguments for and against migration as well as for reconfigurations of existing ties and establishment of new ones. These issues are only comprehensible by studying the Ottoman and the Islamic perspective in the Habsburg period.

This chapter explores debates on migration from the vantage points of Bosnia, Serbia, and the Ottoman Empire, finding that most of those evaluating migration from Bosnia Herzegovina to the Ottoman Empire converged on the same conclusion that migration was unfavorable, albeit for different reasons. Migrations from Bosnia Herzegovina were an outcome resulting from complex considerations by individual migrants who were in a position to make a choice, unlike many other refugees to the Ottoman Empire from the post-Ottoman Balkans and territories conquered by Russia. Since migration had far-reaching consequences regionally as well as for both empires involved, it was not a question debated by Muslims only. The debates highlighted the perceptions on the future of Muslims in Bosnia Herzegovina, in the Balkans, and within the Habsburg and Ottoman Empires. The logic employed in discussing migrations reveals the understanding and the impact of sociopolitical events and their diplomatic reverberations.

As the previous chapter showed, practical circumstances and political events in the province prompted migrations from Habsburg Bosnia Herzegovina. Yet, the contemporary conversation about migration almost exclusively used religious reasoning, rhetoric, and symbolism to discourage, as well as to promote, migration to the Ottoman Empire. Under the surface of Islamic discourse, there were intersecting issues of sovereignty, international law, nationalism, and extraterritoriality. The legally ambiguous position of Bosnia Herzegovina from 1878 to 1908 further complicated the debates on migration, while the flexibility of transimperial identities encouraged Bosnian Muslims to see themselves as both Habsburg and Ottoman subjects, Southeast European Slavs, and members of the reimagined world community of Muslims—the *umma,* headed by a caliph. Pan-Islamic discussions like Rida's fatwa, disseminated in the global Muslim press, corresponded to nationalist fervor expressed in regional publications that influenced Muslims in Bosnia Herzegovina to think of their place in both empires, and their role amid regional and provincial political developments. The many versions of Pan-Islam, Pan-Slavism, and regional nationalisms all tackled questions of territory, identity, and group demographics.[4] Observed more broadly, Bosnian migrations, although comparatively small in number, were part of population movements in the nineteenth and twentieth centuries that critically transformed the structure of population in Southeastern Europe and the Middle East. Bosnian Muslims were well aware of their precarious political position in southeastern Europe, where nationalism triumphed in all of the post-Ottoman lands, more often than not at the expense of Muslims.

Hijra as an Islamic Concept

Rida's was not the first fatwa on migration in Bosnia or elsewhere. In fact, it was one of the latest. Scholars who produced these advisory legal opinions were almost always local scholars familiar with the repercussions of migration be it from Bosnia, Russia, or Bulgaria. Religious rulings on the issue of migration were formed considering Islamic source texts and extensive commentary that entertained classical terms like *Dar al-Islam* (Domain of Peace) and *Dar al-Harb* (Domain of War) to distinguish between regions where Muslims could righteously live and those from which they had to migrate to be able to live as Muslims. Why those who debated migration did so from the viewpoint of the shari'a makes sense only when shari'a is understood as an entirety of institutions, social and religious norms and ethics, ritual and devotional practice, and jurisprudential principles with their evolving interpretation derived from and inspired by the Qur'an and Sunna (collections of traditions attributed to Prophet Muhammad).[5]

The views of jurists relating to the problems of occupation of Muslim lands, or Muslims living outside the areas ruled by Muslim sovereigns, existed since the early times of Islam. The very fact that Prophet Muhammad performed hijra from Mecca to Medina in 622 CE because the safety and the survival of Muslims there was threatened underscored all future discussions on this issue due to the relevance of the prophetic example. The migration from Mecca to Medina was obligatory for all Muslims, while an earlier migration of a small group of Muslims from Mecca to Abyssinia (Ethiopia) in 615 CE was not.

There are several Qur'anic verses and hadith that formed the basis for these discussions and scholarly work on hijra. The Qur'anic verses cited in most scholarly opinions and treatises are the following:

> When angels take the souls of those who die in sin against their souls, they say: "In what (plight) were ye?" They reply: "Weak and oppressed were we in the earth." They say: "Was not the earth of Allah spacious enough for you to move yourselves away (From evil)?" Such men will find their abode in Hell—What an evil refuge! Except those who are (really) weak and oppressed—men, women, and children—who have no means in their power, nor (a guidepost) to their way.
>
> For these, there is hope that Allah will forgive: For Allah doth blot out (sins) and forgive again and again. He who forsakes his home in the cause of Allah, finds in the earth many a refuge, wide and spacious: Should he die as a refugee from home for Allah and His Messenger, his reward becomes due and sure with Allah: And Allah is Oft-forgiving, Most Merciful.[6]

and

> Those who believed, and adopted exile, and fought for the Faith, with their property and their persons, in the cause of Allah, as well as those who gave (them) asylum and aid, these are (all) friends and protectors, one of another. As to those who believed but came not into exile, ye owe no duty of protection to them until they come into exile; but if they seek your aid in religion, it is your duty to help them, except against a people with whom ye have a treaty of mutual alliance. And (remember) Allah seeth all that ye do.[7]

A number of hadith refer to hijra as an obligation, while scholars in later centuries extrapolated on the specific conditions that make hijra obligatory to Muslims. A hadith transmitted by Prophet Muhammad's wife Aisha stated that "There is no hijra after the liberation of Mecca," (*la hijrata ba'd al fathi*). This hadith was most often cited to discourage the necessity of migration. The issue of hijra, and when or whether Muslims are obliged to migrate, was judged differently depending on the circumstances and considering the actual viability of such a move.[8] Whether it was the Muslim lands conquered by the Mongols, the Iberian Peninsula, Central Asia, India, or West Africa, scholars deliberated on the definitions of *Dar al-Islam* and *Dar al-Harb*. The fundamental principle was that righteous existence was possible only within a system that upholds shari'a and where life could be led under its guidance, defined as *Dar al-Islam*. However, scholars differed on what disqualifies such a setting, while the reality of Muslim existence in non-Muslim societies continued to challenge the rigid division of the world into two separate entities.[9] After all, Prophet Muhammad sent a group of Muslims to emigrate to Christian Abyssinia, where they were allowed to practice their faith. The extensive debates continued among scholars and jurists over what circumstances define either domain, considering the social, political, economic, and practical aspects of hijra. Overall, the jurists who adhered to the Hanafi and Shafi'i schools of jurisprudence maintained that as long as Muslims were able to practice their religion, even as a minority under non-Muslim rule, those regions remained *Dar al-Islam*.[10]

Discussions on the issue of hijra became more prominent in the nineteenth century when Muslims around the world became subjects of European colonial empires. At the start of the twentieth century, more Muslims lived in the Russian Empire than in the Ottoman Empire, while British India contained the largest Muslim population in the world at the time. European empires viewed their colonial subjects through a religious lens and worked to integrate Islamic structures into the colonial state. For Muslims it was more than the symbolism of a skewed shari'a that the French and British colonial administrations tried to display with the Droit musulman en Algérie and the Anglo-Muhammadan Law in their colonies.[11] Despite different forms of colonial rule and the heterogeneity of the Muslim inhabited world, many colonized Muslims faced similar predicaments.[12] They considered the future of their existence as Muslims, including the option of migration and whether and where should Muslims migrate, reflecting on migrations' religious, strategic, and political implications. Muslims articulated solutions from within their intellectual tradition and expressed it in a language of familiar symbolism.

Scholars and intellectuals considered contemporary circumstances when debating the future of Muslim presence in areas of the world where they had no sovereignty. Muslims threatened by European expansion in the lost Ottoman territories, and those who were in Muslim majority areas of the world that were never part of the Ottoman Empire, began to look up to the sultan-caliph and the Ottoman Empire as the sole independent Muslim country that had the power to defend them. They regarded the Ottoman Empire not only as the direction of potential refuge, but also as the protector in the nascent system of international laws and treaties focused on populations and minorities.

Deliberations continued among religious scholars, and some rulings and treatises even made it into the popular press where they were publicly debated. It is in the colonial context that the classical terms *"Dar al-Islam"* and *"Dar al-Harb"* came to be used to imply the dichotomous view of the world as a perpetual war against non-Muslims versus a utopian Islamic society, with a modern geopolitical twist, that ominously lingers to present day.[13] When the British seized power from the Mughal rulers of India, some scholars argued that India had become *Dar al-Harb*, very much in the same vein as the preacher who disturbed Tarabar enough to write to Rida and ask for a scholarly clarification on the status of Bosnia Herzegovina under Habsburg rule.[14] However, fatwas recommending hijra remained controversial, and no single fatwa caused any mass migrations.

Bosnia Herzegovina was part of the Ottoman sociopolitical structure since the fifteenth century. The Islam of Muslims throughout the Ottoman domains was a lived experience and was broadly reflected in the social customs and cultural rites that varied throughout time and imperial space. The Ottoman legal and administrative system represented a rather constant structure across the imperial realm that was at the same time adaptable to local conditions and brought a level of uniformity in public affairs. The practice of celebrating religious holidays, pilgrimages, participation in Sufi communal organizations, reciting the communal Friday prayers in the sultan's name, matters of birth, marriage, death, public order, guilds, and trade practices were embedded in the Bosnian social structure beyond pious observance. After the loss of Hungary and Dalmatia in the seventeenth century, Bosnia became the Ottoman border region with Austria-Hungary, with which the Ottomans were often at war. The status of Bosnia Herzegovina as a border region, and its inhabitants as the defenders of the Ottoman Empire, contributed to an extensive consideration of Islamic concepts such as *Dar al-Harb, Dar al-Islam,* and jihad, entertained in the works of the Bosnian and other scholars in southeastern Europe.[15] Hijra was situated within the discussions of social order and the relationships between the state and the subjects.[16]

Migration played an important role in the formation of the Ottoman state, while migrants, including both immigrants and internal nomadic populations, continued to be a viable element within the Ottoman domains.[17] As mentioned, the empire's final century was marked by an influx of millions of refugees transforming it demographically. Because of the centrality of hijra in Islamic history, admitting migrants and refugees (Arabic *muhajir*, plural *muhajirin*) had an additional sense of a religious responsibility beyond humanitarian action throughout Ottoman history, be they Muslim or non-Muslim.[18] The use of the terms "hijra" and "*muhajir*" (*hicret* and *muhacir* in Turkish) symbolically linked Muslim migration and the migrants with the experiences of the early Muslim community. Islamic ethics were extensively relied upon when the Ottoman Empire, faced with managing the many migrants that overwhelmed the empire in its last century, depended on local communities to accept the migrants as *muhajir* and help them settle.[19] Migrants fled because they were Muslim and their plight articulated in Islamic idiom reached the broadest audience and had widespread urgency among Muslims of various class, ethnic, and regional backgrounds. For Habsburg Bosnia Herzegovina in particular, the fact that Ottoman sovereignty over this province was articulated within the religious context at the Berlin Congress, and that the Bosnian subjects' association with the Ottoman Empire was spelled out in the relationship with the Muslim spiritual leaders in Istanbul, added to the weight of religious discourse. Yet, when it came to classical categorizations, most Ottoman scholars adhering to the Hanafi school of jurisprudence held a general view that although *Dar al-Islam* were territories ruled by Muslim rulers, outside territories were not necessarily *Dar al-Harb*.

Migration Debate in Bosnia Herzegovina

Many Muslim migrants cited difficulty of practicing Islam within a non-Muslim state as the principal motivation for leaving Habsburg Bosnia Herzegovina. Reasons for migration discussed in the previous chapter, including conscription and the consequences of economic and legal centralization policies, were frequently related to religious differences between the ruler and the ruled. These policies often resulted in discrimination against Muslims, ultimately concluding that Muslim survival under non-Muslim rule was impossible. While Muslims did experience mistreatment simply for being Muslim, the social, political, and economic transformations and general anxiety about the future also had an important role in considerations of migration. Bosnian ulema and intellectuals were the first to reject migration as the solution to the problem of Habsburg occupation.

One of the earliest reactions to migratory movements appeared in print in 1884. Muhamed Emin Hadžijahić (1837–1892) wrote articles discouraging migration in the Ottoman Turkish-language paper *Vatan* published in Bosnia Herzegovina.[20] A *kurra hafiz* and a professor, he held appointments in two of Sarajevo's major mosques, Begova and Careva. Following the occupation, Hadžijahić then traveled to Istanbul, most likely to protest these acts, staying in the Ottoman Empire several months.[21] Upon return, however, he became active in dispelling illusions about Bosnia's future as part of the Ottoman Empire, underscoring the rights Muslims were already granted under the new administration. Although it seemed that he had come to accept the Habsburg rule, he continued to be identified as an oppositional public figure.[22] In particular he was vocal in criticizing migration as a response to Habsburg occupation, dismissing its reasoning from an economic, social, and religious perspective. He wrote about migration not in the genres of Islamic scholarship but chose to address a broader audience through the paper *Vatan* in Ottoman Turkish.[23]

Hadžijahić was alarmed that migration demographically reduced, and therefore weakened, the Muslim community in Bosnia Herzegovina. Demographic decline lessened Muslims' political importance and rendered them a minority. He rejected the idea that Bosnia Herzegovina became *Dar al-Harb* simply because the provincial administration changed reminding the readers that communal prayers, calls to prayer, and other religious practices were undisturbed. Hadžijahić opposed the idea that migration was a religious obligation, claiming that, on the contrary, migration would contribute to the disappearance of Islam in Bosnia Herzegovina, "a sin before God and shame before the rest of the Muslim world," for which the migrants themselves would be responsible. In Hadžijahić's writings, love of homeland and its protection were thus fundamental religious obligations and the basis for preservation of faith. Although his reasoning was religious, it was not in a form of a religious ruling usually meant for other religious scholars, but in the style of a public address emphasizing patriotism and the connection between Islam and homeland.

After dismissing the religious reasoning for migrations, Hadžijahić analyzed the social and political circumstances that drove the Muslim population to migrate. He stressed the safety and legal rights guaranteed by the Habsburg administration and encouraged those who were wronged in any way to seek justice with the courts and even the emperor. Addressing the introduction of conscription that caused a wave of migration, Hadžijahić recognized that military service was required everywhere else around the world, adding that, at least in this case, the military was for the protection of one's homeland and not for defense of foreign countries. He advised that the safety and freedoms guaranteed by the Habsburg administration in Bosnia Herzegovina were far more promising than the uncertainty and otherness of language and customs that awaited the migrants on the long journey to the Ottoman Empire.[24]

In the same year, the mufti of Tuzla, Mehmed Teufik Azapagić (1838–1918)—later to become the second Reis ul-ulema of Habsburg Bosnia Herzegovina—wrote *Risala fi al-hijra* (Treatise on Migration) in Arabic.[25] Whereas a fatwa is usually initiated by a question and is composed in a form of an authoritative answer, Azapagić chose to write a more comprehensive work. The treatise genre allowed him to construct lengthy and complex arguments reflecting on the body of authoritative legal literature in light of contemporary conditions, in order to grapple with an issue of fundamental importance.[26] Mufti Azapagić disproved claims that Bosnia became *Dar al-Harb* after the Habsburg occupation. He divided the treatise into three parts that analyzed the notion of hijra, *Dar al-Harb,* and *Dar al-Islam* and their use as elements in the discourse on migration.

His approach stressed the need to view the issue of migration through the prism of its own time and circumstance. Azapagić refuted the analogy between the hijra of Prophet Muhammad and that of the Bosnian Muslims by analyzing the period in which these two processes took place: the hijra of the Prophet happened in the early period of Islam and was a necessary step for further development of the community and its ultimate victory. The hijra of Muslims in Bosnia Herzegovina, in contrast, was weakening the Muslim community. In an effort to clear the confusion about the status of Bosnia Herzegovina that followed the occupation of this Ottoman territory by the non-Muslim Habsburg Empire, Azapagić referred to the body of work by Islamic scholars on the notions of *Dar al-Harb* and *Dar al-Islam*. He showed that Bosnia Herzegovina could not be considered *Dar al-Harb* because it was a region where Friday and Eid congregational prayers were performed; where hajj travel was completed; where the recitation of the public call to prayer (*adhan*) was allowed; and where the application of Islamic law existed through the appointment of shari'a judges, even if by a non-Muslim ruler.[27] He established that to call for hijra from such a region was not religiously sanctioned. Azapagić cited the hadith "there is no hijra after the liberation of Mecca" to support his claim, while he considered other Qur'anic verses and hadith that dealt with the notion of hijra as an obligation to have symbolic and spiritual meaning.[28]

Azapagić began the treatise with another hadith: *hubb al watan min al iman* ("Love of the homeland is a part of faith") that became popular with Muslim activists discouraging hijra in other areas of the world where Muslim migration was underway, and that continues to be cited as religious validation in nationalist movements.[29] Although the treatise drew on the tradition of Islamic legal argumentation, the conclusion was spelled out in practical terms: migration was perilous for the individual; it weakened the Muslim community; and it resulted in the loss of property and livelihood. All it brought was a precarious future that would most likely result in defeat.

Risala fi al-hijra was a work of legal nature and written in Arabic for Islamic scholars. It was primarily intended for the ulema, who might not have been unanimous on the issue of hijra but who were able to reach the public through weekly Friday sermons across the province.[30] With similar intentions, muftis across the Russian Empire and encouraged by the Russian authorities, also issued rulings condemning migration in practical terms. Mufti of the Sunni Assembly of the Caucasus stated that migration from the "motherland" was unnecessary and that those who encouraged it actually worked against shari'a. Orenburg Mufti in the Volga region also denounced migration, blaming it on the opportunists, who encouraged migration hoping to make money off transport and by purchasing migrants' properties for less than their worth.[31] These muftis appealed to religious and patriotic sensibilities in practical terms and direct language, hoping to dissuade their apprehensive believers.

While most contributors to the migration debates worked to deter migration, there were scholars who encouraged it. One was Bosnalı Hilmi Baba (Hilmi ibn Huseyn Taşlıcavi Bosnevi), who wrote the treatise *Risala fi al-hijra wa al-muhajirin* (Treatise on Migration and Migrants) in 1885. Of Bosnian origin and residing in Medina, he proposed that migration was a religious obligation for Bosnian Muslims who found themselves under Habsburg rule, comparing the urgency of Bosnian migration to that of the early Muslims under Prophet Muhammad's guidance.[32] Bosnalı Hilmi Baba even considered Russia to be a better destination for Bosnian Muslims than staying in the Habsburg Empire, but he recommended migration to eastern parts of the Ottoman Empire, to the regions of Damascus, Aleppo, and Urfa. He recommended these regions since Istanbul and its surrounding areas—due to Ottoman modernization that he saw as imitation of Europe—had become just as "un-Islamic" as *Dar al-Harb*.[33] This advice in particular is instructive as it points to the issues that pushed so many to migrate: the centralization policies and the state encroachment on the lives of their subjects that both empires were executing.

Concrete events in towns and villages instigated migration for Muslims in Bosnia Herzegovina, while those who wanted to leave and those who decided to stay found religious discourse reassuring. Šerif Arnautović (1847–1935), early Habsburg oppositional activist and later director of the Pious Foundations Administration, described instigators traversing Bosnia Herzegovina as either profiteers who wanted to buy Muslim properties under market value or as those who had "purchased a preacher's mantle" (as opposed to earning the status)—both kinds preying on naïve people and convincing them to migrate. For Arnautović, these men were the reason for surges in migrations especially after the annexation in 1908, when in his view, the positions and opportunities for Muslims in Habsburg Bosnia had already improved.[34]

Bosnian intellectuals also advocated against migration that they considered one of the principal problems of their society. They published in the provincial Ottoman Turkish and Bosnian press, printed brochures, and wrote didactical novels. The intellectuals and writers criticized the lack of Muslim engagement in education and economy and claimed that those who sought their escape from the inevitable change (and "progress") in Habsburg Bosnia did not realize that their illusory sanctuary (in the Ottoman Empire) was transforming as well. Bosnian papers often translated articles from the Ottoman press that discouraged migration. Letters from Bosnian students, migrants, and others in the Ottoman Empire describing the poverty, disease, and other dangers that befell migrants on the long journey and the difficult conditions in their new places of settlement were also given space in the press with a hope that these examples would further dissuade the population from migrating. One such letter from a certain Osman hodža who settled in Ankara province, lamented the decision to migrate and revealed that the representatives of migrant families met to discuss their return and to find possible ways to finance it, ending with an exclamation: "Stay in Bosnia!"[35]

Migration was a problem for Muslim communities in empires and nation-states alike. Ismail Gasprinskii's Crimean reformist paper *Tercüman* ran several articles warning of the dangers of migration and false rumors that encouraged it, also concluding that migration was unwarranted since freedom of religion existed in Russia.[36] Like the Bosnians, Bulgarian Muslim intellectuals condemned migration to the Ottoman Empire. The Bulgarian Turkish language paper *Muvazene* was particularly outspoken in arguing against migration to unfamiliar lands as a solution to the problems Muslims faced and the inappropriate correlation of migration with the historic hijra. The paper warned that migration would lead to Muslim "obliteration" in Bulgaria.[37]

Foremost among the intellectuals discouraging emigration from Bosnia Herzegovina was Mehmed-Beg Kapetanović Ljubušak (1839–1902), who grounded his appeal in three perspectives of Bosnian identity: the landowner-notables, Bosnians, and Muslims. Ljubušak was a landowner who held Ottoman and Habsburg provincial governmental posts, including membership in the first Ottoman parliament. Reaching back to pre-Ottoman and pre-Islamic history of Bosnia Herzegovina, Ljubušak pointed to the connection between the notables and their land possessions in Bosnia Herzegovina. Locating the issue within regional historical narrative, he questioned the notables' reasoning behind migration caused by the Habsburg occupation, stressing that their ancestor notables did not opt to leave upon Ottoman conquest centuries earlier.[38] Emphasizing the continuity of the medieval Bosnian population with the Ottoman Muslim subjects, he asked if it would not be a shame for them to migrate after they had protected their homeland "since the times of the Bosnian kings."[39] Not losing sight of Bosnian Muslim identity, he also claimed the contradiction between the decision to leave one's homeland and what Islamic ethics recommended, reiterating the hadith: "Love of the homeland is a part of faith."[40] Ljubušak's writings shaped the romantic nationalist discourse in Habsburg Bosnia Herzegovina, where discouraging migration was seen as a matter of survival in political and socioeconomic sense and also a matter of Bosnian physical existence. In a vicious circle, Muslim demographic decline and weakening of their social and economic strength reinforced the issues that pushed many to migrate to the Ottoman Empire.

From the perspective of the new administration, mass migration from Bosnia Herzegovina would have been an embarrassment for the Habsburg

Empire. The very excuse for occupying this Ottoman province was that the Ottomans were unable to properly govern, causing peasant migration into Habsburg territories just a few years prior. After the initial wave of emigration in the aftermath of occupation, the Habsburg administration tried to prevent mass migration through a series of policies that regulated the conditions that pushed Muslims to migrate, as well as making migration administratively more burdensome.[41] Capitalizing on this concern, Muslim political opposition often included the possibility of migration in their petitions to the Habsburg as well as the Ottoman authorities. In one such publication in the Hungarian *Pester Lloyd*, Muslim oppositional activists described their grievances concluding that the Habsburg administration in their homeland was so intolerable that it pushed Muslims to leave their homes and "wander about in foreign lands like vagabonds."[42] When the opposition's demands were met in the aftermath of annexation, threats of migration ceased to be part of their petitions.

Political activists—whether those advocating for a return to the Ottoman fold or the nationalists of various persuasions—were engaged in propaganda against migration and sought Ottoman help to deter it. Šerif Arnautović, writing to an Ottoman official, explained that due to the spread of false information (that the Habsburg and Ottoman empires agreed to ban migration and delay property sales after the annexation), some ignorant people decided to migrate before the alleged agreement was put in effect. Arnautović requested a statement from the Ottoman administration strongly condemning emigration from Bosnia Herzegovina. The statement was to be published in the local press and, he hoped, would finally settle the migration issue once and for all.[43] Arnautović wrote that "half the Muslims" from Bosnia Herzegovina would not be able to migrate to the Ottoman Empire anyway, and would be rendered a minority, which would be their end. Predictions that the emigrants would sell their property below value, and that the administration would then settle the abandoned land with Catholic colonists from the empire, revealed his fears of Muslim demographic collapse. Encroaching nationalist aspirations were justified through demographic predominance in the province as was done in the rest of post-Ottoman Balkans.

Arnautović also meant to alarm the Ottoman administrators and arouse Ottoman public opinion with fresh memories of Muslim migration from

Greece, Serbia, Montenegro, and Bulgaria where Muslim properties were often quickly usurped with the approval of their governments, even when bilateral agreements regarding compensation to the Ottoman Empire for Muslim properties were in place. He warned of widespread poverty among the migrants and the negative effect that it had on their moral standards, citing as evidence the prostitutes in Ankara and Skopje, the majority of whom were immigrant women. In his lengthy elaboration, Arnautović underscored that those who already migrated caused more damage than benefit to the Ottoman state: "Half of them . . . became ruined and hit bottom, while a quarter returned to Bosnia in a state deserving of charity. The rest are helpless because they do not speak the [Turkish] language." Members of the Bosnian student club in Istanbul also lobbied with the Ottoman high-ranking officials and even met with the Şeyhülislam, urging them to officially discourage migration from Bosnia Herzegovina.[44] The hope was that a definitive Ottoman statement would resolve the rumors and debates on the necessity of hijra, the lure of free land, or the illusion of an escape to a society that resembled the old times.

The onset of the Balkan Wars (1912–1913) had a significant impact on migration debates in Bosnia Herzegovina and the Ottoman Empire. The most obvious outcome of the wars was that it severed the territorial continuity Bosnia Herzegovina had with the Ottoman Empire. The physical detachment from the empire seemed like a final act in the process of separation. The territorial losses, as well as the horrific atrocities Muslims suffered in these wars, affected Ottoman prestige, leaving Muslims who sought protection from the empire disappointed and abandoned. For others, it was a signal of Muslim demise in Ottoman Europe and a final chance to hold onto the Ottoman ideal by migrating.

Ottoman Attitudes Toward Bosnian Migration

Rumors circulated in Bosnia Herzegovina alleging that the sultan ordered a complete Muslim migration to the Ottoman Empire and that immigrants received free land and money upon arrival. While the improbability of such rumors might have been obvious, they were regularly denounced, testifying to their permanence among the public. Rumors were not limited to Bosnia only. In Russia, rumors circulated about an alleged agreement between the sultan and the tsar allowing baptism of all Russian Muslim subjects, which alarmed the Russian authorities, fearing another wave of migration, to the extent that they asked the muftis of Orenburg and the Caucasus to denounce them.[45] While the press and the activities of the officials and community leaders in Bosnia Herzegovina were quick to deny and condemn such rumors, they stubbornly lingered throughout the Habsburg period, especially in rural regions. Muslims expelled from Crimea and the Caucasus—and those fleeing violence in the lost Ottoman territories in Serbia, Greece, Bulgaria, and Romania who showed up at the Ottoman borders and ports—were always received, and a system of migrant aid and settlement was established through the Ottoman Migrants and Charity commissions and local authorities in the nineteenth century. Brutal treatment of Muslims in the lost territories and their flight to the Ottoman Empire prompted the Şeyhülislam, the highest religious authority in the Ottoman Empire, to address the sultan, arguing in favor of accepting all immigrants from the lost territories based on the Islamic tradition of aiding migrants, especially when they were Muslims fleeing non-Muslim oppressive rule.[46]

Although there was a faint chance of reclaiming the province, relying on the fact that Bosnia Herzegovina was de jure under Ottoman sovereignty until 1908, it was advantageous to use this legal situation for diplomatic purposes, precisely because of the size of its Muslim population. In one such decision, the Ottoman Council of Ministers, considering petitions from Bosnian Muslims and the related government reports, concluded that although migration was beneficial to increase the Muslim population in the Ottoman Empire, migration from Bosnia Herzegovina should not be encouraged.[47] Two years later, in response to a large number of applications for immigration, the council once again determined that completely vacating Bosnia Herzegovina was not politically sound.[48]

Intentions of the Ottoman officials regarding Bosnian migration were best elaborated in the recommendations of the Ottoman consul in Dubrovnik. Being one of the closest officials to the province and having frequent contact with the Bosnian population, he communicated his concerns regarding Bosnian Muslim migration and offered an approach toward migrants from Bosnia Herzegovina. Accepting them was a humanitarian act towards the "poor" and "tyranny-afflicted" Muslims and potentially a way to increase and strengthen the Ottoman population. Though Bosnian immigrants were "useful people," the consul continued to recommend that migration from this province should not be encouraged. He reasoned that Bosnia Herzegovina was legally part of the Ottoman Empire under temporary foreign occupation and that its Muslims maintained a strong connection to the Ottoman Empire, even hoping that their province would once again be a part of the imperial domains.[49]

The consul in Dubrovnik stressed the size of the Bosnian Muslim population, their unity, and adherence to faith as important. In addition, he recommended that the population of closely 400,000 Bosnian Muslims "devoted to the sultan and ready to sacrifice for faith and fellow countrymen" should not be reduced but amplified because the Bosnian Muslims were the key to Ottoman continuity and influence in the region. He suggested that it would be practical to work on discouraging migration and help Bosnian Muslims resolve their problems, protect them, and ensure their legal rights were upheld, while simultaneously maintaining friendly relations with Austria. His key observation was that the Ottoman Empire should keep its sphere of influence in this vital European province by relying on the loyalty and the Ottoman sentiments of its Muslims, finding it to be more beneficial than their migration. The consul's recommendations were consistent with the Ottoman policies during the reign of Sultan Abdülhamid II. For the entire period of Habsburg rule in Bosnia Herzegovina, Ottoman administration did not encourage migration but never outright prohibited it or denied immigration applications. Since migrants continued coming, the policies were adjusted to situations as they arose. The Ottomans tried to expose migration as a consequence of the Habsburg inability to incorporate the province's multi-confessional society and especially its Muslims. Emphasizing a Muslim exodus from a Christian state, the Ottomans once again challenged the European Great Powers' practice of interfering in Ottoman domestic politics on the pretext of defending Ottoman Christian populations under Muslim rule.[50]

A possibility of a voluntary migration sponsored by the state, as sought in some of the petitions, could not have been considered because of high expenses of such an enterprise and because the empire already struggled to handle an almost constant flow of refugees into its domains. The cost of transporting and settling the migrants was substantial and sometimes needed to be expensed even before the migrants reached the Ottoman Empire. Ibrahim Fethi, the Ottoman ambassador in Belgrade, for instance, addressed the authorities in Istanbul, asking for funds to be assigned to facilitate Bosnian Muslims' travel from Belgrade. He wrote that since his arrival in Serbia, a great number of despairing Muslim migrants applied to the Ottoman embassy for help, but because of the lack of funds for such expenses their requests were denied; the rejection also relied on a prior decision of the Refugee Commission not to encourage migration. Seeing that these destitute migrants then became "a tool in Serbian propaganda," and that some returned home, the ambassador began unofficially aiding the migrants from embassy funds, as well with as with his own money. As the migrants continued to come, he requested a monthly budget allocation for transporting the migrants to Skopje.[51]

Similarly, the governor of Salonica requested financial help with the migrants from Bosnia Herzegovina in 1901, describing the Bosnian arrivals "for 5 to 6 months, in 3 or 4 convoys weekly, each consisting of 300–400 people."[52] Being the starting point in the sea route for Balkan migrants headed to Istanbul and other ports in the empire, the province of Salonica was financially strained by the responsibilities of housing and feeding the migrants.[53] Once they completed their journey to the Ottoman territory, the migrants needed to be housed and employed. To illustrate, the cost of settling 1,469 Bosnian migrants in 283 houses in Ankara province amounted to 1,688,575.50 Ottoman lira.[54] In another case, the Ottoman cabinet allotted 2,000 lira per month and an additional 8,000 lira for housing, tools, animals, food, and seed to settle a group of Bosnian migrants along the Anatolian railroad.[55] Local populations and migrants themselves were employed in the construction of housing.[56] As much as the financial and material help that was provided by the state could have bolstered migration, the difficulties of travel, disease, and poverty were a considerable deterrent for those considering the move. Yet the delicate legal position of the province and the rather safe position of Bosnian Muslims under the Habsburgs allowed some to go back and forth and weigh their opportunities in both empires.

Individual migrants also petitioned the Ottoman authorities describing their predicament and asking for assistance, while on the way or within the imperial domains. Certain Abdülkerim, a migrant from Bosnia Herzegovina who could only afford to move to Istanbul by himself, petitioned the Ottoman authorities for help in bringing his family. He was subsequently awarded a gift from the sultan (*atiyye-i seniyye*) in the amount of 1,400 lira.[57]

Others petitioned out of financial need, life events that made them destitute, and simply the wish to improve their condition. The sense that the sultan was responsible for the migrants in need was discernible in appeals where petitioners sought monetary help, job placement, housing, admission to schools, or other support, and in many cases they received a positive reply. The petitioners' expectations were framed in the language that appealed to contemporary Ottoman concerns and the empire's self-image, especially when they wrote from outside of Ottoman domains and sought caliphal protection. In line with the longstanding Ottoman practice, demonstrating the sultan's generosity on the one hand, and imperial magnanimity in responding to petitions on the other, coincided with a need to maintain order in the imperial domains overwhelmed by migrants.

The Ottoman administration's ability to manage large migrant populations that continued arriving throughout the empire's last century was often criticized by increasingly vocal public opinion. The sight of migrants dwelling in major thoroughfares and imperial mosques in Istanbul and other

FIGURE 4. Migrants in the streets of Istanbul waiting to be resettled.

Source: Faik Sabri Duran and Ubeydullah Esat, *Resimli Kitap 43–48* (Istanbul: s.n., 1913), 764.

cities, lingering around ports and train stations with all of their belongings and sometimes even their animals, stimulated a variety of strong reactions in the press. Some journalists compared the increasingly common immigrant presence to an invasion. The Ottoman public generally empathized with the plight of Bosnian Muslims and welcomed the ones who had already arrived, but many directly discouraged migration from Bosnia Herzegovina. Articles in the press criticized the Habsburg treatment of Muslims and predicted the end of Muslim life under their rule. The Ottoman paper *Muhacir* (Migrant) condemned the "bogus" preachers making migration a religious issue in Bosnia Herzegovina and persuading the susceptible poor and rural population to flee.[58] The paper further blamed the well-to-do Bosnian Muslims for not helping the poor and thus allowing migration, locating the issue in class interests, poverty, and ignorance, rather than religion. The same paper, in an article titled "To Migrate or Not," warned that migration would lead to the extinction of the Bosnians: "Perhaps, in a hundred years Bosniak name would be no more, and the historians would refer to them by saying: once upon a time . . ."[59] *Ittihat ve Terraki* (Union and Progress) pointed out that the Bosnian Muslim migration would be beneficial for Habsburg expansion of its sphere of influence in the region because the land that the Muslims left behind would be settled by colonizers from Austria-Hungary. Warning that if the Bosnians were to abandon their homes, there would be no hope for their future and their homeland would be lost forever, the paper confirmed the putative connection between demographic dominance and territorial expansion that came to define the territorial losses in Ottoman Europe in the twentieth century.[60] Nationalists, however, saw migration as the opportunity to strengthen the "loyal" population of the empire, fearing more secessionist wars supported by European powers.

Itself the focus of marginalization from the "family of sovereign nations,"[61] the Ottoman Empire took advantage of the opportunity to claim protection over Muslims worldwide, many of whom were colonial subjects. Militarily and economically weaker, Sultan Abdülhamid II capitalized instead on the caliphal symbolism bolstering his credentials as a spiritual leader and exploiting the fears of European colonial powers anxious about the extent of the caliph's influence and ideas of Pan-Islam on their Muslim subjects.[62]

Nineteenth-century Ottoman Empire was characterized by agricultural labor shortages and contained tracts of uncultivated land that it wanted to make economically viable.⁶³ Instead of foreign investors it originally considered to remedy this situation, the state attempted to direct migrants to fill that void. Ottoman authorities were primarily concerned with settling and integrating the incoming population into the existing local socioeconomic order, testifying to the state's long-term plans. For this purpose, the Ottoman government provided tax and military service exemptions. Tax exemptions were reflected in immigrant agricultural, trade, and artisan activities; the exemptions ranged from ten years to six years to one year at different times and places of settlement.⁶⁴ In some of the settlement regions, disputes arose with the local populations and disturbed existing arrangements.⁶⁵ For the most part though, in addition to manpower, Balkan migrants brought new knowledge including agricultural and artisanal techniques, foodways, and animal husbandry skills.

A similar logic was applied to military service exemptions. The authorities recognized that the men were the family breadwinners; families without men to work the land or earn a wage were usually destined to continuously depend on government aid and charities. Exemptions from military service were approximately six years in duration, pointing to the fact that the Ottoman government was more concerned with integrating immigrants into society than fulfilling its need for military recruits even in wartime. Bosnians who crossed over to Kosovo and volunteered to serve in the army in 1897, for instance, were ordered first to register and be settled as immigrants before their army service could be considered. The same year, a number of volunteers arrived from Bosnia Herzegovina to Shkodër, prompting the local government to telegraph Istanbul to ask what to do with them.⁶⁶ The answer was the same. They were to be treated as other immigrants: they were to be registered, settled, documented, and conscripted only after their exemption had expired.⁶⁷

When the Ottoman Empire entered World War I, some Bosnian migrants sought to volunteer for the military, but their ambiguous status initiated a debate across the Ottoman Ministry of War, the Ministry of Foreign Affairs, and the Sublime Porte Legal Counsel. The issue was that these migrants had arrived from Bosnia Herzegovina without the necessary documentation from the Habsburg authorities, which was attainable only after they had completed the Habsburg military service. According to the Ottoman–Habsburg agreement on migration, these immigrants were illegal. Notwithstanding, it was decided that they should be given "an opportunity to become Ottoman citizens" after they had resided in the Ottoman Empire for five years with good conduct. They were cautioned not to contact the Austrian consulate (and reveal the breach of the agreement), lest the aid and benefits be revoked and they be expelled from the Ottoman domains.[68]

Ottoman attitudes toward Bosnian migration were consistent with their diplomatic and geopolitical priorities. Whereas the "usefulness" of additional Muslims were considered—whether as manpower or for potential homogenization of the diversely populated strategic areas—encouraging migration never became imperative. That is perhaps because the migrants from the Balkans and Russia continued to arrive regardless. The prohibitive cost and challenging logistics of such large-scale population transfers and settlements were also important reasons not to make migration a policy.

Top members of the Committee of Union and Progress (CUP) who ruled the Ottoman Empire after the Young Turk Revolution in 1908, saw urgency in the policies of demographic engineering. In the aftermath of the Habsburg annexation of Bosnia Herzegovina and the indignation that followed, members of the CUP ruling clique suggested settling Muslims from Bosnia in the remaining key regions in Ottoman Europe to reinforce the Muslim population that could boost its territorial claims in the face of brutal nationalist competition.[69] Although no such relocation of Bosnians materialized, the Balkan Wars and World War I that followed realized the Ottoman fears. Forces of Bulgaria, Greece, Serbia and Montenegro expelled and massacred Muslim populations in Ottoman European regions so they could base their territorial claims on the newly achieved demographic dominance of their own group in the region. The migrations that ensued had lasting consequences on the demographic picture of the Balkans and the Middle East in the twentieth century.

Nationalism and Migration: Serbian Attitudes

Serbia, a former Ottoman province that was given independence at the Berlin Congress, transformed from an already autonomous principality into a nation-state. The Serbian approach to the question of Muslim migration from Bosnia Herzegovina was situated in the context of its regional politics marked by its expansionist aspirations. According to some theories of Serbian nation-building, Bosnian Muslims were ethnic Serbs who had converted to Islam in the Ottoman period and were considered to be part of the Serbian nationalist cause. Others saw Bosnian Muslims as allies with the Orthodox Christian population in Bosnia Herzegovina in opposing the Habsburg occupation. In both views, the concern was that Muslim migration would change the ethnic and confessional makeup of Bosnia Herzegovina. There was also the fear that when Muslims left their estates and migrated, their lands would then be open to the (mostly Catholic) agricultural colonizers from the monarchy. Such colonization would demographically change the province and move Bosnia Herzegovina closer to permanently remaining within the Habsburg Empire.[70] For these reasons the Serbian government, activists, and the press closely followed the events in Bosnia Herzegovina and worked on discouraging Muslim migration, sometimes in collaboration with the Bosnian Muslim diaspora in Serbia and the Ottoman Empire.

Serbian agreement with Austria-Hungary regarding prevention of anti-Habsburg activity ceased to be in effect when the king of Serbia, Milan Obrenović, abdicated in 1889. Serbian nationalist organizations and the government itself began openly supporting the oppositional currents in Bosnia Herzegovina. In addition, they also began supporting those working from Serbia, some of whom were Bosnian Muslims. Preventing Bosnian Muslim migration was seen as critical for the Serbian national and political program. These attitudes were part of the Serbian state-building project fashioned in the nineteenth century. Serbia saw itself at the helm of the South Slav struggle for independence. Although defining itself as a resolutely Orthodox Christian nation, the expansionist state-building entailed incorporating populations across ethnic and confessional lines in Macedonia, Kosovo, Bosnia Herzegovina, and Croatia. Consequently, the message of Serbian nationalism was repeatedly revised so that the future co-nationals did not resist Serbian leadership.[71] Similar considerations of (br)othering characterized evolving nationalisms across the Balkans: Croat nationalists also imagined Bosnia Herzegovina as its land and the Bosnian Muslims as ethnic Croats. Bulgaria viewed its Pomak Muslims in similar terms and considered novel theories about ethnic and historical connections between Bulgarians and Turks that would serve its regional interests.[72]

Immigrants from Bosnia Herzegovina established an association in Belgrade in 1889 with the aim of helping the oppositional movement inside

Bosnia Herzegovina.[73] Ties with the Bosnian Muslim diaspora in Istanbul were created through Bosnian and Serbian students and the Serbian consulate there.[74] The consulate voiced criticism of the Habsburg rule in Bosnia Herzegovina in its Ottoman Serbian paper *Carigradski Glasnik* (Constantinople Herald), where the effort was characterized as part of Serbian regional policy that supported Ottoman rights in territories coveted by others: Habsburg occupied Bosnia Herzegovina, as well as Macedonia, to which both Greece and Bulgaria laid claims.[75] However, Serbia also supported movements that disrupted Ottoman hegemony in the region, such as the autonomy-seeking Albanians, whom Serbia supplied with money and arms at low cost.[76]

Serbian nationalist papers, often illegally brought to Bosnia Herzegovina, contributed to the work of Serbian activists, teachers, and priests in spreading nationalist ideas among the Orthodox and Muslim populations, resulting in the Serbian nationalist affiliation of some Muslims too.[77] These papers often discussed migration and explicitly detailed its dangers for the province and the prospective migrants. Habsburg authorities were repeatedly attacked in the Serbian press for encouraging Muslim migration to open the way for agricultural colonization and extend its hegemony in the Balkans. In addition to Muslim migration to the Ottoman Empire, the Serbian nationalists lamented the intensification of migration to the Americas, which further diminished the numbers of potential co-nationals in the province.[78]

Bosnian Muslim emigrants in Serbia published several works about Bosnia Herzegovina, condemning the Habsburg administration. In 1895, Derviš beg Ljubović's brochure, titled "O stanju B.i H. posvećeno madžarskim patriotima" (On the situation in Bosnia Herzegovina dedicated to Hungarian patriots), referred to Bosnia as Serbian land.[79] *Misrule of the Occupational Administration in Bosnia Herzegovina* was published in Novi Sad.[80] Its authors, defined as the Muslim Committee for Bosnia Herzegovina in the foreword, used a pseudonym Ehli-Islam (Arabic, People of Islam).[81] The publication described violations in various regions in Bosnia Herzegovina, naming the abusive Habsburg officials and their victims, showing why they were left with no choice but to emigrate. The authors stated that their activity would not cease until Bosnia Herzegovina was restored to the Ottoman Empire or was given self-rule.[82] Finally, they considered the fact that the province still legally belonged to the sultan as important, not just for Bosnia Herzegovina, but also for all the Balkan peoples. International legal standards, treaties, and agreements were brought forth discrediting Habsburg hegemony in the Balkans. Criticism of the Habsburg inability to satisfy the fundamental needs of its subjects, its Orthodox Christian and Muslim populations, was reiterated in this brochure as an important factor that disqualified the Habsburg Monarchy's right to rule in Bosnia Herzegovina. Breaking international laws as well as the state's unfulfilled responsibilities to its subjects were the reasons used by this Bosnian committee in exile to promote claims of Habsburg illegal usurpation of Bosnia.

Belgrade, the capital of Serbia, was on the migration route from Bosnia Herzegovina via rail to Ottoman Macedonia. Some migrants remained in Belgrade for longer periods of time, having no means to continue their trip to Skopje and Salonica, and from where they would be further resettled. The Serbian government publicized that "out of humanity and brotherly compassion" it was offering these migrants aid in the form of discounted train tickets, as they "go to Istanbul deluded by religious feelings."[83] Moreover, it advised its diplomats to expose Muslim migration abroad as the fault of the Habsburg regime in Bosnia Herzegovina. The Ottoman consul in Belgrade was concerned that the migrants were caught in these political struggles and wanted to hasten their transport to the Ottoman domains. Jovan Cvijić, a prominent Serbian scientist, observing this migration through the Belgrade train station, regretted that the departing Muslim migrants were "forever lost to Serbian nationhood."[84]

But the limits of (br)othering in Serbian nation-building were evident in the way that the Serbian government dealt with its own Muslim population that was decimated in the middle of the nineteenth century. Many Muslim who were forced to leave Serbia settled in Ottoman Bosnia. Some migrants from Habsburg Bosnia desired to settle in Serbia, as it was close to Bosnia Herzegovina and because of the shared language and a familiar climate. However, these requests were denied and justified by the lack of financial means in Serbia for such settlement.[85] One such request came from Jašar-beg Kapetanović, who had migrated from Počitelj in Herzegovina and settled in the province of Manastır in Macedonia. He wrote to the Serbian Ministry of Foreign Affairs explaining that the poverty and hunger they were enduring was unbearable. His letter epitomized the circumstances of the migrant predicament in the Habsburg period:

> Migration, that contagious disease that devastated my exhausted homeland, did not spare my hometown with its surrounding areas. Eighty families of hardworking farmers migrated from there to Turkey, thinking that, after thirty years of oppression, we would find the sanctuary among our coreligionists as the Turkish press continuously depicted.[86]

A range of specifically Serbian efforts at discouraging Muslim migration was stimulated by a combination of ambitious nationalist plans, the delicate confessional balance in Bosnia Herzegovina, and the possibility of including Muslims Slavs as co-nationals. Because the Habsburg expansionist plans clashed with such Serbian plans in the Balkans, support of Ottoman claims often factored into the policies of the Serbian government and activists.

Debating Imperial Diversity

Debates on migration at the turn of the twentieth century exposed the pressing questions and predicaments some Muslims sought to resolve by leaving. Others advocated direct engagement with the new authorities and working to resolve the problems that pushed the Muslims to migrate. The precarious position of Muslim populations in colonial empires and nation-states—dispossession, expulsion, and ethnic cleansing—created the backdrop to these debates. Much of the migration to the Ottoman Empire was also influenced by political and economic circumstances but articulated in religious idiom and Islamic symbolism.

Migration from Habsburg Bosnia Herzegovina differed from the violent episodes that drove many other Balkan Muslims to the Ottoman Empire. In fact, one of the reasons for the continuity of a significant Muslim presence in Bosnia Herzegovina and the preservation of its Islamic and Ottoman heritage was the fact that this Ottoman province came under another imperial administration, rather than a nation-state. This reality was in contrast with the rest of the Balkans, where demographic engineering and de-Islamization were a feature of nation-building. Bosnian Muslims, for the most part, had a choice in deciding whether to move to the Ottoman domains, and they debated their options while they were part of both empires. In many ways, Bosnian Muslims too "spoke shari'a" to both the Habsburg and Ottoman states.[87] They called for Muslim imperial protection and used migration as leverage.

Muslim ulema and intellectuals in Bosnia Herzegovina and diaspora groups in Serbia and the Ottoman Empire fiercely criticized migration as a misguided response to the occupation and saw it as detrimental to the Muslims who remained. They engaged in debates on migration, evaluating circumstances that prompted such migratory movements and embedded their arguments within the regional and provincial discourse influenced by a variety of nationalist, Pan-Slavic, Pan-Islamic, and Young Turk ideologies that circulated across the empires and among their subjects. They supported their positions with religious reasoning and rhetoric that was used to enhance the significance of respective ideological principles.

Debates entertaining migration by former Ottoman subjects and other colonized Muslims at the turn of the twentieth century were set within Islamic discourse referencing the hijra of the Prophet and the concepts of *Dar al-Islam* and *Dar al-Harb*, which came to have new significance in contemporary geopolitics. This rhetoric was employed in the many versions of Pan-Islamic ideologies. Hamidian Pan-Islamism had a role in maintaining Ottoman sovereignty, prestige, and authority among the world powers and upholding these attributes in the eyes of the world's Muslims. Abstract religious considerations and the apparent appeal of the religiously infused political idea of "returning" to the sultan-caliph and, therefore, disturbing the interimperial equilibrium was not necessarily in the Ottoman interest.[88] Bosnian migration in particular was not beneficial for Ottoman diplomatic goals, since the maintenance of the Ottoman spheres of influence in the Balkans rested on a Muslim presence in the region and the expression of their loyalties.

Various forms of (br)othering, migration, and violence were employed to achieve the goals of ethnic and/or confessional homogeneity as the novel logic of nationalism and nation-building. Specifically, debates on migration exhibited the features of transition from imperial to national reasoning, even in the context of empires and their evolving workings of legitimacy. That the Ottoman, Habsburg, and Russian empires understood and devised mechanisms to redirect and adjust accordingly only speaks to their adaptability and resilience. However, the persistence of these debates, the race for regional demographic dominance, and the emerging views on minorities as problematic all had a definitive role in the aftermath of empires marked by large-scale population movements that were seen as corrective to the apparent inadequacies of imperial heterogeneity.

4   Competing Empires

THE HABSBURG MILITARY TAKEOVER in 1878, with the abrupt departure of Ottoman officials and the military, left no doubt over who controlled Bosnia Herzegovina—despite the Berlin Treaty's elusive formulation of a mere occupation of the sovereign Ottoman territory. The internationally sanctioned act of occupation was a new feature of a developing nineteenth-century international law, so the management and magnitude of imperial reach was left to the parties involved and depended on the power of each empire to assert its dominance. Whereas for Austria-Hungary the occupation was a temporary formality until an opportune moment for full territorial annexation, the Ottoman Empire emphasized the lawfulness of its own sovereignty in the province only by calling on international and bilateral treaties. The year 1878 has been observed solely as a political, civilizational, and geostrategic break, where Ottoman continuities, silenced by the postimperial versions of history, do not fit into the confines of modern area studies that cut through the Balkans, oblivious to its transregional history.

After 1878, the province's ambiguous legal position placed it unevenly between and within the Habsburg and Ottoman empires. The situation created the conditions for interimperial competition to shape the nature of the occupation, while the empires' shared subjects took advantage of the situation and worked within both empires to advance their interests. To reinforce their position, the Habsburg Monarchy proceeded to implement policies—many in violation of the Habsburg–Ottoman agreements—that incorporated the province with the state and engaged its inhabitants as imperial subjects. In this vein, inclusion in the monarchy's customs union meant that Austria-Hungary could use the income from the province; conscription integrated young men into the imperial service; and the reorganization of educational and religious institutions involved Bosnian subjects in the monarchy's structural and administrative system. For the Habsburgs, the allegiance of Muslim subjects was an endorsement of the monarchy's success in promoting its multicultural vision, validating its status as a European colonial power.

The Ottoman Empire asserted its de jure sovereignty and claims over Bosnia Herzegovina and—with respect to European political, economic, and territorial encroachments— by way of legal and diplomatic arguments. It also devised its own extraterritorial claims by nurturing the sentiments and political allegiances of Bosnian Muslims. Emphasizing the protection of Muslims and their interests became part of changing directions in Ottoman foreign policy and an important segment in the empire's public image at home and abroad. The fact that the Ottomans' outward image was at stake further enhanced the role of diplomatic exchanges for both empires.

This chapter investigates the imperial strategies and competitions over Bosnia Herzegovina and the Muslim subjects shared by both empires. With no Ottoman representatives in Bosnia Herzegovina until after the annexation, the Ottoman consuls in Vienna, Budapest, and Dubrovnik became the primary address for Muslims in the province and also the Sublime Porte's point of contact with (former) subjects. The competition between empires was prompted by the ambiguities of the Berlin Treaty, wherein Bosnia Herzegovina became the site for both empires professing to act in the interest of its subjects, inadvertently leaving (however limited) space in between the empires for those subjects to advance their own interests.

Habsburg–Ottoman Continuities

The Habsburg occupation did not end the Ottoman presence in Bosnia Herzegovina. In fact, Austro-Hungarian administration made efforts to continue Ottoman laws and institutions in the province. While not uncommon for empires throughout history, analysis of imperial continuities was not part of modern historiography concerning the post-Ottoman period until the turn of the twenty-first century. The Habsburg occupation has long been portrayed as a point of departure from the Ottoman Empire for Bosnia, marking its inclusion in Europe and a beginning of Bosnia's modern period. Although the Habsburg administration depicted this period in such terms, they were guided by practical economic and political considerations. Austria-Hungary treaded carefully around sensitive issues that had previously caused problems for the Ottoman administration in the province, but at the same time they wanted to establish a firm foothold in order to strengthen their position in the Balkan Peninsula. This required them taking certain unpopular steps while at the same time closely following established Ottoman laws and local practices. The Ottoman policies adopted by the Habsburgs—whose principle was to continue the Ottoman ways until they found a better option—created possibilities for Muslims not only to remain oriented toward the Ottoman Empire but also to create new relationships and interpret imperial practices in innovative ways.

Immediately after occupation, an emphatic message from Emperor Franz Joseph I circulated through print and public announcements to the inhabitants of Bosnia Herzegovina, addressing the people directly:

> The Emperor King orders that all sons of this land are given equal rights according to the law, that they are all protected in their lives, in their faith, and property. Your laws and institutions will not be arbitrarily overturned, your ways and customs will be spared. Nothing should be changed by force without careful consideration of what you need. The old laws should apply until new ones are enacted.[1]

Saffet Pasha, the Ottoman foreign minister and a former *sadrazam* (Ottoman prime minister), commenting on the justifications for occupying Bosnia Herzegovina—namely the Ottoman inability to reestablish control through its reform measures—observed that the only real change in the Austrians' reforms in Bosnia Herzegovina was the abolition of the tax that Christian subjects paid in lieu of military service. The tenth tax and other administrative institutions remained.[2] This cautious Habsburg strategy created a situation where, up until 1910, there were numerous sources of law in Bosnia: the laws and decisions of the Habsburg Land Administration in Bosnia Herzegovina; Ottoman and Islamic laws (if previously applied in

Bosnia Herzegovina); family law of the Catholic, Orthodox Christian, and Jewish faiths; and customary law based on old Slavic customs that had been modified by Croatian, Hungarian, Venetian, and Ottoman laws.[3] But the new administration in Bosnia Herzegovina was selective about the Ottoman laws and practices it would uphold: for example, an Ottoman constitutional law of 1876 calling for a provincial assembly was out of the question.[4]

Implementation of Ottoman land regulations and related relationships—including dues, taxes, ownership, and tenant contracts—in this largely agricultural society was one of the most delicate issues for both the Ottoman and the Habsburg administrations in Bosnia Herzegovina. As the primary economic resource, land was a source of livelihood for the majority of subjects and where the state collected its largest income in taxes. Changes in the land regime, even when not associated with imperial occupation (as was the case earlier in the nineteenth century across Ottoman domains), affected all levels of society: peasants and their obligations; divergent regional and local land use and tenure practices; and landowners and their relationship with the state, local authorities, and tenants.

The occupying administration did retain a series of Ottoman reform laws regulating tithe on agricultural products (1862), mining concessions (1869), forest exploitation (1870), and tenant labor obligations (1872).[5] The Austro-Hungarian administration in Bosnia was careful not to create drastic changes in the relationship between landowners (*aga* and *beg*) and their tenants (*kmet*), which could lead to further opposition from Muslim landowners, whose support was considered important for the Habsburg plans in the province. Therefore, the Habsburgs enforced relevant Ottoman laws pertaining to agrarian issues: the Law of Ramazan, or the Land Code of 1858, and the Law of Sefer (1859), which regulated land ownership and agrarian relationships; as well as laws regarding title deeds (*tapu*) from 1859 and 1874, which, beginning in 1884 were integrated and phased out by the Austrian land registry (*grunt*) while retaining the Ottoman categorizations. The Ottoman Land Code had principally changed the classification of land from one based on recipients of revenue grants to one based on access to land and its use. Considering that Ottoman land regulations and expressly the Land Code, altered the allocation of land as a resource—a shift from earlier practice, that signaled total control of the central government over land; they were contested, resisted, and negotiated in different contexts in the

Balkans and across the Ottoman Empire.⁶ In Bosnia Herzegovina after 1878, the contention involved the Habsburg authorities as interpreters of Ottoman codes, and those disputing the codes petitioned both the Ottoman and the Habsburg authorities in negotiating their case.

The Habsburg administration also worked on codifying the customary laws in effect in Bosnia Herzegovina, a process that had still not been completed on the eve of World War I.⁷ The official publication of Ottoman laws, *Düstur*, became a source of law for the Habsburg administrators in Bosnia Herzegovina.⁸ These laws continued to evolve, modified by Austrian and Hungarian regulations and legal practices, as well as specific circumstances in Bosnia Herzegovina. As they were being translated from French to German, parts of the Ottoman Civil Code, Mecelle, were also used as a source of law in certain instances or when the provisions of Austrian and Hungarian laws that were partially applied in Bosnia Herzegovina did not pertain. A report by the Sarajevo Bar Association from 1909 expressed frustration with the uneven use of Habsburg and Ottoman laws, leaving lawyers and their clients uncertain about which laws would apply in their particular cases, a testament to the entangled legal landscape thirty years after the occupation.⁹ Even after the annexation, the province was not included in the Austrian or the Hungarian part of the Dual Monarchy, which would have allowed for full implementation of either part's laws. Yet, the Mecelle outlived its empire, continuing to be used in Bosnian shari'a courts until 1946 and as civil code in other postimperial successor states until the 1970s.

Integral to the Ottoman system of property management were immense endowments. Islamic pious endowments, or *vakuf* in Bosnian (from the Arabic *waqf* and Ottoman Turkish *vakıf*), play a principal role in Islamic societies, and they were crucial in the formation of Balkan and Bosnian Ottoman urban centers, infrastructure, trade, and education. As religious and sociocultural institutions, the role of pious endowments for the Ottomans was intricately involved with the state and its economic affairs, while they afforded a space of engagement for women, who were benefactors as well as pious endowment managers.¹⁰ Building and maintenance of all mosques and religious objects, schools, public baths, orphanages, waterworks, bridges, roads, caravanserais, public kitchens, and hospitals; funds to assist the poor, travelers, and widows; salaries and expenses for imams, teachers, and doctors—all were funded by pious endowments.

Though created as acts of devotion inspired by religious beliefs, pious endowments were legal entities shaped by economic and fiscal constraints.[11] They had to be made in perpetuity, and the endowed status of properties could not revert to any other form or be sold. The endowed properties had to be freehold, and their beneficiaries, managers (often the founder and his or her family members), usage of funds and facilities, and other applicable conditions had to be identified at the time of establishment in an endowment deed that was recorded in court (*sicil*).[12] In addition to imperial pious endowments by the sultans and their families, some of which still stand in Bosnia Herzegovina, government and military officials, as well as well-to-do men and women and even those of more modest means, endowed their properties for charitable purpose. They endowed entire villages, agricultural estates, houses, commercial properties, and valuable items such as books. Individuals also endowed properties or revenue funds for periodic recitation of the Qur'an in specific mosques and Sufi lodges in their towns and villages, recitations of the Mevlud (musically improvised panegyric poem about the life of Prophet Muhammad) on special days of religious significance, and public lectures expounding on Rumi's *Mesnevi*, testifying to their function and role in everyday lives of Muslims as benefactors and beneficiaries.

Pious endowments differed in their purpose from those with a stipulated charity or service (*hayri*); providing for one's family (*zürri*); and neighborhood, village, and guild emergency funds (*avarız*). They also differed by mode of operation and revenue (*icare-i vahide*, *icare-i tavile*, and *mukataa*). By degree of state oversight, the endowments were categorized as *mazbut*, or directly administered by the state, and *mülhak* and *müstesna*, which were privately endowed and managed, and periodically audited by the state. Their categorization and operation were centralized under the Ottoman Ministry of Pious Endowments (Evkaf-ı Hümayun Nezareti), yet another aspect of state oversight of property and revenue with an understanding of shari'a principles that guided such institutions in endowments' formation, designation of beneficiaries, management, and necessary alterations. Efforts to centralize the administration of the great many pious endowments in Bosnia Herzegovina and throughout the empire also encountered resistance and additional critique on the basis of interpretation of shari'a precepts regarding such endowments.[13] In an effort to reorganize the endowments' functioning, the Ministry of Pious Endowments established control over the work and revenues of chiefly the grand imperial endowments, and it also regulated their performance and directed incomes to the treasury, while also taking over some of the services traditionally provided by the endowments, such as education, public health, and infrastructure projects.

Endowed properties (the ones not bestowed by the sultanic household) were generally considered freehold (*mülk*) and treated as private. However, in the lost Ottoman territories, post-Ottoman nation-states regarded pious endowment properties as state property, with no recognition of their elaborate classifications, related expenditures, and fiscal procedures. Islamic pious endowments in regions that were lost earlier in the nineteenth century were indistinctly included in bilateral agreements as part of compensation paid to the Ottoman State and subsequently nationalized—or as in Serbia, converted to church properties.[14] The Berlin Treaty left the issue of endowments to bilateral commissions between the new states and the Ottoman Empire, but its stipulations were simply not implemented by neighboring Serbia and Montenegro. Bulgaria took until 1909 to convene the commission, by which time a number of endowed properties had been usurped.[15] The bilateral convention between the Ottoman and Habsburg empires did not specifically address the treatment of *vakuf* in Bosnia Herzegovina; however, because it was an Islamic institution, the assumption was that its status would likewise be unchanged.

An estimated one third of usable land in Bosnia Herzegovina was endowed in 1878.[16] Considering that the core of every urban center in Bosnia Herzegovina consisted of endowed properties, that the functioning of schools and other religious and charitable institutions were maintained by pious endowments, and that extensive tracts of agricultural land were also endowed, the Habsburg administration was bound to get involved with the *vakuf* organization on several levels. It did so through its efforts to create a land registry; to reform and modify education and educational institutions; to reorganize Islamic institutions and integrate them into the Habsburg administrative-bureaucratic system; and to undertake urban and rural renewal and expansion. The Habsburg administration established a provisional *vakuf* commission in 1884 and made it permanent within ten years. The commission was officially headed by the mayor of Sarajevo, but its work was under the control of Habsburg government officials. The administration and oversight of endowments were seen as necessary by the province's Muslims because the misuse of endowment funds, as well as appropriation of endowment properties by renters or managers, had affected the work of the institutions. Some had even ceased to exist in the tumultuous period before and after the occupation.

The Habsburg administration was successful in registering *vakuf* properties to substantially increase their revenues.[17] However, Muslims objected to the administration's management of *vakuf*, which was focused on increasing revenue at the expense of the charitable and service-oriented spirit of the endowments and for purposes beyond what the endowments' charters specified.[18] The most visible instances of this were endowment properties used as public land: Veliki Park in Sarajevo, the Kalaj Garten in Trebinje, and a livestock market in Bihać were all built atop Muslim graveyards. At Sarajevo's Atmejdan, a mosque, school, and library were torn down to make space for yet another park. Some *vakuf* buildings and properties were converted to postal and government offices (Doboj), a train station (Tuzla), a hotel (Mostar), and so on. The greatest opposition was voiced against the conversion of mosques to storage facilities and, even more provocative, to churches. This was the case of the Fethija mosque in Zvornik, which ultimately became a museum, and the Ottoman armory mosque in Travnik, which became a Jesuit school.

Complications also arose over land classification and usage rights, especially when it came to communal forests, pasture lands, and endowments created for and used by community members. These issues repeatedly appeared in petitions to the Ottoman and Habsburg authorities as violations of international agreements and as desecration of Muslims' religious rights and Ottoman customs. Because the work of endowments characterized the everyday of Muslim society, demands for autonomy in managing the endowment and educational affairs found backers even among the Habsburg administration's supporters. Preserving the endowments as essential to the continuity of the Muslim life was not a uniquely Bosnian realization. Bulgarian Muslims also understood that preserving the endowments from the Bulgarian state's appropriation was a major reason for the reformist campaigns that mobilized numerous Muslims.[19] The material and economic loss of Islamic pious endowments was compounded by the spiritual and psychological effect of the erasure of such an important sociocultural aspect of Muslim existence. Together with the Muslim exodus following the formation of each post-Ottoman state, the decline of endowments became a palpable symbol of the processes of de-Islamization in the Balkans.

Habsburg Organization of the Islamic Community and the Hajj

The Habsburg policy of continuing Ottoman structures and fostering the religious organization of its subjects further assisted in transforming the relationship of Bosnian Muslims with the sultan-caliph and the Ottoman Empire. The Habsburg administration continued to treat its Bosnian subjects as three major religious groups, essentially recreating the Ottoman *millet* system, in an attempt to curtail Slav nationalisms and establish religious hierarchies to bind to the Habsburg state. The bilateral agreement on the occupation of Bosnia Herzegovina following the Berlin Treaty emphasized the rights and continuation of religious relationships between the institutions and believers in Bosnia with the Islamic and Orthodox Christian ecclesiastical authorities in Istanbul. This agreement remained an important base for Bosnian Muslims' appeals to Ottoman and Habsburg governments.[20] The legally ambiguous status of the province and Habsburg and Ottoman persistence in identifying the inhabitants by religion promoted religious identity as the primary path to claiming rights within both empires. This relationship was not only spiritual; it also entailed bureaucratic, administrative, and educational ties. Moreover, muftis, shari'a court judges, imams, *medresa* professors, and other religious officials received their highest education and certification in Ottoman universities and were centrally appointed from Istanbul.

The Habsburgs worked to minimize Ottoman involvement with the province by focusing on severing ties with the religious hierarchy of primarily Muslims and Orthodox Christians, whose Şeyhülislam and Patriarch, respectively, were based in Istanbul. Annulling the crucial item of the 1879 convention that stipulated ties with the Ottoman religious authorities, and instead engaging the population to consider the Habsburg monarch and not the sultan as their protector, was a policy priority as the Habsburgs prepared for the full annexation of Bosnia Herzegovina. The Habsburg administration launched its reorganization with the two Christian hierarchies in Bosnia Herzegovina. Apprehensive of an independent Serbian church that was likely to include Bosnia Herzegovina, Austria-Hungary carefully worked on separating Bosnia from the fold of the Phanar Ecumenical Patriarchate, tying it instead to the monarchy's Orthodox Christian center in Karlowitz, which had been established in 1691. The Patriarchate in Istanbul already faced difficulties asserting its sphere of influence after the establishment of the Bulgarian Exarchate (1870) and was worried about the newly independent Serbia's demands for an autonomous church based on the once-autonomous Peć Patriarchy.

It took not a lot of persuasion, along with a financial incentive, to come to an agreement with the Patriarchate, which was concluded in 1880. The Bosnian Orthodox bishops remained in their positions after the agreement, and the emperor reserved the right to replace them with candidates of his choosing. Likewise, after the 1881 Habsburg agreement with the Vatican, the Catholic hierarchy in Bosnia Herzegovina was to be appointed by the Austrian emperor.[21] The changes, though, were not accepted as smoothly as the administration had hoped. The new Catholic presence, although initially welcomed by the Catholic population and establishment, introduced new power centers to a traditionally Franciscan-dominated Bosnia Herzegovina. Bosnian Orthodox Christians resented the excessive interference of the Habsburg authorities in church and educational affairs, prompting a movement for autonomy in both areas. When they sent representatives to Vienna and the emperor refused an audience, the Bosnian Orthodox Christian delegation visited the Ottoman consul there, requesting Ottoman mediation in reestablishing the Ottoman system.[22]

Bosnian Jews, the smallest religious community in the province, were also promptly taken under the Habsburg authority through government subventions for Jewish institutions. Provincial administration's approval was required for appointments of rabbis and teachers in Jewish schools. Bosnian Jews were Sephardi and predominantly urban. With the Habsburg occupation, there was a prominent increase in the Jewish population due to the arrival of the monarchy's Ashkenazi Jewish subjects, who came as government administrators, merchants, and businessmen, and who often worshipped separately from the local Sephardi.[23]

With the other confessional groups under its control, the Habsburg administration turned its efforts to drawing the Muslim religious establishment into the monarchy's sphere. Because of the bilateral agreement, and because the province was still formally Ottoman, the Habsburg administration decided to unofficially encourage Bosnian Muslims to propose their own religious leadership structure, separate from the Ottoman authorities, and sponsored several petitions to that end. Sarajevo's prominent Muslims and several high religious officials were approached about appointing local religious leadership for Muslims, so they could have "the same respect and high honor" as the Orthodox and Catholic religious leaders appointed by the emperor.[24] The petitions even included the Habsburg vision of the institution, specifying that the Muslims were seeking an establishment of a Reis ul-ulema at its helm and an advisory council, Medžlis-i ulema (Meclis-i ulema, council of scholars), also known as Ulema medžlis.[25] Creation of religious hierarchies under the Habsburg roof would help consolidate religious power centers in Bosnia Herzegovina and draw subjects away from Ottoman influence. At the same time, individual religious groups worried about the lack of oversight within their institutions and wanted to secure their position in relation to the new administration and, increasingly, to the other two groups in the provincial climate of competition.

The Habsburg Monarchy, having experience with heterogeneous populations but for the first time involving Muslim subjects, actively investigated the ways other colonial empires treated Muslims and the tactics and policies they used to control Islamic religious institutions. The French and the British appointed Islamic religious officials in their colonies with no outside influence. The Habsburg consular officer in Cairo thought that the Habsburg and British administrators in Bosnia and Egypt, respectively, could learn from each other because of the "similarity of governmental tasks."[26] Management of Habsburg Muslims was also a model for others: Theodore Roosevelt might have considered Habsburg methods in Bosnia applicable for the United States in the Philippines; Russian foreign ministry officials investigated British, French, and Austrian supervision of Muslim schools and ways of deterring the influence of Pan-Islam;[27] and the British most likely used the Habsburg handling of the Muslims' religious organization as an example in mandate Palestine.[28] Discussing the crafting of the autonomous statute of 1909, Adalbert Shek, the Austro-Hungarian official and the representatives of the Bosnian ulema, compared cases of colonial management of shari'a courts in East Indies, Algeria, and Egypt as analogous to Bosnia Herzegovina, further demonstrating that neither side had any doubts about the province's colonial status.[29]

The Habsburg administrators were particularly interested, though, in the Russian rule of Muslim subjects because of identifiable parallels in their imperial rule of a contiguous occupied territory. Russia used religion to identify the rights and obligations of its subjects. Religious hierarchies associated communities to imperial rule and became an instrument in legitimizing Russian authority in these communities. Russia officially recognized Islam and other non-Orthodox Christian religions, making them the basis for allegiance and discipline.[30] The Russian Empire had formulated a system of institutions that gradually gained access into local Muslim communities and prompted Muslims, who did not have an ecclesiastical structure, to create their own institutions and receive state patronage.[31] This was not unlike other European colonial powers seeking legitimacy and affirmation of their authority over colonized Muslim populations in religion and its hierarchies. From Napoleon's campaign in Egypt, to British rule over Indian Muslims, to Japan's Pan-Asian claims, protection of Muslim populations and Islam was articulated with geopolitical aims in mind.[32]

The Ottoman organization of Islamic religious affairs entailed a hierarchy headed by a Şeyhülislam (Arabic, *shaykh al-islam*), whose role developed over several centuries to include bureaucratic and administrative tasks, in addition to his status as expert advisor in Islamic affairs to the Ottoman sultan. Appointed by the sultan, who was also the caliph, the Şeyhülislam had the authority himself to appoint religious scholars to provincial mufti posts seated in regional capitals, to influence the work of pious endowments and educational institutions, and to interpret shari'a by issuing religious rulings. At the provincial level, the mufti represented the Şeyhülislam, issued fatwas on relevant subjects, and often held professorial appointments. Bosnian religious scholars were part of this Ottoman world and received their education and served throughout the empire until its very end. A Bosnian scholar, Mehmed Refik Hadžiabdić, was named Şeyhülislam as recently as 1866.[33] The Ottoman high inspector Ahmed Cevdet Pasha, a leading architect of Tanzimat and himself an Islamic scholar, described Bosnian Muslims in his memoir as honest and devout people who looked up to the ulema. He also made sure to elicit support from the Bosnian district muftis for the reform measures he worked to realize in Bosnia Herzegovina during his visit in 1863.[34]

Articulating reform in Islamic idiom played an important role in consolidating central authority and reform implementation. The Habsburg administration followed a similar logic. The same muftis who extended support for Ottoman reform measures in Ahmed Cevdet's Bosnian Tanzimat commission were also active in consolidating Islamic institutions, and their continuity, in the aftermath of the Habsburg occupation. The mufti of Mostar Mustafa Sidki Karabeg (1832–1878), who called for calm in response to the imminent Habsburg occupation and in opposition to some ulema, was killed by an agitated mob. The Sarajevo mufti Mustafa Hilmi Hadžiomerović, who had once "threatened a fatwa" against those opposing serving in the reformed Ottoman military, issued a fatwa on the permissibility of serving in the Habsburg army.[35] The administration reacted to the Ottomans' appointment of Ahmed Şükrü Efendi to the post of Bosnian mufti in 1880 by preventing his arrival. They stressed their role as administrators of Bosnia Herzegovina who did not interfere in the religious affairs of Muslims, but they also did not allow others to do so. The argument was supported with an example from Tunisia, where the local *bey*, and not the sultan-caliph, appointed the mufti. Therefore, the authority to appoint muftis lay with the regional administration, which was Habsburg in the case of Bosnia Herzegovina.[36] After a diplomatic exchange between the two empires, the Ottoman Şeyhülislam appointed the existing mufti of Sarajevo, Mustafa Hilmi Hadžiomerović, to the post of mufti of Bosnia in 1881, most likely to avoid a confrontation and having no means to enforce any other appointment; this allowed him to maintain some contribution in the religious life of Bosnia Herzegovina. The mufti of Bosnia Herzegovina had an authorization from the Şeyhülislam to appoint religious officials, including shari'a court judges, throughout the province. It was a practice akin to developments in other regions the Ottomans lost, where the residing mufti, usually in the capital city, was appointed mufti of the country with additional powers to appoint other religious officials.

Minister Benjamin Kállay seized this opportunity to realize the Habsburg Monarchy's goal of separating the Muslims of Bosnia Herzegovina from their religious leaders in Istanbul. He worked out an appointment of Mufti Hadžiomerović, whom the Şeyhülislam had just appointed, to a newly created position of Reis ul-ulema of Bosnia Herzegovina by the Habsburg emperor. He knew that the Şeyhülislam would not oppose Hadžiomerović. At the same time, a four-member council of scholars, Medžlis-i ulema, was created, and the regional mufti posts remained in place. In this manner,

Austria-Hungary created its own Muslim hierarchy with an entirely new position of Reis ul-ulema at its helm—this came to be known as the Rijaset.

Finally, to avoid the need for education in Istanbul, the Habsburg administration considered creating institutions of higher religious education that would produce religious officials to serve in the province. In 1887, Mekteb-i nuvvab was established in order to educate shari'a judges who would work within the Habsburg provincial legal system. The administration anticipated that the Reis ul-ulema would replace the role of the Şeyhülislam, while the officials of the new hierarchies would not need to go to Istanbul for their religious education, thereby those new religious hierarchies would be formed by Muslims entirely supported by the Habsburg Monarchy.

Reis ul-ulema was used for the first time in Bosnia Herzegovina to signify a post, rather than an honorary title. This had been the case in earlier Ottoman practice; as early as the fifteenth century the Şeyhülislam was described as the "Reis ul-ulema" (head of the ulema).[37] Choosing this exalted title was also a challenge to the Ottoman Empire and the sultan's claim to protection and administrative oversight of Muslims affairs in the former territories, and of caliphal protections worldwide. It was a title attractive to Bosnian Muslims, though, as they read it as a sign of high regard shown to them by Austria-Hungary. Under this arrangement, the Habsburg emperor was to appoint the Reis ul-ulema and the Medžlis-i ulema, while other religious officials, teachers, and judges were appointed by the provincial administration. This arrangement left the Muslims in the province and the Ottomans with no say in appointments. What was even more worrisome—and caused a flow of complaints to Istanbul—was that the religious officials, previously appointed after passing relevant examinations, were being appointed by Habsburg administrators without assessment of their religious knowledge and experience needed for the posts. Instead, they were appointed on the basis of their "loyalty" to the Habsburg administration.[38] The legality of the Reis ul-ulema remained an important point of contention because Muslims requested that the Şeyhülislam in Istanbul issue a document of appointment, the Menšura (*menşur*), specifying the details of service and responsibilities of the Reis ul-ulema. The act was important to legitimize the position, and the Bosnian hierarchy as a whole, in the eyes of Muslims, as well as to maintain a link, even a nominal one, to the Ottoman Empire and the sultan-caliph.

When the first Bosnian Reis ul-ulema retired, the new candidate, Mehmed Teufik Azapagić, was appointed by the Habsburg administration with no input by the Şeyhülislam. The Ottoman government requested via diplomatic channels that he seek Ottoman confirmation as per the Istanbul/Novi Pazar Convention, but the Habsburg foreign minister rejected the request.[39] In addition, Kállay suggested that the response by the Habsburg ambassador in Istanbul stressed the independence of this Bosnian institution protected by the Habsburg administration and that such interference by the Şeyhülislam would be an innovation in established practice. Further, he added that if the Sublime Porte did not accept this argument, then a not-so-veiled threat could be used—namely, that the friendly disposition of the Habsburg Empire and its protection of Ottoman interests in its European territories would change. Finally, he suggested that the response to the Ottomans should be verbal to avoid having a written record of the account.[40] The comparison of the archived Ottoman and Habsburg responses on the same matter is yet another illustration of Ottoman reliance on accepted interimperial laws and treaties to maintain its international standing, while the Habsburg administration exercised its power to evade the same legal standards based on its control of the province and influence in European diplomatic circles.

The Habsburgs were successful in establishing a new hierarchy and a new Islamic institution that avoided Ottoman interference in local religious affairs. However, religious authority became a critical issue for Bosnian Muslims, the Habsburg administration, and the Ottoman Empire. Muslims, whether having accepted the Habsburg administration from the start or in opposition to it, recognized the new structure but insisted on greater Muslim participation in the hierarchy's elections and functions, as well as the confirmation from Istanbul. Religious considerations were the basis of seeking these privileges, as there was an awareness that they would also provide political leverage and a degree of independence in religious and communal affairs.

Other Ottoman provinces that became independent states maintained the regional mufti system in which, after agreement with the Ottoman Empire, a head mufti was appointed after receiving confirmation from the Şeyhülislam. In Bulgaria, which had the same Berlin Treaty stipulations regarding continued spiritual connections to Istanbul, a similar Ottoman framework was maintained, and the hierarchy was integrated into the Bulgarian state. The state and the office of the Şeyhülislam interfered in elections (by local Muslims) of muftis and pious endowment commissions. The Ottoman officials protested to the Bulgarian authorities in response to violations and irregularities in Islamic affairs, and the Şeyhülislam sometimes refused to confirm the appointment of muftis, making their work void. Bulgarian muftis directly communicated with Ottoman representatives and the Şeyhülislam to the irritation of the Bulgarian state officials, who banned direct interaction (and then rescinded the decision), instead wanting all affairs to be conducted through the Ministry of Foreign Affairs. The Ottoman state continued to pay the salaries of Plovdiv muftis even after Eastern Rumelia was annexed by Bulgaria, in an effort to maintain influence.[41]

In comparison, the Habsburg administration was more successful in keeping the Ottomans from intervening. From the time of occupation, the Habsburg administration maintained the system, stations, and salaries in place and even appointed candidates to vacant positions. The office of the Şeyhülislam continued to address Hadžiomerović as mufti and not Reis ul-ulema in its correspondence, which was sent through the Ottoman embassy in Vienna rather than directly. In their efforts to counter Ottoman claims to Bosnia Herzegovina and direct the reading of the bilateral agreements toward their interests, Habsburg administrators even engaged in interpreting shari'a principles and Islamic practice. Similar to British efforts to explain Islam to Muslims, they reached back to pre-Ottoman Islamic traditions, excavating historical instances to disqualify the practice of Şeyhülislam's appointments, such as claiming that the title of Şeyhülislam was "of a newer date"—that is, from the fifteenth century—and pontificating on the practices of authorities who had the power of appointment in earlier Islamic empires.[42]

A primary feature of this Habsburg Islamic institutionalization was the organization of the pilgrimage to Mecca and Medina, located in the Ottoman Empire. Already in 1879, the Habsburg administration in Bosnia Herzegovina issued travel documents to those going on hajj and over time developed a systematic way of organizing and monitoring pilgrims for political and epidemiological purposes. Application, registration, and approval for those who wanted to complete the hajj, their travel, and their return all became part of Habsburg administrative procedure. Hajj from Bosnia Herzegovina often included stopovers in Istanbul and sometimes other major cities of the Ottoman Empire with religiously significant sites—such as Jerusalem, Damascus, Cairo, and Konya—and would often take over a year to complete. Some performed the hajj as part of their travel in the Ottoman Empire, staying away for longer periods of time and performing the hajj as Ottomans, thus avoiding the Habsburg hajj records and procedures. Austria-Hungary formalized the existing Ottoman-era practice of appointing a paid hajj leader, *reis ul-hudžadž* (Arabic, *ra'is al-hujjaj*), who facilitated the trip's progress and reported on the pilgrimage to the administration.[43] Public farewell rituals preceded the journey in which locals and officials saluted the pilgrims in a public display of support for their spiritual endeavor.

The pervasiveness of print augmented these local customs, memorialized in postcards and the press.[44] One such Habsburg-era farewell ceremony was described in the official *Sarajevski list* in 1890 and translated by Dženita Karić in her long durée study of the Bosnian hajj:

> The farewell to Hajjis in Sarajevo was remarkably solemn and the people followed them to the railway station in such huge numbers, as has not been remembered since the Occupation onwards. Many horsemen and an innumerable string of coaches with Muhammadan citizens and Reis ul-ulama Hilmi efendi Omerović and almost all other notables showed off these Hajjis to Ali-Pasha's Mosque on the way out of the city, where hajjis performed prayer. All the way from the front of the Palace of the National Government to Ali Pasha's Mosque stood dense rows of Muhammadan citizens, men and women. After the prayer, the Hajjis and other notables went to the grand hall of the National Government. There the suzerain of this country, His Highness Baron Appel waited for the Hajjis, to say goodbye to them on their way out of the city. Together with the governor, there was his deputy, His Highness Baron Kutschera, the administrators of the national government, Sirs Sauerwald and Eichler, and numerous higher clerks from all the government departments who gathered for this solemn ceremony.[45]

During the Habsburg period, major routes to hajj were by sea from the port of Trieste and by land and rail. To better control the movement of subjects and to minimize interactions and travel through the Ottoman Empire, the Habsburg administration preferred a straightforward sea passage directly to the ports of Yanbu and Jidda in the Hijaz. To facilitate this, it negotiated a favorable rate with Österreichischer Lloyd, an Austro-Hungarian shipping company operating out of Trieste.[46] The return increasingly concerned authorities in the province because they feared that the pilgrims could bring back communicable diseases such as cholera. Return from hajj included a number of quarantine stops in El Tor (Sinai), Izmir, Trieste, and the Bosnian northern river port of Bosanski Brod, where a quarantine procedure was set up for this purpose. Austria-Hungary joined other colonial powers in appointing consuls to Jidda to safeguard their Muslim subjects' rights and in sending along doctors to examine the returning hajjis.[47] When Haji Ibrahim passed away while in Mecca, the Austrian consulate argued that, as their subject, Haji Ibrahim's belongings were to be surrendered to the consulate, asserting Habsburg authority over Bosnian subjects even within Ottoman domains and while Bosnia Herzegovina was still legally under Ottoman sovereignty.[48] As did other European empires with Muslim subjects, the Habsburgs challenged the entitlement that the Ottoman sultan, as the Khadim al-Haramayn (Protector of the Two Holy Places) wanted to uphold in the Hijaz and the wider Muslim world in addition to his authority over Ottoman subjects.[49]

With the convenience of steamship travel and rail, the number of hajj pilgrims significantly increased in the nineteenth century, just as Muslims across Africa and Asia became subjects of European colonial powers. The annual pilgrimage to Islam's two holiest cities, Mecca and Medina, under the protection of the Ottoman sultan, was viewed with suspicion by the colonial powers as a place where anticolonial political ideas as well as disease spread.[50] They attempted to further their influence in the Ottoman Empire by extending the extraterritorial reach in the Hijaz, the region of the holy cities forbidden to non-Muslims. European powers did this by claiming protections over their Muslim subjects from the "uncivilized" injunctions of shari'a law, and even over Islam itself from Ottoman despotism.[51] As the annual number of Bosnian pilgrims was about a hundred and never exceeded two hundred, the Habsburg authorities, who lacked standing in the Hijaz relative to Britain and Russia, unequivocally capitalized on their role as facilitating Islamic pilgrimage and protecting pilgrims—a prerogative of the sultan.

Power of the Sultan-Caliph?

The occupation of Bosnia Herzegovina in the aftermath of the Berlin Congress was but one in a series of turbulent events that transformed the Ottoman Empire in the long nineteenth century. Even before introducing Tanzimat, the state had embarked on a series of reform and modernization projects that reverberated at home and abroad. The Ottomans and Habsburgs, along with other European states, consolidated their power and legitimacy through reform and interimperial acknowledgment of their sovereignty and order, which had been mutually confirmed at the Congress of Vienna (1815). Over the course of the nineteenth century, however, European colonial expansion included direct occupation of Ottoman territories as well as forceful reinterpretation of extraterritorial rights in the Ottoman Empire, thereby challenging Ottomans' equal standing in the Concert of Europe. Defeat in the Russo-Ottoman War (1877–1878) led to Ottoman bankruptcy and the creation of the Ottoman Public Debt Administration (1881), further curtailing Ottoman sovereignty and European intervention in Ottoman fiscal affairs.[52]

The loss to Russia exposed the weakness of the Ottoman army and brought humiliation to the Ottoman Empire. As a result, the Berlin Congress endorsed the loss of a number of Ottoman provinces mostly in southeastern Europe, where the majority of Ottoman Christian subjects resided. Together with substantial Muslim immigration, this left the empire majority Muslim. The premise of geopolitical transformation entailed a shift in the notion of sovereignty from one based on territory to one intrinsic in populations—a conceptualization of ethnic or religious homogeneity that was capitalized on by victorious powers in the aftermath of World War I.[53] During the war, the sultan prorogued the Ottoman parliament and suspended the constitution, justifying the actions as an emergency measure, but did not yield to their restoration in peacetime, which ultimately became a rallying point for the diverse oppositionists. This culminated in the Constitutional Revolution (1908) and Sultan Abdülhamid II's dethroning the following year.[54]

These cascading shocks to the Ottoman Empire—loss of imperial territories, economic and military weakness, and questionable ability to exercise full sovereignty in its remaining lands—were often ascribed to the Ottomans' imperial decline and to the fact that the Ottoman Empire vegetated for several decades before its final demise. However, fully cognizant of its shortcomings, the Ottoman Empire asserted its presence in the imperial competition even after the traumatic events that began in the "Age of Empire."[55] Ascending to the throne in 1876, Sultan Abdülhamid II developed policies meant to compensate for the empire's limitations. Continuing the Ottomans' dynamic engagement with an emerging international legal order (see Chapter 1) was an important strategy not only to remain relevant among the imperial powers but also to prevail on the active side of the increasingly racialized international system. That is, the Ottoman Empire was in constant danger of slipping: of becoming the object of European colonialism. Positioning the Ottoman Empire as a critical component of the balance of power in Europe then, the sultan manipulated the concerns of European states to avoid any one of them achieving foremost influence in the Ottoman Empire. Where and when it could, the Ottoman Empire was competitive and forceful in extending its power.[56]

The Ottoman reform projects acquired a new and urgent realization under Sultan Abdülhamid II, who embarked on a comprehensive expansion of the government, bureaucracy, urban renewal, and agricultural reform, all of which allowed the empire to persevere in the face of ongoing challenges and would leave a mark on the Ottoman successor states well into the twentieth century.[57] The notion of Ottomanism, promoted as a unifying identity in a heterogeneous empire challenged by various nationalist movements, assumed an Islamic orientation under Sultan Abdülhamid II in order to win the support—or at least prevent nationalist separatism—of the empire's diverse Muslims. It served as a force of "sociopolitical solidarity" while upholding the legal equality of the empire's non-Muslims, who significantly decreased in number after the loss of territories that had been home to the majority of the empire's Christian subjects.[58] The Islamic sentiment found broad backing domestically in response to European conceptualizations of Muslims' racial inferiority and to the sight of an almost constant influx of diverse Muslim refugees who were fleeing persecution.[59] However, this sentiment was not without consequence: Christian Ottomans became associated with irredentist movements, and they were viewed as suspicious protégés of imperial powers, becoming "internal outsiders." For Ottoman Sephardi Jews this meant solidifying their position as loyal subjects in the climate of Islamic Ottomanism by positioning their interests alongside those of Ottoman Muslims and the state.[60]

The policies of Sultan Abdülhamid II focused on a discourse of protecting non-Ottoman Muslims in his government's foreign policy interactions. Such policies were useful for consolidating the diverse Muslim groups at home, leading to the creation of public opinion concerned with the treatment of Muslims in former Ottoman territories and worldwide. By the end

FIGURE 5. Map of Bosnia vilayet from a 1907 Ottoman atlas.

Source: Mehmed Nasrullah, Rüşdü Mehmed, and Eşref Mehmed, *Memalik-i Mahruse-i Şahaneye Mahsus Mükemmel ve Mufassal Atlas* (Istanbul: Şirket-i Mürettibiye Matbaası, 1907).

of the nineteenth century, the Ottoman Empire was the only remaining Muslim-ruled state with considerable power and territorial reach, which earned it prestige. Muslims living under European colonial rule, and even those who were never part of the Ottoman Empire, looked up to the Ottoman sultan for help, leadership, and material assistance.[61] Some Muslim rulers pledged allegiance to the sultan, and some proposed merging their states with the Ottoman Empire to head off anxiety about being absorbed into expanding colonial domains.[62] Although the Ottoman sultans held the caliphal title for several centuries, paradoxically the title found worldwide recognition in the empire's final 150 years.[63]

Sultan Abdülhamid II reinvented the caliphate, emphasizing his role as a divinely supported ruler, protector of holy places, and defender of shari'a, just as more and more Muslims around the world were coming under colonial rule.[64] The caliph claimed religious but also political jurisdiction over Muslims, prompting the European states that ruled over Muslims to dismiss Ottoman claims and define caliphal authority as spiritual only and limited to religious affairs. However, such claims were in direct contradiction to the extraterritorial practices of those same states in the Ottoman Empire, where Ottoman Christians claimed foreign status and tax and legal exemptions as protégés of their consulates.[65] Reciprocating, the Ottoman state awarded citizenship and protections to non-Ottoman Muslims. However, as Lale Can has shown, "forum shopping," or switching nationalities in a legally pluralist system, was not always successful, since Ottoman protections did not offer comparable benefits. Inadvertently, the process of framing Ottoman citizenship reinforced boundaries between Ottoman and foreign Muslims.[66]

The late Ottoman government worked proactively to create and strengthen connections with Muslims in strategic locations through print media, through scholarships, and through diplomatic, educational, and informal contacts. In this vein, the sultan proposed mediating services to the United States in negotiations with the Philippine Muslims; awarding citizenship to Indian and Afghan Muslims; and providing scholarships to boys from Java to study in Istanbul, who then, returning as Turkish-speaking Ottoman citizens, would unsettle established relationships with the Dutch colonizers.[67] Similar intentions were behind the sultan's envoys' visits to Zanzibar and China. Nevertheless, the Ottomans' top-down Pan-Islamic sentiment and advancement of Ottoman Muslim leadership were aimed at securing Ottoman sovereignty among the European states, not at working against them.[68] Therefore, Ottoman Pan-Islamic polices were carefully tailored for that purpose, while other visions of what is collectively called Pan-Islamism were discounted and their proponents sometimes sanctioned, as was the case with Jamal al-Din Al-Afghani in Istanbul. The policies toward non-Ottoman Muslims were shaped as occasions arose, and Ottoman officials did not engage in widespread Islamic propaganda and mobilization as the European statesmen had feared. Yet, for Muslims in an unenviable position, the image of a powerful Muslim leader was appealing. The notion of *umma*, the community of believers, began to be equated with the idea of the politically united "Muslim world" in reaction to European hegemony in the late nineteenth century.[69]

Sultan Abdülhamid II's policies were labeled "Pan-Islamic," but the term itself was coined by colonial administrators to define their fears of a united action by Muslims against colonial regimes. Its Ottoman approximation, *ittihad-i islam* (Islamic unity), gained traction in policies under Sultan Abdülhamid II and a number of other diverse political, intellectual, and educational movements that worked to modernize their communities within the Islamic intellectual tradition. Pan-Islam(s) played an important role at the turn of the twentieth century in the Islamic intellectual landscape, which involved diverse actors who worked across Muslim-inhabited regions and political boundaries. They were empowered and stimulated by imperial and political circumstances as well as by the proliferation of new forms of communication and print, and the convenience of steamship and rail travel.[70]

The colonial context left a mark on Pan-Islam's early scholarly definitions and study, rendering it traditionalist and militant, and ever opposing "the West" in line with the colonial understanding of Islamic "fanaticism" that remains current today. Later, scholars analyzed it as part of anticolonial struggles and nascent "Islamic" nationalisms.[71] Others contextualized Pan-Islam with concurrent Pan-Turkic, Pan-Asian, Pan-Arab, and Bolshevik movements,[72] distinguishing among different understandings of Pan-Islam as an outcome of European colonial concerns; of Ottoman state policies; and of "public Pan-Islam," a form of solidarity with the Ottoman state among Muslim elites that was tied to the rhetoric of modernization and reform.[73] Newer scholarly analysis reveals a nuanced nature and a broad spectrum of this global phenomenon, departing from the narrow but still dominant attention to the ideologies of the founders of Islam's puritanical reform movements.[74]

The Pan-Islamic global sphere of interislamic networks and the Muslim cosmopolis illustrates a prevalent Islamic social, political, and legal continuity, different from the more common rendering of Pan-Islam as a break from colonialism, or as a distressed reaction to it. Ottoman reform measures set the stage for the development of these networks even beyond Ottoman domains. Tanzimat—together with Mecelle (Ottoman Civil Code) and the 1876 Ottoman Constitution—were produced by commissions of Islamic scholars and administrators who integrated Islamic legal tradition and practices of modern governance as centralizing efforts of a modernizing state, inspiring modernity projects among Muslims in the "Balkans-to-Bengal" region.[75] The Ottoman Empire became the leading model of modernization in an Islamic context, an undertaking initiated at the highest level of the state that affected every aspect of Ottoman life. The importance of the empire as model is even more relevant when considered in the context of colonial projects that co-opted Islamic shari'a and institutions while disallowing its evolving interpretive tradition—a feature of colonial practice but also the successive nation-state's confines of Islam.

In asserting their spheres of influence in the Balkans, Ottoman administrators worked to insert themselves into the affairs of former Ottoman Muslims and emphasized the authority of the caliphate with the new rulers in post-Ottoman states. Bulgaria and Bosnia Herzegovina represent examples of a nation-state and an imperial context, both showing how the Ottoman state keenly used every tool in its proverbial toolbox, but also expended its prerogative wisely, conscious of its reach and limitations. The religious rhetoric and symbolism used in justifying Ottoman policies to safeguard the rights (and not only religious rights) of Bulgarian Muslims and in protesting their mistreatment resembled those of a nation-state concerned with the status of its external minority.[76] The Bulgarian government understood that interference in Muslim life in Bulgaria could trigger Ottoman retaliation, as the government considered Slav Orthodox Christians in Ottoman Macedonia and Thrace to be Bulgarian, and the seat of the Bulgarian Exarchate was in Istanbul.[77] For Bosnia Herzegovina, there was no such reciprocity with the Habsburg Empire, although as an occupied province it was officially under the sovereignty of the sultan, who would have had more legal rights in Bosnia than in Bulgaria. The Habsburg administration was successful in firmly rejecting any official Ottoman involvement in Bosnia, despite Ottoman claims to international agreements and rights. This prompted Ottoman administrators as well as Bosnian Muslims to capitalize on the critical feature of the bilateral agreement between the two empires: stressing of religious ties in a climate of dynamic interislamic networks that were bolstered by Ottoman Pan-Islamic policies.

The sultan's orientation toward those Muslims outside the Ottoman Empire certainly appealed to Bosnian Muslims, who were apprehensive about their future within the Habsburg Monarchy. Bosnian Muslims were under occupation and surrounded by antagonistic nationalist movements in the province and in neighboring regions that were threatening to absorb them. In addition to being Muslim under non-Muslim rule, Bosnian Muslims were also (former) Ottoman subjects, which further affected the attitudes and sentiments of Ottoman administrators, as well as public opinion. These Ottoman attitudes and allegiances professed by Bosnian Muslims worked in correlation with each other. The image of a powerful sultan in the eyes of Muslims was very much on the minds of Habsburg statesmen who were attempting to devise policies to distance Muslim subjects from the Ottoman Empire. Bosnian Muslims claimed the Ottoman state as their Great Power protector in advancing their interests, while the Ottomans projected diplomatic clout by protecting Muslim interests when doing so worked better than calling on internationally recognized agreements. As there were no Ottoman representatives in Habsburg Bosnia Herzegovina, Bosnian Muslims maintained contact with the Ottoman officials in neighboring regions and with Habsburg–Ottoman legations in Vienna, Budapest, and Dubrovnik (Ragusa). These Ottoman officials had a strategic role in state interactions with former Ottoman subjects and those seeking Ottoman patronage.

Role of the Consuls

After the Habsburg–Ottoman wars of the eighteenth century, relations between the two empires were cordial for the rest of their existence. In fact, Austria more often than other European powers supported Ottoman diplomatic positions. Vienna was one of the earliest permanent Ottoman diplomatic posts in Europe. It served as a central point for the physical passage of Ottoman personages and documents in Europe, and as an intelligence center covering the Balkans and Russia.[78] Austrian and Ottoman officials sometimes exchanged related information, as both states were apprehensive of nationalist movements, Pan-Slavism, and Russian schemes, all of which intersected in the Balkans.[79] The ambassador in Vienna reported on the Habsburg developments to Istanbul and represented the attitudes and views of the sultan to the emperor in Vienna. Once the Habsburg Monarchy occupied Bosnia Herzegovina, the embassy in Vienna and the legations in Dubrovnik and Budapest regularly reported on developments in the province and served as the conduit for Ottoman–Bosnian communication.

One of the roles of Ottoman diplomats in Habsburg and other European capitals was to perform Ottoman "image management." The Ottoman Translations Office (Tercüme Odası) and the Ministry of Foreign Affairs Press Office (Hariciye Matbuat Kalemi) monitored the European press and coordinated actions with diplomatic outposts to counter any damaging representations of the Ottomans.[80] Since the begning of the permanent Ottoman diplomatic activity in Europe in the eighteenth century the diplomats worked to counterbalance any undesirable propaganda and promote a modern image of the empire and advancement of its reforms. The events in Bosnia Herzegovina received attention in European newspapers and were translated and analyzed for Yıldız Palace's review.[81] The Habsburg administrators were equally concerned with their imperial image and similarly collected news reports, taking action when the image suffered from unfavorable depictions in the press.[82] References to public opinion (*efkar-i umumiye*) in reports to Istanbul intensified with each crisis reported in the European press, signaling the relevance of public image in diplomatic dealings.

The Habsburgs' handling of Bosnia Herzegovina was also closely examined; when critics of Austria-Hungary scrutinized their solutions to the Eastern Question, Ottoman diplomats saw it as a cue for action and an opportunity for renegotiation. Wanting to influence public opinion, Sultan Abdülhamid II even ordered an investigation into sponsoring the publication of a prominent newspaper that would support the Ottoman position.[83] Maintaining Ottoman authority and influence in Bosnia Herzegovina was seen as important for the Ottoman presence in the Balkans and its prestige in

Europe. After the occupation of its province with a large Muslim population, the Ottoman Empire was able to contest the Habsburg ability to protect the rights and serve the interests of Bosnian Muslims in its domains, once again using the same rhetoric to challenge the European pretense of protecting Ottoman Christian populations in order to interfere in Ottoman affairs.

A show of paternal care for subjects in Bosnia Herzegovina was one goal of the diplomatic corps in the Habsburg capitals. Receiving petitions and grievances; meeting with opposition leaders, notables, and religious officials; and offering advice and recommendations in dealing with the Habsburg administration were all envisioned as positioning the Ottomans as guardians of Bosnian interests. Muslim and Orthodox Christian deputies from Bosnia Herzegovina who visited the capitals hoping for an audience with the Habsburg emperor and the parliaments in Vienna and Budapest also met with the Ottoman representatives in these cities. Diplomats in the Ottoman legations were able to manifest the sultan's concern for Bosnians' well-being and also bolster allegiance to the Ottoman Empire in their interactions with the Bosnians. At the same time, they received detailed reports and grievances about the Habsburg administration in the province, which they addressed with the authorities in Vienna. The engagement of Ottoman officials in Bosnian affairs was not centrally directed and largely depended on the interest and commitment of individual officials in the Ottoman regions bordering Bosnia Herzegovina and diplomats in Habsburg capitals.

Bosnians made frequent informal contacts with the Ottoman officials across the southeastern border, continuing to treat these officials with the familiarity they had with the officials previously stationed in Bosnia Herzegovina. The Ottoman Pljevlje (Taşlica) chief administrative officer who was particularly engaged in Bosnian matters reported that, based on his contacts and intelligence, neither Muslims nor Christians were content with Austrian rule in Bosnia Herzegovina.[84] A similar observation was noted by the British consul, who reported that the population of all faiths, "from the highest to the lowest, regret the Turkish Government."[85] The same Ottoman official relayed that Bosnian notables had secretly asked him whether the Ottomans wanted them all to migrate to the Ottoman Empire in the aftermath of Habsburg occupation.[86] Such intelligence and familiarity with the mood in Bosnia, and more generally the circumstances on the ground, were relevant for crafting policies and diplomatic activity.

The Ottoman legation in Vienna was one of the most important in Europe. Its ambassadors were former and future foreign ministers and grand viziers, a testament to the significance of the European post and the experience it demanded.[87] The embassy in Vienna was staffed by advisors, attachés, and dragomans, in addition to the ambassador. Some were promoted within the ranks of the embassy and had lengthy careers, spanning more than a decade, while some of the positions were passed on in the family.[88] Vienna was also the Ottoman intelligence center in Europe and a "Bosnia-watcher" after the Habsburg occupation, often sending spies to Bosnia Herzegovina for reliable information.[89] In one report, the ambassador summarized, "In my opinion, the state of the Muslims today in the mentioned region is exactly the same as the situation of the Muslims in the regions that are not under Ottoman administration—according to the official explanation maybe a little better." He conveyed that Muslims, whom he calls "our brothers in faith" (*ihvan-i dinimiz*), protested the Habsburg double standard in Bosnia, and that such complaints, though entirely denied by Austrian officials, were not completely baseless—but they could have been exaggerated.[90] Petitions and consular reports were sent to Vienna, but there was less interaction with Bosnian subjects mostly due to the physical distance between Vienna and the occupied Ottoman province. For the diplomatic corps there, Bosnia was one of many issues, even drawing criticism for its alleged ambivalence. In one response to complaints that the embassy in Vienna was not "doing enough," the irritated ambassador explained that they received such petitions "all the time" and that he was engaged in pressing Habsburg authorities on the Bosnian issues more than it was presumed. He found the Habsburg assurances sufficient for the time being and stated that he would urge the authorities again at a politically appropriate time.[91] His other reports supported the Habsburg view of the debates regarding Bosnia Herzegovina, and he continued to express full confidence in the promises of Habsburg officials over reports from the province's petitioners.

The consulate in Budapest, a smaller operation, keenly reported on Hungarian public opinion and oppositional activity against the Habsburgs. The Hungarian half of the monarchy was less enthusiastic about Bosnian occupation than was the Austrian half, and consular reports exposed conflicting public opinions. Once Bosnia Herzegovina became part of the Dual Monarchy, oppositionists from Bosnia visited Budapest and entertained the possibility of cooperating with the opposition there on several occasions. The Habsburg Serbian opposition was also based in Hungary and eager to work with Bosnian Muslims, stirring concern among both the Ottomans and the Habsburgs about Bosnian Muslims' possible political engagement with Pan-Slavism. Budapest consuls frequently received their information directly from the Bosnians, who did not fail to visit the Ottoman consulate, even when they were continuing on to the embassy in Vienna.

Perhaps because of proximity to Bosnia Herzegovina and frequent communication with the population and its representatives, the Ottoman consul in Dubrovnik (Ragusa) seems to have had a far more detailed picture of the situation than the other two consuls, and he ardently recommended Ottoman action in the province, sending reports to the Vienna embassy and to Istanbul.[92] His comprehensive reports included assessment of the situation and policy recommendations. Detailing the situation in Habsburg Bosnia Herzegovina under a limited sphere of Ottoman action, the Ottoman consul in Dubrovnik proposed appointing an Ottoman official with extensive powers and duties that would include protecting the sultan's subjects and maintaining the influence of the Ottoman Empire in the region. If that was not feasible, he recommended that the responsibilities be transferred to officials in the nearest Ottoman province.[93] A realization that a complete return to the Ottoman Empire was highly unlikely motivated the Ottomans and locals to find other ways of extending their influence and maintaining leverage in the province.

The consul described the Habsburg policies in Bosnia Herzegovina as divisive and further agitated by proselytizing activity; he mentioned schools in which Muslims were educated "in the Christian tradition" and taught antagonism toward the Sublime State: "The Muslims' pious endowments were taken away from them, land forcefully appropriated, trade cruelly taken from their hands, craftsmanship ruined, their girls kidnapped, and family honor tarnished." He continued to describe preachers in major mosques as not allowed to mention the sultan's name in their Friday sermons. He added, "Loyal and honorable religious scholars have been taken down from their posts and in their place ambitious and seditious opportunists who would serve Austria's intentions, actions, and recognition were appointed in their stead," describing without directly naming the dismissal of the Mostar mufti Ali Fehmi Džabić, who organized the opposition movement in 1900.[94] Worried about the consequences of Muslim migration in Bosnia Herzegovina, the same consul advised that the Ottoman state should discourage migration and instead offer Ottoman protection, observing that Muslims in Bosnia were a valuable imperial asset in the region.[95] Urging action, the consul appealed to the sentiments that the Ottoman state worked to project: "Surely, the sultan would not allow for half a million of most distinguished and faithful subjects of the Sublime State, who have been guarding the righteous border toward Europe for five hundred years, to perish."[96]

The consul in Dubrovnik seems to have spent a lot of time and energy to relay his views and offer solutions that would be most beneficial to Ottoman interests. The similarity of the consul's reports to Bosnian Muslims' petitions to Istanbul were indicative of a close relationship between the petitioners and the consul: the consul helped draft them and might have used petitions as the basis for his reports. In broadening the effects of Ottoman continuities in Bosnia Herzegovina, the Dubrovnik consul was also concerned about the Ottoman presence in the Balkans as a whole: the persistence of Habsburg divisive policies, he reasoned, would cause further dissatisfaction among the population and spread to other regions, "setting the Balkans on fire."[97] He foresaw a situation in which the Ottoman Empire would intervene to prevent violence, but by that point, it would be too late. Over a decade later, his predictions were somewhat realized during the Balkan Wars.

Finally, to maintain and enhance Ottoman influence in the region, the consul suggested taking advantage of the amicable relationship with Austria-Hungary to negotiate two important points: first, to have the mufti and the religious officials appointed by the Ottoman religious authorities, or at least elected among the religious scholars in Bosnia Herzegovina by Muslims, who were assumed to be loyal to the Ottoman state (aligning with the demands of the oppositional movement); and second, to make the Ottoman state the protector of Bosnian Muslims, the address for their appeals and their refuge. For that, he reiterated ways of extending Ottoman influence by appointing an Ottoman official in charge of Bosnia Herzegovina, sending teachers who would teach religion and the Ottoman Turkish language, and sponsoring education for Bosnian Muslims in the Ottoman Empire.

His policy recommendations, too, were motivated by European extraterritorial policies in the Ottoman Empire and Russian influence in the Ottoman Balkans. Russian policies in the Balkans were personified in the efforts of the Russian ambassador in Istanbul, Count Nikolay Pavlovich Ignatyev (d. 1908), who worked to forge an ideological bond with the Orthodox

Christian population of the Ottoman Empire through Pan-Slavism—this is best recognized in the fact that he is still renowned in Bulgaria.[98] Ottoman diplomats were unable to achieve similar results, if for nothing else, then for sheer frequency of crises that arose, which prevented any consistency in their efforts toward achieving the goal. Constrained, the officials focused available imperial resources, energy, and diplomatic weight on issues that had more of a chance for a beneficial outcome. In short, preventing the loss of more territories took precedence over extending reach in the autonomous and occupied provinces in the Balkans. After all, the Habsburgs had no intention of ever giving Bosnia Herzegovina back to the Ottomans, who had to be content with maintaining a sphere of influence through that region's Muslim population.

The activities of the consular apparatus and the diplomatic corps were two-directional: they positioned themselves as the protectors of Muslims before the Habsburgs by pressing for their rights and representing their interests, and they nurtured and encouraged Ottoman sentiments and loyalties of Muslims (and at times, of Orthodox Christians), making sure they realized that it was the Ottoman state and its representatives in the Habsburg Monarchy that accepted their petitions and heard their grievances. Diplomatic and consular sources point to a prevalent understanding among diplomats that Bosnia Herzegovina would not be restored to the Ottoman Empire in its previous form and that Ottoman sovereignty in the province was a mere formality that the Habsburgs were preparing to eliminate. However, maintaining Muslims' allegiance was important—first, because Ottoman protections of former subjects was a matter of imperial prestige, and second, Muslims' allegiance was a valuable bargaining chip in diplomatic dealings with the Habsburgs. Ottoman diplomats readily borrowed from the approach of those states that threatened Ottoman territorial sovereignty and international standing to maintain leverage and influence.

Treading Spheres of Influence

The Ottoman Empire's inability to retake Bosnia militarily or diplomatically, the criticism that it did not do "enough" for the Bosnian cause and specifically the status of Bosnian Muslims, did not necessarily signal Ottoman resignation. In comparison, Ottoman officials had more success in their parallel efforts to remain relevant in Bulgaria and extend the imperial spheres of influence amid more violent separation followed by annexation. The imperial efforts in the remaining Balkan provinces and the eastern Ottoman borderlands, the Persian Gulf, the Hijaz, and the eastern Sahara show it to be an assertive player in the international imperial competition, finding "a crack in the hardening veneer of European assertions of superiority that allowed it to claim a place at the negotiation table."[99] Time and again, the Habsburgs and other European states failed to uphold treaty agreements and established international laws when it came to the Ottoman Empire, knowing that the Ottomans had no way to enforce them. Partly out of realization of their limitations in the bid to avoid the colonial threat, and partly following their statecraft tradition, and the strategies of nineteenth-century imperial centralization and reorganization reforms, the Ottomans cultivated relationships at the local level and with long-term objectives. They did so by capitalizing on their imperial reputation, the caliphal status of the sultan, religious and educational arrangements and investment, family and Sufi networks, and the South-South political alliances in the face of European encroachment.[100]

Bosnia Herzegovina was one such limited space of action, as Ottoman administrative oversight and political involvement were completely excluded from the province. Carefully weighing their options, Ottomans cultivated Bosnian Muslim allegiances not only by lending an ear to oppositionists (though never instigating conflict with the Habsburgs) but also by trying to mediate the Austro-Hungarian Islamic institutional practice and legitimacy. Not all connections arose by official instigation or in response to petitions. Out of the Hamidian censors' reach, Muslims in Bosnia Herzegovina had access to publications by oppositionist exiles in Paris and Cairo (and Bulgaria and Romania), considered a spectrum of political standpoints, and proposed "solutions" to imperial and local predicaments. They also entertained ideas developing under similar imperial conditions among Russian Muslims. Cultivated Ottoman loyalties—whether top-down, transregional, political, religious, or intellectual—became increasingly important with mass political mobilization and left a permanent mark on sociopolitical life in Bosnia Herzegovina, extending beyond the existence of the Habsburgs and the Ottomans.

5 Negotiating Imperial Ties
Mobilization and Politics

"SIMILAR TO A FOREIGN state's consuls who protect their citizens in the Ottoman Empire, we want an official from our own state [*devlet*] in our native region [*memleket*] who will protect us and keep an eye on our situation"—so declared one petition from Bosnia Herzegovina seeking an appointment of an Ottoman official who would reside in Bosnia Herzegovina and represent Muslims' legal rights.[1] If that were not possible, the petitioners asked for permission to migrate to the Ottoman domains. The *sadrazam* (Ottoman prime minister) responded that the political climate was not yet suitable for such action and that migration was not an option. Disappointed by the unresponsive Porte, an unidentified Bosnian notable spoke informally to an Ottoman official in Istanbul, expressing his frustration. He said that Bosnian Muslims, not able to receive something "as simple as a representative" from the Ottoman Empire, with which they shared "religion and nature," would try to petition the Russian Empire, with which they shared a Slavic language. He roused a sense of urgency in the Bosnian attempts to solicit action from the Sublime Porte, stressing that he knew such an act would be tantamount to surrendering to a sworn enemy.

A reporting Ottoman official summarized the Ottoman Bosnian predicament: the Ottoman government could not accept migration of the entire

Muslim population of Bosnia Herzegovina because Muslims would lose their right to property and land in Bosnia Herzegovina —the majority of which was in Muslim hands; and if all the Muslims were gone from Bosnia Herzegovina, Ottoman claims to the province would become baseless. He also shed light on the constraints under which Ottoman diplomacy functioned: appointing an official and gaining support from European states would take diplomatic effort that, even under the best conditions, would take time.[2] Sending a representative such as a consul would signal Ottoman abandonment of even nominal sovereign rights in Bosnia Herzegovina. But for local Muslims, a representative could protect their rights, reinforcing their relationship with the Ottoman Empire and leveraging the one with the Habsburg administration.

Seeking Ottoman representation in Bosnia Herzegovina, however, indicated that the petitioners understood the limits of imperial reach and their transimperial claims. In contrast to the allegiances that were habitually expressed to the sultan, a call for foreign intervention was not necessarily a denial of Ottoman sovereignty. Instead, it was an act characteristic of imperial petitioning practices, whereas continuous threats of mass migration were a dramatic communication of a sense of urgency. Faced with a new empire ruling their province, Muslims reacted by trying to preserve their status, their established practices, and the continuation of the social, economic, and political life. Their efforts involved attempts to negotiate and form a new space for Muslims in Habsburg Bosnia Herzegovina, and one of the ways they did this was through strengthening and restructuring ties with the Ottoman Empire. Across the Balkans, emerging nationalist groups relied on the support of the European Great Powers. Bosnian Muslims used their religious and political clout as well. For Muslims, the Ottoman Empire became the Great Power protector, and they fashioned a new bond with the Ottoman Empire, in some ways considering it closer and more dependent than it had been in the previous century of Ottoman rule in Bosnia Herzegovina.

In Habsburg Bosnia Herzegovina, where the old sovereign was still sovereign, the population was expected to show allegiance to the new ruler and participate in the new system of administration. Muslims could take advantage of various disparate protections, which were not necessarily mutually exclusive. For the period 1878–1908, Muslims did not have to choose a singular allegiance, and they could, and did, navigate the possibilities of belonging to the Habsburg Monarchy, the Ottoman Empire, and the politically reimagined Muslim *umma*, in addition to myriad local and regional arrangements that affected one's loyalties. Bosnian Muslims petitioned for rights as Ottomans, as Muslims, and as Habsburg subjects, aware of the protections offered by each one in exchange for political recognition and diplomatic influence. As a result, their loyalties and political allegiances developed along the multiple intersections of sovereignty, legitimacy, and subjecthood in Bosnia Herzegovina.

A closer look at sources shows that the imperial overlap allowed their shared subjects to capitalize on imperial continuities and exchanges and to engage both empires in ways that promoted their locally relevant interests. In other words, interimperial contests created opportunities for subjects who "pulled in" empires to pursue their aims.[3] As the Berlin Treaty and the subsequent Habsburg–Ottoman agreement upheld the relationship between Bosnian Muslims and the sultan-caliph in Istanbul as a form of religious freedom of interaction, it made religion the medium of communication and the leverage in negotiation. Contemporary Habsburg administrators and observers often attributed the insistence on religious ties to a specifically Muslim religious zeal, while historiographical accounts even more often uncritically adopted this interpretation. In fact, the Habsburgs' continuation of Ottoman laws and practices further helped facilitate some of the channels through which Muslims were able to maintain their claims as Ottoman subjects. Bosnian Muslims took advantage of Habsburg and Ottoman claims to protect Muslims and fashion new relationships with both. They strategically employed the notion of Muslim protections put forth by the rulers and presented their demands in a language that emphasized religious rights, drawing on imperial concerns with legitimacy and international prestige.

Transregional Constellations

After the Habsburg occupation, Bosnia Herzegovina's physical border became an international one, but cross-border activity and relationships continued as family, trade, pastoral, and agricultural exchanges persisted. Inhabitants of Bosnia Herzegovina maintained relationships with family members who had migrated to the Ottoman Empire. Some of those who resettled in Ottoman territories had businesses and properties in Bosnia, which were often maintained by representatives who traveled between Bosnia and the Ottoman lands. The Habsburg administration implemented an educational program for its interconfessional schools, and it also continued and reestablished some Ottoman-era and confessional schools, in order to integrate Bosnian students into the monarchy's educational system. In this system, there was opportunity to continue one's studies in the imperial schools and at universities in Zagreb and Vienna. Ottoman schools, and especially Istanbul's premier Darülfünun, remained a competitive option for students who received scholarships from the Ottoman state, from benefactors, and later from Gajret, an educational and cultural association of Muslims in Bosnia Herzegovina. In addition, new relationships and connections were created as a consequence of intensified communication, travel, and the circulation of print media. Muslims in Bosnia Herzegovina subscribed to newspapers from the Ottoman Empire, and they participated in Ottoman associations and campaigns, the most prominent of which was the Red Crescent and fundraising for the Hijaz Railway.[4] Students in Habsburg and Ottoman imperial capitals also created student associations that actively tried to influence the Bosnian political landscape through lobbying.

The Bosnian diaspora in Istanbul urged the Ottoman administration to act for the "Bosnian cause." Members of the diaspora wrote petitions, submitted them on behalf of activists in Bosnia Herzegovina, and informally met with members of the Ottoman administration to push for more active Ottoman involvement in defending the rights of Bosnian Muslims, with the ultimate goal of taking the province back into the Ottoman fold, or at least pushing Austria-Hungary through diplomatic channels to cede to their requests. These government and military officials, students, professors, merchants, members of the ulema and dervish orders, writers, and intellectuals all used their influence and connections through Ottoman social and political networks and promoted the significance of Bosnia Herzegovina and Muslim allegiances for the Ottoman Empire. Some were exiles from the period of Ottoman reestablishment of imperial authority midcentury, such as Mehmed Ali Rizvanbegović-Stočević, who was considered a candidate for the post of governor of an autonomous Bosnia Herzegovina, an arrangement exiles were working toward.[5] Others were members of Sultan Abdülhamid II's retinue and high-ranking officials in the Ottoman government of Bosnian origin: Nazif Beg Drača, Emin Aga Travničanin, Omer Aga Plava, and others. Exiles who came after the occupation, such as Mufti Šemsekadić, an organizer of armed resistance to the Habsburg occupation, were also active in Istanbul. Bosnian students lived and studied in Fatih, Istanbul's old quarter, where many Bosnian immigrants resided and gathered, making diasporic connections easy in local reading rooms, student associations, cafés, and barber shops. People engaged and cooperated with various other informal groups too, including the Serbian diaspora, the Young Turks, and even Russians. For Bosnia-based intellectuals who were educated or frequented Istanbul, the city was an important cultural and intellectual metropole, mapping the cultural-religious-intellectual-linguistic constellations that left a lasting mark on the province.

The Young Turk movement attracted students in the empire and those in the Ottoman diaspora, but unlike in Bulgaria, Romania, and other Balkan centers of Young Turk activity, no major cell or movement was formed in Bosnia Herzegovina.[6] This was not for lack of trying: the Committee of Union and Progress (CUP) activists in the Young Turk movement made connections in Sarajevo, Mostar, Travnik, and Banja Luka. They also connected with Bosnian students in Zagreb and Vienna, earning subscribers to their papers, donations, and sympathies among notables and intellectuals as they articulated connections to a "common fatherland" and the caliphate, and "fraternity among Muslims," which resonated among the reading public in Bosnia Herzegovina.[7] However, the CUP's lack of organization in Bosnia Herzegovina did not prevent Habsburg officials, who read the Young Turks' publications and reported on the content regarding Muslims in Bosnia, from trying to discredit the Bosnian Muslim activists by portraying them as Young Turk collaborators. For example, Minister Kállay was involved in a ploy to publish an article in a prominent paper read at the Yıldız Palace, hoping to ruin Bosnians' relationship with the sultan.[8] The plan was not implemented, but it points to Habsburg efforts and resolve to sever all ties to the Ottoman Empire. It also reveals that, even though Bosnian émigrés had an active role in the Ottoman and, later, Turkish political scene, involvement in Ottoman imperial politics from the province was limited.[9]

Habsburg centralization and fiscal measures that affected religious institutions, the land regime, and taxation were at the root of opposition by Muslim activists who had gathered around the movement for religious and educational autonomy working to preserve the Ottoman order as status quo. The Habsburgs introduced modernization and reform processes in Bosnia that were comparable with similar efforts within the Ottoman Empire. A monetized economy, rational system of tax assessment, industrialization, modern banking, and institutional centralization were all features that Bosnian landlords and merchants would have faced under a continued direct Ottoman rule over the province. However, in that case, they would not have had a chance to politically mobilize around the issues and present them as inextricably religious; nor would their grievances have assumed an international dimension, carrying diplomatic weight.

Petitioning the Sultan and the Sublime State

Historians describe the first years of Habsburg occupation of Bosnia Herzegovina as a period of inactivity. Muslims were in shock and disbelief at the swift change to imperial rule in their province, so much so that the only organized movement among the Muslim population was migration to the Ottoman Empire.[10] With no record of a treatise or book publication between 1878 and 1882 among those who stayed, another scholar has described this as a "discourse of silence."[11] However, what the imperial subjects did in such a situation was to petition the sultan, report on their predicament, and implore him to intervene. With the Habsburg conquest of the province, Muslim notables turned to the Ottoman Empire for help and protection, asserting themselves as Ottomans to the Habsburg authorities. Within a few months of the occupation, several Bosnian representatives arrived in Istanbul and submitted a petition to the Sublime Porte. They stated that they were ready to face whatever difficulties might accompany the process of taking back Bosnia Herzegovina. If that were impossible, then they insisted on migrating to the Ottoman Empire. They envisioned migration as a collective act because petitions' signatories asked for settlement regions to be allotted to them, as well as for financial aid for those unable to pay travel costs.[12] Thus ensued a spell of petitioning and lobbying the Ottoman Empire.

Petitioning was long the medium of communication between subjects and ruler, even when legal mechanisms and bureaucratic justice systems existed. Petitioners appealed to a ruler for a variety of reasons: to seek justice in their disputes, to protest abuse by officials, to complain about a personal or communal situation, and to seek explicit benefits and assistance.

For the ruler, granting justice was a means of projecting power and confirming legitimacy, vis-à-vis not only petitioning subjects but also the different levels of administration to which the implementation was entrusted and the oversight of central and provincial bureaucracies.[13] Numerous petitions in the Ottoman archives give historical insights into the ways petitioners understood how imperial power could serve them. They also provide a glimpse into the lives of ordinary subjects and their expectations of the sultan. The petitions reveal government involvement in minute issues and the legal and bureaucratic mechanisms in effect.[14] In the Ottoman Empire, petitioning the sultan had a long and important tradition, assuming a new character in the nineteenth century, when it also became consequential for public opinion and international legitimacy. Sultan Abdülhamid II continued to receive petitions during the Friday prayer ceremony, "where the performance of Ottoman power and Islamic tradition converged," as yet another way of projecting sultanic and caliphal patrimony in the eyes of petitioners and observers.[15]

Petitions sent in the Ottoman Empire had a uniform formula. They addressed the sultan with honorific titles and words of prayer for his health, long rule, and the longevity of the Ottoman state. Petitioners were always described in the third person and referred to themselves as servant (*bende*) and slave (*kul*). The problem and the request were explained, enunciating the understanding of the Ottoman subject–ruler relationship, where subjects performed their duties (serving in the army, trading, working the land, paying taxes), and the sultan had the power to provide them with safety, justice, and prosperity. Sometimes the requests simply sought aid in a time of difficulty: money or a position to help get back on one's feet; letters of introduction or provision for travelers; scholarships and acceptance to schools; and patronage for projects. Petitions concluded with a phrase stating that the final decision lay with the sultan (*emr ü ferman hazret-i veliyyü'l-emrindir*). Date, signature, and sometimes seals were included at the end. Although the formulaic structure and titles were almost identical in many petitions, language in petitions from the turn of the twentieth century reflected an awareness of state practices and Ottoman concerns, as they used particular elements to appeal to the Ottoman sultan and the statesmen who read them. Documents increasingly referred to Sultan Abdülhamid II as the "refuge of the caliphate" (*hilafetpenah*), which he seems to have preferred,[16] or as "the sole refuge and protection of the entire Muslim world" (*bütün alem-i islamiyyetin melce ve penah-ı yeganesi*).¹⁷

Bosnian Muslims employed petitioning strategies that drew on the shared language of rights, justice, and the public good and their understanding of the sultan's responsibilities even after separation from the Ottoman Empire. Although Bosnian Muslims ceased to be part of the Ottoman administrative structure after the Habsburg takeover, they stressed the rights of the Ottoman state in Bosnia Herzegovina, and their own by extension, as Ottoman subjects. They acknowledged their loyalty by referring to Muslims in Bosnia Herzegovina as "faithful subjects of the Sublime State" (*tebe'a-i sadıka-yi devlet-i aliye*), and they drew attention to Bosnian Muslims' illustrious past within the Ottoman Empire: "The Muslims of Bosnia Herzegovina who had been successful in attaining their distinguished position among other imperial subjects by devotion to, and every kind of self-sacrifice for the Sublime sultanate of the august sovereign, for five hundred years."¹⁸

Many petitions reveal negotiations, as petitioners affirm their loyalty and express demands, adding that the consequences of Ottoman inaction would be detrimental. The act of negotiation was articulated with a warning that, in the event that the petitioners' expectations were not met, all Bosnian Muslims would be forced to migrate to the Ottoman domains.¹⁹ They articulated demands based on international agreements relevant to Bosnia Herzegovina, contemporary "civilized norms," and universal "natural rights" of people ruled by "civilized governments." They also expected the sultan's protection as Muslims, which they made clear in the language they employed in petitions that corresponded with Sultan Abdülhamid II's claims as caliph. Finally, the sophistication of the petitioners' exploitation of contemporary politics is evident in their presentations of their grievances, formulated as violations of Ottoman sovereignty and rights in the region, a trampling of Islam and Holy Law, and the slandering of Ottoman reputation and public image.

Petitioners found innovative ways to send their petitions to Istanbul: by way of Ottoman visitors to Bosnia Herzegovina, through family networks and the Bosnian diaspora in Istanbul, through patronage networks and Bosnian-origin confidants of the sultan, via Ottoman consuls in the Habsburg Monarchy, and through Ottoman officials in the regions neighboring Bosnia Herzegovina. Since Ottoman Turkish was not the language of the province, most petitions were written by those who knew the language and, equally important, knew how to formulate such documents; usually these agents were (former) officials themselves, religious scholars, educated provincial notables, and other literati. Near government buildings, professional petitioners (*arzuhalci*) offered their services to those of the lower classes and the illiterate, so that they could also voice their grievances. It is possible that drafts circulated for group petitions, as revealed by repetitive formulations, stock descriptions of major issues, and uniform demands found in many such documents.

Petitions sent to the Ottoman Empire show signs of joint effort and solidarity among the notables who faced the predicaments of the Habsburg administration. Already in April 1879, twelve notables from different parts of Bosnia Herzegovina stated that life for Muslims had become unbearable as the Austrian oppression increased and that the Muslims were the only ones targeted by the Habsburg military regime. They asked for a guarantee that the agreement between states (the Berlin Treaty and the Istanbul/Novi Pazar Convention) would be respected—or, in the opposite case, they asked for permission to emigrate to the Ottoman domains.[20] A petition sent to the sultan just two months earlier, signed by twenty-three notables, flatly requested that an appropriate place be designated in Anatolia for the settlement of Bosnian Muslims, victims of unjust treatment by the Austrians. They also asked for their property to be protected, reflecting awareness of property losses that Muslims in post-Ottoman regions habitually encountered.[21] Likewise, seals of more than 300 signatories appear on a petition listing grievances against the Habsburg administration, stating that, if its rule continued, it meant the end for Muslims.[22]

In petitions to the Ottoman and Habsburg administrations, religious officials and notables specified that they represented Muslims in Bosnia Herzegovina, but the extent to which they truly did so is questionable. However, their efforts to preserve Islam and its symbols in Bosnia Herzegovina earned them popular support and prestige in the province, evidenced by local protest activities and later in provincial elections. This was an important consideration for politically engaged notables, who made sure that their demands, whether of the Ottomans or the Habsburgs, always touched on the preservation of Islam and its features in the province. At the same time,

FIGURE 6. Petition from Mostar with signatories' personal seals.

Source: BOA, Y.PRK.AZJ. 3/97 (27 August 1880).

they put their faith in international agreements, which they understood as assurances of their rights. Calling upon the Habsburgs and the Ottomans to guarantee the treaties and protect the rights and positions of Muslims was a novel situation in the Bosnian Muslims' relationship with the Ottoman Empire. The faith in a positive outcome seems to have been firm because the majority of these petitions involved migration to the Ottoman domains as final resort. The petitioners saw the Ottoman Empire as the ultimate refuge for Muslims and even demanded financial assistance for such an undertaking, signaling that the Ottoman Empire was responsible for the fate of its former subjects. This threat was used in petitions to the Habsburgs as well, counting on the undesirability of such a show of dissatisfaction with the administration.[23] Realizing the necessity of international diplomacy, petitioners went even further, appealing to other European powers. One petition listing accusations against Austria-Hungary was brought, with copies, to Istanbul. It demanded removal of Austrian forces from Bosnia Herzegovina; if that could not happen, petitioners asked for permission to migrate to the Ottoman Empire. The petitioners planned to send their copies to foreign affairs ministers across Europe, and they sought guidance with the Ottoman administration, inquiring whether such action was appropriate.[24]

In 1880, one petition was entrusted to Mirliva Hüsnü Paşa, an Ottoman military official who had returned to Istanbul from Bosnia. The petition was signed by forty-one religious officials (*ulema ve meşayih*) and other "representatives of the people."[25] One of the earliest accounts of Muslims' experiences with Habsburg rule, the petition provides details about Bosnian Muslims' understanding of relevant treaties, the Habsburg administration and its aims, their expectations of the Ottoman Empire, and their understanding of place and the future of Muslims under the new circumstances. The petitioners divided their grievances into religious matters and ones of "worldly law."

Petitioners were writing in response to the "temporary" occupation allowed at the Berlin Congress, evaluating it as a result of "activities of those with bad intentions" who "betrayed the just Sublime state" by maligning it and inviting foreign intervention. The opening grievance referred to the Habsburg military's announcement to the people of Bosnia Herzegovina on their benevolent intentions. Habsburg assurances were meant only to prevent public opposition, stated the petition, and "none of them were observed after the occupation." They wrote: "[the Habsburgs] did not respect honor, integrity, or justice, and exercised cruelty and torture to the level hearts cannot bear." The petitioners continued that Habsburg authorities did nothing to please the people, and they had put to death many innocent Muslims, including women and children, which was "against the civilized norms of the nineteenth century." The Austrians executed religious leaders, notables, and prominent civilians, even after they had surrendered; thousands were taken away as war prisoners, many of whom perished in beatings; and those who made it back were disabled. Even though Sarajevo's military barracks could hold a considerable number of soldiers, the Austrians put up their soldiers and officers in people's homes, completely destroying the properties.

As for the promised religious freedoms, petitioners complained that their religion was being ruined by the "disorderly tyranny." The new authorities were seizing religious schools and even major mosques, and storing pork and alcohol there, thus making them ritually unclean. In this manner, their religion was damaged materially and spiritually. When it came to education—another religious matter—the petition explained that Muslim children were accepted to new schools but received instruction in Austrian and Croatian (as opposed to Ottoman Turkish) by Austrian and Croatian teachers whose intention was "obviously" to orient the children toward Catholicism and detach them from their "true religion."

Moving on to the issues of "worldly law," the petitioners' focus was on landlords who could not collect their dues: "We are not successful in obtaining even one-tenth's tenth of the yield from the land and farms we fully own." When notables appealed to the courts, their rejection was "contemptible": "The temporary Austrian administration does not look at our official documentation [of ownership] to bring justice along." In addition, unlike the "reasonable taxes" of the Ottoman period, Austrian ones were fifteen times higher. Those who were unable to pay had their possessions sold off to fulfill the tax requirements. "If the above-mentioned administration continues this reform and corrupt organization, it will result in the ruin of Muslim people," concluded the petitioners. Finally, it was only the fact that Bosnia Herzegovina was formally still an Ottoman province that compelled Muslims to stay put and not migrate to the Ottoman Empire: "However, not a whiff of the holy [Ottoman] law is seen here," they reiterated. Supporting these details, Russian consular reports gave a similar picture of Austrian behavior toward Muslims during the initial military occupation: the taking of private homes for soldiers; appropriation of mosques for storage; high taxes; significant disrespect of religious objects by introducing religiously unacceptable alcohol and pork; and a consistent disregard by the Habsburg officials.[26]

Although the majority of the population did not belong to the notable class or have a clear opinion on the transformation of educational institutions and religious appointments, discontent stemmed from acts that were changing their immediate circumstances. A copy of a petition signed by more than forty "Bosnian Orthodox Christian students" addressing the Austrian parliament reached Istanbul and listed case-by-case grievances that had agitated their provincial hometowns and villages. The alienation of arable fields by a local commander in a village in southeastern Herzegovina left eleven families without land, and therefore without sustenance; Muslims were required to pay 66 percent or more in taxes, although they could only afford to give about a third of that—unable to pay, they lived in utmost poverty; for example, a certain Ahmed Efendi owed 30 krone in taxes, so the officers seized his possessions valued at 130 krone and sold them for only 30 krone to cover the amount owed; gendarmes on tour in the countryside were especially brutal toward Muslims, arresting the prominent among them for purposes of extortion.[27] Such incidents provided broad support to opposition activities and petitions; they were also the main cause of migration to the Ottoman Empire.

Ottoman sovereignty in the province, no matter how nominal, formed the basis of Muslim appeals. Belonging to the Ottoman Empire became a fact to be proved and defended when petitioning the Ottomans, and increasingly the Habsburgs. The transformation of the Ottoman Empire and its policies to advance its power beyond Ottoman borders—such as through promoting the sultan's position as caliph—also had a role in the development of these attitudes, which petitioners strategically exploited to advance their appeals for protection. Petitions focused on issues of religion, education, pious foundations, and landowners' difficulties in collecting dues and maintaining ownership of their land. The underlying premise was that being Ottoman would protect Muslims and their social and economic standing under the new circumstances, and that the Ottoman Empire had a responsibility to defend Muslims' rights.

Most petitions sent from Bosnia Herzegovina to Istanbul in the first years of the Habsburg period referred to the Habsburg administration as temporary and were rather suspicious of the reform projects and their possibility of success. It was an attitude not so different from the reluctance to go along with Ottoman reforms some two decades before the Habsburgs' arrival to the province. The petitioners' language was firm and their requirements were often inflexible, as they ended each petition with a desire to migrate *en masse* if their demands were not met. Furthermore, they seem to have believed that the Ottoman Empire was, or could have been, much more influential in resolving their immediate problems. They insisted on their rights as Ottoman subjects, and their province as Ottoman, as much as it was becoming clear that that was not the case on the ground. As the Habsburg administration increasingly settled in Bosnia Herzegovina, any hopes of an Ottoman restoration began to fade. Even so, Muslims' relationship with the Ottoman Empire continued on a different level: Muslims persisted in calling upon Ottoman sovereignty in Bosnia Herzegovina by asking for the Ottomans to protect their rights through diplomatic channels with the Habsburg Empire, to appoint governors and representatives, and to endorse former Ottoman practices. With little room to maneuver, both Bosnian Muslims and the Ottomans exploited claims of Ottoman sovereignty and religious protection as an opportunity to stay involved in decisions on the future of Bosnia Herzegovina.

Not discouraged in petitioning the sultan, petitioners also addressed the Habsburg emperor. By the last decade of the nineteenth century, organized movements for religious and educational autonomy that had emerged among Muslim and Orthodox Christian subjects in Bosnia Herzegovina based their demands on Ottoman laws and practices, international treaties and agreements, and even Hungarian laws.[28] The discourse of civilization, citizen rights, and international norms increasingly became part of the traditional petitioning system for Bosnians in both empires. Petitioners used similar honorifics to address the Habsburg emperor and administration in petitions, defining themselves as the "newest faithful subjects of His Highness" of "unwavering devotion." Whereas the political engagement and petitioning of the Habsburg administration has been studied in detail, the Ottoman dimension demonstrates petitioners' dynamic endeavor in a constrained political space and their sophisticated understanding of the international implications of their position. It is clear that they exploited every possible angle to secure their rights, basing them on the "civilized norms of the nineteenth century," their "right" to reform and progress, religious freedoms, mutually recognized local and regional traditions of justice and "people's well-being"—the provision of which was considered the responsibility of the ruler.

Activism and Mobilization

In managing its newest province, the Habsburg joint minister of finance had much latitude, as the province was not part of Austria or Hungary. At the same time, the province's diplomatic and strategic liminal position required him to balance all the moving parts, which reverberated through the monarchy and the region. The imperial administration was motivated by the desire to achieve legitimacy and recognition in Bosnia Herzegovina. Legitimation of Habsburg authority in Bosnia Herzegovina was relevant domestically in Austria-Hungary, and for the Habsburg standing in the eyes of the European public opinion. In the most pressing issues—Serbian and Croatian nationalist projects for Bosnia and its peoples, and policies of reform and centralization—Bosnia's longest-serving administrator, Benjamin Kállay, like the Ottoman governors before him, worked to provide alternatives to nationalist allegiances, schools, and publications, and to acquire the support of religious leaders and notables, integrating them into the reorganization of imperial provincial institutions.[29]

Changes brought about by the Habsburg administration occasioned a range of reactions. Some notables, especially the most powerful in Sarajevo, participated in the new administration, concentrating power in the capital at the expense of other districts of the province.[30] The ulema and intellectuals took advantage of opportunities that the new administration provided in the realm of reorganizing education, journalism, and publishing. They expanded on the efforts initiated during the last decades of Ottoman reform, including publishing local newspapers and printing in Bosnian and Ottoman Turkish. They also continued the project of vernacular education that the administration saw as a useful tool in severing Bosnian Ottoman ties.[31] When it came to ulema, though habitually classified in a singular oppositional and conservative camp, there were discernible divisions between those who supported the modernizing projects and those who opposed them across the Ottoman and Habsburg contexts.[32]

As the Habsburg administration was consolidating its power in Bosnia Herzegovina through a series of centralizing policies, opposition was converging in reaction to developments associated with the reorganization of education, appointments of religious officials, and the administration of pious endowments. Previous opposition to Ottoman centralization policies in Bosnia Herzegovina had taken on a similar tone: defense of religious rights and violation of tradition by policies of centralization and greater oversight. However, the transformation of Islamic institutions by a Christian empire was an interreligious competition that petitioners drew on to rearticulate their relationship with the Ottoman Empire. The preservation of religion, tradition, and property was integrated into political demands that expected the Ottoman state to guarantee petitioners' interests and protect their rights. Bosnian Muslims demanded their rights and protections as Habsburg subjects within the political system of the monarchy and also as (former) Ottoman subjects and Muslims seeking the protection of the sultan-caliph.

Detailed studies of the Muslim movement for religious and educational autonomy were published by Bosnian and other historians, drawing on Bosnian and Austrian archives and analyzing the actors and issues that motivated Muslim political mobilization in the context of developing nationalisms and Muslim processes of nationalization.[33] The mobilization that emerged in the last decade of the nineteenth century led to Bosnian Muslims' participation in Habsburg, Ottoman, and international political arenas. The movement coalesced around the Habsburg administration's takeover of Islamic institutions, and it was further aggravated by cases of conversion to Catholicism—typically via bride kidnappings in rural Herzegovina. In response to the accusations that the conversions of young Muslim women happened with the complicity of the administration and the Catholic clergy, the administration derisively asserted that the conversions were a consequence of faltering Muslim upbringing, and they had become the outsized symbol of public opposition.[34]

Herzegovina-based oppositionists elected a board headed by the mufti of Mostar, Ali Fehmi Džabić, already known to the administration for his vocal opposition to Habsburg policies in earlier years.[35] A proposal was submitted to Habsburg authorities that outlined an autonomous system of schools, pious endowments, and religious organization in Bosnia Herzegovina. Members of the movement for religious and educational autonomy responded with claims that the weak religious education of Muslims was the fault of the Habsburg administration that controlled educational institutions (and the pious endowments that financed them), as well as the incompetent individuals appointed to the religious posts that directed them.[36] The petition presented to Minister Kállay and Emperor Franz Joseph I was quickly rejected. Some of the activists were also government employees, and the most prominent were removed from their government posts: the mayor of Travnik, Muharem-Beg Teskeredžić, had a leading role in landowners' participation in the movement, while the above-mentioned mufti energetically worked in asserting religious rights.[37] This was viewed as further inflexibility by the administration over Muslims' demands.

Seeing no response in the province, activists decided to take the movement outside the borders of Bosnia Herzegovina—not only to the Ottoman Empire where they hoped for the support of the sultan and the Sublime Porte, but also to the Habsburg Empire. They traveled to Vienna and Budapest to lobby the emperor and the Austrian and Hungarian parliaments. One delegation led by Džabić submitted a petition to the emperor objecting to the activity of the Catholic Propaganda Society, which had been active in Herzegovina since 1882. The petition contained a list of Muslim women who had been abducted and forcibly converted to Christianity. Not having success in reaching the emperor, the delegation met with the Ottoman ambassador and relayed that the entire population of Herzegovina would migrate to the Ottoman Empire if they were unsuccessful. In response, the ambassador spoke to the Habsburg minister of foreign affairs, who dismissed the conversions as coincidental and denied any state support of Catholic proselytizing, adding that Austria treated its subjects as equals.[38]

The Ottoman administration followed the developments in Bosnia Herzegovina through its legations in Vienna and Budapest, which received firsthand reports from activists at each visit. Consular staff also provided help and support with petitions, contacts, and publication venues. The Habsburgs knew that opposition leaders were in touch with a Mostar native, Mehmed Fazıl, in service of the Ottoman embassy in Vienna, and they suspected that the Ottomans were behind some of the petitions, especially those calling for appointments of Ottoman officials to Bosnia Herzegovina, as in Egypt and Bulgaria.[39] In 1900, a Bosnian five-day congress of the opposition was organized in Budapest.[40] A statute for religious and educational autonomy was drafted along with a memorandum detailing Muslims' grievances against the Habsburg administration in the province. The representatives warned that if they did not receive a response within two months, they would submit the memorandum to the emperor for the last time. The Ottoman ambassador reported that members of the Hungarian parliament were present at meetings, and that some even suggested that Bosnia Herzegovina be incorporated into the Hungarian Kingdom, which would honor all of their requests.[41]

Muslim representatives set up a permanent office in Budapest funded by Bosnian notables, and the Serbian lobby, experienced in opposing the monarchy, lent them support.[42] While in Hungary, the presence of the activists and sympathy to the Bosnian situation drew press interest, which provided an outlet for activists to voice their complaints in print. An article in *Revue d'Orient* explained Muslims' grievances and demands, stressing the need for autonomy in religious and educational matters.[43] The Ottoman consul in Budapest reported that the article was the work of the Bosnian Muslim committee in the city. They explained that the main reasons pushing Muslims into opposition were fierce Catholic proselytism in Herzegovina and the Habsburg-controlled religious hierarchy, which was responsible for the deterioration of Islamic institutions and schools. As a result, they requested *status quo ante* Berlin Treaty. Like the petitions, the article concluded that if justice were not reached, *en masse* migration to the Ottoman Empire would ensue, so that Muslims could "live free in a hospitable and tolerant country where we can pray to God as we wish, raise children as we see fit, live peacefully and die piously." The Ottoman legations reported on the interactions in the press, the impact of these political exchanges on public opinion, and possible developments involving the Ottoman Empire. Minister Kállay's article in *Budapesti Szemle*, the journal of the Hungarian Academy of Sciences, of which Kállay was a member, praised the success of the Habsburg administration, which made his arguments "more scientific," according to the Ottoman ambassador in Vienna, so much so that another Budapest daily (*Pester Lloyd*) reprinted parts of it in an "elaborate, serious article" that reiterated and interpreted some of its ideas.[44]

The Muslim committee composed a statement describing their grievances explicitly criticizing Minister Kállay and sent it to various European papers with hopes of publicizing their situation.[45] The administration was accused of using the occupation sanctioned by the Berlin Treaty as a pretext to fully incorporate Bosnia Herzegovina into its domain without regard for "people's legal rights" and "well-being"; Minister Kállay was faulted for using the matter of the religious organization of Muslims and Orthodox Christians to exercise individual power; and finally, the Kállay-appointed religious authority in Bosnia Herzegovina was asserted to be completely subservient to the wishes and orders of the administration, which was working to sever ties with the caliphate and the Şeyhülislam. "As if that were not enough," the statement continued, the Habsburg administration took control of the pious endowments administration and appropriated 600,000 francs of its income. Between Habsburg religious organization and control of the pious endowments, religious and educational institutions were under great pressure, and any attempts at reform were hindered. The article strategically used the language of rights, reform, international laws, and common norms of justice to appeal to European public opinion.

The exposure also provided an opportunity to touch on the issue of land. Muslim landowners understood the Habsburg treatment of land and agrarian matters as an attempt to weaken the landowners and diminish the influence of wealthy Muslims so they would be in no position to oppose the Austro-Hungarian administration. The article cited the practice of land being appropriated by the state despite landowners' documentation and witnesses of private ownership, that no appeals were taken into consideration by local authorities, and that the property values had fallen below what they were before the occupation. Finally, a Habsburg policy seen as damaging for both Muslims and Orthodox Christians was the colonization of land "taken away from the Muslims" by newcomers from the monarchy, who were "assisted in every way by the administration which provide for their material and spiritual well-being." In conclusion, the article expressed that Muslims of Bosnia Herzegovina were convinced that the continuation of their society and way of life was threatened and that autonomy in religious and educational matters would protect their future and economic development. Muslim representatives knew that they had to publicize their situation and grievances internationally to elicit a Habsburg reaction, and they hoped for Ottoman diplomatic support in negotiations with the administration in the province.

In response to the negative publicity, Habsburg officials communicated disclaimers to the Ottoman ambassador in Vienna, asserting that if the Habsburg Monarchy were eager to convert anyone, it would have converted its Jewish population already. The Habsburg Ministry of Foreign Affairs emphasized the good treatment of Muslim subjects in the Habsburg Monarchy in comparison to any other Muslim population under Christian rule worldwide.[46] Austrian officials were correct to compare the treatment of Muslims elsewhere, and in the fact that the state was not actively sponsoring proselytism, at least not in the way the Bosnian Archbishop Strossmayer conducted his holy mission. Good relations with the Ottomans over public opinion in the monarchy and Europe mattered, so the administration allowed for the following meetings of the by then fully formed movement to take place in Bosnia, to avoid the publicity of such oppositional activity in Budapest.

Parallel to Muslims' requests for autonomy in religious and educational affairs, a movement for church and educational autonomy among Bosnian Orthodox Christians was also in development. Representatives of the Orthodox Christian community in Bosnia Herzegovina lobbied in Vienna for continuation of the Ottoman system.⁴⁷ They, too, met with the Ottoman ambassador after the emperor refused an audience. There was cooperation among petitioners in this case too: one group of Muslims and Orthodox Christian Bosnians traveled to Vienna to protest the actions of the provincial administration.⁴⁸ Although the Habsburg administration repeatedly rejected their petitions as baseless, there were fears of joint action between Muslims and Orthodox Christians. Serbian and Bosnian Orthodox Christian diaspora in Istanbul lobbied the Porte and supported the Bosnian cause. A priest by the name of Žarko wrote to an Ottoman official suggesting ways for Muslims and Orthodox Christians to cooperate and defend Bosnia Herzegovina from the Austro-Hungarian Monarchy.⁴⁹ Two Muslim notables, Derviš-Beg Miralem and Ali Beg Firdevs, confided in the Ottoman ambassador that the Muslims were not seeing results of their appeals to the Habsburg administration or the emperor, and they decided to accept the invitation of the Bosnian Orthodox Christian committee, which shared some of their community goals under the Habsburgs. The joint Muslim and Orthodox Christian committee, they reasoned, would represent a population of 1.2 million, which the Habsburgs could not ignore. The political goals would include acquiring the status of an autonomous province (*eyalet-i mümtaze*) for Bosnia Herzegovina under the Ottoman sultan, "as it used to be," and alternating governor and vice-governor of Bosnia Herzegovina between Muslim and Orthodox Christian appointees.⁵⁰

Although there was some convergence in the aims of the two autonomous movements, an agreement on cooperation was difficult to achieve, but it kept the Habsburg administration alert. Fundamental differences were not overcome: the Orthodox Christian movement incorporated items from the Serbian nationalist agenda, such as insistence on Serbian as the official language and use of Cyrillic script. Positions on the reform of agrarian relationships—between Muslim landowners and Christian peasants—were a major obstacle. A Muslim notable was reported to have said that Muslims would leave (the alliance) as soon as they obtained their desired autonomy.⁵¹ As news of a possible convergence spread, Muslims were ridiculed for having been duped by nationalists, whose true aim was acquiring Bosnia Herzegovina as part of Serbia.⁵²

Earlier in 1898, a Bosnian writer and intellectual, Osman Nuri Hadžić, derided Serbian support for reestablishing Ottoman rule in Bosnia Herzegovina, claiming that the religious and political idea of Serbian nationalism is in complete opposition to "Mohammedan being, survival, and progress."[53] The Ottoman Ministry of Foreign Affairs learned that Serbia had established a committee in Bosnia Herzegovina with a central focus on attracting European attention, especially the involvement of France, aspiring to incorporate the province into the Serbian state.[54] Ottomans, just like the Habsburgs, did not look favorably on the convergence of the two groups, considering Serbian territorial aspirations to include not only nominally Ottoman Bosnia Herzegovina but also Ottoman Macedonia.

Considering growing support for the movement in Bosnia Herzegovina even among loyalists of the administration, and concerned over possible Muslim–Serbian cooperation, Benjamin Kállay decided to initiate negotiations with the Muslim representatives in 1901. The draft of the statute for Muslim religious and educational autonomy was submitted to the Habsburg administration, proposing solutions for the state of Islamic religious and educational institutions, the lack or poor training of religious officials and teachers, alienation of *vakuf* properties, and migration of Muslims to the Ottoman Empire.[55] The draft adopted the Habsburg regional organization of the endowments but insisted that Muslims elect administrative bodies, including the highest-level officials. Furthermore, the importance of maintaining a relationship between the existing religious authority, the Reis ul-ulema and the Medžlis-i ulema, and the Şeyhülislam in Istanbul was reiterated. An obstacle in the negotiations was the election of religious leadership for Bosnia Herzegovina: the Habsburg policy worked to minimize Ottoman involvement, whereas Muslims desired to strengthen and institutionalize their bond with the sultan. Three months and thirty sessions later, negotiations were suspended.

Disappointed by failed negotiations, members of the movement once again looked to Istanbul and traveled there to solicit support. Resolved to end Džabić's activities in Bosnia Herzegovina and seeing that there was no way to win him over, Minister Kállay proclaimed the Istanbul-bound group "unlawful emigrants." The administration considered Ali Fehmi Džabić the most conservative and "fanatical" of the Muslim opposition and tried to portray him as an instigator of migration to the Ottoman Empire. The Habsburg administration was so alarmed with his activity that it worked to impede his activities in Istanbul by trying to discredit Džabić and his companions as supporters of the Young Turks.⁵⁶ In the meantime, the administration attempted to sow division among members, offering incentives for them to reject the movement, and, when unsuccessful, intimidating and arresting some. In his defense, Džabić petitioned the sultan and denied Habsburg accusations, claiming that he was trying to "maintain the link to the caliphate and strengthen and uphold the right of the Sublime state over Bosnia Herzegovina."⁵⁷

These developments and the intensified petitioning prompted discussions at the meetings of the Ottoman cabinet that scrutinized appointments of religious officials in Bosnia Herzegovina as contradictory to the Berlin Treaty, as well as a number of conditions that drove Muslim migrations to the Ottoman Empire. The cabinet once again upheld its support of rights of Muslims in Bosnia Herzegovina and recommended continued Ottoman involvement, but no decision of immediate action was taken.⁵⁸ Džabić remained in Istanbul as a "guest" of the sultan and was given a professorial appointment, most likely an outcome of diplomatic dealings between the empires, which wanted to keep a close watch on the opposition. His companions were also appointed to Ottoman government posts.⁵⁹

Ottoman officials kept track of the developments, reporting that members of the movement addressed the Austrian and Hungarian parliaments after failed negotiations and divulging efforts to do away with the movement by exiling, arresting, and intimidating its prominent members and banning the return of its leader.⁶⁰ The Ottoman administration likewise received a slew of petitions, which were sent up the administrative ladder with accompanying commentaries on the importance of maintaining protection over Bosnian Muslims but with little content on taking explicit action beyond protests by the ambassador in Vienna. In one such instance, the ambassador in Vienna met with the Habsburg officials—Foreign Minister Goluchowski, Joint Minister of Finance Kállay, and Bosnia Herzegovina Governor Kutchera—to discuss the situation in Bosnia Herzegovina and the many petitions and reports the Ottoman administration received on the deteriorating conditions of Bosnian Muslims. Denying the Muslims' complaints, officials praised the Habsburg administration, claiming that incomes of pious foundations increased during Habsburg tenure (from 300 to 950); that the administration provided for salaries of Muslim religious officials, teachers, and judges; and that it had built 150 mosques and repaired

117. In addition, they claimed that they were not hindering any relationship between Muslims and the Şeyhülislam and that they had conducted negotiations with the Muslims and resolved most of the demands—in fact, they were waiting for negotiations to reopen. Further reversing the situation, Kállay even asked the Ottomans to discourage migrations by lending spiritual support to Bosnian Muslims, which were harmful for both empires.[61]

The events in Bosnia Herzegovina were not immune to developments engulfing neighboring regions. The 1903 toppling of the Obrenović dynasty and the establishment of the Karadjordjevićs opened the way for nationalistic activities aimed at Bosnia Herzegovina and Ottoman domains to its south. In addition, Greek, Bulgarian, and Serbian nationalist activities, exposed in the Ilinden revolt of 1903, worried imperial administrators in the Habsburg and Ottoman empires, who anticipated that the events would further embolden nationalist activity in Bosnia Herzegovina. Such events threatened to involve other European states if the balance of power in the Balkans could not be maintained, which neither empire wanted.

Negotiating Ties with the Caliphate

Joint Minister of Finance Benjamin Kállay died in 1903 and was replaced by Istvan Burián (1903–1912), chosen for his "knowledge of the East."[62] Burián was determined to resolve the issue of Muslim religious and educational autonomy and was more practical in attaining it.[63] Prominent members who were persecuted, in prison, or under house arrest were released in subsequent years and took over the leadership of the movement for religious and educational autonomy. Having been punished for opposing the Habsburg administration, they were deemed "credible" representatives. Even Muslims who had professed their loyalties to the administration supported steps to resolve the leadership vacuum that would finally bring about a solution to religious and educational autonomy for Muslims.[64]

To consolidate and position themselves as representatives of the people before the Habsburg administration, members of the movement for educational and religious autonomy founded the Muslim People's Organization (Muslimanska narodna organizacija, or MNO) in December 1906, taking advantage of Burián's new policy that allowed the formation of political organizations. The leaders elected Ali Beg Firdevs, a notable and landowner, president of the executive board. Elections for local boards of the MNO were held in urban centers in Bosnia Herzegovina, and delegates met in Budapest for the organization's first convention, where they entrusted the executive board to "represent the Muslim people in all matters."[65]

The movement's primary issues under the leadership of Džabić, a former mufti, were religious ties to the caliphate and autonomous management of educational institutions and endowments. Secondary were issues of property ownership and agrarian relations, which, though important, were to be pursued once autonomy in religious matters was achieved. The new leadership dominated by landowners brought their economic interests to the fore in the organization's charter and made it inextricable from the religious issues. They continued to advocate religious and educational autonomy, as these were the issues that won them overwhelming support of the Muslims of all classes throughout the province.

The negotiations that started soon after the party's founding were conducted along two tracks: religious and educational autonomy, and property laws. In both, the issue of Ottoman sovereignty in Bosnia Herzegovina was the focal point for Bosnian Muslim negotiators. Religious autonomy was based on the relationship with the Şeyhülislam and the sultan-caliph, who would have a final say in religious matters (potentially overriding Habsburg authorities), and with an aim to enhance the importance of shari'a law, making enforceable the decisions of the shari'a family courts, already adopted into the Austrian provincial legal practice. Thus, the acceptance of religious autonomy with the inclusion of Ottoman sovereignty—even if only in religious matters—was a means of recognizing Ottoman continuity in Bosnia Herzegovina that would further make way for the acceptance of other Ottoman practices, in particular, landowners' property claims. Property issues were exclusively founded on the interpretation of Ottoman law codes—so much so that even the Habsburg authorities based their counterarguments on interpretations of the same Ottoman laws.

Renewed negotiations began with the issues of religious organization and appointments by the Şeyhülislam. In addition, the Muslim representatives insisted that the institution of the Rijaset, headed by the Reis ul-ulema, be independent and in charge of Bosnian Islamic pious endowments. While the Habsburg administration was comfortable accepting most of the demands regarding education and pious endowments, a point of contention in the negotiations was, once again, the issue of the appointment and confirmation of the Reis ul-ulema by the Şeyhülislam. Since this further blurred the sovereignty of Bosnia Herzegovina and would make Habsburg plans for annexation more difficult, the administration was not ready to accept the request. Established on the premise of Bosnia Herzegovina being an Ottoman province under temporary Habsburg administration, the MNO refused to continue negotiations without confirming that religious appointments would be from Istanbul. The organization's paper, *Musavat* (Equality), published a full page on the occasion of the *cülus-i hümayun*—Sultan Abdülhamid II's accession to the throne—titled "Padişahım çok yaşa" (Long live our sultan), encouraging this celebration, which was punishable by authorities.[66] Even the Habsburg-appointed chief shari'a judge, Sulejman Šarac (along with two other scholars), published an exposition (*takrir*) in Ottoman Turkish claiming that only the Şeyhülislam was authorized to appoint the religious officials in Bosnia Herzegovina—a move that got him suspended.[67]

Amid negotiations, the Young Turk Revolution in 1908 served as a cue for the Habsburg Monarchy to annex Bosnia Herzegovina. With the sovereignty issue finally resolved, the Habsburg administration had no reason to object to Muslims' aspirations of an association with the Şeyhülislam. Not to prolong the standstill, which neither the Habsburg administration nor the MNO saw as productive, a letter was sent to the Şeyhülislam asking for guidance. The recommendation of the Şeyhülislam was published in the paper *Sarajevski list*, and although it reflected the Bosnian Muslims' requests, the lobbying of the Habsburg diplomats made an impression as well. The Şeyhülislam suggested a compromise: he proposed that the council, Medžlis-i ulema, elect three members. The emperor would select one, who would then be recommended to the Şeyhülislam for confirmation and presentation of the Menšura.[68] Arbitration by the Şeyhülislam was beneficial to both sides, as it demonstrated Habsburg consideration of Muslim religious sensitivities and the fulfillment of Bosnian Muslims' requests that Ottoman interlocutors be included in their communal matters.

In 1909 an official statute was ratified by Emperor Franz Joseph I that allowed for Muslim autonomy in religious and educational affairs, as well as pious endowments (*Štatut za autonomnu upravu islamskih vjerskih, vakufskih i mearifskih poslova*). The electoral curia would nominate three candidates, the emperor would appoint one, and the electoral curia would request confirmation from the Şeyhülislam. The Reis ul-ulema could assume his post after he received the Menšura from the Şeyhülislam. Though symbolic, this document of appointment continued to be issued by the Şeyhülislam until the abolition of the caliphate in 1924, and it was ceremonially handed to appointees in Sarajevo's central mosque. The importance of this act was illustrated in the charter of the Islamic Community of Kingdom of Yugoslavia (1918–1941), in reaction to the abolition of the caliphate after the establishment of the Turkish Republic. A council of prominent members of the ulema was instituted to name the Reis ul-ulema and issue the document of appointment "until the reestablishment of the caliphate."[69] Fatwas issued by the Bosnian Reis ul-ulema continued to include a preamble confirming the power and legitimacy of the Reis ul-ulema based on the Menšura and "in the absence of universal caliph," while the formulaic Arabic supplication in Friday prayers mentioned the sultan-caliph well beyond the Ottoman Empire's existence. Even to this day, the document of appointment of the Reis ul-ulema is issued, and the ceremony is performed in attendance of religious officials, religious leaders of other confessions, and prominent representatives from other Muslim countries as a way of legitimizing the Bosnian religious organization.[70]

The institution that came to be known as Islamic Community (Islamska zajednica)—a product of negotiation between Habsburgs, local actors, and Ottomans—ended up being a partially autonomous Habsburg institution, with its legitimacy rooted in the Ottoman system. The Habsburg approach to *vakuf* and Islamic education and Muslims' achievement of a level of autonomy after annexation were exceptions in the larger post-Ottoman world. In comparison, the life of Islamic institutions in other areas in southeastern Europe ceased to be under Ottoman jurisdiction. Moreover, zooming out even farther to the postimperial world, the Habsburg management of Islam and Muslims in its territories—along with the post-Ottoman yet still-imperial activities of Bosnian Muslims—is even more striking. In the aftermath of World War I and with the demise of both Ottoman and Habsburg empires, Bosnia Herzegovina was included in the Kingdom of Serbs, Croats, and Slovenes (later Yugoslavia). Despite the kingdom's language of liberation and the triumph of nation-state over empire, Bosnian Muslims' communal and institutional rights were much diminished in comparison to their status under the Habsburg rule.[71]

Mobilizing Across Empires

Changes in the province brought about by the Habsburg takeover and the incorporation of the province into the Habsburg domains allowed the shared subjects room to maneuver and the capacity to engage both empires in order to preserve and advance their interests. Bosnian subjects engaged in active petitioning and lobbying in the Ottoman Empire, following established practice, and they also employed a similar approach with the Habsburg administration. The Muslim petitioners and activists capitalized on the fact that the sovereignty of the province was still legally Ottoman: to the Habsburgs, they insisted on the execution of Ottoman laws and practices and ties with the sultan-caliph. To the Ottomans, they appealed for protection as Ottoman subjects and as part of the *umma*, stimulating Ottoman diplomatic activity in their direction and often trying to attract international attention. Whereas it was clear to many that a return to the Ottoman Empire was becoming less realistic, Ottoman legal sovereignty remained important leverage and a feature of petitions and negotiations.

A return to the Ottoman fold and insistence on continuing Ottoman practice was a way of preserving the status quo. This stance was, however, older than the Habsburg occupation and had been expressed in the resistance to the implementation of Ottoman reforms in the decades prior. While reform and modernization were goals for a broad swath of activists across the rupture that marked the end of Ottoman rule and Habsburg occupation, the ways these aims were to be achieved varied. Autonomy in religious and educational affairs was supported by ulema, landowners, and the intelligentsia, but they extensively differed on the management of these institutions and the role of the Ottoman Empire. Often collectively labeled conservative, even reactionary, the ulema in fact had its own divisions. in particular, the younger, Ottoman-educated generation of ulema, along with intellectuals and progressive politicians, wanted to carve out a Bosnian space in the Habsburg Monarchy by cooperating with the administration in building their institutions while still fostering intellectual ties to the Ottoman Empire.

Oppositional activity in the province was sparked by conversions and developed around the control and management of Islamic religious organization, pious endowments, and education. The movement for autonomy grew into a party, the MNO—its popularity resting in the achievement of autonomy. Notables inserted their economic interests into the movement, and later into party politics, and positioned themselves as defenders of Muslims of all classes. For them, the Habsburg regime turned out to be "the best guarantor of the landlord privileges that the Muslims could have hoped for."[72] Considering the processes of modernization and reforms of the Ottoman Empire, which became more visible after Bosnia Herzegovina fell to Habsburg rule, it was likely that the Bosnian ulema and notables would not have had the opportunity to hold on to as much of their advantages had they remained in the Ottoman Empire. However, they relied on Ottoman backing when attempting to preserve their privileges in the Habsburg context. Far from being passive observers, the Muslims engaged both empires on different levels. Religious connection and Ottoman sovereignty in Bosnia Herzegovina, the Habsburg legal and political system, and international legal considerations became the basis for seeking protection, diplomatic activity, autonomy, political alliances, and even restoration into the Ottoman Empire. Participation in Habsburg institutions and petitioning the emperor legitimized the Habsburg administration in Bosnia Herzegovina, where Muslims saw the monarchy as the protector of their privileges—the emperor did not become the protector of Islam but was definitely called on to defend Bosnian Muslims' religious and legal rights.

Bosnian Muslim endeavors, when observed within a broader regional and transimperial political landscape, highlight Muslim initiative and resourcefulness in a notedly constrained sphere of activity. Such an outlook also draws attention to similarities in the activities of Bosnian Muslims and those of Muslims worldwide who worked to respond and actively partake in the conception of their modern societies. They were familiar with developments in other regions with similar circumstances allowing various approaches to travel across the Muslim inhabited landscape. Muslims insisted on their legal and political rights; participation in state representative bodies; and control of the property and functioning of Islamic institutions, including pious endowments and *madrasas*. Many created cultural, religious, and humanitarian associations, some with transregional reach. Muslims negotiated their rights and place in the modern system, lobbied for Ottoman backing, and emphasized the universality and preeminence of the Ottoman caliphate, making their claims a matter of international and diplomatic relevance.

Commonalities can be discerned among the Russian and Habsburg Muslims who worked within the imperial systems of the two multicultural empires with contiguous territories inhabited by Muslim subjects. Their predicament differed from Muslims under British and French colonial control or from those in nation-states. The Habsburg emperor and the Russian tsar offered protections and participatory institutions to their Slav and Turkic Muslim subjects, eager to counter the real and imagined power of the caliph and the growing authority of the Ottoman state among Muslims worldwide. The efforts of these empires and their Muslim subjects resulted in novel considerations of Islamic institutions. Ottoman connections and the role of local Ottoman-educated ulema, intellectuals, and activists were vital in these processes at the turn of the twentieth century. Autonomous Islamic religious institutions were a product of negotiations among ulema, notables, political activists, intellectuals, and the state. Resulting imperial laws and institutions continued to exist beyond the empires themselves, including some to the present day in the nation-states that succeeded them.

6   Allegiances and Final Separation

ON OCTOBER 7, 1908, *Servet-i Fünun* and *Tanin,* followed by other Ottoman papers, called for boycotting Austrian "foul" goods. Crowds gathered in front of government buildings in Istanbul and moved to the gates of European consulates protesting the breach of the Berlin Treaty. Soon, the port workers refused to unload Austrian goods and to service Austrian ships. Shops that carried Austrian merchandise were boycotted. The boycott lasted five months and spread to other port cities across the empire—Salonica, Izmir, Trabzon, Beirut, Yafa, and Tripoli—and even beyond that, when the Indian press picked up on the news and called on Indian Muslims to join the boycott.[1] As the most popular Austrian import was the fez, protestors across the Ottoman Empire symbolically tore their fezzes, while locally produced alternatives were recommended in the popular press, starting a campaign for a national headgear (*serpuş-ı milli*).[2]

Following the Young Turk Revolution the boycott reinvigorated the notion of Ottoman national unity and inspired revolutionary potential, even though it was at first observed with hesitation by the Committee of Union and Progress.[3] Driven by the newly de-censored press, the 1908 Ottoman boycott was an expression of indignation at the European political and economic encroachment, contravening international law, as well as their brazen exercise of extraterritorial rights in the Ottoman Empire, all of which had motivated the revolution. Thirty years after the occupation and de facto rule by Austria-Hungary, Ottoman custody of Bosnia Herzegovina was in the limelight once again.

Exhilaration of the revolutionary success in the Ottoman Empire was deflated with blow after blow in early October 1908: Bulgaria announced its independence on October 5, Habsburg Monarchy annexed Bosnia Herzegovina the following day, and on October 7, Crete declared union with mainland Greece. Russia wanted to renegotiate their access to the straits leading from the Black Sea to the Mediterranean. The reestablishment of the Ottoman constitution and the parliament also included the Ottoman provinces that had a special status like Bosnia Herzegovina, causing anxious reactions to the restoration of provincial and administrative ties to Istanbul. Emperor Franz Joseph I announced that Bosnia Herzegovina officially became part of the Habsburg Monarchy and that, as such, it would have its own provincial constitution.[4]

In Bosnia Herzegovina, the annexation put an end to speculations, hopes, and fleeting dreams of return to the Ottoman fold. The legal basis for Muslims' claims to Ottoman sovereignty and protections of the previous thirty years ceased to be valid. Yet, even the annexation did not mean an end to relationships between the Muslims of Bosnia Herzegovina and the Ottoman Empire. Muslims continued to see developments in the Ottoman Empire as relevant in Bosnia Herzegovina, and the Ottoman Empire continued to be involved with the province even after it had no official claims over its former territory. This chapter looks at these transformations and continuities after 1908, a world in many ways different from the initial years of Bosnian occupation, characterized by widespread press, active associational life, and representative party politics, as well as intensification of regional nationalist politics and the violence it roused.

Annexation

As soon as the Ottoman constitutional regime was established, Bosnian Muslim and Serbian national organizations presented a joint request to Minister Burián for a Bosnian constitution based on Bosnia's status as an Ottoman province—exactly what the Habsburg administration feared might happen if also pursued by the new Ottoman government. Representatives of the two Bosnian parties were planning to push for their demands in

Budapest when the news of annexation reached them. Muslims were in disbelief as their expectations were quite the contrary—that the Young Turk movement would revitalize the empire and even repossess Bosnia Herzegovina. Muslims in Bosnia Herzegovina were divided over how to respond to annexation. The influential Muslim People's Organization (MNO) advised the public through its official paper and announcements not to overreact and hoped that an international conference would correct Austria's breach of the Berlin Treaty.[5] The Muslim Progressive Party (Muslimanska Napredna Stranka) expressed support for the annexation, and called on people to accept their position, having been hopelessly "captivated with thoughts of Istanbul and the Ottoman state for thirty years."[6] Still waiting for the Ottomans to act, MNO's president, Ali Beg Firdevs, traveled to Istanbul to press the Bosnian case with the Young Turks. According to Habsburg intelligence reports, he asked the new leadership in Istanbul whether to "stay put, migrate, or accept the administration's offer to negotiate."[7] The former leader of the movement for autonomy, Džabić, still banished from Bosnia Herzegovina, lobbied for the rejection of the Habsburg annexation, proposing international arbitration and even war before accepting the loss of Bosnia Herzegovina. Both suggested coming up with solutions for Bosnia Herzegovina that involved the protection and guarantees of the Ottoman administration.

Annexing Bosnia Herzegovina was not a new consideration by Austria-Hungary as part of its Balkan policy. Activities of Italy, Serbia, and the Ottoman Empire in southeastern Europe were monitored in order to identify the right moment for annexation. The first years of the twentieth century witnessed active extension of Italian spheres of interest in the Adriatic Ottoman provinces: Serbian nationalist activity focused on expansionist projects into Ottoman and Habsburg lands, and there was an escalation in destructive nationalistic activity in Ottoman Macedonia. They all affected the Habsburg presence in the Balkans. Deliberations about restructuring the Dual Monarchy to include the South Slav bloc and Bosnia Herzegovina were considered, while administrative and military reorganization in the province took war readiness into account.[8] In an effort to establish a firmer stand in the Balkans, annexation was seen as a necessity, often discussed in governmental correspondence in the years leading up to the annexation. The opportune moment came when the Ottoman Empire was in no position to respond.

Although the annexation of Bosnia Herzegovina by the Habsburg Monarchy might have been a surprise to those in Bosnia Herzegovina, it was less so in the Ottoman Empire. The possibility of Habsburg annexation had been discussed in European diplomatic circles and the press from the onset of the Habsburg occupation in 1878. Considerations of such action focused not on Austrian plans, as they seemed apparent, but on reaction of the European powers and the effect it would have on the balance established by the Berlin Treaty.[9] In 1886, Italian consent of the Habsburg annexation of Bosnia Herzegovina was discussed in the press.[10] Illustrative of such discussion was one by the Ottoman ambassador in Rome, reporting on speculations in *Pester Lloyd* and *Patrie* about the possibility of Habsburg annexation. Whereas *Patrie* maintained that Austria-Hungary was preparing the ground for annexation, *Pester Lloyd* argued that it was not so easy: even though Russia was not in the position to respond, other countries would not allow any divergence from the Berlin Treaty changing the status quo and causing turmoil across the Balkans.[11] Despite obvious Habsburg intentions, the complications that a breach of the Berlin Treaty would bring seemed to have been an assurance for the European powers, and to some extent for the Ottomans. Russian reactions were the most condemnatory, although in the heat of territorial partition in 1908, Russia too desired to take advantage of the situation.[12]

Ottoman reports from the two parts of the Habsburg Monarchy were conflicting: The ambassador in Vienna did not give much significance to discussions about the annexation and relied on denunciations of any such plans by the Austrian officials. He reported that no importance was given to annexation speculations by foreign ambassadors, politicians, or press in Vienna.[13] However, Ottoman reports from Budapest related that annexation was openly discussed in the Hungarian parliament and that the consensus there was that Bosnia Herzegovina should become part of Hungary upon annexation.[14] According to this report, such discussion often aroused nationalist feelings of Austrians and Croats, and some even suggested leaving Bosnia Herzegovina to Serbia. Citing an analysis in *Wiener Allgemeine Zeitung*, and assuming that a dispute over an introduction of legal regulations in Bosnia Herzegovina would develop in the future, the Ottoman consul believed that both Austria and Hungary needed to work together to reinforce the permanence of occupation without violating Article 25 of the Berlin

Treaty; the consul added that the Habsburgs would not lack precedent if they desired to take the annexation route, reminding his superiors of Tunisia, Egypt, and Cyprus.

Turhan Pasha, the Ottoman ambassador in St. Petersburg, prompted by an article in the Russian press about Habsburg intentions to annex Bosnia Herzegovina, spoke to the representative of the Russian Foreign Ministry. He confirmed that although there was talk of annexation, it was believed that any action would be taken with signatories' consent; however, Russia was still concerned. The Russian official conveyed to the ambassador that, while earlier Russia was alone in opposition, France, England, and Italy came to have similar concerns, and Germany was about to join them. "In order to look good to the Slavs," continued Turhan Pasha, "the Russians would do anything to hinder Austria's undertaking." He could not confirm if Russia would react with more than just a protest in the case of annexation.[15]

Young Turks, as the collective opposition to Sultan Abdülhamid II was known, was formally the Committee of Union and Progress (CUP) organized in 1889 by the students of the Imperial Medical Academy in Istanbul. Operating mostly in exile, their activities grew fragmented, leaving the deposition of Sultan Abdülhamid II their only common goal.[16] The activist wing of the CUP advocated more radical action, enlisting army officers in Ottoman Macedonia in 1906–1907 and directing oppositional activity toward constitutionalism with the top-down military leadership, which ultimately carried out the revolution.[17] The Young Turk Revolution was part of global democratic movements that included Russia (1905), Iran (1906), Mexico (1910), and China (1911), and although an outcome of local phenomena, they all shared overarching political ideals, resulting in their insistence on constitutional political form.[18] The revolutionary mood and the change it promised in the language of reform, science, and the cultural projects envisioned as Europeanization, both inspired and alienated imperial subjects, including former Ottoman subjects who followed the developments in the Ottoman Empire that could affect them.

In the immediate aftermath of the revolution, CUP was bracing to maintain control of the sultan and the Sublime Porte behind the scenes, amid worker strikes and protests in major cities of the empire. Ottoman rivals attempted to take advantage at the time the Ottoman Empire was unable to respond. Even before declaring independence, Bulgaria seized Ottoman

FIGURE 7. "The Awakening of the Eastern Question: Bulgaria Proclaims Its Independence—Austria Takes Bosnia Herzegovina." Habsburg Emperor Franz Joseph I and the Russian Tsar Nicolas II tear away Ottoman European lands as the Ottoman Sultan Abdülhamid II looks on.

Source: Le Petit Journal, supplément illustré du quotidien (18 October 1908).

railways in Eastern Rumelia and began military mobilization, alarming the Ottoman and other European states. With its eye on Ottoman Macedonia, Bulgaria represented the greatest threat to the empire's territorial integrity and peace, to which it was in no position to respond but diplomatically.[19] However, in much of the scholarly analysis, these events are known as the annexation crisis, focusing on the European apprehensions about the Habsburg expansion.[20]

The Austrian ambassador in Istanbul sent an official note to the Ottoman Foreign Affairs Ministry stating that the Vienna cabinet was withdrawing its soldiers from Novi Pazar, amending Article 25 of the Berlin Treaty: The Habsburg cabinet sensed that a new era had started for the Ottoman state with the second constitutional period, and that the Ottomans were finally ready to maintain order on their own in said county.[21] Withdrawal from Novi Pazar was thought to be enough compensation for annexing Bosnian territory, which was only nominally under the sovereignty of the Ottoman sultan and would not present much of a change.

The same day, the Ottoman ambassador in London met with the British foreign affairs minister to discuss the annexation of Bosnia Herzegovina and Bulgaria's independence. The British minister relayed that his country did not approve of Austria's "deceitful act," and advised the Ottomans to protest and seek compensation, but to avoid war. It seemed to him that there was some talk of a conference in light of the events, although it appeared that Russia, Italy, and Germany had already accepted the annexation of Bosnia Herzegovina and the independence of Bulgaria. The head interpreter in the French embassy confirmed his government's similar stance.[22] Italy, having comparable interests with Austria in the Balkans, had to be reassured. The emperor personally informed the Italian ruler of the establishment of a legislative system in Bosnia Herzegovina as part of the Habsburg Empire. The fact that Italy, whose interests in the Ottoman Balkans overlapped with the Habsburgs, did not react to annexation was evaluated as a tradeoff for consent to Italy's colonization of Trablusgarb (Ottoman Libya).[23]

The Ottoman Empire gauged the attitudes of European states and hoped for a conference where the interests of other signatories of the Berlin Treaty would deter Habsburg advancement, or at least create an opportunity for negotiation.[24] A pact with the other Balkan states—namely Romania, Serbia, and Greece—was considered to keep the possibility of Bulgarian war plans and expansion in check.[25] However, the Ottoman administration did not have much choice except for formal diplomatic objections. Protest notes were sent to the European press and agencies, while prominent pro-government papers—*Tanin, Ikdam,* and *Ittihad ve Terakki*—published them on their front pages.[26] There was an expectation that public opinion would help instigate diplomatic action in a manner beneficial to the Ottomans. Regardless, no European state openly opposed Austria-Hungary, and talks of convening a conference waned.

Reactions to Annexation

Protests in reaction to Austro-Hungarian annexation of Bosnia Herzegovina and Bulgarian proclamation of independence were organized across the Ottoman Empire in major urban centers, often by local CUP members.[27] Papers and posters that placated major cities called for boycotting their goods. Austrian banks, goods, and ships arriving in Ottoman ports were targeted: Austrian shops were blocked, while the port workers refused to carry goods to the quays and service Austrian carriers.[28] The post-revolutionary unrest was a response to the change in government that inspired claims to rights, especially among those who felt disadvantaged under the old administration, including guilds and workers who were increasingly marginalized due to the enforcement of European extraterritorial rights.[29] The boycott provided wider participation especially for the port workers who used public revolutionary enthusiasm and discourse of freedom to secure their rights impacted by these concessions to mostly foreign companies. Hence, their grievances found expression in the collective stance against Austria-Hungary and Bulgaria.

The CUP realized it could channel the port workers' dissatisfaction against an embarrassing foreign policy setback and supported the boycott activities, but it also positioned itself as the arbitrator between the workers, government, and foreign companies, bolstering its prestige.[30] The Ottoman boycott was the first comprehensive expression of Ottoman public opinion, mobilizing segments of society who were not traditionally part of the imperial political discourse, sustained by modern means of communication and political action.[31] Evocative of the Iranian tobacco protest (1892), the Bengali boycott of British goods (1905), and the Chinese boycott of U.S. goods (1905), it was a public response to Western encroachments that consolidated disparate groups to action when there were few options for an official Ottoman response.³² The government and the press capitalized on the fact that the boycott was an outcome of the "people's will" and an expression of the "national opinion," particularly when they were pressed by the Habsburg diplomats to end it.³³ Mobilization encouraged solidarity beyond Ottoman borders and further encouraged boycott activities and the abundant press coverage. The paper *Tercüman-ı Hakikat* published telegrams from Bosnia Herzegovina and wrote that the Muslims there supported the boycott and remained loyal to the Ottoman state.³⁴ Serbia and Montenegro also halted trade and boycotted Austrian goods, dissatisfied that the annexation complicated their plans for territorial expansion.³⁵

The five-month boycott had a diplomatically useful dimension: the Sublime Porte was able to negotiate the terms of annexation with Austria-Hungary and received monetary compensation. The agreement between Austria-Hungary and the Ottoman Empire was signed in February 1909 by the new newly appointed Sadrazam Hüseyin Hilmi Pasha and interim Foreign Affairs Minister Gabriyel Noradonkyan on the Ottoman side and the Habsburg envoy Johann von Pallavicini. The articles addressed Bosnians' citizenship and property ownership; religious rights, including religious official appointments in Bosnia Herzegovina by the Şeyhülislam in Istanbul and permission to mention the sultan's name in the Friday sermons; monetary compensation to the Ottoman Empire in the amount of 2.5 million Ottoman lira; and trade, postal, and customs agreements.³⁶

In demonstrative response, the "Memorandum by the People of Bosnia Herzegovina" was submitted to the Ottoman parliament that same month, expressing shock and disappointment at the "shameful sale" of "faithful subjects" for a few millions, extolling Bosnian history as part of the Ottoman state, and emphasizing their continued readiness to sacrifice for the Ottoman Empire and Islam.³⁷ The document warned that by annexing Bosnia Herzegovina, the Austrian intention was to give "mortal blows" to the Ottoman state and completely destroy its Bosnian Muslim subjects. Most painful seemed to be the monetary compensation that the memorandum depicted as the sale of land earned by blood, by those who have no rights to sell it. Finally, the memorandum expressed hope that the Ottoman people would not accept such a disgraceful act. The memorandum derisively suggested offering several times the sum of compensation, wondering if the state was in such need of money that it had to sacrifice its land and its subjects.³⁸

The most fervent reaction outside of the Ottoman Empire came from Serbia, because it had direct interests in the annexed territory. Annexation made Serbian plans to appropriate Bosnia Herzegovina more difficult once it became Habsburg, since nationalist states with expansionist plans in southeastern Europe understood that enlarging their territories on account of the Ottoman state was more palatable to European arbitrators. The Ottoman consul in Belgrade sent an urgent telegram to Istanbul saying that the Serbian foreign affairs minister notified him that if necessary Serbia would support, even militarily, any action the Ottoman Empire would take in response to the Bulgarian independence proclamation and the Austrian annexation of Bosnia Herzegovina.[39] Protests erupted in Belgrade when the news spread. Protestors shouted "Long live the Sublime State, long live England and Serbia," and they chanted slogans against Austria and Bulgaria. The protestors cheered in front of the Ottoman embassy, and the ambassador related that he had to appear on the balcony to greet them several times.[40]

Belgrade's *Politika*, known to express official opinion, reported that Serbian envoys were to deliver official requests to the European states demanding autonomy for Bosnia Herzegovina. The same paper reported calls to increase the Serbian military budget, raising concern in neighboring regions.[41] Although Serbia did not approve of annexation and was supportive of the Ottoman protests, the Ottoman cabinet instructed its ministry of war that measures needed to be taken in order to prevent Serbian and Montenegrin territorial plans for Novi Pazar in light of the Habsburg withdrawal from the district coveted by both.[42] The annexation caused more anxiety and mobilization among the Muslim population in Novi Pazar than in Bosnia Herzegovina, because they feared Serbian and Montenegrin territorial encroachment and the violence directed at Muslims that usually came with it.

Public protest against the annexation and critique of Austria-Hungary continued in the Ottoman press and other publications. In "A patriotic plea against the Austrian annexation of Bosnia Herzegovina," Ali Ulvi, an Ottoman judge of Bosnian origin, emphasized the importance of Bosnia Herzegovina as a core province that was Ottoman before Istanbul itself and whose inhabitants performed the holy duty of guarding its borders.[43] In light of the Habsburg infringement of the Berlin Treaty, he contemplated a possible "executive power" (*kuvve-i icraiye*) that would correct the breach of international law and reprimand the Habsburg Monarchy.[44] Condemning the acceptance of monetary compensation from the Habsburg Monarchy, he warned that the sale of land would not only remain a disgraceful act in Ottoman history, but that the abandonment of Bosnia Herzegovina would pain the entire Muslim world. Optimistic about the effect of the boycott, Ali Ulvi suggested that the Ottoman Empire seek to reclaim the territory or at least work out an autonomy under an Ottoman prince.[45]

Ali Rüşdü, a Bosnian scholar and an Ottoman official with CUP ties, addressed the Ottoman parliament in a brief confirming Bosnian Muslim–Orthodox Christian unity and a commitment to achieving Ottoman rule or autonomy for Bosnia Herzegovina "until the last drop of their blood." He appealed to the parliamentarians' integrity and likened the acceptance of monetary compensation to treason.[46] Situating the annexation of Bosnia Herzegovina in the context of the international relations, Ali Şadi's *Bosnia Herzegovina or Ottoman Alsace-Lorraine*, predicted that the annexation could cause Ottoman–Habsburg enmity akin to that between France and Germany. He concluded his publication to avenge Bosnia Herzegovina.[47] The former mufti of Mostar and exiled leader of the Bosnian movement for religious and educational autonomy also published a short work in Arabic, critical of the Habsburg administration condemning its annexation of Bosnia Herzegovina.[48]

Publications and the daily press that reported on the protests set the annexation in the discourse of international law, that is, the possible legal consequences of the Habsburg and Bulgarian infringement of the Berlin Treaty and the rights of the Ottoman Empire in such situations. Furthermore, the boycott was presented as a spontaneous expression of national outcry sparked by flagrant alienation of Ottoman territory, and in disapproval of the longer history of the capitulatory system with its broad economic and legal rights benefiting the European states at the expense of local industries and particularly Muslim merchants and workers. In calling for a firmer Ottoman response, the authors emphasized the consequences of previous territorial losses, most important being the refugees that were certain to follow. Human plight in the process of migration, and burden on the treasury and the local population, were concerns the government was asked to consider.

Émigré Bosnians in Istanbul were already motivated by the revolutionary potential to strengthen the empire and by extension Bosnia Herzegovina. They founded the Bosnian Club of about three hundred prominent

Bosnian Ottomans. Its youth branch was named "Hope of the East."[49] They lobbied through their Ottoman networks and organized to keep the protest against annexation current, hoping for change, or at least an opportunity to negotiate what seemed like a fait accompli. To this end they made contacts with other Balkan émigrés, namely Serbian and Albanian, who viewed annexation as an unfavorable development for their own home regions, although stemming from significantly different motives. Connections were made between the Vienna-based Bosnian scholars' association Zvijezda and the Bosnian Club in Istanbul in order to come up with lobbying strategies against the annexation. One of the public protests organized by the Istanbul Bosnians attracted a crowd of 50,000, marching from the central Fatih neighborhood to the Parliament building and European embassies.[50] However, an order was issued not to allow the demonstrators to appear in the vicinity of the imperial palace.[51] Bosnia Herzegovina Ottoman Beneficent Association published brochures and sent them to the Ottoman government and the parliament, as well as informative material for public distribution, in hopes of keeping the issue of Bosnia Herzegovina on the agenda.[52] The pamphlets highlighted the attachment and allegiance of the Bosnian people to the Ottoman state and argued that both Muslims and Orthodox Christians in Bosnia would not accept a solution for the province without Ottoman involvement and protection.

In response to criticism of his handling of the Bosnian and Bulgarian issues, seventy-six-year-old Sadrazam Kamil Pasha summarized Ottoman powerlessness in the matter and reliance on European public opinion:

> I know there are those who object by ascribing the [Ottoman] soft attitude to my old age. They are mistaken. If it were that way, it would be easy to find a young Sadrazam. Yet, it is not me who is old—it is the Sublime State: our age is not that of Sultan Süleyman the Magnificent. Secondly, Bosnia Herzegovina is indeed our possession, but a possession that we do not own. It is possible to preserve and protect a possession that is under one's control by way of war. However, it is not so easy to take back the land we did not govern. Even if it were possible to form an international conference [*mahkeme-i düveliyye*] to deal with the political issues, its actions would have been bound by mutual benefits [of the members]. Certainly the principle of "the victor has the last word" is the rule, no matter what. Protracting this issue is not rooted in our soft attitude, but is a result of expecting a positive outcome by showing a friendly and pacifist attitude and relying on the fairness of European public opinion.[53]

After Bosnia Herzegovina officially became a Habsburg province, the legal relationships of Bosnian Muslims with the Ottoman Empire transformed along the lines of the Habsburg–Ottoman agreement signed in 1909. This bilateral agreement became the legal criterion for all interactions, including citizenship, land ownership, and other official business between the Ottoman Empire and its former subjects in Bosnia Herzegovina. Yet, the realization was slow especially among the Bosnian immigrants to the Ottoman Empire who desired to travel or settle their affairs in Bosnia Herzegovina. One Abdullah, son of Mahmud, immigrated to the Ottoman Empire before the annexation but petitioned the Ottoman authorities to settle his inheritance in Bosnia Herzegovina, calling upon Ottoman laws. He was advised to address the Bosnian courts directly or to apply to the Austrian consulate with official documents concerning inheritance.[54] Others petitioned the Ottoman authorities after finding no legal response in the Habsburg system. Such was Süleyman Efendi who petitioned regarding his property that was seized by the Habsburg officials under the premise that it was state land (*miri*), although he was in possession of an Ottoman title deed. Legal Counsel of the Sublime Porte responded that said property needed to be returned to its owner according to the Ottoman–Habsburg agreement of 1909, which stipulated the continuation of property rights, and directed the Ottoman embassy in Vienna to take the necessary steps.[55] There were so many issues regarding property that continued to be contested after the annexation that the previously established committee within the Legal Counsel of the Sublime Porte, which solely focused on resolving petitions and issues relating to property in Bosnia Herzegovina, continued to operate after the annexation.[56]

Bosnian Muslims also sought Ottoman legal protections after the annexation. They filed complaints with the Ottoman authorities regarding travel to Bosnia Herzegovina when they were denied visas or entrance.[57] In some cases, the petitioners were, or had recently become, Ottoman citizens, giving the Ottoman state legal basis to safeguard its citizens' rights. Often though, the Ottoman officials advocated on behalf of and in protection of Muslim rights. When the provincial constitution was announced in Bosnia Herzegovina, the Legal Counsel of the Sublime Porte instructed the ambassador in Vienna to investigate whether the articles of the constitution contradicted the agreement from 1909, and whether the new provincial constitution was in any way changing the previously established protocol between the two empires. Most importantly, the ambassador was to look into whether the needs and demands of the Muslims were met.[58]

After the Young Turk takeover, the Ottoman policy of claiming protections over Muslims beyond Ottoman borders continued, carrying over the Hamidian understanding of its diplomatic and political influence, in a less spectacular but a more pragmatic way. The rhetoric of the Committee of Union and Progress often lauded plans for settling Muslim refugees in demographically mixed regions such as Macedonia, to achieve a majority and deter the activities of nationalist movements engaged in violence toward civilians and subversion of Ottoman authority. However, no migration of such scale took place from Bosnia Herzegovina. Soon, the new Ottoman administration was met with significantly more territorial losses in southeastern Europe and a fresh wave of migrants into its remaining territories after the Balkan Wars, during World War I, and its turbulent aftermath.

The Ottoman consulate was opened in Sarajevo in 1910, confirming the foreign status of its former province.[59] The Habsburg administration did not look favorably on Ottoman plans for opening two legations in Sarajevo and Mostar, although the Habsburgs had their consulates in several cities across Bosnia Herzegovina before the occupation, as did other European states in Bosnia and other Ottoman regions of interest to them.[60] Ottoman representation in Bosnia Herzegovina was useful in speeding up the resolution of many migration applications and legal cases involving applicants who were subjects of the two empires.

The incoming consul Suad Bey set to work immediately. Even before he was officially confirmed, he had contacted a district court about a case. This initiated correspondence among the district and the supreme court and the provincial administration about interaction with a representative of a foreign state. Habsburg authorities were adamant about making sure that all correspondence went through the provincial government to prevent the Ottoman consul from acting as if Bosnia Herzegovina was still an Ottoman province.[61] Resul Efendi, appointed the following year, was to be joined later by a military officer with a bureaucratic title, for the purpose of intelligence gathering in addition to growing staff.[62] Resul Efendi too, frustrated the Habsburg authorities with his interpretations of intraimperial authority over legal issues and matters of migration. Bosnian migration to the Ottoman Empire—as well as Ottoman refugees and civilian and Ottoman government employees and officers from the regions affected by the Balkan Wars—had their travel facilitated by the consulate.[63]

The Ottoman consul also addressed inheritance and custody issues, attempting to resolve them according to Ottoman interpretation of international and bilateral norms; but his actions and even his personal circumstances were scrutinized by the Habsburg authorities, who were concerned over his influence on the Muslim population in Bosnia Herzegovina.[64] An Ottoman official residing in the Bosnian capital was a new point of contact for Muslims in the province but also for those in the neighboring regions. In addition, the Ottomans and the Bosnians worked to maintain connections between the Ottoman Empire and Bosnia Herzegovina, no matter how nominal. Illustrative of the Ottoman resolve to maintain its prerogative were awards of Ottoman medals for "tolerance and service to the Muslims" to Habsburg officials in Bosnia Herzegovina.[65] Although symbolic, they were often requested by Bosnians to indicate their Ottoman connection in the precarious political climate of Habsburg Bosnia Herzegovina.

Provincial Assembly and Party Politics

Seeing no reaction from the Ottoman Empire or the European states, at the time when the Habsburg administration was preparing a Bosnian constitution and a provincial assembly, MNO leaders realized that they had to recognize the annexation in order to continue functioning in Bosnia Herzegovina. Other Bosnian parties had already sent their representatives to Vienna to express allegiance and acknowledge their acceptance of the new political order. It took MNO more than a year to accept the act of annexation and pledge loyalty to the Habsburg Monarchy. The Bosnian provincial constitution was announced just a few days after MNO's acceptance of the annexation in 1910, but it did not bring much of a change in governing and administrative structure in Bosnia Herzegovina. Compared to other Habsburg provincial constitutions of the same period (in Moravia and Bukovina, for example), Bosnia's was the most restricted.[66]

Because Bosnia Herzegovina did not belong to either part of the monarchy, its inhabitants did not become Austrian or Hungarian citizens but had a special status, lacking the full extent of rights Habsburg subjects in Austria, Hungary, and abroad enjoyed. Furthermore, the Habsburg administration continued the division of Bosnian subjects into confessional groups, which were considered national: Catholicism was equated with Croats, Orthodox Christianity with Serbs, and Islam with Bosnian Muslims (Bosniaks). The administration planned to expand the rights and participation in the province gradually, in the form of "rewards" to its subjects who were not considered ready for full democratic institutions.[67] Insistence on treating the subjects in the province as religious groups in competition for imperial favor was not a novel approach by colonial powers ruling the diverse post-Ottoman regions. The "unfortunately" mixed societies were observed strictly through the lens of religious communities, which needed to be brought out of their backwardness with European guidance.[68]

In Habsburg Bosnia Herzegovina, Muslims were seen as the "state-building element" but also as exotic Orientals whose presence interfered with Bosnia's position compared to other Habsburg provinces. It also allowed for the continuation of efforts at appropriating Muslims by different South Slavic nationalist projects.[69] Imperial subjects in Bosnia as well as across colonized and semi-colonized Ottoman domains, however, were not passive recipients of Ottoman Tanzimat or European colonial policies but understood the new categories as avenues through which it was possible to advance their interests, further reinforcing such categories. Flattening provincial inhabitants and the complex historical meaning of community and geography into color-coded maps that assumed monolithic predominance of one or another group across the region, European imperial powers set out to provide solutions to the problems they had helped devise. They reinforced confessional divisions through policies such as the so-called national/confessional key that awarded dominance to a group in a region, its top-down awards, and political representation in governmental bodies. The inadequacy of such an approach was not unintentional: it assured a need for colonial arbitrators even after the demise of the formal colonial status, in Mt. Lebanon and Bosnia alike.[70]

The Habsburg administration introduced a provincial assembly (Sabor), with restricted powers and authority. Both Austrian and Hungarian governments needed to approve drafts of laws to be discussed in the assembly—which already had a limited sphere of issues it could tackle. Before any decisions could be ratified by the emperor, they needed to be vetted in the same manner.[71] Interests of Austria and Hungary, and their increasingly opposing views over the province's management, stemmed from the growing economic, strategic, and political relevance of the province in the imperial internal and foreign policy.[72] Despite these limitations, until the beginning of World War I, Muslim political activity in Bosnia Herzegovina was expressed through work in the Bosnian assembly.[73] Members were elected based on religious proportion of the population, divided among the landowners and city and rural dwellers. Whereas voting rights were reserved for men, women landowners who paid at least 140 krone in taxes were also allowed to vote.[74] In line with the Habsburg confessional politics, representatives of religious hierarchies also participated in the work of the assembly; these included the Reis ul-ulema, head of the provincial Islamic pious endowments administration, and muftis; metropolitans and the president of the Orthodox Christian community; the archbishop and Franciscan representatives; and the Bosnian chief rabbi. The elections took place in 1910: thirty-one seats went to the Serbian People's Organization (Srpska narodna organziacija), twenty-four to the Muslim People's Organization (Muslimanska narodna organizacija, MNO), twelve to the Croatian People's Organization (Hrvatska narodna zajednica), and four to the Croatian Catholic Association (Hrvatska katolička udruga). Representatives of the Habsburg government also participated in the provincial assembly. The work of the assembly was characterized by alliances among the parties divided along confessional and ethnic lines and influenced by nationalist support coming from outside Bosnia Herzegovina, in particular those from Croatia and Serbia both coveting Bosnia Herzegovina as their national right.

The Muslim People's Organization that emerged out of the movement for autonomy in the previous decade was successful in attaining all of its goals in negotiations with the Habsburg administration leading to the adoption of autonomy in Islamic religious and educational affairs. The success brought unprecedented prestige to MNO, in such measure that no other party claiming to represent Muslims had a chance at competing in the first assembly elections in 1910—MNO won all twenty-four seats. In the context of the Ottoman constitutional revolution, MNO was not discredited for siding with the ousted sultan, because its former opposition to the Habsburg authorities provided it credibility in the eyes of émigré lobbyists. After achieving preeminence and the desired autonomy, MNO was comfortable pledging loyalty to the Habsburg state and engaged in coalition politics supporting most Habsburg policies.[75] New forms of sociability and communal association, as advocated by modernist and educated activists and intellectuals, became the main vehicle of political mobilization and organization. Likewise, writers, teachers, and provincial administrators actively engaged in party politics, many becoming members of the assembly and regional party representatives. The new political climate in the province created conditions for convergence among previously disagreeing Muslim factions ultimately creating the United Muslim Organization (Ujedinjena muslimanska organizacija).

Agrarian reform, the most prevailing issue discussed during the sessions of the assembly, was at the same time the most sensitive topic for the landlords controlling the dominant Muslim party, and it was the primary issue for the dominant Serbian party, which claimed to champion the interests of the Orthodox Christian peasants. Land or agrarian reform, discussed at length throughout the existence of the assembly, was principally about restructuring the relationship between the majority Muslim landowners (*aga* and *beg*) and their tenants (*kmet*), most of whom were Orthodox Christian.[76] The issue reached back into the Tanzimat reforms to include Ottoman laws

FIGURE 8. Address by Ali Beg Firdevs, the first president of the Bosnian assembly, at the opening ceremony, 1910.

Source: Arhiv BiH. Reprinted with permission.

FIGURE 9. Members of the assembly, June 15, 1910.

Source: Arhiv BiH. Reprinted with permission.

and their interpretation of the legal relationship and the nature of the contract between the landowners and their tenants; land buyout options; and definitions of usufruct, private, communal, and state land rights.

Furthermore, land and the related dues were the cause of the disturbances integrated in the Eastern Question that ultimately led to Bosnia Herzegovina's occupation by Austria-Hungary in order to resolve the issues that the Ottoman Empire was supposedly not able to accomplish. Redistribution of Muslim land was expected by the tenants who withheld work and dues in the immediate period after the occupation because that became the norm in the territories lost to the Ottoman Empire. Differing from the approach of the nation-states carved out of Ottoman territories, the Habsburgs upheld the legal system and the existing socioeconomic relationships, working to resolve them gradually. Already in the last decade of the nineteenth century, the Habsburg administration devised opportunities for voluntary buyouts that showed some limited results. The class divide that overlapped with the religious identities that were then presumed to be national presented a predicament for the Habsburg as it did for the Ottoman authorities previously. The Habsburg administration treaded the middle line throughout its rule, careful not to alienate the Muslim landlords, but also to exhibit an aspiration to resolve the grievances of the *kmet* as part of its mandate. The relevant Ottoman land regulations known as Ramazan and Safer laws were interpreted by the landlords, the state, and the self-proclaimed defenders of tenant rights, in the manner that protected their interests the most.[77]

Just over half of privately held land in Bosnia (900,000 hectares) was owned by landlords with tenants. Over 90 percent of those landowners were Muslim in 1910.[78] Muslim landlords saw their land ownership as a source of economic and political power and projected the idea that the preservation of their properties was crucial for all Muslim interests in Bosnia Herzegovina. They insisted that the landlords' relationship with their tenants was based on a private contract and therefore could not be changed by the state or anyone else. However, as collecting dues became increasingly difficult and sometimes even dangerous, landlords desired to come to a solution sooner than later.[79] They supported voluntary land buyouts, which would be based on an agreement between the landlord and the tenant. In opposition, Serbian parties pushed for a mandatory buyout of Muslim land, defining the tenant–landlord relationship as being in the domain of the state and therefore within its authority to change it. Their hope (and urgency) was that Muslim dispossession would also weaken them politically, while the transfer of land into the hands of Orthodox Christian peasants—seen by Serbia and its Bosnian acolytes as potential Serbs, would fortify the claims of Bosnia as Serbian land. They envisioned it to be a government-financed project. To that end they tried to take political advantage of a peasant protest action in 1910 in northern Bosnia when tenants refused to pay dues, hoping to put additional pressure on the government to adopt an obligatory buyout solution.[80]

The state considered the consequences of resolutions that would drastically change the established relationships, as well as how a change in land ownership would potentially empower Serbian expansionist aims into Habsburg territory. Habsburg administration was also interested in interpreting the various classifications of land and its usage, relying on Ottoman laws and practice in Bosnia Herzegovina. This was the case with *miri* lands, which according to Ottoman categorization were owned by the state over which the notables had rights under certain conditions but which the Habsburg administration coveted from the start of the occupation. Furthermore, the administration wanted to keep for itself vast forests with landlord and communal rights as a significant source of income.[81]

The parties engaged in creating alliances to achieve the desired outcomes. One compromise entailed Muslim acceptance of a change in designation of the provincial language to Croatian or Serbian, attesting to nationalist aspirations at appropriating the land and the people of Bosnia Herzegovina. The administration supported the voluntary option and encouraged alliances between Muslim and Croat parties. A majority was achieved with the help of representatives of the Serbian party who did not want to end the possibility of aligning with the Muslim party to achieve majority, or worse, letting it ally with the Croat bloc. To complicate matters, some in the Serbian parties were themselves landowners with tenants.[82] Political maneuvering led to the promulgation of voluntary buyouts with the state providing low interest loans in 1911. However, that did not end the land question, and various representatives of Serbian parties continued to bring up the prospects for revising the agrarian buyout regulations.

The impatience with which the land was expected to change hands was encouraging nationalists to question the ways in which Muslims became landowners, falsely claiming that Bosnian Muslims hailed from Asia and therefore had less right to land than the Orthodox Christian peasants who moved to Bosnia Herzegovina during the Ottoman period.[83] Such chauvinistic talk became louder with the Serbian successes in the first Balkan War (1912), when most Ottoman Balkan territories were conquered by the Serbian, Montenegrin, Bulgarian, and Greek forces, who indiscriminately dispossessed and massacred Muslims of all ethnicities. The Habsburg administration did not want to appear to be lagging behind because the land ownership was being resolved in a "swift and radical" manner in the neighboring regions lost to the Ottoman Empire.[84] However, for the Bosnian Muslims, the expulsion, massacres, dispossession of Muslims, and annihilation of entire villages in these regions signaled what was in store for Muslims in the new nation-states in the Balkans. The Serbian socialist-oriented paper *Radničke Novine* published eyewitness accounts of its editor, Dimitrije Tucović, who was conscripted in the Serbian army. The editor's accounts concluded that the "barbarian" activities of the Serbian and Montenegrin forces realized within that war year were a more persuasive argument for desiring Austro-Hungarian presence in Montenegro and northern Albania than the efforts of the Habsburg consuls and friars who had worked for an entire century to expand Habsburg spheres of interest in that region.[85] The Balkan Wars contributed to some Bosnian Muslims' realization that Bosnia Herzegovina within the Habsburg Monarchy was a more favorable alternative than any version of a nation-state dominated by their neighbors.

Claiming Autonomy

Annexation resolved the tenacious issue of Muslim religious and educational autonomy in Bosnia Herzegovina. Concerned that the requests for an autonomous religious hierarchy in Bosnia Herzegovina tied to the Ottoman sultan-caliph would strengthen Bosnians' connection to the Ottoman state, as well as Ottoman territorial claims over the occupied province before 1908, the Habsburg administration prolonged the negotiations with Bosnian Muslim representatives for years preceding the annexation. As Ottoman sovereignty ceased to be an issue for Austria-Hungary after the annexation, Bosnian Islamic Community's religious ties with the sultan-caliph and the Şeyhülislam were accepted together with the autonomy in Muslim religious and educational affairs.

The promulgation of the statute regarding the Islamic Community after the annexation required a new election of Reis ul-ulema and its officers. It included community elected and district representatives, pious endowment boards and offices, Medžlis-i ulema members, and the ulema electoral curia. The press followed these elections not only as a relevant issue for religious organization but also as critical for the social and political being of all Muslims in Bosnia Herzegovina. *Musavat*, the paper of MNO, hailed them as having an utmost influence "on the future of our people" (*budućnost našega milleta*).[86] The electoral curia ended up proposing an unforeseen lineup of candidates: Hafız Sulejman Šarac, supreme shari'a judge, who was suspended for writing an exposition confirming the absolute authority of the caliph in appointing religious officials in Bosnia Herzegovina; former mufti Ali Fehmi Džabić, founding leader of the oppositional movement for autonomy in Islamic affairs, a political exile, and a professor in Istanbul;[87] and Ali Ruždi Kapić, a high-ranking Ottoman justice.

The paper *Bošnjak* reacted with condemnation of the electoral curia's choices of scholars known for their opposition to the Habsburg Monarchy, two of whom were not even residing in Bosnia Herzegovina.[88] The Habsburg administration expectedly nullified the election because Džabić and Kapić were Ottoman citizens. In a repeat selection, two local scholars were proposed along with Šarac, who was ultimately elected to the post of Reis ul-

ulema.[89] The Habsburg administration was hoping that the annexation would sever any claims to Ottoman citizenship and to a constitution of its Bosnian subjects, and that the authorization of a limited autonomy in Islamic affairs and its institutions would further attract Muslim loyalties the Habsburg way. However, the first election showed that Muslims wanted to push the boundaries of their autonomy and reaffirm ties to the Ottoman Empire by including Ottoman scholars as candidates, which they most likely knew would nullify the election.[90]

Autonomy was an important boost for an Islamic institution in the Habsburg Empire. In its broadest structure, it allowed for communal participation and oversight of pious endowments and educational institutions in collaboration with the members of the newly established Bosnian provincial assembly and the Habsburg administration. The power was not uncontested from the start, as ulema, the state, political leaders, and members of the assembly all vied for dominance in the work of Islamic institutions that affected so much of Muslim life in the province. The ulema united to guard their independence, to the point that Reis ul-ulema Šarac rejected any involvement of the assemblymen in plans for educational reform in Islamic schools. A proposed women's high school fell victim to the infighting, earning the ulema a reactionary label. Even prominent religious scholars such as Džemaludin Čaušević (1870–1938), who endorsed women's emancipatory policies as part of his reformist efforts, closed ranks with the ulema in order to uphold their prerogatives in the organization of the Islamic Community. Political representatives and the reformist ulema increasingly diverged from the views of the Reis ul-ulema, ultimately calling for his resignation, leading to yet another election in 1913.[91]

Subsequent elections exhibited the political relevance of the position of the Reis ul-ulema and the extent of public investment. Debates in the press, political struggles, and backroom deals, as well as petitions from across Bosnia Herzegovina, factored in the election of the Reis ul-ulema. The electoral curia and the overwhelming public support went to the reformist Mehmed Džemaludin Čaušević, but the Habsburg authorities did not respond for several months as they explored other options, including vetting another Ottoman-based candidate who could appease the Muslim members of the assembly, as a counter to Čaušević's Ottoman Islamic prestige.[92] The authorities then offered a choice of high-ranking positions to Čaušević in return for his withdrawal from the Reis ul-ulema election, his reassurance that "his friends" would not nominate him again, and his promise that he would not oppose the annulment of the election. Čaušević responded that he found such "bargaining with public trust contrary to human dignity," but that he would not oppose annulment in the interest of settling the issue and electing a head of Islamic Community, as its operations were brought to a halt without guidance. Seven months later the elections were annulled.[93] Public outcry at the actions of the administration, seen as pleasing local politicians' personal ambitions and party aspirations at the expense of broader Muslim interests, ultimately led to the nomination and appointment of Čaušević in the repeat elections, despite the opposition of the government and the leading politicians.[94]

Appointment of a prominent Pan-Islamist reformer like Čaušević to the Reis ul-ulema post exposed the strength of the reformist current among the ulema and the popularity of their modernization efforts. Inspired by the ideas of Pan-Islam, their locally rooted activism represented the middle road among the increasingly widening gap between the conservative ulema rejecting any institutional reform and the progressive intellectuals who shunned ulema's steadfast "backwardness." Čaušević's communal reform agenda was influenced by the developments in the Ottoman Empire and the issues grappled with by Muslims elsewhere, as reflected in the globally connected Muslim publications he enthusiastically introduced in Bosnia Herzegovina upon his return from Istanbul in 1901. Harun Buljina observed the local events around Čaušević's activities and his leap to the highest Islamic position in the Habsburg hierarchy in 1914 in a transregional and cross-imperial milieu as having initiated a "micro-revolution" in Bosnia Herzegovina, taking part in the global wave of constitutional revolutions to attain local autonomy with an aim of instituting a modernizing program.[95]

As much as the Habsburg authorities hoped that annexation, granting autonomy to Islamic institutions, and the establishment of the provincial assembly would further sever ties with Istanbul and direct Muslim allegiances toward Vienna, the Young Turk Revolution and the Second Constitutional Period in the Ottoman Empire reinvigorated the Bosnian Muslim–Ottoman connection. This was most notable in the physical travel by students at schools in the Ottoman Empire who were active in the political and associational life of Istanbul and Sarajevo, as well as the intensified print culture that made the link to the Ottoman Empire and the broader Muslim world more intimate than it ever was previously. The Ottoman constitution and the atmosphere of freedom and revival in the immediate aftermath of the revolution was an important example of modernity and potential for reform in an Islamic idiom. In the Bosnian provincial context it established a discourse of constitutionalism that served to secure institutional autonomy and promote Muslims' own confessional identity that was local yet Ottoman-backed and integrated into the broader "Muslim world." However, the direction was not necessarily anti-Habsburg as it was situated and legitimized within the Habsburg imperial and provincial structure. Čaušević was awarded the "rank of Mecca and Medina" (*Haremeyn-i muhteremeyn payesi*)—one of the highest titles of honor for Islamic scholars in the Ottoman Empire, which came with a formal mantle gifted by the sultan-caliph.[96] Wearing this mantle symbolizing sultanic legitimacy, Čaušević was ceremonially confirmed by Emperor Franz Joseph I in Vienna as the Reis ul-ulema of Bosnia Herzegovina, a post that he would continue to hold beyond the existence of both the Habsburg and Ottoman empires.[97]

Muslim Loyalties and Ottoman Ties

Telling of the post-annexation attitudes in Bosnia Herzegovina were activities and opinions of the controversial activist and politician, Mehmed Šerif Arnautović. As a veteran high-ranking member of the movement for autonomy from its earliest days, Mostar native Arnautović was imprisoned for his oppositional activity. At different times in his career, he advocated for cooperation with Serbian and Croatian nationalists, as it became advantageous to Muslim interests but without endorsing Serbian and Croatian Muslim nationalization, which earned him criticism.[98] After the annexation, when the Habsburg authorities accepted the demands of the autonomous movement, he was appointed director of the Islamic Pious Foundations Administration and became a member of the provincial assembly. His political career of Habsburg oppositionist, pro-Ottomanist, and Habsburg bureaucrat and politician demonstrates how he gauged political opportunities for Muslims and the ways in which he fused loyalty to the Ottoman Empire and the Habsburg Monarchy as relevant to Bosnia Herzegovina.

Concerned about yet another wave of migration after the annexation and the negative effect it had on the status of those who stayed, Arnautović wrote to the Sublime Porte with explicit plans to discourage migration.[99] In particular, he was concerned about the Habsburg approach where confessional differentiation among the provincial subjects was tied to their political representation, and closely related to their demographic presence. Dismissing the need for migration, Arnautović explained that the position of Muslims in Bosnia Herzegovina had improved, so much so that they prospered. The landowning class was still strong, he claimed: Muslims comprised one third of the population and were in possession of three quarters of Bosnian agricultural land; 100,000 Christian families worked Muslim-owned land, and roughly half of trade was in Muslim hands. Serbs and Croats, he continued, having mutual political and nationalist animosities, needed a coalition with Muslims. For this reason, Muslims were able to consolidate their position and fortify their political presence through political alliances.

Pleased to describe the achievements of the movement for autonomy that allowed the relationship with the Şeyhülislam to continue, he also went on to say that pious foundations and education were finally flourishing: yearly *vakuf* income was over 1,900,000 francs, and the Muslim educational institutions followed the Ottoman school program. Gajret, a beneficent society with a yearly income of 70,000 francs, was sponsoring students in various universities in Europe—in the year of his writing there were more than sixty students being supported by Gajret funds. Finally, Arnautović confirmed with pride that Bosnia Herzegovina was still Muslim: "The lovely view of Sarajevo's 120 minarets reveals the Muslim essence of the city in one gaze to a foreign eye." Arnautović's depiction of the Bosnian Muslim situation concluded with a proposal with mutual benefits for Bosnian Muslims and the Ottomans: "There is no Ottoman who would not want Muslims to become strong and influential in this region bordering the Ottoman Empire—in a country that for the past two hundred years had had an eye on Ottoman territory."[100] He reasoned that strong Muslim presence in the Habsburg Empire was more beneficial to the Ottoman Empire than migration, which was damaging to Bosnian Muslim political influence.

Arnautović's confidence in reclaimed Muslim preeminence in Bosnia Herzegovina was not entirely baseless, even if it was enthusiastic. Statistics from the period show that the number of landowners, *aga* and *beg*, dwindled from 8,000 in 1879 to 4,000 in 1918.[101] When it came to education, out of 56,000 students in 568 elementary schools, only about 10,000 were Muslim in

1913, even though elementary education became compulsory in 1911.[102] The "Muslim essence of the city" continued to be fused with new directions in the monarchy's image making, blending Sarajevo and other Bosnian urban centers into the central European architectural landscape where Ottoman heritage protruded as exotic and Oriental.[103]

Soon after Arnautović's letter, territorial changes that occurred as a consequence of the Balkan Wars (1912–1913) left a sizable Muslim population in the Balkans outside the Ottoman Empire. Although taking place outside Bosnian territory, the Balkan Wars caused concern among Muslims and the Habsburg administration in Bosnia Herzegovina. Victories of the Serbian and Montenegrin forces were greeted with enthusiasm among the Slavophiles and Serbian nationalists in Bosnia Herzegovina, who organized celebrations in the streets of Sarajevo. Muslims gathered the next day in the same streets to protest the Ottoman aggressors and seek Habsburg support for the Ottoman Empire.[104] The administration heightened security measures and introduced a curfew in the province while trying to maintain a neutral attitude, especially after volunteers to Serbian and Ottoman armies were seen off with public celebrations in cities across Bosnia Herzegovina.

Drawing on the Bosnian experience of post-Ottoman Muslim life, Arnautović addressed Muslims who remained in the territories occupied by the victors in the Balkan Wars. In a newspaper column, he warned Muslims who had become citizens of new states to learn from the Bosnian "bitter experience" and avoid their mistakes:

> Thirty-five years ago we were also occupied by a foreign power. We too were faced with a new way of life and work.... Everything new that came our way we hated and despised, and there was no thought of accepting any of it.... It took us 20–25 years to come to our senses: our children started attending schools in greater number and going for modern vocations, and we seriously took hold of our work and started competing with the rest of the world—to at least preserve what was left.... Now we bitterly regret not being able to quickly find our way under new circumstances.[105]

Arnautović further advised Balkan Muslims to realize that they would only prosper through hard work, education, and acceptance of the "new," especially in the Balkans, describing it as "part of Europe where someone else's accounts are being settled mostly to your disadvantage."[106]

Arnautović's political career throughout the Habsburg period was highlighted by assertion of Bosnian ties to the Ottoman Empire: requesting the acknowledgment of Bosnia Herzegovina as Ottoman, then autonomy within the Habsburg system, and insistence on religious appointments by Istanbul. Even after the annexation, he encouraged Gajret society to give scholarships for studies of theology (by default at Ottoman universities) seeing it as a way of continuing and strengthening relationships with Istanbul.[107] Having been labeled by the authorities as the second most extreme oppositional member, after Mufti Džabić in the early period of Habsburg occupation, Arnautović transformed his exclusive pro-Ottoman political stance over the course of the Habsburg occupation. After his trip to Istanbul, Arnautović wrote: "Istanbul is our holy ground. . . . Istanbul is where our caliph, our religious leader is enthroned. . . . Istanbul is our symbol and ideal, although we are faithful, proper, and most loyal subjects of our high Habsburg dynasty!"[108]

In light of discussions regarding possible Habsburg political reordering, Muslim political representatives lobbied for Bosnian autonomy within the Habsburg system. South Slav unity and the possibility of such a political union were appealing to many in political and intellectual circles, including Reis ul-ulema Čaušević, who although welcoming Ottoman–Habsburg union at the beginning of the war, was frustrated with the imperial ineffectiveness in the face of Muslim losses and war sacrifices by the end of the war, opting for supporting "whatever brings freedom to our people."[109] Others, feeling endangered by Serbian and Croatian nationalisms, saw the future of Bosnia Herzegovina as an autonomous region, and as part of the Habsburg Monarchy, which seemed more secure than the possibility of becoming part of a Slav nation-state. Territorial discontinuity with the Ottoman Empire that followed the Balkan Wars was an important element in reorientation of many political activists as union with the Ottoman Empire, however ephemeral, was also finally physically impossible. By the end of World War I, reordering in the Balkans emerged under the influence of ideas of Pan-Slavism, nationalism, the Soviet revolution, and Woodrow Wilson's Fourteen Points.

Arnautović favored an autonomous status for Bosnia Herzegovina within the monarchy, as was the political course of many in the merged political party, the United Muslim Organization. After the announcement of a declaration envisaging union of South Slav lands in 1917, Arnautović submitted a memorandum to Emperor Karl I during his audience in Vienna, seeking autonomy for Bosnia Herzegovina. He supported this claim by expounding Bosnia's historical and cultural autonomous status separate from its neighboring South Slav entities. Contrary to the pride in Muslim advancement in the descriptions of Bosnian circumstances to the Ottomans, his portrayal of the Bosnian Muslim state seven years later as economically, politically, and educationally disadvantaged warranted the reestablishment of the provincial assembly (suspended at the beginning of the war), greater participation of Muslims in the administration of the province, and proposed resolutions of its most pressing problems.[110]

According to Austrian sources, autonomy was a course followed by the majority of Muslim representatives resisting nationalist projects as late as 1918.[111] Muslims in the Sandžak of Novi Pazar evaluated their prospects and petitioned Austria-Hungary for their region to be incorporated into Bosnia Herzegovina, rather than Montenegro, as they "belonged to it by history and language."[112] An imperial system they knew was seen as safer for the future of Muslims in Bosnia Herzegovina than the new nation-state. In addition, treatment of minorities in each nation-state in southeast Europe did not bode well for Bosnian Muslims considering their future in nation-states. Ultimately, Bosnian Muslims became citizens of the Kingdom of Serbs, Croats, and Slovenes (later Yugoslavia), which did not recognize Slav Muslims as constitutive people. However, their Habsburg political experience was of great value for reconstituting their rights and safeguarding their interests.

Composite Allegiances

Habsburg annexation of Bosnia Herzegovina was the last stage in the occupation of this province and its separation from the Ottoman Empire. Occurring in response to the Young Turk revolution, it provoked strong reactions across the Ottoman domains. Annexation and other territorial losses that transpired in the revolutionary turmoil were the last in line of decades-long territorial contraction and European political and economic encroachment associated with the faults of the previous administration. Revolutionary elation projected a new chapter in imperial history and reinvigorated the imperial project. The Ottoman mood extended to the domains beyond its borders, to its former regions, and it inspired its former subjects. Not solely an Ottoman instance, constitutionalism as a global wave of ideas and institutions, assumed lives of its own adapting to local conditions.¹¹³ Although part of Habsburg long-term plans in the region, the annexation was timed out of concern that the Bosnian provincial subjects would also seek constitutionally sanctioned representation, possibly even in the Ottoman parliament. The Habsburg administration offered a version of their own constitution, together with religious institutional autonomy. Bosnian Muslim activity in response to the new circumstances reflected their efforts to push the boundaries of the limited religious autonomy and the restricted parliamentary politics in order to advance their interests and safeguard their precarious influence in the province by relying on old and new allegiances. Analyzed from this perspective, it also challenged the presumption that the local political sphere was entirely nationalized.

History of turn-of-the-twentieth-century Bosnia Herzegovina and Bosnian Muslim activities have exclusively been evaluated through the lens of nationalist politics and the extent to which Muslims were or were not able to articulate their national belonging—assuming that nationalization was the inevitable end result of the period's historical processes. Their Muslimness as a political category was often deemed a consequence of delayed development of national consciousness. Although these assumptions have been challenged in scholarship, they are still presumed to be an exception to the nationalist convention and an obstacle to full participation in modern mass politics. Bosnian Muslims' composite allegiances were not unique: scholars have identified "national indifference" and a myriad of multiple and hybrid identities in case studies of Eastern and Central Europe not caused by the absence or immaturity of national identity, but in the face of forceful competition among nationalist movements.¹¹⁴

Serbian and Croatian nationalisms tried to lure Muslims (as well as Catholics and Orthodox Christians) to acknowledge their Serbian or Croatian nationhood useful to their respective nation-building projects in the region and to legitimize their claim to Bosnia Herzegovina. They also discriminated against them and equated them to the "terrible Turk" of nationalist lore.¹¹⁵ The Habsburg administration gave up on trying to prevent national factionalization in Bosnia Herzegovina by allowing political parties with national designations and naming Bosnian language "Serbian" and "Croatian," a significant element of national self-definition. Bosnian Muslim local identity and the modernizing agenda that defined it—embedded in the globally diffused ideas variously named Pan-Islam, Islamic cosmopolitanism, and defined in the context of interislamic intellectual networks as promoted by Čaušević—provided one of the responses to these nationalisms backed by Ottoman and Islamic prestige. The overlap of composite allegiances was to some extent possible in a state that cherished a multicultural vision of society such as the Habsburg Monarchy.

Observing religious minorities in post-imperial environments, the Muslim situation was comparable to the Jewish situation in post-Habsburg Austria, where Austrian Jews wished to continue to identify as Austrians by political loyalty, as Germans by cultural affinity, and as Jews by ethnicity. Unable to do so, while not accepting the German ethnic label, they increasingly identified primarily as Jews, which was further intensified by anti-Semitic exclusionism.[116] Habsburg Muslims, too, saw a need to unite in the face of nationalizing classifications that were not only unnatural to them but were seen as politically detrimental. Robin Okey observed that "the inner lack of sympathy with Muslims as Muslims which marked the Austrian administrators, Serbs, and Croats" was an important factor in the maintenance of Muslim solidarity.[117] Identifying as Muslim people (*Muslimanski narod, islamski millet*) was not based on religion alone, but encompassed cultural, historical, and regional features that in the politically precarious position helped redefine their connection to the Ottoman Empire. Muslims saw the preservation of their preeminence in the province closely tied to religious institutions and the landowning elite—the cultural and economic backbone legitimized by the Ottoman system as vital to their survival in the post-Ottoman world. Whereas the Ottoman *millet* designations created the confessional categorization that later served as basis for various ethno-confessional claims of nationhood, it was as if Muslims became a *millet* only *after* they ceased to be a part of the Ottoman system—a Habsburg *millet* of sorts.

Epilogue
Alternative Muslim Modernities

IDEAS OF MODERNITY, CONVEYING novel ways of imagining the world and one's place within it, together with new forms of societal organization and intellectual production, first reached Bosnia in the Ottoman and Habsburg period. The two empires that overlapped in Bosnia Herzegovina shared some features in their respective modernization practices, with both pursuing such state interests as centralization and an intensified control over their subjects' lives, but they diverged in their strategies and outcomes. The two distinct imperial conceptions also differed from the ways in which notions of modernity were internalized locally, as well as from the discourses of modernization theory and developmentalism that often plagued European scrutiny of non-European regions, including the Balkans. The modernity envisioned by the Muslim intellectuals in Habsburg Bosnia Herzegovina not only represented an alternative to the historiography's modernity narrative, but it was also an alternative to the contemporaneous understanding of modernity in imperial Ottoman and Habsburg visions.

This chapter focuses on the individuals who, in diverse ways, articulated Bosnian Muslim modernity during the Habsburg period; they came to a nuanced understanding of what modernity signified for them and in what ways it informed their definitions of Bosnian Muslim society and shaped cultural and political activity. The actors examined here are considered intellectuals because of their concern for their society and for how they proposed ideas and devised solutions to societal problems in their capacity as notables, educators, writers, religious officials, journalists, and administrators. Many saw themselves as reformers pursuing the task of enlightening their society and making it compatible with the requirements of the "new age," redefining it in the process. In contemporary Bosnian historiography, these thinkers are considered guardians of national identity. They had differences and rifts that sometimes spilled over into the public realm, but they often cooperated to form new social and cultural organizations and to publish papers, and they shared political interests that frequently brought them together. Although not a unified or formally organized group, these actors singled out similar problems and struggles in Bosnian society, offered comparable solutions to them, and tapped into related cultural and religious imagery. This analysis adopts Paul Rabinow's perspective that, rather than attempting the impossible task of defining modernity, one must explore how it has been understood and used by self-proclaimed modernists.[1]

The Muslim intellectual elite of Habsburg Bosnia Herzegovina, in addition to their new Eastern and Central European position, remained active in the Ottoman intellectual context, and they considered themselves to be part of a broader community of the world's Muslims. Although there have been extensive analyses of the Muslim world's reform movements of this period, Bosnian Muslim intelligentsia have yet to be studied as part of them.[2] Their concerns with the future of their culture, education, and society in general—all the while working to reconcile Islam with modernity—have much in common with the modernist movements across the Muslim world at this time. These intellectuals were influenced by developments in Istanbul and Cairo, and they closely followed the activities of Muslims ruled by non-Muslims in tsarist Central Asia, Russia, and independent Bulgaria. Discursive approaches to experiences of Volga Tatars, Turks in Bulgaria, Malayan Muslims, and others in relation to Muslim issues in Bosnia provide insights for comparing different Muslim lives under non-Muslim rule in the last decades of empires and in new nation-states. Comparative analysis shows that Bosnian Muslim experiences not only ran in parallel with those of other groups, but also influenced and shaped the broader Muslim modernist discourse, prompting a need for Bosnia Herzegovina to be integrated into scholarly debates on Islam and modernity that are usually limited to the Middle Eastern or South Asian contexts.

The trajectory of intellectual life in Bosnia Herzegovina was structured by multiplicity of social environments and imagined communities Muslims had at their disposal: being part of the Habsburg and Ottoman imperial context, but also being Slavs (and Slavic-speaking) and members of the universal Muslim community (the *umma*). The significant Habsburg influence on the modernization and transformation of the intellectual outlook in the province has been studied and documented in depth. What has been neglected is the lasting effect that Islamic intellectual discourse in Bosnia Herzegovina has had on the understanding and expression of modernity there (and in Southeastern Europe, for that matter). Historiography conceives of Bosnia's modern period as dating from its break with the Ottoman Empire, and as a consequence of European influences that began with Austria-Hungary's occupation. According to this narrative, the Habsburgs, as the representatives of what was modern, European, and enlightened, took over the derelict province from the Ottomans, who after 1878 seem to have disappeared from the Bosnian scene in every significant respect.

Scholarly work on the post-Ottoman period in the Balkans has been hampered by analyses limited by national and disciplinary boundaries, and it almost always centers on the break with the Ottoman Empire and the otherness of "Asiatic Islam." Means by which European modernist discourse reached different social and intellectual groups across Eastern Europe and the Middle East and the nuanced ways in which that discourse was received and modified locally are seldom considered.

Treating the transition from one empire to another not as a radical break, but rather as a process that displayed many continuities, allows for moving away from a fixation on modernity as simply an outcome of Habsburg rule. It lets us to reconsider conventional historiography's portrayal of Muslim subjects as passive recipients of European modernization and sociopolitical organization, disconnected from former Muslim centers. This is to discount neither the effects of top-down Ottoman reforms, nor how the Habsburg imperial, colonial context shaped and nurtured ideas and activities associated with modernity.[3] Structures the state set in place for administrative organization, the treatment of individuals and groups (the Ottoman *millet* system and its continuation in the Habsburg period), and education, print media, and social associations affected how new intellectual elites defined the notions of tradition and modernity and the place of individuals in the community and the world. By examining how the modernist discourse developing in the Ottoman Empire and the wider Muslim world influenced Bosnian Muslim intellectuals' conceptions of their particular Muslim modernity in a European context, we see that Habsburg Bosnia Herzegovina was not only a particular response to modernity, but also a unique location in which intellectuals, in interaction with other sites and struggles, forged their own European Islamic intellectual tradition.

Islamic Reform and Ottoman Modernization

While reform was a recurrent aspiration throughout Islamic history, the need for reform beginning in the eighteenth century was understood in the context of the European encroachment that threatened Muslim societies on all fronts: militarily, economically, politically, and culturally.[4] Muslim reformers at the turn of the twentieth century, from the Balkans to Southeast Asia and from Sub-Saharan Africa to Central Asia, articulated reasons for Muslim weakness vis-à-vis Europeans in terms of a fundamental opposition between tradition and modernity within their own societies. Sayyid Jamal al-Din al-Afghani (1839–1897), Muhammad Rashid Rida (1865–1935), and Ismail Bey Gasprinski (1851–1914) were influential figures of this intellectual movement, attracting the most attention from scholars. They were known across the Muslim world through their publications in the ever-growing Muslim press. Their opinions were lauded, debated, and sometimes dismissed by local authors who engaged with questions about modernity and its effects on their immediate environments.[5] These activists sought to make their societies compatible with modernity, which they understood as a set of ideas and practices that included cultural revival, modern education, women's rights, various institutional and associational developments, and science. How these ideas reached different areas where Muslims lived varied considerably. So too, Muslims' interpretations and strategies of modernization were quite diverse both geographically and also among local and regional proponents of modernity.

In Bosnia Herzegovina, the foundations of modernizing reforms and intellectual concepts were laid out in the last decades of Ottoman rule. Although the Tanzimat period in Bosnia was brief, it laid the foundation for modernization of all aspects of society. Most importantly, in this period the fundamentals of reforms, as well as of opposition to them, were articulated in the context of the Islamic state and in Islamic terms (see Chapter 4). Many Bosnian notables opposed the Tanzimat; they wanted to maintain autonomy in local affairs and taxation as well as their military privileges, and they expressed their resistance to Ottoman centralization efforts as a rejection of "un-Islamic" Ottoman practices. By the 1860s, however, Bosnia Herzegovina had become a model province, and advanced Ottoman modernization policies took root there.

The Ottoman reform introduced multi-level representative councils, while modern elementary and higher-level schools were established alongside the traditional *mekteb* (elementary school) and *medrese* (seminary).[6] An administrative school (Mekteb-i hukuk) and a teachers' school (Dar ul-muallimin) opened in Sarajevo and educated the first generation of modern bureaucrats and teachers in the spirit of the Ottoman reform. These new schools met little resistance from religious officials, who continued to control education in the traditional schools, especially the elementary *mekteb* that most students attended. Nonetheless, the new schools were an important departure in education in that they treated religion as only one of many elements in the curriculum.

During the tenure of Governor Topal Şerif Osman Pasha (1861–1869), the province experienced the most successful features of the Tanzimat. In addition to reorganizing the province and building roads, railways, schools, hospitals, and libraries, this Ottoman governor founded an inter-religious provincial assembly and executive council. The intensity of anti-Ottoman nationalist propaganda emanating from Croatia and Serbia through textbooks for confessional and missionary schools, and the increasingly relevant role of the press, compelled the governor to introduce comparable local sources of Ottoman influence. Among his important legacies were the founding of the official *vilayet* (provincial) printing press in 1866, the initiation of the papers *Bosnaski vijesnik* (Bosnian herald) in Bosnian Cyrillic script and *Bosna* (Bosnia) in Bosnian and Turkish, and the publication of the Ottoman official yearbook, *Salname-i vilayet-i Bosna*.[7] As a local response, journalist and educator Mehmed Šakir Kurtćehajić (1844–1872) launched *Sarajevski cvjetnik—Gülşen-i saray* in 1868.[8] By 1878, the provincial press had published more than twenty titles, textbooks, and administrative publications in Turkish and Bosnian.[9]

These Ottoman top-down measures—the establishment of a provincial printing press, educational reform, and enhanced communication systems—created the conditions for greater intellectual production that continued during the Habsburg era. The Austro-Hungarian state retained a top-down approach, which significantly aided Muslims in furthering the modernist intellectual development initiated during the Ottoman period. The Ottomans invoked reforms to reaffirm their authority throughout their domains, but also in response to European encroachment and the increasingly relevant public opinion, to preserve the state's global imperial position. Similarly, Austria-Hungary aspired to exhibit its new province as a successful model of the multicultural Dual Monarchy that for the first time incorporated Muslims. The Habsburg occupation in 1878 did not discontinue the reform efforts of the last Ottoman years. The administration carried over Ottoman practice in most areas and planned to gradually implement changes.

Habsburg Modernization

The Habsburg administration worked to integrate Muslims into its imperial sphere and, like the reformist Ottomans had, make Bosnia Herzegovina into its model province (Musterstaat).[10] Soon after the occupation, vigorous development began in areas ranging from industrialization, to infrastructure, to education. Provincial folk poetry compendiums were commissioned, and even customary carpet patterns were redesigned in Vienna for weavers in Bosnia Herzegovina.[11] In encouraging Muslim participation in the new state, the Habsburgs sought to define Muslim culture as integral to the empire's new image.

Bulgaria provides comparative evidence for the Muslim minority position under imperial and national rule. It was also created as an outcome of the Berlin Congress—first as the Bulgarian Principality and Eastern Rumelia, later annexed to form the Bulgarian nation-state. The Ottoman Danubian province, most of which later became Bulgaria, was, like Bosnia, one of the Ottomans' exemplary modernization provinces. Under governor Midhat Pasha (1864–1867), the province led the way in the number of post-elementary *rüşdiye* schools attended by both Muslims and non-Muslims. The Russo-Ottoman War (1877–1878) and the subsequent Berlin Treaty created an independent Bulgaria. Though the new state had a constituent assembly and over a dozen Muslim deputies, it largely disregarded Muslims and hoped they would ultimately all emigrate. The authorities rarely responded to cases of violence, illegal property alienation, religious discrimination, or other acts against its Muslim population, and then only when it damaged the new Bulgarian state's international image.[12] Most Muslims there spoke Turkish, and so when the official language became Bulgarian, that further alienated Muslims from participating in the new society.

Bulgaria discouraged the publication of Turkish papers by introducing measures that required editors to have a high school or university education, even though no schools in Bulgaria offered Muslims that level of education. When newspapers tried to bypass the requirement by employing Bulgarian or Greek editors (who did not perform any editorial work), the administration tightened the requirements by demanding that editors be fluent in the language of their paper.[13] The Habsburg administration, on the other hand, encouraged and financed the publication of Muslim papers even in Turkish, and they advanced similar local initiatives with a long-term goal of drawing Muslim leaders and educated elites into the Habsburg and Central European intellectual circles and away from Ottoman influences.

The Habsburg administration started the *Bosansko-hercegovačke novine*—later the *Sarajevski list,* as well as a cultural magazine *Nada*. In addition to relevant news, it promoted the administration's particular civilizing mission with Europeanization, Latin script, and modern education as the basis of progress and separation of the province from its "Oriental" heritage. There were sporadic dedications of articles to stylized "Eastern" themes in poems and short stories ("Stories from the Arab desert," "Story from Persia") written by non-Muslim authors, and other articles examined Turkish influences on the Bosnian language ("Turcizmi u Bosni"). These testify to the administration's earliest efforts to represent and include Muslims as a constituent element in the province.[14] More importantly, the administration was adopting the strategies and tools of nationalist movements as a way to counter them.[15]

Austria-Hungary supported the printing of a yearbook in Turkish that continued from 1882–1893. It took its original purpose from the Ottoman period, and even its official character, publishing statistical and administrative information in addition to a calendar of yearly events and articles on history and culture.[16] Muslim writers at first felt more comfortable publishing in this yearbook in Turkish than in the *Bosansko-hercevacke novine* in its Bosnian Latin script. The yearbook's articles were written by late Ottoman scholars and former Ottoman officials such as Salih Sidki Hadžihuseinović Muvekkit (1825–1888), its editor and the official Ottoman timekeeper; Ibrahim Beg Bašagić (1840–1902), a member of the Ottoman parliament and a district governor in both the Ottoman and Habsburg administrations; Mehmed Hulusi (1849–1907), editor of the Ottoman paper *Neretva*, journalist, and an official in the Habsburg pious endowments administration; and Mehmed Teufik Azapagić (1838–1918), an Istanbul-educated religious scholar, mufti of Tuzla, and Reis ul-ulema of Bosnia Herzegovina.

Muslim writers also began publishing in *Vatan* (Homeland), established in 1884 in Turkish, which was supported by subscriptions and donations. Though papers printed in Ottoman Turkish receded over time, the names of many remained Turkish: *Behar* (Blossom), *Musavat* (Unity), *Gajret* (Endeavor), *Tarik* (Path), *Muallim* (Teacher), and *Misbah* (Lantern). Discussions about the place of Turkish language in Bosnian education and print—as a link with the Ottoman Empire, Islam, and even political stances—continued throughout the Habsburg era in Bosnia Herzegovina.[17] Although the administration saw Turkish as a threatening bond to Ottoman influences in the province, it tolerated it, probably because literacy levels in Turkish were low and its importance was diminishing on its own.[18]

That the first publications were in Turkish, and that their content and their authors' writing styles closely followed the trends of Ottoman literary and journalistic currents, indicate that they inhabited the Ottoman as much as the new Habsburg Bosnian world. Muslim activists who supported the Habsburg modernizing measures were part of late Ottoman reform efforts. Some of them had been educated in Istanbul and were therefore affected by trends at the heart of the Ottoman Empire. Whereas the Ottoman sociocultural framework continued to be relevant, many Bosnian Muslim intellectuals did not claim, or work toward, a political bond with the Ottoman Empire. They were acutely aware of their new regional circumstances and worked to preserve their former status and to actively participate in Habsburg developments relevant to their future.

Intellectuals' understandings of modernity did not develop as a linear process of rejecting the Ottoman, Islamic, or Eastern in favor of the Habsburg, European, or Western. Their modernity was a complex response to, first, their immediate sociopolitical environment in the province; second, the reformist currents in the Ottoman Empire and the wider Muslim world; and finally, the administration's efforts to cultivate them in hopes of attracting and integrating them into the Habsburg imperial setting.

The Habsburg administration supported the Muslim intelligentsia and worked to separate the religious establishment from Istanbul. To that end, it restructured the existing Ottoman educational institutions (*mekteb, ruždija,* and *medresa*) and established new ones that would end the need to travel to Istanbul for education.[19] Key to this effort were the separation of the provincial Islamic hierarchy from the authority of the Ottoman Şeyhülislam in Istanbul and the creation of institutions of higher religious education that would produce religious officials to serve in the province. In 1887, Mekteb-i nuvvab was established with the main purpose of educating shari'a judges who would work within the Habsburg provincial legal system, which had adopted some of the shari'a laws. The students at this school studied subjects related to shari'a and Habsburg jurisprudence, Arabic, Bosnian, Turkish, Persian, German, and French, as well as subjects in the sciences and humanities. The school was an outcome of the Habsburg effort to accomplish its political aims while also satisfying the demands of the local religious establishment. It became an exemplar of modern education in the Muslim world, so much so that Muhammad 'Abduh (1849–1905), a Muslim reformer and mufti of Egypt, named it as an example when he proposed to the Egyptian government that it establish a school for shari'a judges.[20] For comparison, the first Muslim higher education school in Bulgaria, the Medresetünnüvvab, was not founded until 1920.[21]

The graduates of this and other schools in Bosnia Herzegovina continued their higher education in Zagreb, Vienna, Istanbul, and Cairo. Although educational patterns are often explained to account for the split between the modernist and traditionalist factions (the Ottoman educated being the traditionalists), the fact is that many of those educated in the Ottoman capitals were part of the reformist intellectual elite that was active beyond the Habsburg period.[22] Those studying in Vienna and Zagreb often attained specializations in Oriental languages, which gave them access to developments in the Muslim world through literature and the press.

As noted earlier, the religious officials and notables who opposed the Habsburg administration of Bosnia Herzegovina organized a movement for religious and educational autonomy. They insisted that Ottoman rather than Habsburg authorities appoint religious officials, to ensure that the pious foundations and the educational system did not lose their Islamic character and legitimacy. These issues were fused into a struggle to preserve tradition that also included positions about opposing land reform—issues portrayed as inextricable from the interests of Bosnian Muslims as a whole and indistinguishable from the perpetuation of Islam in the province. Intellectuals criticized the oppositionists for misinterpreting Islam, for an unreasonable reliance on the Ottoman Empire, and for their insistence on an archaic Ottoman system. Yet they voiced no opinion about land reform, which was likely to involve Muslim notables losing land to their mostly Orthodox Christian tenants or to the state.

Even after the establishment of the provincial parliament, land reform remained the major point of contention in debates among the nationally divided parties. Muslim intellectuals, religious officials, and notables of differing ideological backgrounds all assumed the same stance, evocative of the Muslim faction in the Russian Duma: though they belonged to different parties, they united on issues relating to Muslims. Even advocates of modernization did not promote land reform, which would result in Muslim economic collapse. This selective adoption and rejection of features considered fundamental to the modernization process supports the claim that, for its advocates, modernity did not represent an abstract set of ideas, but instead was related to specific local conditions creating a concrete possibility and materiality of modernity.[23]

Reformists

One of the most prominent Muslim reformers in Habsburg Bosnia Herzegovina was Mehmed- Beg Kapetanović Ljubušak (1839–1902), a notable and an Ottoman and Habsburg official, whose writings on deterring migration were introduced in Chapter 3. He described the implications of the Habsburg occupation for Bosnian Muslims and compared their fate to that of Muslims in the rest of the Balkans: "Never before have over half a million Mohammedans lived in full freedom under the protection of a Christian ruler, as we live today in our homeland."[24] This realization is reminiscent of that of Muhammad Iqbal (1877–1938), who, referring to the South Asian Muslim experience, wrote in 1909, "It is not the number of Muhammadans that it protects, but the spirit of the British Empire that makes it the greatest Muhammadan Empire in the world."[25] Russian Muslims, too, found that they could advance within the framework of a non-Muslim state, while Ottoman intellectuals such as Şemseddin Sami Fraşëri (1850–1904), advocated for a focus on eradicating ignorance, which had once been a European problem as much as it was a contemporary problem for Muslim societies.[26] The idea that Islam and Muslims could thrive under non-Muslim rule was a principle readily promoted by Muslim thinkers concerned with the diminishing socioeconomic status of Muslims who failed to adjust to their new circumstances.

Ljubušak served as district governor and as mayor of Sarajevo and was elected to the first Ottoman parliament. He was awarded the Ottoman Third Class Order of Mecidiye for his participation in Ottoman reform efforts. After the Habsburg occupation of Bosnia Herzegovina, he was one of the Muslim representatives who traveled to Vienna for an audience with the emperor. He was subsequently reappointed as Sarajevo's mayor, this time by the Habsburgs. The administration awarded him the Habsburg Order of the Iron Crown Third Class, and upon his request for an Austrian title, he was granted a place in the Austrian knighthood (österreichischen Ritterstandes).[27]

This almost seamless transition from one empire to another was characteristic of notables and officials who distinguished themselves in Ottoman reformist cultural and educational activities and who continued their endeavors into the Habsburg period. The development of print brought about the growth of the press and the circulation of literature, along with greater ease of travel. These facilitated new ways of recognizing one's place within overlapping communities—religious, economic, linguistic, and regional—in ways that had been impossible before. Bosnian intellectuals' understandings of modernity, as initiated by Ottoman reform measures that further expanded within the Habsburg framework, developed around concrete and immediate social, political, and economic struggles involving Muslims. They engaged with tangible issues such as convincing Muslims to send more of their children to modern schools that would provide them opportunities to become active participants in their future, the province, and the new empire. They worked to counter Muslims' economic decline that was caused by disparities in the Habsburg economic and trade system, but also by Muslim landlords and merchants being slow to adopt modern agriculture and market capitalism. Finally, Bosnian Muslim thinkers and activists espoused Habsburg institutions and features of provincial sociopolitical life, insisting that these were not inconsistent with Islam and that only by embracing the "new" could Muslim existence in the province be preserved.

Though the Bosnian–Ottoman experience with neighboring Austria in earlier centuries had included expulsion and the forceful conversion of Muslims, Ljubušak now saw the Habsburg administration in a new light: "Everyone knows that religious wars and the Crusades ended a long time ago."[28] He reasoned that the authorities' promise of equality and impartial treatment for all, regardless of religion, should be the basis of Muslims' loyalty to the monarchy.[29] By voicing such a definitive attitude regarding the end of Bosnian territorial existence within the Ottoman Empire, Ljubušak firmly resolved the limbo in which some Muslims were lingering, still hoping for an Ottoman return, or at least Ottoman support in their political endeavors. He wrote: "As for the thoughts and hopes of Bosnian return to Turkish hands, everyone here knows that in the past two centuries, whatever the Turkish government lost, or was taken away from it, was never returned. Bosnia can be a lot of things, but never Turkish."[30] Instead, he advised focus on improving Muslim economic and political positions under Habsburg rule by taking advantage of the opportunities the administration provided. Comparable to the Crimean Tatar reformers in the Russian Empire, Bosnian reformers focused on promoting educational, cultural, and social reform and engaged in political mobilization and participation only later, when political associations became legally sanctioned in the Habsburg Empire. In this they differed from Bulgarian Muslims, who were involved in the political activities of the Bulgarian constituent assembly from its inception in 1879.[31]

The encounter with a foreign, occupying power was a common theme among Muslim modernizers at the turn of the twentieth century, and some saw it as an opportunity to improve their own societies. Malayan Muslim modernists advised that Muslims there should take advantage of British colonial justice and freedom and improve themselves so as to be able to assist the British in projects that brought benefits to their country. They even praised the British as God's "righteous servants."[32] Muhammad Iqbal, the visionary of Pakistan's independence, stressed the British "civilizing factor" in a similar context.[33]

Press and Print

Bosnian intellectuals of the Habsburg period were graduates of modern Ottoman and Habsburg schools and universities in Zagreb, Vienna, and Istanbul. Many came from notable families and were employed in the offices of the provincial administration and educational institutions. Their ideas and political attitudes were expressed in the ever-growing provincial press, where they published literary essays and translations, most often from Turkish, but also from French, German, Hungarian, English, and Japanese.[34] Publications by Bosnian authors referenced classical and modern Islamic sources, but also European ones, demonstrating their familiarity with and acceptance of European intellectual heritage as relevant to and supportive of their arguments.[35]

The first individual works and publications written exclusively by Muslims in Bosnian and Cyrillic/Latin script appeared in the 1890s. The spread of Latin script literacy and a rise in readership followed publishing activities, which drew interest to a number of books printed in the 1890s by Bosnian Muslim writers, about and for Muslims.[36] Popularizing Bosnian in the Latin script opened up a growing readership to a variety of new print sources, both provincial and regional, and the literary, political, and social influences that they projected. Bosnian was not a new language in the province, but its Latin rendition was. Movement for adopting the provincial language in education and publications appeared during the implementation of the Ottoman reforms. The textbook *Sehletul Vusul* (Effortless approach), printed in 1875 in Arebica (Bosnian Arabic script), proposed that Bosnian be the official language of education.[37] Throughout the Ottoman period a body of literature known as Bosnian *alhamijado* literature in Arabic script existed alongside literature in Turkish, Arabic, and Persian,[38] and Bosančica (Western, or Bosnian Cyrillic) was used in pre-Ottoman and Ottoman-era epistolary literature.

These forms of writing and literature in Bosnian did not disappear with the Habsburg occupation. Moreover, Džemaludin Čaušević standardized Bosnian Arabic script suitable for the printing press, and works were published in Arebica until World War II. Ljubušak himself used Bosančica.[39] Many of the Muslim intellectuals writing in Bosnian also wrote, published, and translated from Turkish. Arabic remained the language in which religious scholars wrote their treatises and official opinions, while Persian literary output and study, associated with the dervish orders, and particularly the Mevlevi, receded with the marginalization of Sufi institutions and its educational establishments in Bosnia Herzegovina.

In 1900, a group of eminent writers led by Safvet Beg Bašagić (1870–1934), a notable who studied Islamic languages in Vienna and was later president of the Bosnian assembly (1910–1919), established an independent paper of primarily literary content, intended to influence and educate the young, corresponding to the "spirit of time and needs of the people."[40] In the words of one of the founders, *Behar* (Blossom) was to be "exclusively ours, Islamic, and arranged in a clear and sensible Islamic spirit," and written and read by Muslims.[41] Considered the arena of Muslim literary renaissance, *Behar*, through its popularity and wide readership, influenced educational and cultural developments and shaped Muslim political views.

In addition to poetry and prose authored by Bosnian Muslim contributors, *Behar, Biser, Gajret*, and other periodicals also offered literary critiques and translations, with a special focus on contemporary Ottoman Turkish literature. The Ottoman avant-garde literary-political periodical *Servet-i Fünun* (Wealth of knowledge) was widely read and had considerable influence on Muslim writers in Bosnia Herzegovina. Assessing Turkish literary directions and European influences, Bašagić expressed his vision of Muslim literary production in Bosnia Herzegovina by following Turkish modern writers who "do not blindly follow the French decadents, but take from them what is beautiful, and according to their eastern tastes, complement the unrefined in decadence, with Eastern gaiety and poignancy."[42] This understanding of the "juncture of East and West" in Turkish literature affected the work of Bašagić and other writers in the generations that followed.[43]

Most influential were translations of poetry, prose, and literary criticism published as serials, predominantly from Turkish, but also Arabic and Persian. Theater became popular, not least due to the high rate of illiteracy, and many amateur theater associations were established in cities. Muslim audiences, however, were not attracted by Serbian and Croatian plays, which habitually portrayed Muslims and the Ottoman period in a negative light. Muslim actors often refused to play non-Muslim or immoral characters, and a need emerged for content that would appeal to an exclusively Muslim audience.[44] Plays by Namık Kemal (1840–1888), a prominent Ottoman advocate of constitutionalism and reform, were among those most translated from Turkish, while local authors readily espoused the new form of expression and its wide-ranging audience.[45] European plays also appeared in Muslim literary publications, among the first being Henrik Ibsen's *A Doll's House* and *An Enemy of the People*. The first rendition of Molière's *Les Fourberies de Scapin* in Bosnian was actually a translation of a Turkish adaptation of the play for Muslim audiences.[46] Looking at these phenomena in theater and literature, scholars have found that Western literary influences did not reach Bosnia Herzegovina directly, or at least not only, from Europe, but by way of Ottoman Turkish literary agency.[47]

Some Bosnian Muslim thinkers voiced in their works the need to free women from traditionalist constrains so they could perform their role in a modern society. Bosnian authors translated poetry and prose by Ottoman women writers such as Fatma Aliye (1862–1936) and Nigar (1856–1918) and expressed hope that the Muslim women in Bosnia Herzegovina would follow in their steps. Editors often lauded the reputations of their publications, claiming that "even the women read them," while some maintained that popular serialized novels encouraged many women to learn the Latin script.

Muslim women began appearing as authors: Vahida, Nafija Zildžić, and M. Munira in *Behar*; Hatidža Djikić, Šefika Nesterin Bjelavac, and P. K. Fatma in *Gajret*; and Nafija Sarajlić in *Zeman* and *Biser*. They wrote poetry and prose, often under pseudonyms, and distinguished themselves from earlier Bosnian Muslim women writers by writing in Bosnian and publishing in provincial journals.[48] The first women's organizations and magazines appeared after World War I, although girls' education, women's activism, and public appearances were encouraged in the Habsburg period. Women were teachers and educators, writers, and activists in women's chapters of cultural associations.[49]

Bosnian Muslim reformers, similarly to reformers around the Muslim world, criticized the conditions of women in their society. The focus of their efforts was education for girls and women, and they argued that Islam already granted it to them. The Ottoman Empire was leading the way in the emancipation of Muslim women, which had the first women's publication staffed and edited entirely by women in 1895, as was Crimea, where Pembe Bolatukova, sister of the prominent reformer Ismail Gasprinski, started the first New Method girls' school in 1893. Gasprinski's daughter Şefıqa edited a women's magazine, *Alem-i Nisvan* (Women's world). Appeals to improve the status of women in reformers' writings, however, had little impact on Bosnian society. The editors of *Biser* distanced themselves from the prolific Istanbul-educated author Hifzi Bjelavac (1886–1972) because his liberal outlook, which included support for the full emancipation of women, was not in line with the editorial board's views.[50] These and other debates concerning women, such as that surrounding (un)veiling, had to wait until social and political circumstances brought them to the fore during the interwar period.[51]

Education

While the Habsburg oppositionists warned of the disappearance and ruin of the Muslim community because of its separation from the Ottoman Empire and the loss of the traditional Muslim way of life, reformists warned of the destruction of Muslim society on another level. Edhem Mulabdić (1862–1954), renowned for his didactic prose, defined the key idea of his entire generation of intellectuals engaged in the Muslim cultural-literary reform movement through one of his characters:

> Gone are the times when we defended our land, fame, reputation, and might with a sword.... [T]oday is the time to defend these with education. Only education can safeguard them for us. If we are not hard working and accept it, there would be no one else to blame but ourselves if we lose all these to others who had accepted education in time.[52]

A Bulgarian reformer, Tırnovalı Osman Nuri, advised in almost the same words: "In our age the extent of the power of a nation and the guarantee of its future is no longer determined by the possession of cannon, guns, and ammunition but by education!"[53]

Analogous arguments in much of the Muslim world at the time focused on the damage that was occurring by misidentifying tradition with Islam, which undermined attempts at reform. They all saw education as key to reconciling these two conceptualizations. Education was also the focus of nationalist projects: teachers were the earliest agents of such movements and had a crucial role in spreading ideas of national identity in the Balkans. Newly formed nation-states in the Balkans, as well as in the Habsburg

Empire, made elementary education compulsory and free. Yet, only a fraction of Muslims attended. Ljubušak warned, "One should not ceaselessly hold on to the old ways, that meant something in the past, but should move on as the occasion requires,"[54] and critiqued fanatical adherence to tradition when it led to passivity in the face of progress. The harshest critique came from the pen of Osman Nuri Hadžić (1869–1937), a law graduate of Zagreb and Vienna universities and a productive writer who held various posts in the provincial administration. His novels and short stories condemned Muslim dissoluteness and resignation during the Habsburg period. He summed up the problem at the beginning of his work *Muslimansko pitanje u Bosni i Hercegovini* (The Muslim question in Bosnia Herzegovina):

> It is obvious that in the last twenty years the Muslims have overwhelmingly stagnated, and are perishing day in and day out. The fortunes and properties they owned until the occupation began to shrink and by now have largely slipped out of Muslim hands. The new cultural innovations in our lands are not being used by us, Muslims, or are used very little, whilst trade is slipping from our hands daily. Consequently, two main factors of human society, and two main aspects of a modern state: material wellbeing and spiritual intelligence, are missing among the Muslims in Bosnia Herzegovina.[55]

Hadžić and other intellectuals saw the roots of Muslim stagnation in the lack of education and the ignorance of the ulema, who rejected everything associated with modernity yet had control over Muslim primary education and a monopoly on defining what was Islamic. Hadžić's descriptions in his prose of decaying *medresas*, with inept students wasting their lives in an irrational educational system with inadequate, corrupt teachers, were his gloomiest and represent the most relentless critique of the clerical class.[56] He directly blamed the "lazy" and "self-indulgent" ulema, ignorant of Islam, for the intellectual and material downfall of the Muslim people.[57] These descriptions are strikingly similar to those found in the Singapore paper *Al-Imam*, which published equally unsympathetic critiques of the seminaries and their teachers,[58] and the Bulgarian *Muvazene*, which expressed matching feelings of doom and anger and comparable views of a dire Muslim predicament.[59]

The Bosnian cultural reformists saw in the thinking and preaching of the ulema, on whose advice the common folk greatly relied, a blind adherence to a distorted tradition, a rejection of everything new and modern, and a paralyzing reliance on the prospect of an Ottoman return. From South Asia to Egypt, to the Ottoman Empire and Central Asia, Muslim intellectuals reassessed cultural-religious values and offered unique understandings of Islam as consistent with modernity, with modern education being its most important aspect. In addition to writing about how education was the basis of reform, Bosnian Muslim thinkers actively worked to realize such goals by taking up teaching positions, funding students, and participating in organizations that supported educational endeavors. Muslims worldwide likewise saw education as the first step in reform to be followed by economic and political mobilization that would allow Muslims to effectively participate in their societies.

A noticeable feature of the change taking place in the sociocultural landscape was the disintegration of the ulema's control of education about religion, which was at the core of the reformists' efforts. Although moral and Islamic education was relevant for the reformists, what this meant for them was different from the traditional *mekteb* and *medresa* instruction based on memorization in Arabic and Turkish. One of the first works Ljubušak authored for the Habsburg school board was *Risale-i ahlak* (Tract on moral conduct), based on Ottoman textbooks and modern curricula. The visionaries of modern education dismissed rote recitation and encouraged education in Bosnian rather than Turkish, which the Habsburg oppositionists continued to insist upon more for its political connection to the Ottoman Empire than for any practical merit.

Like the modern Ottoman and the New Method schools in Central Asia, the modern schools of Habsburg Bosnia Herzegovina, especially the Mekteb-i nuvvab described earlier, taught Islam as well as other subjects unrelated to Islam—"marking off Islam from the rest of knowledge," as Adeeb Khalid observed in the Central Asian case.[60] Ottoman schools and Habsburg–mixed elementary and secondary schools in Bosnia Herzegovina had separate religious education classes, while other subjects were taught without regard to students' religion. In this manner, Islam was "situated squarely in a desacralized world defined by progress through history."[61]

In Russia, the Volga-Ural Muslims worked to reform their existing *madrasas* and to operate independently instead of establishing parallel lay educational institutions, since those would have required unwanted supervision of Russian authorities.[62] However, the reform efforts limited to existing schools reinforced the divisions between the modernists and the traditionalists as they fought for control over the same spheres. Bulgarian Muslim education was also limited to schools established during the Ottoman period. Many of these once-flourishing schools were destroyed in the Russo-Ottoman War, or were closed due to migration or lack of funding. The remaining schools that taught in Turkish were classified as private and were contingent on local Muslim initiative, with nominal support from the state.[63] Left to their own devices, Bulgarian Muslim educators established the Muslim Teachers Association in 1906, which worked to coordinate reform in schools and implement the New Method curriculum.[64] The Bulgarian government did take an interest in the minority Bulgarian-speaking Pomak Muslims. It founded Bulgaro-Muhamedan schools to encourage their Bulgarian affiliation based on Slavic origin and language rather than religion, with limited results.[65]

The Habsburgs, by contrast, supported and encouraged Muslim reformist endeavors so long as they were articulated within the discourse of a religious community (rather than a nation). In this the Habsburg administration differed from other national or colonial administrations that ruled over Muslim populations, which saw Muslim reformists as a possible threat to their hegemony.[66] Although the intellectual elite was contemptuous of traditionalists, personified in the image of the (usually lower-ranking) ulema, many high-ranking Ottoman-educated religious officials did engage in reformist efforts, and thus enjoyed popular and institutional support.[67] After all, the Ottoman Tanzimat, its civil code, and the constitution were created with input from religious scholars working within the framework of Islamic modernism. In Bosnia, too, the split between the so-called traditionalists and modernists was less precise. Especially after the province was annexed in 1908, the ulema took up an active role in Muslim mobilization and toward achieving reformist goals.

Likewise, Sunni and Shi'a religious scholars in British India, Iran, Egypt, and Iraq saw the need to reform in practical terms and acknowledged the critique that blind imitation and rigid interpretation were unfit for the modern world.[68] The Qur'an, hadith, and examples from Islamic history and literature were employed to rationalize, justify, and organize new cultural and political undertakings. These reformists, however, did not engage in theological debates or intellectual deliberations on abstract ideas and theories—the urgency of the dismal Muslim situation led them to focus on practical aspects that produced direct results.

Islam, Modernity, and Associational Life

What characterized all Muslim reformers was their use of Islamic discourse in their articulations of modernity and their insistence on upholding Islam's "true" principles as essential in modernizing societies. For the cultural reformists, modernity, progress, and advancement were all rooted in "genuine" and "unspoiled" Islam. They did not criticize traditionalists for their religiosity, but rather for what they saw as an understanding of Islam that had become distorted. They advised that modernity, progress, and Islam were in a mutually conditional relationship: Islam warrants progress, and knowledge and community—in its unity, proper organization, and prosperity—enable the true understanding of Islam. Ljubušak pointed out that Islam had no boundaries when it came to progress, and he quoted Qur'anic verses to illustrate that there were no hardships in religion, which he further supported by citing examples from Islamic history and Islam's emphasis on education.[69] Bašagić wrote that Islam was "founded on democratic institutions" and that it preached "realistic socialism," which was the reason for its equal "appeal to an African and to a European."[70]

By employing Islamic discourse and interpreting the scriptures in reference to contemporary issues, these thinkers engaged in an intellectual exercise that had until then been monopolized by religious scholars. Muslim reformists in Bosnia and elsewhere claimed the right to contribute new interpretations as part of the Islamic discourse, and they made this the central issue of the Muslim reformist movement worldwide.[71] In Bulgaria, which became one of the most important centers of CUP activity in the Balkans, Young Turk exiles were keenly involved in local reform endeavors and shared the reproachful attitude toward the ulema. However, because Islam and its discourse were central to the identity of the Bulgarian Muslim minority, the exiled Ottoman oppositionists were careful not to denounce religion and promote positivism, as they did in the Ottoman Empire and Europe. Instead, they also employed Islamic discourse to communicate their ideas.[72]

Muslim reformist thinkers defined education and hard work, based on Islamic principles, as essential to the existence of Muslim communities.

Islamic discourse informed new ways of organizing and keeping the community united. To maintain the community, they urged, it was essential for Muslims to participate in new schools, economic establishments, social and cultural institutions, and ultimately political parties. Bašagić often quoted hadith to demonstrate that congregation was envisioned as a duty of the faithful not only for the purpose of performing prayer, but also to develop mutually beneficial social and ethical values.[73] Associations, organizations, and clubs proliferated in Bosnia Herzegovina as a consequence of these concrete efforts to modernize society.

One such development was the founding of *kiraethana* (Turkish *kıraathane*), an Ottoman concept of a public reading room, first in Sarajevo in 1888 and then in other cities. The reading room was a public space that offered its patrons newspapers, journals, and books and organized lectures and discussions. It served as a public forum, elevating public consciousness about issues relevant to Muslims, and it was the birthplace of the movement for educational and religious autonomy. Most importantly, the *kiraethana* was intended to combat illiteracy, and important material was often read aloud and discussed. Such reading rooms also opened in Russe, Vidin, Shumen, and Varna in Bulgaria, and in Samarqand and Tashkent in Russian Central Asia. They were an outcome of new forms of sociability that characterized the reformers' circles, promoting communication through print in societies with established oral traditions.

Based on the notion of uniting, Bašagić worked on expanding associational life through supporting, funding, and initiating clubs, societies, and other organizations that promoted modern values among Bosnian Muslims. He supported the work of the reading rooms, and in 1903 was a founding member of Gajret, an association with the primary purpose of financially helping students gain education in modern schools.[74] Soon after, an association of Muslim academics, Zvijezda, was founded in Vienna, followed by the cultural association El Kamer in Sarajevo and the Islamska dionička štamparija (Islamic printing house) in 1905. Bašagić also participated in founding the Association of Muslim Youth in 1906 and the Muslim Central Bank and Združena Tiskara (Joint printing house) in 1911. Trade and workers' associations were established bearing Turkish/Arabic names: Ittihad (Unity) in Mostar in 1906, and Hurrijet (Freedom) in Sarajevo in 1908. The first Muslim charitable society, Merhamet (Compassion), was started in 1913

FIGURE 10. Interior of the Sarajevo reading room (kiraethana), 1901.

Source: Muzej Sarajeva. Reprinted with permission.

to fight poverty, a modern version of the work that Islamic pious endowments traditionally performed.

That new forms of sociability were beginning to dominate the social and cultural landscape in Bosnia Herzegovina was obvious when the so-called traditionalists, who had opposed the founding of Gajret and other modern associations that they deemed un-Islamic, effectively took control over Gajret's board through organized voting blocs in local chapters. Under the influence of modernist reformist current among the ulema led by Džemaludin Čaušević, the central figure of Bosnian Pan-Islamism, members of the ulema also established their own associations: Muslimansko muallimsko-imamsko društvo za Bosnu i Hercegovinu (Muslim teachers and clerics association of Bosnia Herzegovina) in 1909, and Udruženje bosansko-hercegovačke ilmije (Association of religious scholars of Bosnia Herzegovina) in 1912. They published papers as well: *Muallim* (Teacher) and

Misbah (Lantern). Such organizations and the intensive interaction they offered contributed to a rapid exchange of ideas and efforts to reach out to the broader Muslim population.

Creating an intellectual elite and a prosperous economic community that would support it, both modern and Muslim, were key aims of the intellectuals in their efforts to regenerate society. Muslims' attitude toward capitalism and acquiring wealth was one aspect of society that reformists thought needed to change. In this case too, Bašagić reminded his readers of the hadith that presented poverty as being close to faithlessness, and the necessity of acquiring wealth in order to do good.[75] The emphasis on financial prosperity was rooted in the weakening economic state of contemporary Muslims, and the intellectuals' own experiences had made them realize that reform and modernization needed financial backing to be successful: Bašagić financed his own education in Vienna; Ljubušak, Bašagić, and Hadžić self-financed the publications of their first works; and many of the papers and societies were fully dependent on contributions from their subscribers and members. Ademaga Mešić, a prominent merchant and patron of reformist endeavors, set an example of such investment: he owned the leading paper *Behar* and was majority owner of the Islamic Printing House and was a generous donor to Gajret. The First Muslim Publishing House and Bookstore in Mostar was also founded in 1911 by a business entrepreneur, Muhamed Bekir Kalajdžić, and he brought about another wave of publishing activity through his paper *Biser* (Pearl) and editions of the *Muslimanska biblioteka* (Muslim library), which published works that catered to Muslim audiences.

The circumstance of Bosnian Muslims was indicative of Muslim conditions elsewhere. For example, Muslim industrialists and merchants were instrumental in financing Muslim reform efforts in the Volga–Ural regions in Russia and Azerbaijan.[76] In Bulgaria, the Ahmetbegov brothers of Vidin bequeathed a considerable sum wills to support the work of the local reading room and an Islamic pious endowment, while politically engaged tobacco industrialists used their position of economic power to negotiate advantages for Muslims.[77] The understanding that social and cultural advancement and participation in the increasingly integrated economy demanded skilled and modern-educated individuals encouraged Muslim industrialists and merchants to finance reform initiatives and fund schools and students.

Principles of market capitalism factored into the discourse of modernity and were put into practice by reformist thinkers and their supporters.

Modern Ideologies

In addition to these sorts of issues that were occupying Muslims worldwide, Bosnian Muslims faced the polarizing agendas of South Slav nationalisms that were present in the region for much of the nineteenth century. In an environment gradually defined by ethno-confessional nationalisms, these Slav Muslims engaged in related ideological activism. Their notions of romantic nationalism blended with the ideas of Pan-Slavic, Pan-German, and Pan-Turkic movements, but they were also inspired by Pan-Islamisms in which Muslim intellectuals of Bosnia Herzegovina found issues comparable to those with which their own community wrestled. Muslim writers were often branded Serbian or Croatian when their pieces appeared in the Serbian or Croatian publications, though few declared themselves Serbs or Croats, switched back and forth, or participated in nationalist activities. Political differences caused disagreements and rifts that sometimes became personal. Poet and playwright Osman Đikić (1879–1912), educated in Belgrade, Istanbul, and Vienna, was barred from publishing in *Behar* after Osman Nuri Hadžić, one of the paper's founders, harshly criticized his compilation of politically charged patriotic poetry. Another prominent writer of this period, Musa Ćazim Ćatić (1878–1915), subtitled his poem "I Am a Bosniak" with "To Traitor Avdo S. Karabegović," to condemn that writer's Serbian nationalist leanings. Whereas nationalism was only one of the many overlapping identities an imperial subject could assume, Muslims' political galvanization became a pressing issue.

In their efforts to thwart the emerging forces of nationalism, both Ottomans and Habsburgs engaged with and adopted strategies of nationalist movements.[78] Both administrations encouraged regional Bosnian identification so as to deflect nationalist movement attempts to fragment the allegiance to the empire. For instance, the Ottomans introduced a Cyrillic standard in the Bosnian provincial press even before it was accepted by other South Slavs, thus appropriating a form of nationalist cultural production (language and script) for the purposes of imperial reform.[79] The Habsburgs also founded the paper *Nada* (Hope), which promoted Bosnia as the center of South Slavic culture, its Bosnian language, and regional affiliation within the imperial domain.[80] Bosnian Muslim reformers readily accepted the idea of regional association, which repelled the nationalist Serbian or Croatian appropriation of Bosnia and more specifically of its Muslims.[81] Even more importantly, Bosnianism provided a base for the promotion of reform and modernization efforts articulated in contemporary forms of patriotic language and consistent with changing ideas of identity and loyalty.

The Muslim intellectuals' characterization of a Bosnian, multi-religious nation was ridiculed in the non-Muslim press, and in the first years of the twentieth century the Habsburg administration officially abandoned it as a policy of countering Serb and Croat nationalism. The Bosnian/Bosniak identity then increasingly came to be understood as equivalent to Muslim. The nation was imagined within the boundaries of the province in territorial and linguistic terms, but also in confessional terms. Islam gained importance as an essential part of identity and a link to the Bosnian Muslims' moral, cultural, and historical heritage. For instance, tolerance and equality, as elemental characteristics of Ljubušak's Bosnianism, were also rooted in Islam.[82] In his poem "Šta je Bošnjak?" (What is a Bosniak?), Bašagić depicted Bosnian Muslims as "One small branch / of the great Slav tree."[83] He also defined Bosnian people as Muslims with a shared past and a common fatherland, and he established patriotism as a religious responsibility when he cited the hadith "Love of the fatherland is part of faith."[84] National identity was rationalized through references to the Islamic cultural and intellectual heritage and the history of Bosnian Muslims' contributions to the Ottoman and Islamic civilizations. Association with Islam alternated between an emphasis on the ethno-confessional individuality of Muslims in Bosnia Herzegovina and the importance of belonging to the community of Muslims (the *umma*).

Bosnian Muslim reformers looked eastward and reprinted Islamic literature and journalism in translation, both to share their cultural heritage and because the writings focused on sociocultural issues that were also current in Bosnia Herzegovina. Publications featured a section of news from the Muslim world. One of the first treatments of the notion of Pan-Islam in the press was "Pan-Islamska Ideja" (Pan-Islamic idea) in *Behar*. Its author, Fehim Spaho (1877–1942), elaborated on cultural and religious unity as the focus of twentieth-century Pan-Islamism and linked it to Muslims in Bosnia Herzegovina living under non-Muslim rule.[85] Articles published in *Biser* indicate a profound interest in Pan-Islam as an idea and related debates, as seen in the choice of translated articles: "Pan-Islamism and Pan-Turkism" translated from French; "Muslim Woman" by Muhammad Farid Wajdi (1875–1954), and "Pan-Islamism and Europe" by Rafiq Bey al-'Azm (1865–1925). The editor of *Behar* and *Biser*, Musa Ćazim Ćatić, who used the pseudonym "Panislamista," translated Muhammad Abduh's poem expressing discontent with the ulema, finding its message close to the Bosnian reformists' attitudes toward the clerics.[86]

There was interest in and fascination with other Muslims around the world, and with the advent of presses and postal mail, the rapid spread of information about their circumstances became possible. This was facilitated by educated Muslims of the time having mastered the Turkish, Arabic, and Persian languages. *Gajret* published articles about the conditions of Muslims in Russia, reform of the *medrese* system in the Ottoman Empire, and Islamic education in Bukhara.[87] *Behar* ran a report about Bakhchysarai in Crimea, and about the paper *Tercüman/Perevodchik* and its editor, Ismail Gasprinski.[88] *Tercüman* often printed articles in translation, and it published letters to the editor from as far away as Cairo. Papers ran stories that mentioned the Bosnian Muslims, from Crimean papers like *Tercüman* and *Sabah*, and discussions of Bosnian Muslims from the Bulgarian press.[89] Likewise, the Bulgarian papers *Uhuvet* and *Tuna* stressed the importance of maintaining links with the Jadid movement among the Russian Tatars,[90] while the Bulgarian paper *Gayret* criticized attempts to divide Muslims between various nations, which was particularly harmful to the multi-ethnic Bulgarian Muslims.[91]

Bosnian Pan-Islamist reformers placed importance on maintaining association with the rest of the Muslim world. Whereas Bosnian papers attentively followed the worldwide Muslim press, the press in Bosnian language was largely inaccessible and had limited readership beyond the Balkans, unlike the Crimean *Tercüman*, or the Bulgarian *Gayret* published in Turkish, which were widely read and had contributors from other regions. There was a need to continue publishing in Ottoman Turkish as a way of taking an active part in Muslim intellectual activities on a global scale. In Bosnia, *Vatan* and *Rehber* were published entirely in Turkish, *Misbah* ran in Turkish and introduced Bosnian Latin and Cyrillic script, while others, like *Behar*, only later began to publish a few extra pages in Turkish. *Tarik* was printed in standardized Arebica, as a way to connect Bosnian readership to the script used by most Muslims in the world. *Biser*, although published in Bosnian Latin script, ran its heading with two mottos in transliterated Arabic: "True believers are brothers" and "Islam triumphs over everything, and nothing triumphs over it." The press increased the linkage between different Muslim communities and awareness of Muslims and their issues in other regions. The result of these efforts and increased circulation created a globally interconnected Muslim community that had not previously existed.

This heightened the challenges and need for action in the face of escalating threats to Muslim existence and rights. It also deepened the belief that Muslim populations around the world needed a Great Power protector. Sultan Abdülhamid II's construction of the Hijaz Railway, which connected parts of the Ottoman Empire with the holy cities of Mecca and Medina and facilitated the Muslim pilgrimage, was followed with interest in the Muslim press; calls for donations to the project appeared in Bosnian papers.[92] The press also brought news from the Ottoman fronts in Libya in 1912 and the Balkan Wars of 1912–1913. Young men from Bosnian Herzegovina volunteered in the Ottoman army, and the Bosnian Red Crescent committees collected donations for Ottoman defense efforts and refugees.[93] Čaušević pointed out the magnitude of the Ottoman predicament and the understanding of its relevance for the entire Muslim world:

> It is obvious that the attacks the great Ottoman State is facing are aimed at destroying the Islamic world, because Turkey is the hope for the liberation of the entire Muslim world. Turkey is the heart of the whole Islamic world. The ability of Muslims to live like Muslims is tied to the perpetual existence of the Turkish government. That is why the Muslim world truly desires the Ottoman State and the caliphate to be strong, and excel in its prosperity and honor. Those enemies of Islam, aware of this, are taking action in every way. To diminish it, they engage in all kinds of deceit and conspiracy. Their aim is to weaken and make Turkey—the basis and support of the Muslim world—wretched. Our coreligionists in Turkey are defending the honor of the caliphate with their lives. They are dealing with unexpected attacks from four kingdoms and one million enemies.[94]

For Bosnian readers, their ties to the Ottoman Empire, existing by way of their past affiliation, were further encouraged by the Pan-Islamic sentiment that placed the Ottoman state and the caliphate at the center of Islamic existence and Muslim struggles. Antagonistic Balkan nationalisms and the horrific violence perpetrated against Muslims during the Balkan Wars polarized Muslim public opinion and sparked interest in how Muslims in other parts of the world overcame similar threats to their existence. In the eyes of many Muslims, the Ottoman Empire played a symbolic role as the powerful Muslim state defying European powers, with the caliphate as the symbol of Muslim unity and community, and the sultan-caliph as its leader. Istanbul, then one of the most cosmopolitan cities of the world, was also a junction of ideas, peoples, and ideologies: it was where the Central Asian and Balkan Muslims stopped over on their way to the hajj, where exiled Iranians wrote and published, and where Arab and many other Muslims came for advanced education.[95]

As discussed in Chapter 4, the stage for the development of a global sphere of interislamic networks was set with the nineteenth-century Ottoman reforms that positioned the Ottoman Empire as the leading example of Islamic modernization. Yet the Pan-Islamic policies of Sultan Abdülhamid II focused on the features of Pan-Islamism that served Ottoman political interests, while it contained facets of Pan-Islamic activity it deemed unnecessary or harmful to its affairs. Top-down as well as bottom-up continuities related to Muslim reform activities in Bosnia Herzegovina reveal the year 1878, then, to be much about continuity—transimperially and cross-regionally. Reform features enabled by the Tanzimat and continued in local settings found backing as part of Habsburg imperial projects in Bosnia Herzegovina. Connections maintained through educational and familial lineages, and along trade and Sufi networks that Bosnian Muslims maintained with the Ottoman Empire, paved the way for interislamic exchange of reformist ideas, ones not always in tune with the policies of Sultan Abdülhamid II. The various notions of what counted as Pan-Islam in Bosnia Herzegovina were rarely anti-Habsburg, nor were they an outcome of Ottoman agitation. Rather, they were a locally originated approach to reform and a mode of sociocultural perseverance under changing circumstances specific to this locality. Furthermore, Bosnian Pan-Islamists were found among the ulema and the Vienna-educated literati, which challenges the common yet erroneous historiographical distinction between religious resistance to "European" reform and the notion that transplanting European practices was the sole force of modernity.

Pan-Islamists endeavors around the world were likewise molded according to the circumstances of their immediate environments and the different concerns of Muslim communities in Bosnia Herzegovina, tsarist Central Asia, Bulgaria, Egypt, Malaya, or India. Pan-Islam was one way to reconcile Muslim identity with ideas of modernity. For Bosnian Muslims, Pan-Islam focused on bridging the internal differences within the Bosnian Muslim community, as well as neutralizing appropriations of Muslims by other national programs. It provided an alternative political formation that was not necessarily devoid of its linguistic, geographic, and ethnic characteristics. Since Pan-Islam spread through the printed word, it was confined to the reading elites, for whom it was only one of multiple identities and ways through which modernity was mediated. Contrary to the fears of European countries with Muslim colonies, or Ottoman efforts to monopolize Pan-Islam, it was not a movement of the masses, but rather of the reformist-inclined elites who were shaping local modernist discourses.

Continuities and Reform

The turn-of-the-twentieth-century reform movement among Muslim intellectuals in Bosnia Herzegovina was an outcome of the encounter with modernity in the context of Ottoman and Habsburg imperial policies, and of the intellectual currents extending across Eurasia and the Middle East impelled by improved communications and an interconnected market economy. Enhanced circulation of information, greater ease of travel, and new forms of associational life all enabled Bosnian Muslim intellectuals to envision themselves as part of overlapping global communities of Muslims, Slavs, and citizens of the "civilized" world, as well as Habsburg and Ottoman subjects. By reconstructing a nuanced picture of this intellectual milieu, we can place it at the juncture of seemingly contradictory European, Ottoman, Balkan, and Muslim intellectual tracks. The overlap mediated by the imperial and national environments shaped their experience of modernity.

These alternative modernities developed when intellectuals used the potentials of their intersecting but delineated environments. The initial introduction of reforms within the Ottoman and Islamic framework weakened opposition to modernization based on religious reasoning, while the modernists' insistence on interpreting Islamic discourse in new ways made it one of the main approaches to promoting modernization. In an effort to deter nationalistic aspirations within a multi-religious province, both the Ottomans and Habsburgs selectively adopted forms of nationalist ideology, while continuing to treat their subjects as religious groups. Furthermore, in response to the progressively polarizing South Slav nationalist agendas, Muslim thinkers engaged in ideological debates that stimulated the Bosnian Muslim political self-formation. The result was a unique, modern response.

Even upon separation from the Ottoman Empire, reformers remained within the intellectual spheres of the Ottoman and Muslim world. Awareness that Muslims elsewhere faced similar challenges helped Bosnian Muslim intellectuals to compare and define problems. They expressed solutions through an Islamic prism, but also influenced the Muslim modernist discourse through model intellectual and political developments in Bosnia Herzegovina. Correspondingly, the Habsburg pragmatic approach that viewed Muslims as the key element of state-building in the province, and the administration's sponsorship of Muslim culture as integral to the image of the empire, played a vital role in shaping Muslims' understandings of their place in the new regional and intellectual realignments, despite the limitations placed on Bosnians in the imperial system.

In Bosnia Herzegovina, the realization that Muslim cultural reform was a path to attaining membership in the modern world, combined with the precariousness of Muslims' socioeconomic and demographic positions, focused the intelligentsia's approach to challenges facing the community and how they articulated their urgency through localized cultural and religious interpretations. The most significant realization of these modernist reformists was that Islam and Muslim life were compatible with, and could even be enhanced, in the Austro-Hungarian and European settings, as witnessed by achievements and institutional development in Bosnia Herzegovina. Muslims developed a cross-regional modernity rooted in Ottoman and Muslim thought not despite Europe, but to hold onto their place in Europe, even though they were not considered of Europe. They came to see themselves within overarching identity formations that were comprehensible only from a cross-regional perspective encompassing Southeastern Europe and the Middle East. What emerged was an Islamic intellectual discourse that became integral to twentieth-century Europe.

Notes

Introduction

1. Leopold von Ranke, *The History of Servia, and the Servian Revolution: With a Sketch of the Insurrection in Bosnia; the Slave Provinces of Turkey,* trans. Mrs. Alexander Kerr (London: Bohn, 1853), 459.

2. Karl Marx, and Eleanor M. Aveling, *The Eastern Question: A Reprint of Letters Written 1853–1856 Dealing with the Events of the Crimean War* (London: S. Sonnenschein & Co., 1897), 4.

3. J. A. R. Marriott, *The Eastern Question: An Historical Study in European Diplomacy* (Oxford: Clarendon Press, 1940), 3.

4. For Ottoman contemporaneous responses to Orientalism, see Zeynep Çelik, *Europe Knows Nothing About the Orient: A Critical Discourse from the East, 1872—1932* (Istanbul: Koç University Press, 2021). On how the Orientalist continuities in the Balkans inform ongoing georacial imaginaries, see Piro Rexhepi, *White Enclosures: Racial Capitalism and Coloniality along the Balkan Route* (Durham and London: Duke University Press, 2023).

5. Maria Todorova, *Imagining the Balkans* (New York: Oxford University Press, 2009), 182. Also, Fikret Adanir and Suraiya Faroqhi, eds., *The Ottomans and the Balkans: A Discussion of Historiography* (Leiden: Brill, 2002).

6. Mark Mazower, *The Balkans: A Short History* (New York: Modern Library, 2000), xxxviii–xli.

7. Todorova, *Imagining the Balkans*, 180. Mazower, *The Balkans*, xxxviii.

On the processes see Machiel Kiel, *Studies on the Ottoman Architecture of the Balkans* (Aldershot, Hampshire: Variorum, 1990); Ahmet Kuş, Ibrahim Dıvarcı, and Feyzi Şimşek, *Rumeli'de Osmanlı Mirası: Bosna Hersek—Kosova / Ottoman Heritage in Rumelia: Bosnia Herzegovina—Kosovo* (Istanbul: Nildem Brokerliği, 2010); Dijana Alić and Maryam Gusheh, "Reconciling National Narratives in Socialist Bosnia and Herzegovina: The Baščaršija Project, 1948–1953," *Journal of the Society of Architectural Historians* 58:1 (1999): 6–25; and Rusmir Mahmutćehajić, "On Ruins and the Place of Memory," *East European Politics and Societies* 25:1 (2011): 153–192. For contemporary continuities see: András Riedlmayer, "Convivencia Under Fire: Genocide and Book Burning in Bosnia." In *The Holocaust and the Book: Destruction and Preservation*, ed. Jonathan Rose, 266–291 (Amherst: University of Massachusetts Press, 2001); András J. Riedlmayer, "Crimes of War, Crimes of Peace: Destruction of Libraries During and After the Balkan Wars of the 1990s," *Library Trends* 56:1 (2007): 107–132; and Lejla Gazić, "Destruction of the Institute for Oriental Studies During the Aggression Against Bosnia Herzegovina, 1992–1995," in *Orijentalni Institut u Sarajevu, 1950–2000*, eds. Amir Ljubović and Lejla Gazić, 30–35 (Sarajevo: Orijentalni Institut, 2000).

8. Suhnaz Yilmaz and Ipek K. Yosmaoglu, "Fighting the Specters of the Past: Dilemmas of Ottoman Legacy in the Balkans and the Middle East," *Middle Eastern Studies* 44:5 (2011): 677. Also see, L. Carl Brown, ed., *Imperial Legacy: The Ottoman Imprint on the Balkans and the Middle East* (New York: Columbia University Press, 1996).

9. On Bosnian borders throughout centuries, Ratimir Gašparović, *Bosna i Hercegovina na geografskim kartama od prvih početaka do kraja XIX vijeka* (Sarajevo: Akademija nauka i umjetnosti Bosne i Hercegovine, 1970).

10. Adem Handžić, *Population of Bosnia in the Ottoman Period: A Historical Overview* (Istanbul: Organisation of the Islamic Conference, Research Centre for Islamic History, Art, and Culture, 1994). On Ottoman population and demographic categories, see Kemal H. Karpat, *Ottoman Population, 1830–1914: Demographic and Social Characteristics* (Madison: University of Wisconsin Press, 1985).

11. Đorđe Pejanović, *Stanovništvo Bosne i Hercegovine* (Beograd: Naučna knjiga, 1955), 12–28.

12. Mark Pinson, *The Muslims of Bosnia-Herzegovina: Their Historic Development from the Middle Ages to the Dissolution of Yugoslavia* (Cambridge, MA: Harvard University Press, 1994), 81–82.

13. For an overview, see Selim Deringil, "From Ottoman to Turk: Self-Image and Social Engineering in Turkey," in Deringil's *The Ottomans, the Turks and World Power Politics: A Historical Dictionary of Titles and Terms in the Ottoman Empire* (Piscataway: Gorgias Press, 2010), 165–176.

14. Seema Alavi, *Muslim Cosmopolitanism in the Age of Empire* (Cambridge, MA: Harvard University Press, 2015); Faiz Ahmed, *Afghanistan Rising: Islamic Law and Statecraft between the Ottoman and British Empires* (Cambridge, MA: Harvard University Press, 2017).

15. Christoph Kamissek and Jonas Kreienbaum, "An Imperial Cloud? Conceptualizing Interimperial Connections and Transimperial Knowledge," *Journal of Modern European History* 14:2 (2016): 164–182.

16. Alan Mikhail and Christine Philliou, "The Ottoman Empire and the Imperial Turn," *Comparative Studies in Society and History* 54:4 (2012): 738. Also, Dominic Lieven, *Empire: The Russian Empire and Its Rivals* (New Haven: Yale University Press, 2001).

17. Benedict Anderson, *Imagined Communities: Reflections on the Origin and Spread of Nationalism* (London and New York: Verso, 1991).

18. Tara Zahra, "Imagined Noncommunities: National Indifference as a Category of Analysis," *Slavic Review* 69:1 (2010): 93–119; Pamela Ballinger, *History in Exile: Memory and Identity at the Borders of the Balkans* (Princeton: Princeton University Press, 2003); and Dominique Reill, "A Mission of Mediation: Dalmatia's Multi-National Regionalism from the 1830s–60s," in *Different Paths to the Nation: Regional and National Identities in Central Europe and Italy, 1830–70*, ed. Laurence Cole (Basingstoke: Palgrave Macmillan, 2007), 16–36.

19. Edin Hajdarpasic, *Whose Bosnia?: Nationalism and Political Imagination in the Balkans, 1840–1914* (Ithaca: Cornell University Press, 2015), 17; employing nationalism as a never-ending process: Étienne Balibar, *Masses, Classes, Ideas: Studies on Politics and Philosophy Before and After Marx* (New York: Routledge, 1994), 203; and the liminal "other," Zygmunt Bauman, *Modernity and Ambivalence* (Ithaca: Cornell University Press, 1991), 65–73.

20. Hajdarpasic, *Whose Bosnia?*, 197–198.

21. Caroline Humphrey, "Loyalty and Disloyalty Along the Russian–Chinese Border," *History and Anthropology* 28:4 (2017): 402.

22. Ibid.

23. Michel-Rolph Trouillot, *Silencing the Past: Power and the Production of History* (Boston: Beacon Press, 2015), 24.

24. Saba Mahmood, *Politics of Piety: The Islamic Revival and the Feminist Subject* (Princeton: Princeton University Press, 2005), 18; and Timothy Mitchell, *Colonising Egypt* (Cambridge and New York: Cambridge University Press, 1988), xi.

25. I borrow the description recognized by Faiz Ahmed in "Contested Subjects: Ottoman and British Jurisdictional Quarrels in Re Afghans and Indian Muslims," *Journal of the Ottoman and Turkish Studies Association* 3:2 (2016): 328.

26. Pierre Bourdieu, *The Logic of Practice* (Stanford: Stanford University

Press, 1990); and Pierre Bourdieu, *In Other Words: Essays Towards a Reflexive Sociology* (Stanford: Stanford University Press, 1990).

27. For the late Ottoman context, see Selim Deringil, *The Well-Protected Domains: Ideology and the Legitimation of Power in the Ottoman Empire, 1876–1909* (London: I. B. Tauris, 2011); Isa Blumi, *Foundations of Modernity: Human Agency and the Imperial State* (Hoboken: Taylor & Francis, 2011); and Michelle U. Campos, *Ottoman Brothers Muslims, Christians, and Jews in Early Twentieth-Century Palestine* (Stanford: Stanford University Press, 2010).

28. Péter Hanák, "Die Parallelaktion von 1898. Fünfzig Jahre ungarische Revolution und fünfzig Jahre Regierungsjubiläum Franz Josephs," in *Der Garten Und Die Werkstatt: Ein Kulturgeschichtlicher Vergleich Wien Und Budapest Um 1900* (Wien: Böhlau, 1992), 101–115, also discussed in Laurence Cole and Daniel L. Unowsky, eds., *The Limits of Loyalty: Imperial Symbolism, Popular Allegiances, and State Patriotism in the Late Habsburg Monarchy* (New York: Berghahn, 2007), 2–3.

29. Michael Brenner and Derek J. Penslar, eds., *In Search of Jewish Community: Jewish Identities in Germany and Austria, 1918–1933* (Bloomington: Indiana University Press, 1998).

30. Michael Hanagan and Charles Tilly, eds. *Extending Citizenship, Reconfiguring States* (Lanham: Rowman & Littlefield, 1999).

31. Karen Barkey and Mark von Hagen, eds., *After Empire: Multiethnic Societies and Nation Building: The Soviet Union and the Russian, Ottoman and Habsburg Empires* (Boulder: Westview Press, 1997); Uri Ra'anan, Maria Mesner, Keith Armes, and Kate Martin, eds., *State and Nation in Multi-Ethnic Societies: The Breakup of Multinational States* (Manchester, New York: Manchester University Press, 1991); Aviel Roshwald, *Ethnic Nationalism and the Fall of Empires: Central Europe, Russia and the Middle East, 1914–1923* (London: Routledge, 2001); Lieven, *Empire*.

32. David Henig traces contemporary continuities in "Crossing the Bosphorus: Connected Histories of 'Other' Muslims in the Post-Imperial Borderlands of Southeast Europe," *Comparative Studies in Society and History* 58:4 (2016): 908–934; and in the context of the Middle East: Michael Provence, *The Last Ottoman Generation and the Making of the Modern Middle East* (Cambridge, UK: Cambridge University Press, 2017). For non-Muslim loyalties see: Eva Anne Franz, "Catholic Albanian Warriors for the Sultan in Late-Ottoman Kosovo: The Fandi as a Socio-Professional Group and Their Identity Patterns." In *Conflicting Loyalties in the Balkans: The Great Powers, the Ottoman Empire and Nation Building*, edited by Hannes Grandits, Nathalie Clayer, and Robert Pichler, 182–202 (London and New York: I. B. Tauris, 2011).

33. Ann Laura Stoler, *Imperial Debris: On Ruins and Ruination* (Durham: Duke University Press, 2013); Mikhail and Philliou, "The Ottoman Empire and the Imperial Turn"; Nile Green, "Rethinking the 'Middle East' After the Oceanic Turn," *Comparative Studies of South Asia, Africa and the Middle East* 34:3 (2014): 556–564; Karen Barkey, *Empire of Difference: The Ottomans in Comparative Perspective* (New York: Cambridge University Press, 2013).

34. Alavi, *Muslim Cosmopolitanism*; James L. Gelvin and Nile Green, eds., *Global Muslims in the Age of Steam and Print* (Berkeley: University of California Press, 2014); Ahmed, *Afghanistan Rising*; and Lale Can, *Spiritual Subjects: Central Asian Pilgrims and the Ottoman Hajj at the End of Empire* (Stanford: Stanford University Press, 2020).

35. Peter Loizos, "Ottoman Half-Lives: Long-Term Perspectives on Particular Forced Migrations," *Journal of Refugee Studies* 12:3 (1999): 237–263.

36. Nicolas Argenti, ed., *Post-Ottoman Topologies: The Presence of the Past in the Era of the Nation-State* (New York: Berghahn, 2019).

37. Comprehensive works on different aspects of the Habsburg period appeared in Bosnian already in the first half of the twentieth century. See works cited here by Adem Handžić, Hamdija Kapidžić, Hamdija Kreševljaković, Dževad Juzbašić, Muhsin Rizvić, and Nusret Šehić.

38. Peter F. Sugar, *Industrialization of Bosnia-Hercegovina: 1878–1918* (Seattle: University of Washington Press, 1963); Robert J. Donia, *Islam Under the Double Eagle: The Muslims of Bosnia and Hercegovina, 1878–1914* (Boulder: East European Quarterly, 1981); Robin Okey, *Taming Balkan Nationalism: The Habsburg Civilizing Mission in Bosnia, 1878–1914* (Oxford: Oxford University Press, 2007); Hajdarpasic, *Whose Bosnia?*

39. Willem van Schendel, "Geographies of Knowing, Geographies of Ignorance: Jumping Scale in Southeast Asia," *Environment and Planning D: Society and Space* 20 (2002): 655.

40. Ibid.

41. Ahmed, *Afghanistan Rising*, 4; and van Schendel, "Geographies of Knowing," 652.

42. van Schendel, "Geographies of Knowing"; Green, "Rethinking the 'Middle East,'" 557–558; and Magnus Marsden and David Henig, "Muslim Circulations and Networks in West Asia: Ethnographic Perspectives on Transregional Connectivity," *Journal of Eurasian Studies* 10:1 (2019): 11–21.

Chapter 1

1. Muhamed Enveri Kadić, *Tarih-i Enveri*, manuscript, vol. 14, Gazi Husrevbegova Biblioteka (GHB) (1931), 30.

2. Ibid., 34.

3. Sandra Biletić, "Dolazak austro-ugarske vojske u Fojnicu 1878. godine: odlomak iz dnevnika fra Marka Kalamuta," *Bosna Franciscana* 51 (2019): 150.

4. BOA, Y.EE. 103/36 (4 August 1878).

5. Husejn Bračković and Zejnil Fajić, "Mala istorija događaja u Hercegovini," *Prilozi za orijentalnu filologiju* 34 (1984): 187. Karbala refers to the battle in 680 CE when the grandson of Prophet Muhammad, Huseyn ibn Ali, and his family were killed by the Umayyad forces in an ongoing succession struggle. The martyrdom of Muhammad's grandson is commemorated by Sunni and Shi'a Muslims as one of the saddest events in Islamic history.

6. Kadić, *Tarih-i Enveri*, 37–38.

7. Ibid., 43.

8. Ibid., 46, 48.

9. Amand Schweiger-Lerchenfeld, *Bosnien: das Land und seine Bewohner: geschichtlich, geographisch, etnographisch und social-politisch* (Vienna: Verlag von L.C. Zamarski, 1878), 193–194; also, BOA, HR.SYS. 256/2 (11 May 1880).

10. Hamdija Kreševljaković, *Sarajevo u doba okupacije Bosne* (Sarajevo: Naklada piščeva, 1937), 128.

11. Kadić, *Tarih-i Enveri*, 64.

12. Safet Bandžović, "Pljevaljski Muftija Šemsekadić u otporu austrougarskoj okupaciji Bosne i Hercegovine i zaposjedanju novopazarskog sandžaka," *Novopazarski Zbornik* (1992): 100–111.

13. BOA, Y.EE. 103/42 (12 August 1878).

14. A version of this section appeared in Leyla Amzi-Erdoğdular, "Ottoman Bosnia Herzegovina and Its Muslims," in *Routledge Handbook of Balkan and Southeast European History*, eds. John R. Lampe and Ulf Brunnbauer (London: Routledge, 2020).

15. Snježana Buzov, "Ottoman Perceptions of Bosnia as Reflected in the Works of Authors Who Visited or Lived in Bosnia," in *Ottoman Bosnia: A History in Peril,* eds. Marcus Koller and Kemal H. Karpat (Madison: University of Wisconsin Press, 2004), 84–85.

16. On the critical role of Sufi networks in Bosnia's urbanization and Islamization see Ines Aščerić-Todd, *Dervishes and Islam in Bosnia: Sufi Dimensions to the Formation of Bosnian Muslim Society* (Leiden: Brill, 2015); and Adem Handžić, "O ulozi derviša u formiranju gradskih naselja u Bosni u XV stoljeću," *Prilozi za orijentalnu filologiju* 31 (1981): 170–178.

17. For comprehensive studies of Islamization in Bosnia Herzegovina: Nedim Filipović, *Islamizacija u Bosni i Hercegovini* (Tešanj: Centar za kulturu i obazovanje, 2005); Muhamed Hadžijahić, *Porijeklo Bosanskih Muslimana* (Sarajevo:

Bosna, 1990); and a discussion in Mark Pinson and Roy P. Mottahedeh, *The Muslims of Bosnia-Herzegovina* (Cambridge, MA: Harvard Center for Middle Eastern Studies, 1996), 11–19.

18. Halil Inalcık, "Impact of the Annales School on Ottoman Studies and New Findings (with Discussion)," *Review* (Fernand Braudel Center) 1:3/4 (1978): 78. On Ottoman Bosnian population see, Adem Handžić, *Population of Bosnia in the Ottoman Period: A Historical Overview* (Istanbul: Organisation of the Islamic Conference, Research Centre for Islamic History, Art, and Culture, 1994).

19. On Franciscan Ottoman legitimacy and authority in Bosnia see Ana Sekulić, "From a Legal Proof to a Historical Fact: Trajectories of an Ottoman Document in a Franciscan Monastery, Sixteenth to Twentieth Century," *Journal of the Economic and Social History of the Orient* 62:5–6 (2019): 925–962.

20. For the Ottoman institution of *devşirme*, see İsmail H. Uzunçarşılı, *Osmanlı Devlet Teşkilatından Kapukulu Ocakları: Acemi Ocağı Ve Yeniçeri Ocağı* (Ankara: Türk Tarih Kurumu, 1988), 13–30. For *devşirme* in Bosnia Herzegovina, see Hadžijahić, *Porijeklo Bosanskih Muslimana*, 72–74.

21. Ayelet Zoran-Rosen, "The Emergence of a Bosnian Learned Elite: A Case of Ottoman Imperial Integration," *Journal of Islamic Studies* 30:2 (2019): 176–204.

22. Buzov, "Ottoman Perceptions of Bosnia," 86–87.

23. Nedim Filipović, "Ocaklık timars in Bosnia and Herzegovina," *Prilozi za orijentalnu filologiju* 36 (1986): 149–180.

24. Hamdija Kreševljaković, *Kapetanije u Bosni i Hercegovini* (Sarajevo: Naučno Društvo NR Bosne i Hercegovine, 1954).

25. On the practice of holding council, see Fatma Sel Turhan, *Ottoman Empire and the Bosnian Uprising: Janissaries, Modernisation and Rebellion in the Nineteenth Century* (London: I. B. Tauris, 2015), 105–112.

26. On the causes and consequences of the war, see Enes Pelidija, *Banjalučki boj iz 1737: uzroci i posljedice* (Sarajevo: El-Kalem, 2003); and Ömer Bosnavî, *Tarih-i Bosna der zaman-i Hekimzade Ali Paşa* (İstanbul: Süleyman Efendi'nin Matbaası, 1876).

27. Wendy Bracewell, "Friends, Lovers, Rivals, Enemies: Blood-Brotherhood on an Early-Modern Balkan Frontier," *Caiete de Antropologie Istorică* 3 (2003): 104; on the changing political and social fabric in the eighteenth century, see Edin Hajdarpasic, "Frontier Anxieties: Toward a Social History of Muslim-Christian Relations on the Ottoman-Habsburg Border," *Austrian History Yearbook* 51 (2020): 25–38.

28. Elma Korić, "Bosansko pograničje u vrijeme Dubičkog rata, 1788–1791," *Prilozi za orijentalnu filologiju* 65 (2016): 223.

29. Noel Malcolm, *Bosnia: A Short History* (New York: New York University

Press, 1994), 87. Also, Virginia H Aksan, *Ottoman Wars, 1700–1870: An Empire Besieged* (London: Routledge, 2014), 92.

30. Galib Šljivo, "Prvi pokušaj bosanskih krajišnika da vrate Cetingrad u sastav bosanskog vilajeta (26. april 1809–14. maj 1810)," *Prilozi* 31 (2002): 113.

31. Ibid., 114.

32. Ibid., 117–130.

33. Ibid. 130–131, according to Austrian sources.

34. For the global context, see Immanuel Wallerstein, Hale Decdeli, and Reşat Kasaba, "The Incorporation of the Ottoman Empire into the World Economy," in *The Ottoman Empire and the World-Economy*, ed. Huri İslamoğlu-İnan (Cambridge, UK: Cambridge University Press, 2004), 88–100.

35. Huri İslamoğlu and Çağlar Keyder, "Agenda for Ottoman History," in *The Ottoman Empire and the World-Economy*, ed. Huri İslamoğlu-İnan (Cambridge, UK: Cambridge University Press, 2004), 58–59. More broadly, Ali Yaycioglu, *Partners of the Empire: The Crisis of the Ottoman Order in the Age of Revolutions* (Stanford: Stanford University Press, 2016).

36. Hajdarpasic, "Frontier Anxieties," 26.

37. Ahmed S. Aličić, "Manuscript *Ahval-i-Bosna* by Muhamed Emin Isević (Early 19th Century)," *Prilozi za orijentalnu filologiju* 50 (2002): 258–259.

38. Ibid.

39. Turhan, *Ottoman Empire and the Bosnian Uprising*, 341.

40. BOA, HAT 406/21191 (21 March 1831), cited in Turhan, *Ottoman Empire and the Bosnian Uprising*, 192.

41. Turhan, *Ottoman Empire and the Bosnian Uprising*, 358–359.

42. According to Ahmed Cevdet Pasha, a distinguished Tanzimat statesman, intellectual, and scholar, even in the "problematic" northwestern border region army volunteers exceeded quotas. In his memoirs, Cevdet Pasha commented: "Look at these simple borderland people, how they hold the sultan sacred, and what reverence they show to imperial orders." Ahmed Cevdet Paşa and Cavid Baysun, *Tezakir* (Ankara: Türk Tarih Kurumu Basımevi, 1991), 86.

43. Ibid., 38–39.

44. On Osman Pasha, see a contemporary account by Osman Pasha's confidant, Josef Koetschet, *Osman Pascha, Der Letzte Grosse Wesier Bosniens, Und Seine Nachfolger* (Sarajevo: Studnička, 1909).

45. Raymond Detrez, "Reluctance and Determination: The Prelude to the Austro-Hungarian Occupation of Bosnia Herzegovina in 1878," in *Wechselwirkungen: Austria-Hungary, Bosnia-Herzegovina, and the Western Balkans, 1878–1918*, eds. Clemens Ruthner, Diana Reynolds-Cordileone, Ursula Reber, and Raymond Detrez (New York: Peter Lang, 2015), 27.

46. Malcolm, *Bosnia*, 132.

47. Arthur Evans, *Through Bosnia and the Herzegovina on Foot* (London: Longmans, 1876), 86–87; and Hasan Škapur, *Odnos osmanskih vlasti prema Bosanskom ustanku, 1875–1878* (Sarajevo: Centar za osmanističke studije, 2017). Representative reports in HR.SYS. 250/1, for northern cross-border activity: document 96 (25 May 1876) and 323 (29 May 1877).

48. Edin Hajdarpasic, *Whose Bosnia?: Nationalism and Political Imagination in the Balkans, 1840–1914* (Ithaca: Cornell University Press, 2015), 105–114.

49. For detail, see David Harris, *A Diplomatic History of the Balkan Crisis of 1875–1878* (Stanford: Stanford University Press, 1936); and Robert W. Seton-Watson, *The Role of Bosnia in International Politics, 1875–1914* (London: Milford, 1931).

50. Evans, *Through Bosnia and the Herzegovina on Foot*, 250. See also, Janos Asboth, *An Official Tour Through Bosnia and Herzegovina* (Lon: Swan Sonnenschein, 1890); Edmund Spencer, *Travels in European Turkey: Through Bosnia, Servia, Bulgaria, Macedonia, Thrace, Albania, and Epirus* (London: Hurst and Blackett, 1853); and Midhat Šamić, *Francuski putnici u Bosni i Hercegovini u XIX stoljeću (1836–1878) i njihovi utisci o njoj* (Sarajevo: Veselin Masleša, 1981).

51. Peter F. Sugar, *Industrialization of Bosnia-Hercegovina: 1878–1918* (Seattle: University of Washington Press, 1963), 20.

52. Dževad Juzbašić, *Politika i privreda u Bosni i Hercegovini pod austrougarskom upravom* (Sarajevo: ANUBiH, 2002), 50.

53. Ibid., 52.

54. Maureen Healy, "Europe on the Sava: Austrian Encounters with "Turks" in Bosnia," *Austrian History Yearbook* 51 (2020): 81.

55. Juzbašić, *Politika i privreda*, 14.

56. On these debates in the monarchy, see Pieter Judson, *Exclusive Revolutionaries: Liberal Politics, Social Experience, and National Identity in the Austrian Empire, 1848–1914* (Ann Arbor: University of Michigan Press, 1996), 184–191.

57. Schweiger-Lerchenfeld, *Bosnien: das Land und seine Bewohner*, 193–194.

58. BOA, Y.EE. 103/29 (9 July 1878).

59. BOA, Y.PRK.EŞA. 1/28 (19 September 1878).

60. BOA, Y.EE. 76/55 (15 August 1878).

61. BOA, Y.EE. 103/32 (25 July 1878). He also conveyed that nine Hungarian soldiers who refused to fight were executed. BOA, Y.EE. 103/50 (21 August 1878).

62. BOA, Y.EE. 103/45 (11 August 1878).

63. BOA, Y.PRK.ASK. 2/9 (16 September 1878).

64. BOA, Y.EE. 103/33 (27 July 1878).

65. BOA, HR.TO. 498/38 (7 October 1878).

66. Juzbašić, *Politika i privreda,* 479.
67. BOA, Y.EE. 3/67 (2 October 1878).
68. BOA, Y.EE. 5/1 (3 November 1878).
69. BOA, Y.EE. 103/56 (30 October 1878); Y. PRK. ASK. 2/7 (7 September 1878).
70. BOA, Y.EE. 3/67 (2 October 1878).
71. BOA, I.MMS. 60/2849 (14 February 1879).
72. Ibid.
73. BOA, Y.EE. 77/68 (19 April 1879).
74. Isa Blumi, *Reinstating the Ottomans: Alternative Balkan Modernities, 1800–1912* (Basingstoke: Palgrave Macmillan, 2011), 139–143.
75. BOA, Y.A.HUS. 160/86 (5 April 1879).
76. Mary Edith Durham, *Twenty Years of Balkan Tangle* (London: G. Allen and Unwin, 1920), 164.
77. BOA, Y.EE. 77/68 (19 April 1879).
78. BOA, Muahedenameler, 56/15 (21 April 1879).
79. BOA, Y.PRK.HR. 7/47 (17 February 1884); MV 17/10 (9 February 1887); Y.PRK.HR. 11/64 (10 February 1889).
80. James G. C. Minchin, *The Growth of Freedom in the Balkan Peninsula: Notes of a Traveler in Montenegro, Bosnia, Servia, Bulgaria and Greece* (London, 1886), 51.
81. Nedim Ipek, *Rumeli'den Anadolu'ya Türk Göçleri, 1877–1890* (Ankara: Türk Tarih Kurumu Basımevi, 1994), 40.
82. Fikret Karčić, "Pitanje javnopravnog priznanja islama u jugoslovenskim krajevima nakon prestanka osmanlijske vlasti," *Anali Gazi Husrev-begove biblioteke* XI-XII (1985): 114–115; and Blumi, *Reinstating the Ottomans,* ch. 4.
83. Nicole Immig, "The 'New' Muslim Minorities in Greece: Between Emigration and Political Participation, 1881–1886," *Journal of Muslim Minority Affairs* 29:4 (2009): 511–522.
84. Mehmed-Beg Kapetanović Ljubušak, *Budućnost ili napredak Muhamedovaca u Bosni i Hercegovini* (Sarajevo: Spindler & Löschner, 1893), 5.
85. See Martti Koskenniemi, *The Gentle Civilizer of Nations: The Rise and Fall of International Law 1870–1960* (Cambridge, UK: Cambridge University Press, 2010); and Turan Kayaoglu, *Legal Imperialism: Sovereignty and Extraterritoriality in Japan, the Ottoman Empire, and China* (Cambridge, UK: Cambridge University Press, 2014).
86. Mustafa Serdar Palabıyık, "The Emergence of the Idea of 'International Law' in the Ottoman Empire Before the Treaty of Paris (1856)," *Middle Eastern Studies* 50:2 (2014): 233–251; and Will Smiley, *From Slaves to Prisoners of War: The Ottoman Empire, Russia, and International Law* (Oxford: Oxford University Press, 2018).

87. Aimee M. Genell, "The Well-Defended Domains: Eurocentric International Law and the Making of the Ottoman Office of Legal Counsel," *Journal of the Ottoman and Turkish Studies Association* 3:2 (2016): 258–260.

88. Aimee M. Genell, "Autonomous Provinces and the Problem of 'Semi-Sovereignty' in European International Law," *Journal of Balkan and Near Eastern Studies* 18:6 (2016): 538. On late Ottoman autonomy, see Elektra Kostopoulou, "Armed Negotiations: The Institutionalization of the Late Ottoman Locality," *Comparative Studies of South Asia, Africa and the Middle East* 33:3 (2013): 295–309.

89. Robert J. Donia, "The Proximate Colony Bosnia-Herzegovina Under Austro-Hungarian Rule," in *Wechselwirkungen: Austria-Hungary, Bosnia-Herzegovina, and the Western Balkans, 1878–1918*, eds. Clemens Ruthner, Diana Reynolds-Cordileone, Ursula Reber, and Raymond Detrez (New York: Peter Lang, 2015), 67–82.

90. On the conceptualization of the colonial project, see the full volume Clemens Ruthner, Diana Reynolds-Cordileone, Ursula Reber, and Raymond Detrez, eds., *Wechselwirkungen*; and Clemens Ruthner and Tamara Scheer, eds., *Bosnien-Herzegowina und Österreich-Ungarn: Annäherungen an eine Kolonie* (Tübingen: Narr Francke Attempto, 2018).

91. Robert Donia, *Islam Under the Double Eagle* (Boulder: East European Monographs, 1981), 14.

92. Larry Wolff, *The Idea of Galicia: History and Fantasy in Habsburg Political Culture* (Stanford: Stanford University Press, 2010), 6.

93. Robin Okey, *Taming Balkan Nationalism: The Habsburg Civilizing Mission in Bosnia, 1878–1914* (Oxford: Oxford University Press, 2007), 26–28.

94. Most notably, Eugen Weber, *Peasants into Frenchmen: The Modernization of Rural France 1870–1914* (Stanford: Stanford University Press, 1976).

95. Pieter M. Judson, *The Habsburg Empire: A New History* (Cambridge, MA: Harvard University Press, 2016), 272.

96. Daniel L. Unowsky, *The Pomp and Politics of Patriotism: Imperial Celebrations in Habsburg Austria, 1848–1916* (West Lafayette: Purdue University Press, 2005); and Laurence Cole and Daniel L. Unowsky, eds., *The Limits of Loyalty: Imperial Symbolism, Popular Allegiances, and State Patriotism in the Late Habsburg Monarchy* (New York: Berghahn, 2009).

97. Selim Deringil, *The Well-Protected Domains: Ideology and the Legitimation of Power in the Ottoman Empire 1876–1909* (London: I. B. Tauris, 2011); Michelle U. Campos, *Ottoman Brothers: Muslims, Christians, and Jews in Early Twentieth-Century Palestine* (Stanford: Stanford University Press, 2010); and a comparative study, Karen Barkey and Mark von Hagen, eds., *After Empire: Multiethnic Societies and Nation Building in the Soviet Union and the Russian, Ottoman, and Habsburg Empires* (Boulder: Westview Press, 1997).

98. Hajdarpasic, *Whose Bosnia?*, 163.

99. BOA. HR.SYS. 256/2 (11 May 1880).

100. BOA, Y.EE. 43/73 (22 August 1882). For a discussion on Kállay's own views regarding Bosnian notables and their potential conversion, see Okey, *Taming Balkan Nationalism*, 60–61.

101. Ebru Boyar, *Ottomans, Turks and the Balkans: Empire Lost, Relations Altered* (London: I. B. Tauris, 2007), 14–15.

102. For example: BOA, Y.MTV. 39/50 (26 June 1889); MV. 44/27 (13 June 1889), in *Bosna-Hersek ile Ilgili arşiv belgeleri*, 112–116.

103. Edward W. Said, *Orientalism* (New York: Vintage Books, 1978).

104. Larry Wolff, *Inventing Eastern Europe: The Map of Civilization on the Mind of the Enlightenment* (Stanford: Stanford University Press, 1994); and Maria Todorova, *Imagining the Balkans* (New York: Oxford University Press, 2009).

105. Blumi, *Reinstating the Ottomans*, 58–59. Also, Ussama Makdisi, *The Culture of Sectarianism, Community, History and Violence in Nineteenth-Century Ottoman Lebanon* (Berkeley: University of California Press, 2000), 67–69.

106. For example, BOA, HR.HMŞ.İŞO. 177/10 (24 December 1892); DH.MKT. 563123 (20 August 1902); HR.HMŞ.İŞO. 199/59 (1 March 1910); HR.SYS. 141/49 (3 March 1911); A.MKT.MHM 608/10 (21 May 1912); HR.HMŞ.İŞO. 199/59 (1 March 1910).

107. Blumi, *Reinstating the Ottomans*, 157–159. On the role of American missionaries, see Nevila Pahumi, "Constructing Difference: American Protestantism, Christian Workers, and Albanian-Greek Relations in Late Ottoman Europe," *Journal of Modern Greek Studies* 36:2 (2018): 293–328.

108. Isa Blumi, "The Great Powers' Fixation on Ottoman Albania in the Administration of the Post-Berlin Balkans, 1878–1908," in *Ottoman-Russian War of 1877–1878*, ed. Ömer Turan (Ankara: Middle East Technical University Press, 2006), 191–192. Theodor Ippen, a Habsburg Albanology scholar and diplomat—a consul in Shkodër, Jerusalem, Istanbul, and Athens—had a number of his works on Albanian history and ethnography published by the Habsburg provincial press in Sarajevo. His ethnographic map of Albania was used for negotiating borders at establishment of independent Albania in 1913, while a flamboyant Hungarian aristocrat, Baron Franc Nopcsa, who created the first geological map of Albania, hoped to become its first king. Robert Elsie, "The Viennese Scholar Who Almost Became King of Albania: Baron Franz Nopcsa and His Contribution to Albanian Studies," *East European Quarterly* 33:3 (1999): 327–345.

109. Ruthner, et al., *Wechselwirkungen*, 10.

110. Sugar, *Industrialization of Bosnia-Hercegovina*, 29.

111. Kreševljaković, *Sarajevo u doba okupacije*, 11. Such expropriation came after empire, in both Yugoslav states, with drastic consequences for Muslim landlords, small and large.

112. Aydin Babuna, "The Berlin Treaty, Bosnian Muslims, and Nationalism," in *War and Diplomacy: The Russo-Turkish War of 1877–1878 and the Treaty of Berlin*, ed. M. Hakan Yavuz (Salt Lake City: University of Utah Press, 2011), 208, 219–220; Donia, *Islam Under the Double Eagle*, xii.

113. BOA, BEO Gelen Giden Kataloğu, 1003/63–1, 70–71 (29 March 1896). Also, HR.HMŞ.İŞO. 20/25 (30 November 1894).

114. BOA, HR.SYS. 259/1–65 (27 April 1903); HR.HMŞ.İŞO. 20/28 (3 March 1905).

115. Amila Kasumović, "Zemaljska pripadnost stanovnika Bosne i Hercegovine u prvim godinama austrougarske uprave," *Historijska traganja* 6 (2010): 14. Archive of Bosnia Herzegovina (ABiH), ZMF 10441, 10947 (29 May 1880), and ZMF 5825 (1880); on Ottoman subjects, ABiH, ZMF 6263, 7061, 7278 (1880).

116. On the Ottoman Nationality Law (*Tabiiyet-i Osmaniye Kanunnamesi*), see Will Hanley, "What Ottoman Nationality Was and Was Not," *Journal of the Ottoman and Turkish Studies Association* 3:2 (2016): 277–298.

117. HR.HMŞ.İŞO. 20/31 (23 December 1898)

118. Hanley, "What Ottoman Nationality Was," 286.

119. Umut Özsu, "The Ottoman Empire, the Origins of Extraterritoriality, and International Legal Theory," in *The Oxford Handbook of the Theory of International Law*, eds. Anne Orford and Florian Hoffman (Oxford: Oxford University Press, 2016), 129.

120. Malte Fuhrmann, "Vagrants, Prostitutes, and Bosnians: Making and Unmaking European Supremacy in Ottoman Southeast Europe," in *Conflicting Loyalties in the Balkans: The Great Powers, the Ottoman Empire and Nation-Building*, eds. Hannes Granditis, Nathalie Clayer, and Robert Pichler (London and New York: I. B. Tauris, 2011), 43.

121. BOA, Y.A.HUS. 411/107 (27 December 1900); HR.SYS. 259/1, 26–31 (27 June 1906).

122. For such practices by contemporary monarchs, also see John Plunkett, *Queen Victoria: First Media Monarch* (Oxford: Oxford University Press, 2003); and Richard Wortman, *Scenarios of Power: Myth and Ceremony in Russian Monarchy* (Princeton: Princeton University Press, 1995).

123. BOA, HR.SYS. 259/1 (8 April 1901).

124. For example: BOA, Y.PRK.MYD. 15/81 (1 December 1894) and Y.PRK.AZJ. 41/95 (19 April 1901).

Chapter 2

1. The descendants of the Yanoun Bosnians moved to Nablus but still own most of the land in Yanoun.

2. The Yugoslav anthropologist Nina Seferović interviewed the descendants and relatives of Herzegovinian migrants in Jordan, Lebanon, and Yugoslavia in

the late 1970s; in Nina Seferović, "Kolonija Hercegovačkih Muslimana u Kajzeriju u Palestini," *Zbornik radova Etnografskog instituta* 12 (1981): 47–64.

3. Ilan Pappé, *The Ethnic Cleansing of Palestine* (Oxford: Oneworld, 2007), 75.

4. Pieter M. Judson, *The Habsburg Empire: A New History* (Cambridge, MA: Harvard University Press, 2016), 275.

5. Jared Manasek, "Protection, Repatriation and Categorization: Refugees and Empire at the End of the Nineteenth Century," *Journal of Refugee Studies* 30:2 (2017): 301–317.

6. For Ottoman reports, see BOA, HR, SYS. 250/1 doc. 221 (11 December 1875); doc. 152 (16 March 1876); doc. 146 (1 April 1876); doc. 95 (22 April 1876); doc. 93 (27 April 1876), doc. 96 (25 April 1876); doc. 323 (29 May 1877/18 May 1878) in *Bosna-Hersek ile ilgili arşiv belgeleri*, 50–69; and Hasan Škapur, *Odnos osmanskih vlasti prema Bosanskom ustanku, 1875–1878* (Sarajevo: Centar za osmanističke studije, 2017).

7. Justin McCarthy, "Archival Sources Concerning Serb Rebellions in Bosnia 1875–76," in *Ottoman Bosnia: A History in Peril*, ed. Markus Koller and Kemal H. Karpat (Madison: University of Wisconsin Press, 2004), 144. Also, Justin McCarthy, "Ottoman Bosnia, 1800–1878," in *The Muslims of Bosnia-Herzegovina: Their Historical Development from the Middle Ages to the Dissolution of Yugoslavia*, ed. Mark Pinson (Cambridge, MA: Harvard University Press, 1994), 54–83.

8. TNA/FO 424/75 (4 October 1878) in Bilâl N. Şimşir, *Rumeli'den Türk Göçleri: Belgeler/Emigrations Turques Des Balkans/Turkish Emigrations from the Balkans: Documents*, vol. I (Ankara: Türk Tarih Kurumu Basımevi, 1989), 629.

9. TNA/FO 424/77 (7 December 1878) in Şimşir, *Rumeli'den Türk Göçleri*, 714–715.

10. Hana Younis, "Brez nikoga u dijaru gurbetu," *Prilozi* 45 (2016): 51.

11. Ibid., 54–55.

12. Ibid., 54.

13. Ibid., 55.

14. Robert Donia, *Islam Under the Double Eagle* (Boulder: East European Monographs, 1981), 166.

15. BOA, Y.A.RES. 3/7 (27 April 1879).

16. BOA, Y.A.HUS. 163/29 (17 December 1879).

17. BOA, Y.A.HUS. 163/29 (6 January 1880).

18. BOA, HR.SYS. 256/2 (11 May 1880) in *Bosna-Hersek ile ilgili arşiv belgeleri*, 86–89.

19. Ibid.

20. Kemal H. Karpat, *Studies on Ottoman Social and Political History: Selected Articles and Essays* (Leiden and Boston: Brill, 2002), 702.

21. Kosovo, North Macedonia, and northeastern Greece today.

22. Şimşir, *Rumeli'den Türk Göçleri*, 737.

23. Izet Šabotić, "Bosanske muhadžerske enklave u Makedoniji: Nekad i sad," *Glasnik Arhiva i Arhivističkog Udruženja Bosne i Hercegovine* 48 (2018): 134.

24. TNA/FO 424/79 Confidential 3910 (26 December 1878) in Şimşir, *Rumeli'den Türk Göçleri*, 742.

25. See Hamdija Kreševljaković, *Sarajevo u doba austrougarske okupacije 1878–1914* (Sarajevo: Naklada piščeva, 1937), appendix compares consumer prices before and after the occupation in Sarajevo.

26. Safet Bandžović, *Iseljavanje Bošnjaka u Tursku* (Sarajevo: Institut za istraživanje zločina protiv čovječnosti i međunarodnog prava, 2006), 127.

27. Nehrudin Rebihić, "Između orijentalizma i okcidentalizma: Narativi o iseljavanju Bošnjaka u Tursku u bošnjačkoj književnosti prve polovine 20. stoljeća," *Društvene i humanističke studije: časopis Filozofskog fakulteta u Tuzli* 3:12 (2020): 31–58.

28. Donia, *Islam Under the Double Eagle*, 8–10.

29. For an Ottoman report of the events, see BOA, Y.A.HUS. 169/87 (16 February 1882).

30. For Ottoman reaction see: BOA, Y.A.HUS. 167/46 (20 April 1881); Y.A.HUS. 169/4 (25 November 1881); Y.A.HUS. 169/13 (27 November 1881).

31. BOA, Y.PRK.MŞ. 5/108 (20 April 1895).

32. *Sarajevski list* (4 November 1881) and (11 November 1881).

33. Omer Nakičević, *Istorijski razvoj institucije Rijaseta* (Sarajevo: Rijaset Islamske zajednice u RBiH, 1996), 83. The same mufti was also engaged in encouraging conscription into the Ottoman reformed military during Tanzimat implementation in Bosnia.

34. Quoted in Dževada Šuško, "Bosniaks & Loyalty: Responses to the Conscription Law in Bosnia and Herzegovina 1881/82," *The Hungarian Historical Review* 3:3 (2014): 538.

35. Šuško, "Bosniaks & Loyalty," 537; Kapidžić, *Hercegovački ustanak 1882* (Sarajevo: V. Masleša, 1958), 81.

36. Ahmed Cevdet Paşa and Cavid Baysun, *Tezakir* (Ankara: Türk Tarih Kurumu Basımevi, 1991), 44.

37. BOA, Y.A.HUS. 380/11 (28 December 1897); DH. MKT. 785/53 (2 November 1903); DH.MKT 1026/59 (22 November 1905).

38. BOA, HR. HMS. ISO 165/16 (11 November 1882).

39. Tomislav Kraljačić, "Iseljavanje muslimana iz Bosne i Hercegovine u Albaniju za vrijeme austrougarske uprave," in *Stanovništvo slovenskog porijekla u Albaniji: zbornik radova sa međunarodnog naučnog skupa održanog u Cetinju 21,*

22. *i 23. juna 1990,* ed. Jovan R. Bojović (Titograd, Montenegro: Istorijski Institut SR Crne Gore, 1991), np. n.4.

40. Ibid.

41. BOA, Y.PRK.ASK 13/23 (7 July 1882).

42. BOA, Y.A.HUS. 169/87 (17 April 1882).

43. Galib Šljivo, "Sprovodjenje zakona o vojnoj obavezi u banjalučkom i bihaćkom okrugu 1881–1882," in *Naučni Skup 100 godina ustanka u Hercegovini 1882. godine: Sarajevo, 21–22. X 1982,* ed. Hamdija Ćemerlić et al. (Sarajevo: Akademija nauka i umjetnosti Bosne i Hercegovine, 1983), 121.

44. Vojislav Bogićević, "Emigracija Muslimana Bosne i Hercegovine u Tursku u doba austro-ugarske vladavine 1878–1918," *Historijski zbornik* 1:4/3 (1950): 183–184.

45. BOA, A.MKT. MHM 486/92 (12 March 1882)

46. Kemal H. Karpat, "Migration of the Bosnian Muslims to the Ottoman State, 1878–1914: An Account Based on Turkish Sources," in *Ottoman Bosnia: A History in Peril,* eds. Markus Koller and Kemal H. Karpat (Madison: University of Wisconsin Press, 2004), 130.

47. BOA, Y.PRK.ASK. 10/55 (17 January 1882).

48. For an illustrated overview, see Christoph Neumayer and Erwin A. Schmidl, *The Emperor's Bosniaks: The Bosnian-Herzegovinian Troops in the K.u.k. Army History and Uniforms 1878 to 1918* (Vienna: Militaria, 2008).

49. BOA, BEO 44/3262 (4 August 1892).

50. BOA, Y.MTV. 137/68 (25 February 1896).

51. BOA, BEO. 2314/173503 (16 April 1904).

52. BOA, DH.EUM.EMN. 15/26 (6 January 1913).

53. For example, there were 35 Catholic churches in Bosnia Herzegovina before the occupation; by 1900 the number rose to 135. Tomislav Kraljačić, *Kalajev režim u Bosni i Hercegovini 1882–1903* (Sarajevo: Veselin Masleša, 1987), 316.

54. Hamdija Kapidžić, *Hercegovački ustanak 1882* (Sarajevo: V. Masleša, 1958), 72–73.

55. ABiH, Kv (Konverzije) contains administration's files and statistics regarding conversions in Bosnia Herzegovina, 1878–1910.

56. Hivzija Hasandedić, "Četiri slučaja pokrštavanja Muslimanki u Hercegovini za vrijeme austrougarske uprave," *Glasnik Rijaseta Islamske Zajednice u SFRJ* 54 (1991): 726–730.

57. Kraljačić, *Kalajev režim,* 322.

58. For comparative attitudes of the state see, Selim Deringil, *Conversion and Apostasy in the Late Ottoman Empire* (Cambridge, UK: Cambridge University Press, 2012).

59. Zoran Grijak, *Politicka djelatnost vrhbosanskog nadbiskupa Josipa Stadlera* (Zagreb: Hrvatski institut za povijest, 2001), 573–579.
60. Ibid.
61. Kraljačić, *Kalajev režim,* 323.
62. Ibid., 328–329, 322.
63. Ibid., 329. For discussion of conversions in the late Ottoman–Habsburg period, see Philippe Gelez, "Vjerska preobraćenja u Bosni i Hercegovini (c.1800–1918)," *Historijska Traganja* 2 (2008): 17–75.
64. BOA, A.MTZ.BN. 1/13 (13 May 1901).
65. Bandžović, *Iseljavanje,* 139.
66. For colonists' distribution, see Josef K. Heimfelsen, *Die Deutschen Kolonien in Bosnien* (Wien: Gerold, 1911).
67. For example, Frater Franz Pfanner, "Bosnien, ein Land für Ansiedlung," *Weckstimmen für das katholische Volk* 9:11 (1878): 4. Frater Franz was a Trappist monk who founded the Kloster Maria Stern in 1869 near Banja Luka in Bosnia Herzegovina. That he went on to South Africa after Bosnia further points to the trans-colonial missionary networks that included Austria-Hungary.
68. For intentions and methods, see contemporary discussion in Alfred Brenning, *Innere Kolonisation* (Leipzig: B. G. Teubner, 1909).
69. Priscilla T. Gonslaves, "A Study of the Habsburg Agricultural Programmes in Bosanska Krajina, 1878–1914," *The Slavonic and East European Review* 63:3 (1985): 367.
70. Šaćir Filandra, *Bošnjačka politika u XX. stoljeću* (Sarajevo: Sejtarija, 1998), 29.
71. BOA, MV. 121/15 (21 October 1908).
72. ABiH ZMF Präs BH 1308/09 (16 May 1909).
73. Ibid.
74. Bandžović, *Iseljavanje,* 190–191.
75. Ibid., 191.
76. ABiH ZMF Präs BH 280/10 (22 February 1910).
77. ABiH ZVS 47 20-2 1911.
78. ABiH ZMF Präs BH 280/10 (22 February 1910).
79. ABiH ZVS 38 20–15 1910 (29 January 1910)
80. BOA, HR.HMŞ.IŞO.29/2–4, 20/1 a, b (10 September 1910), in *Bosna ile ilgili arşiv belgeleri,* 315–316.
81. BOA, HR.HMŞ.IŞO. 29/2–4, 18/2 a, b (11 October 1910), in *Bosna ile ilgili arşiv belgeleri,* 317–318.
82. BOA, HR.HMŞ.IŞO. 29/2–1, 16/1, 2 (1 October 1912); and HR.HMŞ.IŞO. 29/2–1, 14/1, 2 (2 January 1913), in *Bosna ile ilgili arşiv belgeleri,* 323–327.

83. BOA, HR.HMŞ.IŞO. 29/2–4, 1 a, b, c (1 December 1911), in *Bosna ile ilgili arşiv belgeleri*, 321–323.

84. See cases in ABiH ZVS 43 20–134 and 20–120 (1913).

85. Ryan Gingeras, *Eternal Dawn: Turkey in the Age of Atatürk* (New York: Oxford University Press, 2020), 34.

86. ABiH ZMF Präs BH 280/1910 (22 February 1910).

87. ABiH ZMF Präs BH 1175/1910 (19 July 1910).

88. On the Macedonian Question, see Ipek Yosmaoglu, *Blood Ties: Religion, Violence, and the Politics of Nationhood in Ottoman Macedonia, 1878–1908* (Ithaca: Cornell University Press, 2013).

89. M. Şükrü Hanioğlu, *Preparation for a Revolution: The Young Turks, 1902–1908* (New York: Oxford University Press, 2001), 44 and n.137.

90. BOA, Y.EE.KP. 35/3433 (28 January 1911).

91. Mustafa Imamović, *Pravni položaj i unutrašnjo-politički razvitak Bosne i Hercegovine od 1878. do 1914* (Sarajevo: Bosanski Kulturni Centar, 1997), 110–111.

92. Esad Zgodić, *Bosanska politička misao: Austrougarsko doba* (Sarajevo: DES, 2003), 33.

93. "Agitator na seobu," *Musavat* (18 January 1911): 4.

94. ABiH ZVS 100 20–47 1911 (13 July 1911).

95. Mary Edith Durham, *Twenty Years of Balkan Tangle* (London: G. Allen and Unwin, 1920), 163.

96. "Iseljavanje kod nas," *Srpska Riječ* 31 (26 February 1906): 1–2; "Kako je u Americi?," *Srpska Riječ* 43 (19 March 1906): 2–3; "Seljenje," *Srpska Riječ* 45 (22 March 1906): 1.

97. BOA, Y.PRK.HR. 17/40 (29 June 1893); Y.A.HUS. 407/9 (1 June 1900).

98. Samira Puskar, *Bosnian Americans of Chicagoland* (Charleston: Arcadia, 2007).

99. Bandžović, *Iseljavanje*, 146.

100. ABiH ZMF Präs BH 280/1910 (22 February 1910).

101. Nusret Šehić, *Autonomni pokret Muslimana za vrijeme austrougarske uprave u Bosni i Hercegovini* (Sarajevo: Svjetlost, 1980), 142–143.

102. On the difficulties of Ottoman citizens traveling to Bosnia, see BOA, HR.HMŞ.IŞO. 20/28 (26 February 1904).

103. Tomislav Kraljačić, "Povratak muslimanskih iseljenika iz Bosne i Hercegovine u toku prvog balkanskog rata," in *Migracije i Bosna i Hercegovina: materijali s naučnog skupa migracioni procesi i Bosna i Hercegovina od ranog srednjeg vijeka do najnovijih dana—njihov uticaj i posljedice na demografska kretanja i promjene u našoj zemlji, održanog u Sarajevu 26. i 27. oktobra 1989. godine*, ed. Nusret Šehić (Sarajevo: Institut za istoriju u Sarajevu, 1990).

104. BOA, HR.HMŞ.İŞO. 29/2-1, 23 a, b (13 February 1911), in *Bosna ile ilgili arşiv belgeleri*, 319–320.

105. BOA, A.MKT.MHM. 513/12 (21 April 1901).

106. ABiH, ZVS 100 20–47 1911.

107. Kraljačić, "Povratak," 152–153.

108. Ibid., 154.

109. Ibid., 155.

110. Noel Malcolm, *Kosovo: A Short History* (New York: New York University Press, 1998), 258.

111. Kraljačić, "Povratak," 157.

112. Ibid., 158.

113. AbiH ZVS 43 20–120 1913.

114. AbiH ZVS 41 20–90 1913. 1 dunum = 1,000 square meters; from Ottoman Turkish dönüm.

115. Joint Ministry of Finance report on the administration in Bosnia Herzegovina contains statistical information on migrants and returnees beginning in 1881; *Izvjestaj o upravi Bosne i Hercegovine* (Zagreb: Zajednicko Ministarstvo Financija, 1906), 9–10.

116. Nikola Jarak, *Poljoprivredna politika Austro-Ugarske u Bosni i Hercegovini i zemljoradničko zadrugarstvo* (Sarajevo: Naučno društvo NR Bosne i Hercegovine, 1956), 41.

117. Ferdinand Schmid, *Bosnien und Herzegovina: Unter Der Verwaltung Österreich-Ungarns* (Leipzig: Veit, 1914), 249–250.

118. Ibid., 249.

119. Karpat, "Migration of the Bosnian Muslims to the Ottoman State," 139–140.

120. Đorđe Pejanović estimated 140,000; Vojislav Bogićević, 150,000; Sulejman Smlatić, 160,000; and Mustafa Imamović and Enes Pelidija, 180,000; as cited in Safet Bandžović, "Uzroci muhadžirskih pokreta iz Bosne i Hercegovina 1878–1912," *Almanah-Časopis za pručavanje, prezentaciju i zaštitu kulturno-istorijske baštine Bošnjaka Muslimana* 48/49 (2010): 102–103.

121. Dževad Juzbašić, "O iseljavanu iz Bosne I Hercegovine poslije aneksije 1908. godine," in *Migracije i Bosna i Hercegovina: Naučni skup Migracioni procesi i Bosna i Hercegovina od ranog srednjeg vijeka do najnovijih dana—njihov uticaj i posljedice na demografska kretanja i promjene u našoj zemlji, održan 1989*, ed. Nusret Šehić (Sarajevo: Institut za Istoriju, 1990), 617.

122. Jarak, *Poljoprivredna politika*, 41.

123. Ibid.

124. BOA, Y.A.HUS. 426/15 (15 March 1903).

125. BOA, MV 109/52 (7 June 1904).
126. AbiH ZMF Präs BH 280/1910 (22 February 1910).
127. Reşat Kasaba, *A Moveable Empire: Ottoman Nomads, Migrants & Refugees* (Seattle: University of Washington Press, 2009), 11–12.
128. Eric D. Weitz, "From the Vienna to the Paris System: International Politics and the Entangled Histories of Human Rights, Forced Deportations, and Civilizing Missions," *American Historical Review* 113:5 (2008): 1320–1321.
129. Anna M. Mirkova, "'Population Politics' at the End of Empire: Migration and Sovereignty in Ottoman Eastern Rumelia, 1877–1886," *Comparative Studies in Society and History* 55:4 (2013): 962, 965–966.
130. Before 1877, 1.5 million Muslims or 37 percent of the population lived in the region that became Bulgaria. Justin McCarthy, *Death and Exile: The Ethnic Cleansing of Ottoman Muslims, 1821–1922* (Princeton: Darwin Press, 1999), 89–91.
131. Karpat, *Studies on Ottoman Social and Political History*, 377.
132. Halil Inalcık and Donald Quataert, eds., *An Economic and Social History of the Ottoman Empire*, vol. 2 (Cambridge, UK: Cambridge University Press, 1997), 793.
133. Karpat, *Studies on Ottoman Social and Political History*, 322. On Muhacirin Komisyonu, see Erdal Taşbaş, *Halifenin Gölgesine Sığınanlar: Göçler ve Muhacirin-i İslamiye Komisyonu* (Ankara: Berikan, 2017).
134. BOA, İ.DH. 751/61326 (28 July 1877).
135. For example, BOA, Y.EE. 44/124 (4 December 1879); Y.PRK.AZJ 12/76 (27 January 1888); Y.PRK.AZJ 28/58 (4 May 1894).
136. BOA, Y.EE. 14/13 (31 May 1899).
137. BOA, Y.EE. 43/70 (23 January 1880).
138. McCarthy, *Death and Exile*, 164.
139. Leyla Amzi-Erdoğdular, "Muslim Migration and Nation-Building in Interwar Yugoslavia and Turkey," in *Borders, Boundaries and Belonging in Post-Ottoman Space in the Interwar Period*, eds. Kate Fleet and Ebru Boyar (Leiden: Brill, 2023), 258–259.

Chapter 3

1. Muhammad Rashid Rida, "Al hijratu wa hukumu muslimi busna fiha," *Al-Manar* 12 (1909): 410–415. On Rida see Malcolm H. Kerr, *Islamic Reform: The Political and Legal Theories of Muḥammad 'abduh and Rashīd Riḍā* (Berkeley: University of California Press, 1966); and on his view of Bosnia in the pages of *Al-Manar*, Enes Karić, "Muḥammad Rašid Riḍā (1865.-1935.) i tematiziranje Bosne i Hercegovine i Balkana u časopisu "Al-Manār" (1898.-1935.)" *Godišnjak Bošnjačke zajednice aroda »Preporod«* 1 (2009): 223–238.

2. Fikret Karčić and Mustafa Jahić, "Jedna vazna fetva o pitanju iseljavanja bosanskih Muslimana u vrieme austrougarske uprave," *Prilozi instituta za istoriju* 27 (1991): 41–48.

3. Cemil Aydin, *The Idea of the Muslim World: A Global Intellectual History* (Cambridge, MA: Harvard University Press, 2017), 3–7.

4. Pan-Islam overlapped with concurrent ideologies including Pan-Turkism, Pan-Asianism, and Pan-Arabism and shared the anti-colonial bent, as shown by Cemil Aydin, *The Politics of Anti-Westernism in Asia: Visions of World Order in Pan-Islamic and Pan-Asian Thought* (New York: Columbia University Press, 2007); and Adeeb Khalid, *The Politics of Muslim Cultural Reform: Jadidism in Central Asia* (Berkeley: University of California Press, 1999).

5. Translating shari'a as solely Islamic law, in the sense of state legal codes, is insufficient. See, Samira Haj, *Reconfiguring Islamic Tradition: Reform, Rationality, and Modernity* (Stanford: Stanford University Press, 2009), 4–7; and Wael B. Hallaq, *Authority, Continuity and Change in Islamic Law* (Cambridge, UK: Cambridge University Press, 2001).

6. Qur'an (4:97–100), trans. Yusuf Ali.

7. Qur'an (8:72), trans. Yusuf Ali.

8. Discussed in Muhammad Khalid Masud, "The Obligation to Migrate: The Doctrine of Hijra in Islamic Law," in *Muslim Travelers: Pilgrimage, Migration and Religious Imagination*, eds. Dale F. Eickelman and James Piscatori (London: Routledge, 1990), 29–49.

9. Khaled Abou El Fadl, "Islamic Law and Muslim Minorities: The Juristic Discourse on Muslim Minorities from Second/Eighth to the Eleventh/Seventeenth Centuries," *Islamic Law and Society* 1:2 (1994): 141–187.

10. Some Maliki jurists insisted that Muslims should migrate from non-Muslim ruled lands into Muslim-ruled territories. Muhammad Qasim Zaman, *The Ulama in Contemporary Islam: Custodians of Change* (Princeton: Princeton University Press, 2002), 36. Muslims in southeast Europe predominantly follow the Hanafi school.

11. See Wael B. Hallaq, *An Introduction to Islamic Law* (Cambridge, UK: Cambridge University Press, 2009), 85–114.

12. David Motadel, ed., *Islam and the European Empires* (Oxford: Oxford University Press, 2014), 2–4.

13. Faiz Ahmed, *Afghanistan Rising: Islamic Law and Statecraft Between the Ottoman and British Empires* (Cambridge, MA: Harvard University Press, 2017), 356 n.102.

14. Barbara D. Metcalf, *Islamic Revival in British India: Deoband, 1860–1900* (Princeton: Princeton University Press, 1982), 49–52.

15. Muhamed Mufaku Al-Arnaut, "Islam and Muslims in Bosnia 1878–1918: Two Hijras and Two Fatwās," *Journal of Islamic Studies* 5:2 (1994): 245.

16. For such widely circulated classical works, see Kınalızade Ali Çelebi, *Ahlak-ı alai* (Istanbul: Tercüman, 1974); and by a Bosnian author, Hasan Kafi Aq-Hissari (Pruščak), *Usūl El-Hikam Fī Nizām Al-Ālam* (Istanbul, 1868).

17. Reşat Kasaba, *A Moveable Empire: Ottoman Nomads, Migrants & Refugees* (Seattle: University of Washington Press, 2009).

18. Masud, "The Obligation to Migrate," 33–34. Critically, the *Hijri* Islamic calendar starts with the migration of the early Meccan Muslims led by Prophet Muhammad in 622 CE.

19. Kemal H. Karpat, "Commentary: Muslim Migration: A Response to Aldeeb Abu-Sahlieh," *International Migration Review* 30:1 (1996): 88.

20. Ibrahim Kemura, "Dva patriotska apela bosanskih muslimanskih prvaka iz prvih godina austrougarske okupacije," *Glasnik Vrhovnog islamskog starješinstva u SFRJ* 9–10 (1970): 436–443.

21. Hamdija Kreševljaković, "Hadži Hafiz Džemaludin Hadžijahić," *Glasnik vrhovnog islamskog starješinstva u FNRJ* 8–10 (1955): 336–337. Incidentally, his famed ancestor, Mustafa Muhlisi participated in a critical war with Austria in 1737 and was part of the commission that negotiated the Ottoman–Habsburg border.

22. Enes Pelidija, "Dr. Muhamed Hadžijahić—Dostojan nastavljač porodične tradicije," *Znakovi vremena* 10:38 (2007): 17.

23. "Vatan mühabbeti," *Vatan* 4 (4 October 1884): 2; "Vatan ve muhaceret hakkinda," *Vatan* 5 (11 October 1884): 2; and three articles titled "Hicret" in *Vatan* 15 (19 December 1884): 3; *Vatan* 16 (24 December 1884): 4; and *Vatan* 18 (9 January 1885): 3, 8.

24. Esad Zgodić, *Bosanska politička misao: austrougarsko doba* (Sarajevo: DES, 2003), 30–34.

25. The manuscript of the treatise is in Gazi Husrev-beg Library, Sarajevo (R1343); Mehmed Teufik Azapagić, "Risala o Hidžri," trans. Osman Lavić, *Anali Gazi Husrev-begove biblioteke* 16-17 (1990): 197–222.

26. On the *risala* genre and its use, see Wael B. Hallaq, *Authority, Continuity and Change in Islamic Law* (Cambridge: Cambridge University Press, 2001), 169.

27. Azapagić, "Risala o Hidžri," 202–203.

28. Ibid., 200, 221.

29. Although the soundness of this hadith is disputed, its mention is found as early as 1595 in an Islamic pious endowment charter from Bosnia Herzegovina, where the benefactor cited the hadith as motivation for building a major complex in his hometown; in Lejla Gazić, ed., *Vakufname iz Bosne i Hercegovine (XV I XVI vijek)* (Sarajevo: Orijentalni Institut u Sarajevu, 1985), 15–16.

30. Fikret Karčić, *The Bosniaks and the Challenges of Modernity: Late Ottoman and Hapsburg Times* (Sarajevo: El-Kalem, 1999), 112. The treatise was published two years later in the Bosnian *Vatan* in an edited form in Ottoman Turkish to reach a wider literate public, but it was translated to Bosnian only in 1990, over a hundred years later.

31. James H. Meyer, "Immigration, Return, and the Politics of Citizenship: Russian Muslims in the Ottoman Empire, 1860–1914," *International Journal of Middle East Studies* 39 (2007): 17–18.

32. Karčić, *The Bosniaks and the Challenges of Modernity*, 116. *Risala fi al-hijra wa al-muhajirin* is in Süleymaniye Library, Istanbul, Ibrahim Efendi Collection, no. 421.

33. Karčić, *The Bosniaks and the Challenges of Modernity*, 117.

34. BOA, Y.KP. 3433 (29 January 1910).

35. Osman Hodža, "Pismo iz Ankare," *Musavat* (18 December 1909): 2.

36. Meyer, "Immigration, Return, and the Politics of Citizenship," 18.

37. Milena B. Methodieva, *Between Empire and Nation: Muslim Reform in the Balkans* (Stanford: Stanford University Press, 2021), 212–213.

38. Mehmed-Beg Kapetanović Ljubušak, *Šta misle muhamedanci u Bosni* (Sarajevo: Spindler & Löschner, 1886), 15.

39. Ibid., 17.

40. Mehmed-Beg Kapetanović Ljubušak, *Budućnost ili napredak Muhamedovaca u Bosni i Hercegovini* (Sarajevo: Spindler & Löschner, 1893), 25.

41. See BOA, Y.PRK.EŞA. 33/22 (14 April 1900); Y.PRK.EŞA. 35/103 (17 July 1900).

42. BOA, Y.A.HUS. 510/76 (31 March 1907). The opposition is discussed in "Muhammedaner in Budapest," *Pester Lloyd* 73 (29 March 1907): 9.

43. BOA, Y. Kamil Paşa Evraki 3433 (29 January 1910).

44. Haran Buljina, *Empire, Nation, and the Islamic World: Bosnian Muslim Reformists Between the Habsburg and Ottoman Empires, 1901–1914*, PhD dissertation (Columbia University, 2019), 174.

45. Meyer, "Immigration, Return, and the Politics of Citizenship," 17.

46. Kemal H. Karpat, *Studies on Ottoman Social and Political History: Selected Articles and Essays* (Leiden and Boston: Brill, 2002), 661.

47. BOA, Y.A.RES. 117/77 (14 August 1902).

48. BOA, MV. 109/52 (7 June 1904).

49. BOA, Y.A.HUS. 413/134 (17 March 1901).

50. Also see Malte Fuhrmann, "Vagrants, Prostitutes, and Bosnians: Making and Unmaking European Supremacy in Ottoman Southeast Europe," in *Conflicting Loyalties in the Balkans: The Great Powers, the Ottoman Empire and Nation-Building*, eds. Hannes Granditis, Nathalie Clayer, and Robert Pichler (London and New York: I. B. Tauris, 2011), 39–40.

51. BOA. Y.MTV. 175/183 (4 May 1898), in *Bosna ile ilgili arşiv belgleri*, 127–130.

52. BOA, A.MKT.MHM. 512/5 (17 January 1901).

53. BOA, A.MKT.MHM 514/24 (23 July 1901).

54. For the turn of the twentieth century: 1 gold lira = 100 kuruş; 0.229 gold lira = 1 U.S. dollar, Şevket Pamuk, *A Monetary History of the Ottoman Empire* (Cambridge, UK: Cambridge University Press, 2000), 191, 208–209. BOA, A.MKT.MHM. 510/27 (29 August 1900), in *Osmanlı belgelerinde Bosna Hersek: Bosna i Hercegovina u osmanskim dokumentima*, eds. Yusuf Sarınay, Mustafa Budak, and H. Y. Ağanoğlu (İstanbul: T.C. Başbakanlık, Devlet Arşivleri Genel Müdürlüğü, Osmanlı Arşivi Daire BaşkanlığI, 2009), 285.

55. BOA, MV. 101/36 (20 December 1900).

56. BOA, Y.PRK.MYD. 24/5 (14 May 1901).

57. BOA, DH.MKT. 1567/61 (22 October 1888).

58. Fahriye Emgili, *Yeniden Kurulan Hayatlar: Boşnakların Türkiye'ye Göçleri, 1878–1934*. (Istanbul: Bilge Kültür Sanat, 2012), 201–202.

59. Ibid., 237.

60. Ibid., 271.

61. Mostafa Minawi, "International Law and the Precarity of Ottoman Sovereignty in Africa at the End of the Nineteenth Century," *International History Review* 43:5 (2021): 1098–1121.

62. Aydin, *The Idea of the Muslim World*, 103; and Lale Can, *Spiritual Subjects: Central Asian Pilgrims and the Ottoman Hajj at the End of Empire* (Stanford: Stanford University Press, 2020); Selim Deringil, *The Well-Protected Domains: Ideology and the Legitimation of Power in the Ottoman Empire, 1876–1909* (London: I. B. Tauris, 1998).

63. Korkut Boratav, A. Gündüz Ökçün, and Şevket Pamuk, "Ottoman Wages and the World-Economy, 1839–1913," *Review* (Fernand Braudel Center) 8:3 (1985): 397. Ottomans created immigration-friendly policies to attract agricultural capital from abroad. Kemal H. Karpat, *Studies on Ottoman Social and Political History*, 785–788.

64. H. Yıldırım Ağanoğlu, *Osmanlı'dan Cumhuriyet'e Balkanlar'ın Makûs Talihi Göç* (Istanbul: Kum Saati, 2001), 264–265.

65. For instance, see Vladimir Hamed-Troyansky, "Circassian Refugees and the Making of Amman, 1878–1914," *International Journal of Middle East Studies* 49:4 (2017): 605–623.

66. BOA, BEO 966/72388 (17 June 1897); BEO 965/72333 (16 June 1897).

67. BOA, BEO 967/72525 (22 June 1897).

68. BOA, HR.HMŞ.IŞO. 36/4 (27 October 1915), in *Bosna ile ilgili arşiv belgleri*, 327–336.

69. Fuhrmann, "Vagrants, Prostitutes, and Bosnians," 41.

70. Tomislav Kraljačić, "Stav srpske vlade prema iseljavanju Muslimana iz Bosne i Hercegovine u posljednjoj deceniji XIX vijeka" *Godišnjak društva istoričara BiH* XXXIX (1988): 142.

71. Edin Hajdarpasic, *Whose Bosnia?: Nationalism and Political Imagination in the Balkans, 1840–1914* (Ithaca: Cornell University Press, 2015), 95.

72. Milena B. Methodieva, "How Turks and Bulgarians Became Ethnic Brothers: History, Propaganda and Political Alliances on the Eve of Young Turk Revolution," *Turkish Historical Review* 5 (2014): 221–262.

73. Kraljačić, "Stav srpske vlade prema," 142.

74. Muhsin Rizvić, *Bosansko-muslimanska književnost u doba preporoda (1887–1918)* (Sarajevo: Mešihat islamske zajednice BiH, El-Kalem izdavačka djelatnost, 1990), 151.

75. Klara Volarić, "Between the Ottoman and Serbian States: Carigradski Glasnik, an Istanbul-based Paper of Ottoman Serbs, 1895–1909," *Hungarian Historical Review* 3:3 (2014): 560–586.

76. Nader Sohrabi, "Reluctant Nationalists, Imperial Nation-State, and Neo-Ottomanism: Turks, Albanians, and the Antinomies of the End of Empire" *Social Science History* 42:4 (2018): 860.

77. Rizvić, *Bosansko-muslimanska književnost*, 149–150.

78. "Iseljavanje kod nas," *Srpska riječ* 31 (26 February 1906): 1–2; "Kako je u Americi?," *Srpska riječ* 43 (19 March 1906): 2–3; "Seljenje," *Srpska riječ* 45 (March 22, 1906): 1.

79. Rizvić, *Bosansko-muslimanska književnost*, 149–50.

80. "Ehli-Islam," *Bezakonja okupacione uprave u Bosni i Hercegovini* (Novi Sad: Srpska štamparija dra. Sv. Miletića, 1901).

81. Salih Kazazovć, a writer, was arrested in relation to the publication of this brochure; Zgodić, *Bosanska politička misao*, 318.

82. Ehli-Islam, *Bezakonja*, 9.

83. Safet Bandžović, *Iseljavanje Bošnjaka u Tursku* (Sarajevo: Institut za istraživanje zločina protiv čovječnosti i međunarodnog prava, 2006), 131. Attitudes about Muslim "backwardness" and "fatalism" as adopted from the European Orientalist discourse, supported the Serbian bid to enlightened guidance toward liberation among the South Slavs. On the hierarchies of "otherness" and nesting Orientalisms, see Milica Bakić-Hayden, "Nesting Orientalisms: The Case of Former Yugoslavia," *Slavic Review* 54:4 (1995): 917–931.

84. Jovan Cvijić and Milorad Vasović, *Govori i članci, I* (Beograd: Srpska akademija nauka i umetnosti, 1987), 15.

85. Bandžović, *Iseljavanje*, 131; Kraljačić, "Stav srpske vlade prema," 138–142.

86. Bandžović, *Iseljavanje*, 158–159.
87. To borrow from James H. Meyer, "Speaking Shari'a to the State: Muslim Protesters, Tsarist Officials, and the Islamic Discourses of Late Imperial Russia," *Kritika* 14:3 (2013): 485–505.
88. Aydin, *The Idea of the Muslim World*, 97–98.

Chapter 4

1. Amand Schweiger-Lerchenfeld, *Bosnien: das Land und seine Bewohner: geschichtlich, geographisch, etnographisch und social-politisch* (Vienna: Verlag von L.C. Zamarski, 1878), 193–194.
2. BOA, Y.EE. 43/73 (22 August 1882).
3. Mustafa Imamović, *Historija države i prava Bosne i Hercegovine* (Sarajevo: Magistrat, 2003), 224.
4. Mustafa Imamović, *Pravni položaj i unutrašnjo-politički razvitak Bosne i Hercegovine od 1878. do 1914* (Sarajevo: Bosanski Kulturni Centar, 1997), 61; Dževad Juzbašić, *Politika i privreda u Bosni i Hercegovini pod austrougarskom upravom* (Sarajevo: ANUBiH, 2002), 15.
5. Peter F. Sugar, *Industrialization of Bosnia-Hercegovina: 1878–1918* (Seattle: University of Washington Press, 1963), 8.
6. Huri Islamoğlu, "Property as a Contested Domain: A Reevaluation of the Ottoman Land Code of 1858," in *New Perspectives on Property and Land in the Middle East*, eds. Roger Owen and Martin Bunton, 3–62. (Cambridge, MA: Harvard Center for Middle Eastern Studies, 2000), 20–21, 28–29, 34–35.
7. Mehmed Bećić, ""Osmansko tanzimatsko pravo i austrougarski pravni poredak u Bosni i Hercegovini," *Anali Pravnog Fakulteta Univerziteta u Zenici* 12 (2009): 195–196.
8. AbiH, ZVS-11 24/19 (1881).
9. Mehmed Bećić, "Primjena Medželle u postosmanskoj Bosni i Hercegovini," *Godišnjak Pravnog fakulteta u Sarajevu* LVII (2014): 60.
10. Adem Handžić, "O formiranju nekih gradskih naselja u Bosni u XVI stoljeću," *Prilozi za orijentalnu filologiju* 25 (1976): 133–169; and Adem Handžić, "Vakuf kao nosilac određenih državnih i društvenih funkcija u Osmanskom carstvu," *Anali Gazi Husrev-begove biblioteke* 9-10 (1983): 113–119.
11. Amy Singer, *Constructing Ottoman Beneficence: An Imperial Soup Kitchen in Jerusalem* (Albany: State University of New York Press, 2002), 25.
12. Ibid., 20–21.
13. For Ottoman reorganization of the pious endowments, see Hilmi Ömer, *Ahkâmü'l-evkaf* (İstanbul: Matbaa-yı Amire, 1889); and Ahmet Akgündüz, *İslâm hukukunda ve Osmanlı tatbikatında vakıf müessesesi* (Ankara: Türk Tarih Kurumu, 1988).

14. Fikret Karčić, "Medjunarodnopravno regulisanje vakufskih pitanja u jugoslovenskim zemljama," *Anali Gazi Husrev-begove biblioteke* IX-X (1983): 144.

15. Ibid., 146–147; Milena B. Methodieva, *Between Empire and Nation: Muslim Reform in the Balkans* (Stanford: Stanford University Press, 2021), 32.

16. Robert Donia, *Islam Under the Double Eagle* (Boulder: East European Monographs, 1981), 23.

17. Nusret Šehić, *Autonomni pokret Muslimana za vrijeme austrougarske uprave u Bosni i Hercegovini* (Sarajevo: Svjetlost, 1980), 19–30.

18. In a memorandum submitted to Minister Kallay, conversion of *vakuf* properties is one of the key complaints: *Memorandum nj. preuzvišenom ministru Kallayu predan 19.12.1900 u Sarajevu od predstavnika i zastupnika muslimanskog naroda okupiranih zemalja* (Novi Sad: Srpska štamparija dra. Svetozara Miletića, 1901).

19. Methodieva, *Between Empire and Nation*, 177.

20. Donia, *Islam Under the Double Eagle*, 10–11.

21. For a detailed account, see Berislav Gavranović, *Uspostava redovite katoličke hijerarhije u Bosni I Hercegovini 1881. godine: prilog političkoj historiji Austro-Ugarske Monarhije na Balkanu* (Beograd: Univerzitet u Beogradu, 1935).

22. BOA, Y.A.HUS. 364/34 (5 January 1897).

23. To illustrate, by 1895 Ashkenazi Jews made up around 30 percent of all Jewish inhabitants of the province totaling over 8,000 people; in Avram Pinto, *Jevreji Sarajeva i Bosne i Hercegovine* (Sarajevo: Veselin Masleša, 1987), 16–17.

24. Omer Nakičević, *Istorijski razvoj institucije Rijaseta* (Sarajevo: Rijaset islamske zajednice u RBiH, 1996), 74.

25. Ibid., 45; ABiH ZMF Präs BH 1087/1881 (18 October 1881).

26. Edin Hajdarpasic, *Whose Bosnia?: Nationalism and Political Imagination in the Balkans, 1840–1914* (Ithaca: Cornell University Press, 2015), 177–178.

27. James H. Meyer, *Turks Across Empires: Marketing Muslim Identity in the Russian-Ottoman Borderlands, 1856–1914* (Oxford: Oxford University Press, 2019), 148.

28. Ibid., 178; Fikret Karčić, *Studije o šerijatskom pravu* (Zenica: Bemust, 1997), 173.

29. Nacionalna i sveučilišna knjižnica u Zagrebu (NSK) R 5698 Enquete über die Reform der Scheriatsgerichte, abgehalten vom 2. März 1908 bis 27. April 1908. I thank Edin Hajdarpasic for pointing out this document.

30. For "religious toleration" as a core attribute of Russia's state identity, see Paul W. Werth, *The Tsar's Foreign Faiths: Toleration and the Fate of Religious Freedom in Imperial Russia* (New York: Oxford University Press, 2014).

31. Robert Crews, "Empire and the Confessional State: Islam and Religious

Politics in Nineteenth-Century Russia," *American Historical Review* 108 (2003): 50–83; and Robert Crews, *For Prophet and Tsar: Islam and Empire in Russia and Central Asia* (Cambridge, MA: Harvard University Press, 2006).

32. Selçuk Esenbel, "Japan's Global Claim to Asia and the World of Islam," *American Historical Review* 109:4 (2004): 1140–1170.

33. Kasim Dobrača, "Mehmed Refik-efendi Hadžiabdić šejhul-islam," *Anali Gazi Husrev-begove biblioteke* V-VI (1978): 109.

34. Paşa and Baysun, *Tezakir*, 25, 29.

35. Husejn Bračković, and Zejnil Fajić. "Mala istorija događaja u Hercegovini," *Prilozi za orijentalnu filologiju* 34 (1984): 187; Haran Buljina, *Empire, Nation, and the Islamic World: Bosnian Muslim Reformists Between the Habsburg and Ottoman Empires, 1901–1914*, PhD dissertation (Columbia University, 2019), 27, 57.

36. Imamović, *Pravni položaj*, 107–108.

37. Rumeli Kazasker (chief military judge for Rumelia) was also noted to have this title; Ismail Hakki Uzunçarşılı, *Osmanli devletinin ilmiye teşkilatı* (Ankara: Türk Tarih Kurumu Basimevi, 1988), 159.

38. BOA, A.MTZ.BN. 1/20 (18 July 1903).

39. BOA, HR.TH. 149–142 (11 November 1894).

40. ABiH, ZMF BH 85/1895.

41. Methodieva, *Between Empire and Nation*, 59–64.

42. ABiH, ZMF Präs BH 85/1891.

43. ABiH, ZVS 146, 11–263 (1906); Zijad Šehić, "Putovanje bosanskohercegovačkih hodočasnika u Meku u doba austrougarske uprave 1878–1918," *Saznanja: Časopis za historiju* 2 (2008): 69–85.

44. Dženita Karić, *Bosnian Hajj Literature: Multiple Paths to the Holy* (Edinburgh: Edinburgh University Press, 2022), 115.

45. "Mali vjesnik," *Sarajevski list* (11 June 1890), cited in Dženita Karić, *Bosnian Hajj Literature*, 115.

46. Hana Younis, "Smrtni slučajevi tokom hadža u Mekku kroz primjere iz građe Vrhovnog šerijatskog suda u Sarajevu u periodu austrougarske uprave," *Anali Gazi Husrev-begove biblioteke* 37 (2016): 201.

47. Ibid., 199.

48. A.MTZ.BN 1/14 (30 July 1901).

49. BOA, A.MKT.MHM. 572/17 (28 August 1895).

50. Michael Christopher Low, *Imperial Mecca: Ottoman Arabia and the Indian Ocean Hajj* (New York: Columbia University Press, 2020).

51. Michael Christopher Low, "Unfurling the Flag of Extraterritoriality: Autonomy, Foreign Muslims, and the Capitulations in the Ottoman Hijaz," *Journal of the Ottoman and Turkish Studies Association* 3:2 (2016): 307.

52. See, Murat Birdal, *The Political Economy of Ottoman Public Debt: Insolvency and European Financial Control in the Late Nineteenth Century* (London: I. B. Tauris, 2010).

53. Eric Weitz, "From Vienna to the Paris System: International Politics and the Entangled History of Human Rights, Forced Deportations and Civilizing Missions," *American Historical Review* 113:5 (2008): 1313–1343.

54. Erik Jan Zürcher, *Turkey: A Modern History* (London: I. B. Tauris, 2004), 74–75. See also M. Şükrü Hanioğlu, *Preparation for a Revolution: The Young Turks, 1902–1908* (Oxford: Oxford University Press, 2001); and Nader Sohrabi, *Revolution and Constitutionalism in the Ottoman Empire and Iran* (New York: Cambridge University Press, 2011).

55. Eric Hobsbawm, *The Age of Empire, 1875–1914* (London: Weidenfeld and Nicolson, 1987).

56. M. Şükrü Hanioğlu, *A Brief History of the Late Ottoman Empire* (Princeton: Princeton University Press, 2008), 129; and Selim Deringil, *The Well-Protected Domains: Ideology and the Legitimation of Power in the Ottoman Empire 1876–1909* (London: I. B. Tauris, 2011).

57. Engin Akarlı, "The Tangled Ends of an Empire: Ottoman Encounters with the West and Problems of Westernization—an Overview," *Comparative Studies of South Asia, Africa and the Middle East* 26:3 (2006): 362.

58. Ibid., 357.

59. Cemil Aydin, *The Idea of the Muslim World: A Global Intellectual History* (Cambridge, MA: Harvard University Press, 2017), 61–62.

60. Julia Phillips Cohen, *Becoming Ottomans: Sephardi Jews and Imperial Citizenship in the Modern Era* (New York: Oxford University Press, 2017), 78–80.

61. Selim Deringil, "Legitimacy Structures in the Ottoman State: The Reign of Abdülhamid II (1876–1909)," *International Journal of Middle East Studies* 23 (1991): 350.

62. Kemal H. Karpat, "Yakub Bey's Relations with the Ottoman Sultans: A Reinterpretation," *Cahiers du Monde russe et soviétique* 32:1 (1991): 30.

63. Dariusz Kołodziejczyk, "Khan, Caliph, Tsar and Imperator: The Multiple Identities of the Ottoman Sultan," in *Universal Empire: A Comparative Approach to Imperial Culture and Representation in Eurasian History*, eds. Peter F. Bang and Dariusz Kołodziejczyk (Cambridge, UK: Cambridge University Press, 2015), 180.

64. Deringil, "Legitimacy Structures in the Ottoman State," 353–354; for disputes, see, Ş. Tufan Buzpınar, "Opposition to the Ottoman Caliphate in the Early Years of Abdülhamid II: 1877–1882," *Die Welt des Islams* 36:1 (1996): 59–89.

65. Will Hanley, "Papers for Going, Papers for Staying: Identification and

Subject Formation in the Eastern Mediterranean," in *A Global Middle East: Mobility, Materiality and Culture in the Modern Age, 1880–1940*, eds. Liat Kozma, Avner Wishnitzer, and Cyrus Schayegh, (London: I. B. Tauris, 2014), 177–200; and Ziad Fahmy, "Jurisdictional Borderlands: Extraterritoriality and "Legal Chameleons" in Precolonial Alexandria, 1840–1870," *Comparative Studies in Society and History* 55:2 (2013): 305–329.

66. Lale Can, *Spiritual Subjects: Central Asian Pilgrims and the Ottoman Hajj at the End of Empire* (Stanford: Stanford University Press, 2020), 97, 105; Deringil, *The Well-Protected Domains*, 57–60.

67. Hanioğlu, *A Brief History of the Late Ottoman Empire*, 130; Deringil, "Legitimacy Structures," 351.

68. Aydin, *The Idea of the Muslim World*, 97.

69. Ibid., 3.

70. James L. Gelvin and Nile Green, eds., *Global Muslims in the Age of Steam and Print* (Berkeley: University of California Press, 2014).

71. Kemal H. Karpat, *The Politicization of Islam: Reconstructing Identity, State, Faith, and Community in the Late Ottoman State* (Oxford: Oxford University Press, 2001); Niyazi Berkes, *The Development of Secularism in Turkey* (Montreal: McGill University Press, 1964), 267–268; Nikki R. Keddie, "The Pan-Islamic Appeal: Afghani and Abdülhamid II," *Middle Eastern Studies* 3:1 (1966): 50.

72. Cemil Aydin, *The Politics of Anti-Westernism in Asia: Visions of World Order in Pan-Islamic and Pan-Asian Thought* (New York: Columbia University Press, 2007); and Adeeb Khalid, *The Politics of Muslim Cultural Reform: Jadidism in Central Asia* (Berkeley: University of California Press, 1999).

73. Adeeb Khalid, "Pan Islamism in Practice: The Rhetoric of Muslim Unity and Its Uses," in *Late Ottoman Society: The Intellectual Legacy*, ed. Elisabeth Özdalga (London: Routledge, 2005), 204–205, 222.

74. Faiz Ahmed, *Afghanistan Rising: Islamic Law and Statecraft Between the Ottoman and British Empires* (Cambridge, MA: Harvard University Press, 2017), 209.

75. On the Balkans-to-Bengal complex, see Shahab Ahmed, *What Is Islam? The Importance of Being Islamic* (Princeton: Princeton University Press, 2016), 81–83.

76. Methodieva, *Between Empire and Nation*, 55.

77. Ibid., 52.

78. Roderic H. Davison, "Vienna as a Major Ottoman Diplomatic Post in the Nineteenth Century," in *Habsburgisch-osmanische Beziehungen: Relations Habsbourg-Ottomanes*, ed. Andreas Tietze (Wien: Verlag des Verbandes der wissenschaftlichen Gesellschaften Österreichs, 1985), 253–256.

79. Ibid., 256.

80. Houssine Alloul and Roel Markey, "'Please Deny These Manifestly False Reports': Ottoman Diplomats and the Press in Belgium (1850–1914)," *International Journal of Middle East Studies* 48:2 (2016): 268.

81. Some of the press reports on Bosnia Herzegovina: BOA, Y.PRK.TKM. 2/17 (6 August 1878)—*Le Monde*; Y.A. HUS 179/129 (9 October, 1884)—the British press; Y.A.HUS 180/27 (15 November, 1882)—reports in French, Italian, Belgian, and Egyptian press; Y.A.HUS 187/38 (15 January 1886)—Vienna's *Fremdenblatt* and Prague's *Politik* on Bosnia and Crete; Y.A.HUS 203/47 (8 June 1887)—*Allemagne du Nord*, the British press; Y.A.HUS 210/39 (29 January 1888)—St. Petersburg's *Novoye Vremya*; 235/25 (5 May 1890)—*Correspondance Gazette*; Y.PRK.TKM 9/38 (12 January 1886)—Rome's *Dirito*.

82. On Habsburg press monitoring regarding Bosnia Herzegovina, see Hajdarpasic, *Whose Bosnia?*, 186–187.

83. BOA, Y.PRK.BŞK. 35/44 (6 March 1894).

84. BOA, Y.PRK.MYD. 6/5 (9 January 1887).

85. Robin Okey, *Taming Balkan Nationalism: The Habsburg Civilizing Mission in Bosnia, 1878–1914* (Oxford: Oxford University Press, 2007), 27.

86. BOA, Y.PRK.MYD. 4/35 (9 May 1885)

87. Davison, "Vienna as a Major Ottoman Diplomatic Post," 251–281, 254, 262.

88. Mahmud Nedim was ambassador to Vienna from 1896 to 1907. Davison, "Vienna as a Major Ottoman Diplomatic Post," 261, 267–268.

89. Ibid., 255. BOA, Y.PRK.HR. 3/84 (23 December 1878); Y.PRK.HR. 5/7 (22 July 1880).

90. BOA, Y.A.HUS. 408/22 (9 July 1900); HR.SYS. 259/1–78–80 (7 July 1903), in *Bosna ile ilgili arşiv belgeleri*, 201–203.

91. BOA, HR.SYS. 259/1–63, 64 (21 April 1903).

92. For reference, the approximate distance by air from Sarajevo to Dubrovnik is 84 miles (135 km), from Mostar to Dubrovnik is 50 miles (80 km); whereas Sarajevo to Vienna is 315 miles (507 km), and Sarajevo to Budapest is 254 miles (409 km).

93. BOA, HR.SYS. 259/1 (8 April 1901).

94. Ibid.

95. BOA, Y.A.HUS. 413/134 (17 March 1901); A.MTZ.BN 1/12 (11 May 1901).

96. BOA, A.MTZ.BN. 1/13 (13 May 1901).

97. BOA, HR.SYS. 259/1 (8 April 1901).

98. Ebru Boyar, *Ottomans, Turks and the Balkans: Empire Lost, Relations Altered* (London: I. B. Tauris, 2007), 106.

99. Mostafa Minawi, *The Ottoman Scramble for Africa: Empire and Diplo-*

macy in the Sahara and the Hijaz (Stanford: Stanford University Press, 2016), 10. Also, Isa Blumi, *Rethinking the Late Ottoman Empire: A Comparative Social and Political History of Albania and Yemen, 1878–1918* (Istanbul: Isis Press, 2010); Gökhan Çetinsaya, "The Ottoman View of British Presence in Iraq and the Gulf: The Era of Abdulhamid II," *Middle Eastern Studies* 39:2 (2003): 194–203; Tufan Buzpınar, "The Hijaz, Abdülhamid II and Amir Hussein's Secret Dealings with the British, 1877–80," *Middle Eastern Studies* 31:1 (1995): 99–123.

100. Minawi, *The Ottoman Scramble for Africa*, 146.

Chapter 5

1. BOA, Y.PRK.AZJ. 31/32 (23 June 1895).

2. Ibid.

3. I borrow the description recognized by Faiz Ahmed in "Contested Subjects: Ottoman and British Jurisdictional Quarrels in Re Afghans and Indian Muslims," *Journal of the Ottoman and Turkish Studies Association* 3:2 (2016): 328.

4. See Hamza Karčić, "Supporting the Caliph's Project: Bosnian Muslims and the Hejaz Railway," *Journal of Muslim Minority Affairs* 34:3 (2014): 282–292.

5. Murat Ramadanović, "Bosanska emigracija u Osmanskom carstvu i sultanov suverenitet u Bosni i Hercegovini," *Znakovi vremena* 9–10 (2000): 324.

6. On the connections with Austria-Hungary, see Harun Buljina, "Bosnia's 'Young Turks': The Bosnian Muslim Intelligentsia in Its Late Ottoman Context, 1878–1914," in *The Turkish Connection: Global Intellectual Histories of the Late Ottoman Empire and Republican Turkey*, eds. Deniz Kuru and Hazal Papuççular (Berlin and Boston: De Gruyter Oldenbourg, 2022).

7. Şükrü M. Hanioğlu, *Preparation for a Revolution: The Young Turks, 1902–1908* (Oxford: Oxford University Press, 2001), 161–163.

8. Ibid.,76.

9. A prominent Young Turk of Bosnian origin was Mehmed Kadrija "Nâsih" Pajić (1855–1918), known as Hoca Kadri who published in Ottoman Turkish and Arabic from exile in Cairo and Paris. In addition to being Mehmet Akif Ersoy's teacher, his prominent work *Sarayih* (Paris: Librairie Geuthner, 1910), discussed some of the later developments in post-Ottoman Turkey. See Cahit Tanyol, *Hoca Kadri Efendi'nin Parlamentosu* (Istanbul: Gendaş, 2003).

10. Mustafa Imamović, *Pravni položaj i unutrašnjo-politički razvitak Bosne i Hercegovine od 1878. do 1914* (Sarajevo: Bosanski Kulturni Centar, 1997), 104.

11. Enes Karić, "Aspects of Islamic Discourse in Bosnia-Hercegovina from the Mid-19th Till the End of the 20th Century: A Historical Review," in *Şehrayin. Die Welt der Osmanen, die Osmanen in der Welt; Wahr-nehmungen, Begegnungen und Abgrenzungen*, ed. Yavuz Köse (Wiesbaden: Harrassowitz, 2012), 286.

12. BOA, Y.PRK.AZJ. 2/40 (24 December 1878).

13. Yuval Ben-Bassat, *Petitioning the Sultan: Protests and Justice in Late Ottoman Palestine, 1865–1908* (London: I. B. Tauris, 2013), 4.

14. James E. Baldwin, "Petitioning the Sultan in Ottoman Egypt," *Bulletin of the School of Oriental and African Studies* 75:3 (2012): 501.

15. Lale Can, *Spiritual Subjects: Central Asian Pilgrims and the Ottoman Hajj at the End of Empire* (Stanford: Stanford University Press, 2020), 43.

16. M. Şükrü Hanioğlu, *A Brief History of the Late Ottoman Empire* (Princeton: Princeton University Press, 2008), 128.

17. For example, BOA, HR.SYS. 259/1 66 (22 April 1902).

18. BOA, HR.SYS. 259/1 66 (22 April 1902).

19. On such petitions by non-Ottoman Central Asian Muslims, see Can, *Spiritual Subjects*, 125–148.

20. BOA, Y.PRK.BŞK. 2/27 (15 July 1879).

21. BOA, Y.PRK.BŞK. 2/13 (26 April 1879).

22. BOA, Y.PRK.AZJ. 4/75 (23 June 1881).

23. Robert Donia, *Islam Under the Double Eagle* (Boulder: East European Monographs, 1981), 97.

24. BOA, Y.PRK.AZJ. 4/87 (7 June 1881).

25. BOA. HR.SYS. 256/2 (11 May 1880).

26. Ibrahim Tepić, "Uspostavljanje austrougarske okupacione vlasti u Bosni i Hercegovini u izvjestajima ruskog konzulata u Sarajevu (1879–1880)," *Prilozi instituta za istoriju* 24 (1988): 125.

27. BOA, HR.SYS.259/1, 26–31 (27 June 1906); petition was written in 1902.

28. BOA, Y.A.HUS. 510/76 (31 March 1907).

29. For Kállay's relations with each of the major groups, see Robin Okey, *Taming Balkan Nationalism: The Habsburg Civilizing Mission in Bosnia, 1878–1914* (Oxford: Oxford University Press, 2007).

30. Donia, *Islam Under the Double Eagle*, 41–43.

31. So far, the only transimperial study on vernacular projects in Bosnia Herzegovina is Haran Buljina, *Empire, Nation, and the Islamic World: Bosnian Muslim Reformists Between the Habsburg and Ottoman Empires, 1901–1914*, PhD dissertation (Columbia University, 2019).

32. Ibid., 70.

33. Building on the meticulously researched major studies of the movement for Muslim religious and educational autonomy, this analysis contributes the previously unexplored Ottoman connections. These are: Nusret Šehić, *Autonomni pokret Muslimana za vrijeme austrougarske uprave u Bosni i Hercegovini* (Sarajevo: Svjetlost, 1980); Imamović, *Pravni položaj*; Donia, *Islam Under the*

Double Eagle; Okey, *Taming Balkan Nationalism*; and Ferdo Hauptmann, *Borba Muslimana Bosne i Hercegovine za vjersku vakufsko-mearifsku autonomiju* (Sarajevo: Arhiv Socijalističke Republike Bosne i Hercegovine, 1967).

34. Mustafa Imamović, *Historija države i prava Bosne i Hercegovine* (Sarajevo: Magistrat, 2003), 241; Donia, *Islam Under the Double Eagle*, 115. On the metaphor of sexual violence as symbolic territorial appropriation, see Irvin Cemil Schick, "Christian Maidens, Turkish Ravishers: The Sexualization of National Conflict in the Late Ottoman Period," in *Women in the Ottoman Balkans: Gender, Culture and History*, eds. Amila Buturović and Irvin C. Schick (London: I. B. Tauris, 2007), 274–304; on conversions, Selim Deringil, *Conversion and Apostasy in the Late Ottoman Period* (Cambridge, UK: Cambridge University Press, 2012).

35. Less known is that his father Ahmed Šaćir, also a scholar and a mufti, opposed the Tanzimat measures during the Ottoman period; Buljina, *Empire, Nation, and the Islamic World*, 70, n.165.

36. Imamović, *Historija države i prava*, 241–242.

37. Following his dismissal, Teskeredžić emigrated to the Ottoman Empire, while Džabić was exiled.

38. BOA, Y.A.HUS. 408/22 (9 July 1900).

39. Donia, *Islam Under the Double Eagle*, 97, 74.

40. BOA, Y.A.HUS 412/8 (26 December 1900).

41. Ibid. Džabić was noted to have rejected the offer, saying that the Muslims were concerned with religious and not political issues; Donia, *Islam Under the Double Eagle*, 134.

42. Ibid.; Imamović, *Historija države i prava*, 243.

43. "Les Musulmans de Bosnie-Herzégovine: Leurs doléances—Leurs voeux," *La Revue d'Orient et de Hongrie* (20 June 1900): 139–141; BOA, Y.A.HUS 411/115 (30 October 1900).

44. BOA, Y.A. HUS. 411/115 (30 October 1900).

45. BOA, Y.A.HUS. 413/8 (28 January 1901).

46. BOA, Y.A.HUS. 411/115 (30 October 1900).

47. BOA, Y.A.HUS. 364/34 (15 June 1896).

48. BOA, Y.A.HUS. 367/2 (18 February 1897).

49. BOA, Y.PRK.AZJ. 5/32 (6 May 1882).

50. BOA, Y.A.HUS 413/8 (28 January 1901).

51. ABiH, ZMF Präs BH 510/1909.

52. *Obzor*, 210:XLII (13 May 1901), quoted in Nusret Šehić, *Autonomni pokret Muslimana za vrijeme austrougarske uprave u Bosni i Hercegovini* (Sarajevo: Svijetlost 1980), 127–128.

53. Osman Nuri Hadžić, "Srpsko-muhamedanska sloga," *Hrvatsko Pravo* 790 (24 June 1898).

54. BOA, Y.PRK.HR. 33/21 (1903–1904); on nationalization, see Edin Hajdarpasic, *Whose Bosnia?: Nationalism and Political Imagination in the Balkans, 1840–1914* (Ithaca: Cornell University Press, 2015).

55. "Nacrt štatuta bosansko-hercegovačkih muslimana," analyzed in Šehić, *Autonomni pokret Muslimana za vrijeme austrougarske uprave u Bosni i Hercegovini*, 70–109.

56. Šehić, *Autonomni pokret Muslimana za vrijeme austrougarske uprave u Bosni i Hercegovini*, 144.

57. BOA, HR.SYS. 259/1–66 (22 April 1902).

58. BOA, Y.A.RES. 117/77 (14 August 1902).

59. BOA, BEO 2179 163389 (28 September 1903).

60. BOA, HR.SYS. 258/1 37–58 (26 August 1902).

61. BOA, Y.A.HUS. 426/15 (15 March 1903).

62. *Sarajevski list* 89 (31 July 1903).

63. While much of scholarly analysis focuses on the Kállay regime, Istvan Burián term is covered in Okey, *Taming Balkan Nationalism*; also, Robin Okey, "A Trio of Hungarian Balkanists: Béni Kállay, István Burián and Lajos Thallóczy in the Age of High Nationalism," *Slavonic and East European Review* 80:2 (2002): 234–266.

64. See discussion in *Bošnjak* 8 (22 February 1906).

65. Imamović, *Pravni položaj*, 137.

66. *Musavat* 29 (30 August 1907), text transmitted in Imamović, *Pravni položaj*, 141.

67. The printout of the statement by Šarac and the transcript of the opinion are in Muhammed Enveri Kadić, *Tarih-i Enveri*, manuscript, vol. 14, Gazi Husrev-begova Biblioteka (GHB) (1931), 412.

68. *Sarajevski list* 118 (2 October 1908).

69. Fikret Karčić, *Šerijatski sudovi u Jugoslaviji, 1918–1941* (Sarajevo: Vrhovno starješinstvo Islamske zajednice u SFRJ, 1986), 83.

70. Omer Nakičević, *Istorijski razvoj institucije Rijaseta* (Sarajevo: Rijaset Islamske zajednice u RBiH, 1996), 58.

71. Fikret Karčić, "Medjunarodnopravno regulisanje vakufskih pitanja u jugoslovenskim zemljama," *Anali Gazi Husrev-begove biblioteke* IX-X (1983): 150.

72. Donia, *Islam Under the Double Eagle*, 194.

Chapter 6

1. Roderic H. Davison, "The Ottoman Boycott of Austrian Goods in 1908–09 as a Diplomatic Question," in *Third Congress on the Social and Economic History of Turkey: Princeton University, 24–26 August 1983*, eds. Heath W. Lowry and Ralph S. Hattox (Istanbul: Isis Press, 1990), 10.

2. Merve Çidem, "II. Meşrutiyet'in İlanı Sırasında Kaybedilen Balkan Toprakları ve Olayların Basına Yansıması," *Vakanüvis-Uluslararası Tarih Araştırmaları Dergisi* 3 (2018): 88; Y. Dogan Çetinkaya, *1908 Osmanlı Boykotu: Bir Toplumsal Hareketin Analizi* (Istanbul: Iletişim, 2004), 169.

3. Palmira Brummett, *Image and Imperialism in the Ottoman Revolutionary Press, 1908–1911* (Albany: State University of New York Press, 2000), 175.

4. Ottoman report on the emperor's handwritten note: BOA, YA.HUS. 525/70 (7 October 1908).

5. Mustafa Imamović, *Pravni položaj i unutrašnjo-politički razvitak Bosne i Hercegovine od 1878. do 1914* (Sarajevo: Bosanski Kulturni Centar, 1997), 191–192.

6. Ibid., 194.

7. Ibid., 196.

8. Dževad Juzbašić, *Politika i privreda u Bosni i Hercegovini pod austrougarskom upravom* (Sarajevo: ANUBiH, 2002), 266–319.

9. For example: BOA, Y.EE.KP. 33/3250 (23 October 1908); BOA, HR.TO. 19/64 (23 March 1886); HR.TO 19/91 (27 June 1886); Y.PRK.TKM 30/24 (19 December 1893); HR.SFR.3 287/26 (20 March 1882); HR.TO 22/42 (18 June 1889); Y.EE.KP. 33/3258 (2 November 1908); HR.SYS. 59/6 (17 April 1885); Y.A.HUS. 209/50 (4 January 1888); HR.SFR.3 287/25 (19 March 1882).

10. BOA, HR.TH. 65/70 (25 August 1886); for other examples, see HR.SFR.1 80/93 (5 September 1890); HR.SFR.1 83/71 (31 August 1891); HR.TO. 91/35 (30 December 1887); HR.TO. 111/28 (3 September 1885);

11. BOA, Y.A.HUS. 507/5 (19 October 1906).

12. For Russian reactions as reported by Ottoman administrators, see BOA, HR.SFR.1, gömlek 147, 153 (1908/1909); also, A.MTZ. (04) 171/6 and 171/7 (29 September 1908).

13. BOA, Y.A.HUS. 511/48 (4 May 1907).

14. BOA, Y.A.HUS. 513/99 (5 August 1907).

15. BOA, Y.A.HUS. 525/56 (4 October 1908); sent 30 September 1908.

16. On the Young Turks, see M. Şükrü Hanioğlu, *Young Turks in Opposition* (Oxford: Oxford University Press, 1995); M. Şükrü Hanioğlu, *Preparation for a Revolution: The Young Turks, 1902–1908* (Oxford: Oxford University Press, 2001); and Nader Sohrabi, *Revolution and Constitutionalism in the Ottoman Empire and Iran* (New York: Cambridge University Press, 2011).

17. Sohrabi, *Revolution and Constitutionalism*, 73–74.

18. Ibid., 3–4.

19. Hasan Ünal. "Ottoman Policy During the Bulgarian Independence Crisis, 1908–9: Ottoman Empire and Bulgaria at the Outset of the Young Turk Revolution," *Middle Eastern Studies* 34: 4 (1998): 135–176.

20. Ibid., 139–140.

21. BOA, Y.A.HUS. 525/67 (7 October 1908).

22. BOA, Y.A.HUS. 525/66 (7 October 1908).

23. BOA, Y.A.HUS. 525/70 (7 October 1908).

24. BOA, HR.SYS. 261/1 (25 October 1908).

25. BOA, Y.EE.KP. 33/3242 (October 10, 1908).

26. "Cemiyetin Ittirazi," *Ittihat ve Terakki* 28 (8 October 1908): 1; "Bosna-Hersek Kıtaları ve Babıali'nin Protestosu," *Tanin* 72 (11 October 1908): 1; "Protestoname," *Ikdam* 5167 (12 October 1908): 2.

27. Davison, "The Ottoman Boycott," 5.

28. Ibid., 6–7.

29. Mehmet Emin Elmaci, "1908 Avusturya Boykotunda Liman İşçileri," *Kebikeç* 5 (1997): 155–162.

30. Sohrabi, *Revolution and Constitutionalism*, 186–188.

31. Çetinkaya, 35–36.

32. Palmira Brummett, *Image and Imperialism in the Ottoman Revolutionary Press, 1908–1911* (Albany: State University of New York Press, 2000), 175; Davison, "The Ottoman Boycott," 6.

33. Çetinkaya, *1908 Osmanlı Boykotu*, 111–113. Over 21 percent of Ottoman imports in 1907 were from the Habsburg Empire, Juzbašić, *Politika i privreda*, 425.

34. Fahriye Emgili, *Yeniden Kurulan Hayatlar: Boşnakların Türkiye'ye Göçleri, 1878–1934* (Istanbul: Bilge Kültür Sanat, 2012), 174.

35. Davison, "The Ottoman Boycott," 10.

36. BOA, HR.HMŞ.IŞO. 36/4–9 (26 February 1909), BOA, HR.HMŞ.IŞO. 36/4–8 (26 April 1909).

37. Gazi Husrev-begova Biblioteka (GHB), "Memorandum Muslimana iz Bosne i Hercegovine: predan osmanlijskom parlamentu mjeseca februara 1909. god. u Carigradu," II-3373.

38. Mustafa Imamović, *Historija Bošnjaka* (Sarajevo: Preporod, 1996), 430

39. BOA, Y.A.HUS. 525/68 (7 October 1908).

40. BOA, Y.A.HUS. 525/78 (15 October 1908).

41. BOA, Y.A.HUS. 526/77 (9 February 1909).

42. BOA, MV. 125/38 (7 Mart 1909).

43. Ali Ulvi, *Avusturya'nın Bosna Hersek'i ilhakına karşı bir müdafaa-ı vatanperverane* (Dersaadet [Istanbul]: Ruşen Matbaası, 1324 [1908]).

44. Ibid, 8.

45. Ibid., 10–12.

46. Ali Rüşdü, *Bosna Hersek'in memâlik-i Osmaniyye'den tefrîkiyle Avusturya'ya satmak fikrinde bulunanların vücûb-ı tel'inini nâtık Bosna Hersek ahâlisi nâmına Meb'ûsân ve Ayân-ı Osmanî Meclislerine verilen lâyıhadır* (Dersaadet [Istanbul]: Ruşen Maatbasi, 1324 [1909]).

47. Ali Şadi, *Bosna Hersek yahud Osmanlı'ların Alsas Loren'i* (Dersaadet [Istanbul]: Süha Matbaası, 1327 [1911]).

48. Esad Zgodić, *Bosanska politička misao: austrougarsko doba* (Sarajevo: DES, 2003), 69, n.1.

49. Murat Ramadanović, "Bosanska emigracija u Osmanskom carstvu i sultanov suverenitet u Bosni i Hercegovini," *Znakovi Vremena* 9–10 (2000): 331.

50. Ibid., 332–333.

51. BOA, I.HUS. 171/20 (1 November 1908).

52. Emgili, *Yeniden Kurulan Hayatlar* 174–176.

53. BOA, Y.KP. 3319 (1908).

54. BOA, HR.HMŞ.İŞO. 29/2–4, 27/2 (17 April 1910), in *Bosna ile ilgili arşiv belgeleri*, 312.

55. BOA, HR.HMŞ.İŞO. 29/2–1, 30/1 (24 April 1910), in *Bosna ile ilgili arşiv belgeleri*, 314.

56. BOA, BEO 456/34193 (16 August 1894).

57. For example, BOA, HR.HMŞ. IŞO 29/2–4, 31/2 (5 December 1909), in *Bosna ile ilgili arşiv belgeleri*, 306.

58. BOA, HR.HMŞ. IŞO. 29/2–3, 2 (6 March 1910), in *Bosna Hersek ile ilgili arşiv belgeleri*, 311–312.

59. BOA, BEO 3788/284049 (4 August 1910).

60. Amila Kasumović, "Carski osmanski generalni konzulat u Sarajevu (1910–1918)," *Prilozi* 44 (2015): 63.

61. Ibid., 67.

62. BOA, BEO 3984/298789 (30 December 1911); BEO 3989/299173 (13 January 1912).

63. BOA, HR.SYS. 2038/12 (11 September 1913); HR.SYS. 2032/1 (6 October 1913); HR. SYS. 2038/16 (18 October 1913); HR.SYS. 2039/1 (7 December 1913).

64. Kasumović, "Carski osmanski generalni konzulat u Sarajevu," 72.

65. For example, Šerif Arnautović requested such medals for the Habsburg Bosnian governor and commander in chief, Stefan von Sarkotić, and for the director of internal affairs, Karl Baron Collas. BOA, DH.KMS. 39/10 (18 May 1916).

66. Robert A. Kann, *The Multinational Empire: Nationalism and National Reform in the Habsburg Monarchy, 1848–1918*, vol. 1 (New York: Octagon Books, 1964), 432.

67. Imamović, *Pravni položaj*, 213.

68. See Ussama Makdisi, *The Culture of Sectarianism: Community, History, and Violence in Nineteenth-Century Ottoman Lebanon* (Berkeley: University of California Press, 2000).

69. Edin Hajdarpasic, *Whose Bosnia?: Nationalism and Political Imagination in the Balkans, 1840–1914* (Ithaca: Cornell University Press, 2015), 197.

70. As a colonial device, this method continues to plague contemporary Bosnia after the partition within independent Bosnia Herzegovina by the Dayton Peace Accords that ended the war on Bosnia Herzegovina, 1992–1995.

71. Juzbašić, *Politika i privreda*, 292.

72. Ibid., 248.

73. On the work of the assembly, see Imamović, *Pravni položaj*, ch. 5.

74. Imamović, *Pravni položaj*, 216.

75. Robert Donia, *Islam Under the Double Eagle* (Boulder: East European Monographs, 1981), 194.

76. On the transformation of the Ottoman categories of *çiftlik* and *çiftçi* (*čifluk* and *čifčija* in Bosnian), see Husnija Kamberović, *Begovski zemljišni posjedi u Bosni i Hercegovini od 1878 do 1918. godine* (Sarajevo: Ibn Sina, 2005), 109–137.

77. See Hamdija Kapidžić, ed., *Agrarni odnosi u BiH, 1878–1918* (Sarajevo: Arhiv Bosne i Hercegovine, 1969).

78. Edin Radušić, "Agrarno pitanje u Bosanskohercegovačkom Saboru 1910–1914," *Prilozi* 34 (2005): 122.

79. Ibid., 131.

80. Ibid., 140. Todor Kruševac, "Seljački pokret—štrajk u Bosni 1910. godine," *Pregled* 7 (1948): 369–405.

81. Kamberović, *Begovski zemljišni posjedi*, 119–122. The government earned 6.5 million krone per year from Bosnian forests at the eve of World War I; Radušić, "Agrarno pitanje," 127–128 and n. 27.

82. Radušić, "Agrarno pitanje," 145.

83. Ibid.,138–139.

84. Juzbašić, *Politika i privreda*, 471–472.

85. Dimitrije Tucović, "Crnogorski bes," *Radničke Novine* 239 (9 November 1913), quoted in Safet Bandžović, *Iseljavanje Bošnjaka u Tursku* (Sarajevo: Institut za istraživanje zločina protiv čovječnosti i međunarodnog prava, 2006), 231.

86. "Pred izbore naše uleme," *Musavat* (6 November 1909): 1.

87. On his career as a scholar of early Arabic poetry, which earned him praise as far as Cairo, see Lejla Gazić, "Ali-Fehmija Džabić kao kritičar klasične arapske poezije," *Prilozi za orijentalnu filologiju* 35 (1985): 29–50.

88. Meho Manjgo, "O imenovanju hafıza Sulejman-ef. Šarca za reisu-l-ulemu u Bosni i Hercegovini," *Anali Gazi Husrev-begove biblioteke* 48:40 (2019): 127–128.

89. Ibid., 128–130.

90. Ibid., 129.

91. Adnan Jahić, "O imenovanju Džemaludina Čauševića za reisul-ulemu 1913. godine," *Prilozi* 41 (2012): 63.

92. Haran Buljina, *Empire, Nation, and the Islamic World: Bosnian Muslim Reformists Between the Habsburg and Ottoman Empires, 1901–1914*, PhD dissertation (Columbia University, 2019), 215.

93. Jahić, "O imenovanju Džemaludina Čauševića," 66–72.

94. Ibid., 73, 77.

95. Buljina, *Empire, Nation, and the Islamic World*, 155–156.

96. BOA, BEO 4275/320586 (7 April 1914).

97. Buljina, *Empire, Nation, and the Islamic World*, 219–221.

98. Adnan Jahić, "Usponi i padovi zagonetnog Mostarca—skica za biografiju Šerifa Arnautovića," *Arhivska Praksa* 18 (2015): 458.

99. BOA, Y.KP. 3433 (29 January 1910).

100. Ibid.

101. Nikola Jarak, *Poljoprivredna politika Austro-Ugarske u Bosni i Hercegovini i zemljoradničko zadrugarstvo*, (Sarajevo: Naučno društvo NR Bosne i Hercegovine, 1956), 39. Ferdo Hauptmann quoted an increase in landowners from 8,162 in 1885 to 10,463 in 1910, but an overall drop in their economic power and prestige. Ferdo Hauptmann, *Die österreichisch-ungarische Herrschaft in Bosnien und der Herzegowina: Wirtschaftspolitik Und Wirtschaftsentwicklung, 1878–1918* (Graz: Institut für Geschichte der Universität Graz, Abt. Südosteuropäische Geschichte, 1983), 116–118. On landowners, also see Kamberović, *Begovski zemljišni posjedi*.

102. Nusret Šehić, *Autonomni pokret Muslimana za vrijeme austrougarske uprave u Bosni i Hercegovini* (Sarajevo: Svijetlost 1980), 36.

103. See Robert J. Donia, "Fin-de-Siècle Sarajevo: Habsburška transformacija grada," *Prilozi* 32 (2003): 149–178; Diane Reynolds, "Kavaljeri, kostimi, umjetnost: kako je Beč doživljavao Bosnu 1878–1900," *Prilozi* 32 (2003): 135–148; and Clemens Ruthner, " 'Naš' mali 'Orijent' jedno postkolonijalno čitanje austrijskih i njemačkih kulturalnih narativa o Bosni i Hercegovini 1878–1918," *Prilozi* 37 (2008): 149–167.

104. Imamović, *Pravni položaj*, 255.

105. Šerif Arnautović, "Muslimani na Balkanu," *Vakat* 1 (2 January 1914): 2.

106. Ibid.

107. Zgodić, *Bosanska politička*, 81.

108. BOA, DH.EUM.1.Şb. 3/25, 3/28, 3/29 (18, 25, 29 April 1916); Zgodić, *Bosanska politička*, 81, n. 51.

109. Husnija Kamberović, "Projugoslavenska struja među muslimanskim političarima 1918. godine," *Historijska traganja* 3 (2009): 95.

110. Adnan Jahić and Edi Bokun, "Memorandum Šerifa Arnautovića caru Karlu 1917. godine," *Prilozi* 44 (2015): 145–179.

111. Zgodić, *Bosanska politička*, 89, n.86.

112. Kamberović, "Projugoslavenska struja," 94–95.

113. Sohrabi, *Revolution and Constitutionalism*.

114. Tara Zahra, "Imagined Noncommunities: National Indifference as a Category of Analysis," *Slavic Review* 69:1 (2010): 93–119. For such examples in nearby Istria and Dalmatia, see Pamela Ballinger, *History in Exile: Memory and Identity at the Borders of the Balkans* (Princeton: Princeton University Press, 2003); and Dominique Reill, "A Mission of Mediation: Dalmatia's Multi-National Regionalism from the 1830s-60s," in *Different Paths to the Nation: Regional and National Identities in Central Europe and Italy, 1830–70*, ed. Laurence Cole (Basingstoke: Palgrave Macmillan, 2007), 16–36.

115. On the century-long (br)othering of Slav Muslims in Bosnia Herzegovina at the time, see Hajdarpasic, *Whose Bosnia?*.

116. Marsha L. Rozenblit, "Jewish Ethnicity in a New Nation-State: The Crisis of Identity in the Austrian Republic," in *In Search of Jewish Community: Jewish Identities in Germany and Austria, 1918–1933*, eds. Michael Brenner and Derek J. Penslar (Bloomington and Indianapolis: Indiana University Press, 1998), 135.

117. Robin Okey, *Taming Balkan Nationalism: The Habsburg Civilizing Mission in Bosnia, 1878–1914* (Oxford: Oxford University Press, 2007), 244–245.

Epilogue

Material from the Epilogue originally appeared in Leyla Amzi-Erdoğdular, "Alternative Muslim Modernities: Bosnian Intellectuals in the Ottoman and Habsburg Empires," Comparative Studies in Society and History 59:4 (2017): 912–943.

1. Paul Rabinow, *French Modern: Norms and Forms of the Social Environment* (Cambridge, MA: MIT Press, 1989), 9.

2. For example, Şerif Mardin, *The Genesis of Young Ottoman Thought: A Study in the Modernization of Turkish Political Ideas* (Princeton: Princeton University Press, 1962); Albert H. Hourani, *Arabic Thought in the Liberal Age: 1798–1939* (London: Oxford University Press, 1970); Nikki R. Keddie, *An Islamic Response to Imperialism: Political and Religious Writings of Sayyid Jamāl Ad-Dīn "al-Afghānī"* (Berkeley: University of California Press, 1968); Malcolm H. Kerr, *Islamic Reform:*

The Political and Legal Theories of Muḥammad ʿabduh and Rashīd Riḍā (Berkeley: University of California Press, 1966); Hamid Algar, *Mīrzā Malkum Khān: A Study in the History of Iranian Modernism* (Berkeley: University of California Press, 1973); and Adeeb Khalid, *The Politics of Muslim Cultural Reform: Jadidism in Central Asia* (Berkeley: University of California Press, 1999).

3. Timothy Mitchell remarked that colonial subjects are formed "within the organizational terrain of the colonial state, rather than some wholly exterior social space." Timothy Mitchell, *Colonising Egypt* (Cambridge and New York: Cambridge University Press, 1988), xi.

4. See John O. Voll, "Renewal and Reform in Islamic History: Tajdid and Islah," in *Voices of Resurgent Islam*, ed. John L. Esposito (New York: Oxford University Press, 1983), 32–47. For a treatment of the Bosnian Muslims' encounter with modernity, see Fikret Karčić, *The Bosniaks and the Challenges of Modernity: Late Ottoman and Hapsburg Times* (Sarajevo: El-Kalem, 1999).

5. See, for example, Ömer Turan and Kyle T. Evered, "Jadidism in South-Eastern Europe: The Influence of Ismail Bey Gaspirali Among Bulgarian Turks," *Middle Eastern Studies* 41:4 (2005): 481–502.

6. On provincial administration, see Stanford J. Shaw, "Local Administration in the Tanzimat," in *150. yılında Tanzimat,* ed. Hakki Dursun Yildiz (Ankara: Türk Tarih Kurumu Basımevi, 1992); Milen V. Petrov, "Everyday Forms of Compliance: Subaltern Commentaries on Ottoman Reform, 1864–1868," *Comparative Studies in Society and History* 46 (2004): 730–759; on Bosnia, Ahmed Aličić, *Uređenje Bosanskog ejaleta od 1789 do 1878. godine* (Sarajevo: Orijentalni institut, 1983).

7. On the official printing press, see: Mujo Koštić, "Državna štamparija i službene i polusužbene novine u Bosni i Hercegovini od 1866. do 1945. godine" *Novi Muallim* 18 (2004): 96–110.

8. See Senada Dizdar, "Mehmed Šaćir Kurtćehajić: (1844–1872)," *Godišnjak Bošnjačke zajednice kulture »Preporod«* 1 (2014): 314–324.

9. Đorđe Pejanović, *Štamparije u Bosni i Hercegovini, 1529–1951* (Sarajevo: Svjetlost, 1952), 11–16.

10. Edin Hajdarpasic, *Whose Bosnia?: Nationalism and Political Imagination in the Balkans, 1840–1914* (Ithaca: Cornell University Press, 2015), 186–196.

11. See Robert J. Donia, "Fin-de-Siècle Sarajevo: Habsburška transformacija grada," *Prilozi* 32 (2003): 149–178; Diane Reynolds, "Kavaljeri, kostimi, umjetnost: kako je Beč doživljavao Bosnu 1878–1900," *Prilozi* 32 (2003): 135–148; Clemens Ruthner, "'Naš' mali 'Orijent' jedno postkolonijalno čitanje austrijskih i njemačkih kulturnih narativa o Bosni i Hercegovini 1878–1918," *Prilozi* 37 (2008): 149–167.

12. See Kemal H. Karpat, *The Turks of Bulgaria: The History and Political Fate of a Minority* (Istanbul: Isis Press, 1990).

13. Milena Bogomilova Methodieva, *Reform, Politics, and Culture Among the Muslims in Bulgaria, 1878–1908*, PhD dissertation (Princeton University, 2010), 170–173.

14. Muhsin Rizvić, *Bosansko-muslimanska književnost u doba preporoda (1887–1918)* (Sarajevo: Mešihat islamske zajednice BiH, El-Kalem izdavačka djelatnost, 1990), 20–23.

15. Hajdarpasic, *Whose Bosnia?*, 163.

16. Bisera Nurudinović, "Bosanske salname (1866–1878 i 1882–1893)," *Prilozi za orijentalnu filologiju* 10/11 (1960–61): 253–265.

17. See Ismail Eren, "Turska štampa u Jugoslaviji (1866–1966)," *Prilozi za orijentalnu filologiju* 14–15 (1964–1965): 359–395.

18. When the statute of Sarajevo was adopted in 1884, the administration approved the proposal to translate it into Turkish and distribute it to representatives. Todor Kruševac, *Sarajevo pod austrougarskom upravom 1878–1918* (Sarajevo: Muzej grada, 1960), 271.

19. For Muslim elementary and higher schools for girls, see Mina Kujović, "Muslimanska osnovna i viša djevojačka škola sa produženim tečajem (1894–1925)—prilog historiji muslimanskog školstva u Bosni i Hercegovini," *Novi Muallim* 41 (2010): 72–79.

20. Karčić *The Bosniaks and the Challenges of Modernity*, 62–63.

21. Milena B. Methodieva, *Between Empire and Nation: Muslim Reform in the Balkans* (Stanford: Stanford University Press, 2021), 120.

22. For a comprehensive analysis of Bosnian Muslim educational networks in this period, see Haran Buljina, *Empire, Nation, and the Islamic World: Bosnian Muslim Reformists Between the Habsburg and Ottoman Empires, 1901–1914*, PhD dissertation (Columbia University, 2019).

23. These fears became reality when interwar agrarian reform and post–World War II land nationalization caused Muslim economic decline followed by their sociopolitical marginalization and systematic discrimination in the Kingdom of Yugoslavia and the Socialist Federative Republic of Yugoslavia.

24. Mehmed-Beg Kapetanović Ljubušak, *Budućnost ili napredak Muhamedovaca u Bosni i Hercegovini* (Sarajevo: Spindler & Löschner, 1893), 4–5.

25. Charles Kurzman, *Modernist Islam, 1840–1940: A Sourcebook* (Oxford: Oxford University Press, 2002), 312.

26. Ibid., 149–151.

27. Husnija Kamberović, *Begovski zemljišni posjedi u Bosni i Hercegovini od 1878 do 1918. godine* (Sarajevo: Ibn Sina, 2005), 60–63.

28. Ljubušak, *Budućnost ili napredak*, 5.
29. Ibid., 17.
30. Ibid., 6.
31. Hakan Kırımlı, *National Movements and National Identity among the Crimean Tatars, 1905–1916* (Leiden: Brill, 1996), 59.
32. Ibrahim bin Abu Bakar, *Islamic Modernism in Malaya as Reflected in Hadi's Thought*, PhD dissertation (McGill University, 1992), 258.
33. Kurzman, *Modernist Islam*, 312.
34. On the role of Japan as a model of "non-Western" modernity and success, after its 1905 victory over Russia, see Renée Worringer, *The Islamic Middle East and Japan: Perceptions, Aspirations, and the Birth of Intra-Asian Modernity* (Princeton: Markus Wiener, 2007); and Cemil Aydin, *The Politics of Anti-Westernism in Asia*.
35. Fikret Karčić, *Islamske teme i perspektive* (Sarajevo: El-kalem, 2009), 27.
36. These include Safvet Beg Bašagić's poems "Trofanda" (1896) and a 1900 historical work, *Kratke upute u prošlost Bosne i Hercegovine* (A short instruction into the past of Bosnia Herzegovina); Edhem Mulabdić's 1898 novel *Zeleno Busenje* (Green turf), set during the early days of the Habsburg occupation; Osman Nuri Hadžić's *Islam i kultura* (Islam and culture) in 1894; and in collaboration with Ivan Aziz Miličević, *Bez nade* (Without hope) in 1895, *Na pragu novog doba* (At the doorstep of a new age) in 1896, *Bez svrhe* (Without purpose) in 1897, and *Pripovijesti iz bosanskog života* (Tales from Bosnian life) in 1898.
37. See Omer Humo, *Sehletul-vusul: grafija i leksika sehletul-vusula* (Mostar: Muzej Hercegovine, 2010).
38. The first Bosnian-Turkish dictionary was published in 1631; Muhamed H. Uskufi, Ahmet Kasumović, and Svein Mønnesland, *Bosansko-turski rječnik* (Tuzla: Općina Tuzla, 2011). For an overview of Bosnian Alhamijado literature, see Werner Lehfeldt, *Das Serbokroatische Aljamiado-Schrifttum Der Bosnisch-Hercegovinischen Muslime: Transkriptionsprobleme* (München: R. Trofenik, 1969); Alen Kalajdžija, "O klasifikaciji bosanske književnojezičke tradicije," *Anali Gazi Husrev-begove biblioteke* 33 (2012): 277–289; and Svein Mønnesland, ed., *Jezik u Bosni i Hercegovini* (Sarajevo: Institut za jezik u Sarajevu, 2005).
39. See Srđan Janković, "Ortografsko usavršavanje naše arabice u štampanim tekstovima," *Prilozi za orijentalnu filologiju* 38 (1988): 9–40. On standardization of Arebica for reformed vernacular religious education to Pan-Islamic reform, see Harun Buljina, "Writing Bosnian in Arabic: The Standardization of the Arebica Script in the Long 19th Century," *Turcica* 54 (2023).
40. Muhsin Rizvić, *Behar: književnoistorijska monografija* (Sarajevo: Svjetlost, 1971), 14.

41. Ibid., 15.

42. Muhsin Rizvić, *Bosansko-muslimanska književnost u doba preporoda (1887–1918)* (Sarajevo: Mešihat islamske zajednice BiH, 1990), 201.

43. Rizvić, *Behar*, 82.

44. Rizvić, *Bosansko-muslimanska književnost*, 212.

45. On Namık Kemal's reformist role, see Mardin, *The Genesis of Young Ottoman Thought*, 283–336.

46. Rizvić *Bosansko-muslimanska književnost*, 212–213. On the adaptation, see Midhat Šamić, "Jedna prerada Molijerovih *Skapenovih podvala* u Bosni početkom XX stoljeća," *Radovi Filozofskog fakulteta u Sarajevu* 1 (1963).

47. Rizvić *Behar*, 244.

48. Fabio Giomi, "Daughters of Two Empires: Muslim Women and Public Writing in Habsburg Bosnia Herzegovina (1878–1918)," *Aspasia* 9 (2015): 6.

49. See Nusret Kujraković, "*Osvitanje*—prvo udruženje Muslimanki u Bosni i Hercegovini," *Prilozi* 39 (2009): 145–164.

50. Rizvić, *Bosansko-muslimanska književnost*, 253.

51. For some of these debates, see Xavier Bougarel, "Farewell to the Ottoman Legacy? Islamic Reformism and Revivalism in Inter-War Bosnia-Herzegovina," in *Islam in Inter-War Europe*, eds. Nathalie Clayer and E. Germain (New York: Columbia University Press, 2008), 313–343.

52. Rizvić, *Bosansko-muslimanska književnost*, 93.

53. Methodieva, *Between Empire and Nation*, 139.

54. Ljubušak *Budućnost ili napredak*, 12.

55. Osman Nuri Hadžić, *Muslimansko pitanje u Bosni i Hercegovini* (Zagreb: Tisak Dioničke Tiskare, 1902), 4.

56. This is most notably in the novel *Bez svrhe* (Without purpose), coauthored with Ivan Miličević under the pseudonym Osman-Aziz, Osman Nuri Hadžić, *Bez svrhe: Slika iz života* (Zagreb: Matica hrvatska, 1897).

57. Hadžić, *Muslimansko pitanje*, 53.

58. Kurzman, *Modernist Islam*, 342.

59. Methodieva, *Between Empire and Nation*, 205.

60. Adeeb Khalid, *The Politics of Muslim Cultural Reform: Jadidism in Central Asia* (Berkeley: University of California Press, 1999), 173. He explained, "In the maktab, all knowledge was sacral and tenets of Islam pervaded everything taught. In new method schools, Islam became an object of study, knowledge of which could be acquired in the same way as all other knowledge." For Ottoman modern education, see Benjamin C. Fortna, *Imperial Classroom: Islam, the State, and Education in the Late Ottoman Empire* (Oxford: Oxford University Press, 2002); and Selçuk A. Somel, *The Modernization of Public Education in*

the Ottoman Empire, 1839–1908: Islamization, Autocracy, and Discipline (Leiden: Brill, 2001).

61. Khalid, *The Politics of Muslim Cultural Reform*, 175.

62. See Mustafa Tuna, "Madrasa Reform as a Secularizing Process: A View from the Late Russian Empire," *Comparative Studies in Society and History* 53:3 (2011): 540–570; also see Danielle Ross, *Tatar Empire: Kazan's Muslims and the Making of Imperial Russia* (Bloomington: Indiana University Press, 2020).

63. Methodieva, *Reform, Politics, and Culture*, 218–219.

64. Ibid., 204–205.

65. Ibid., 234.

66. For example, Guy Imart, *Islamic and Slavic Fundamentalisms: Foes or Allies? The Turkestanian Reagent* (Bloomington: Research Institute for Inner Asian Studies, Indiana University, 1987).

67. On the Ottoman Westernized elite, see M. Şükrü Hanioğlu, "Garbcılar: Their Attitudes Toward Religion and Their Impact on the Official Ideology of the Turkish Republic," *Studia Islamica* 86 (1997):133–158; and Ismail Kara, "Turban and Fez: Ulema as Opposition," in *Late Ottoman Society: The Intellectual Legacy*, ed. Elisabeth Özdalga (New York: Routledge Curzon, 2005).

68. See Yaşar Sarıkaya, *Medreseler ve Modernleşme* (Istanbul: İz Yayıncılık, 1997); Muhammad Qasim Zaman, "Religious Education and the Rhetoric of Reform: The Madrasa in British India and Pakistan," *Comparative Studies in Society and History* 41:2 (1999): 294–323; Indira F. Gesink, "Islamic Reformation: A History of Madrasa Reform and Legal Change in Egypt," *Comparative Education Review* 50: 3 (2006): 325–345; and Said A. Arjomand, "Ideological Revolution in Shi'ism," in *Authority and Political Culture in Shi'ism*, ed. Said A. Arjomand (Albany: State University of New York Press, 1988), 178–209.

69. Ljubušak, *Budućnost ili napredak*, 14.

70. Quoted in Esad Zgodić, *Bosanska politička misao: austrougarsko doba* (Sarajevo: DES, 2003), 104.

71. Kurzman, *Modernist Islam*, 5.

72. M. Şükrü Hanioğlu, *Preparation for a Revolution: The Young Turks, 1902–1908* (Oxford: Oxford University Press, 2001), 76.

73. Zgodić, *Bosanska politička misao*, 104–107.

74. On the role of Gajret in Muslim life, see Ibrahim Kemura, *Uloga "Gajreta" u društvenom životu Muslimana Bosne i Hercegovine* (Sarajevo: Veselin Masleša, 1986).

75. Zgodić, *Bosanska politička misao*, 105; also see Hadžić, *Muslimansko pitanje*, 5–6.

76. Tuna, "Madrasa Reform as a Secularizing Process," 544; and Audrey Alt-

stadt, "The Azerbaijani Bourgeoisie and the Cultural-Enlightenment Movement in Baku," in *Transcaucasia, Nationalism, and Social Change*, ed. Ronald Grigor Suny (Ann Arbor: University of Michigan Press, 1996), 199–209.

77. Methodieva, Between *Empire and Nation*, 117–118.

78. Hajdarpasic, *Whose Bosnia?*, 163.

79. Ibid., 167.

80. Ibid., 161–163.

81. An article titled "Patriotism" ran in one of the first local papers in Ottoman Bosnia. See Mehmed Šakir Kurtćehajić, "Patriotizam," *Sarajevski cvjetnik* 30 (25 July 1870).

82. Esad Zgodić, *Bošnjacko iskustvo politike, osmansko doba* (Sarajevo: Euromedija, 1998), 56.

83. "Jedna mala grana / Velikoga stabla Slavljana," in Rizvić, *Bosansko-muslimanska književnost*, 86.

84. Safvet Beg Bašagić, "Hubb-ul vatani min-el iman / Ljubav otadžbine s vjerom je skopčana." *Bošnjak* 2 (1891): 2–3.

85. Fikret Karčić, *Društveno-pravni aspekt islamskog reformizma: pokret za reformu šerijatskog prava i njegov odjek u Jugoslaviji u prvoj polovini XX vijeka* (Sarajevo: Islamski teološki fakultet, 1990), 205.

86. Rizvić, *Behar*, 328.

87. Karčić, *The Bosniaks and the Challenges of Modernity*, 146.

88. The report, signed "Garib," appeared in *Behar* 4 (15 June 1903).

89. Methodieva, *Reform, Politics, and Culture*, 340–341.

90. Ibid., 206.

91. Ibid., 202–203.

92. Hamza Karčić, "Supporting the Caliph's Project: Bosnian Muslims and the Hejaz Railway," *Journal of Muslim Minority Affairs* 34:3 (2014): 282–292.

93. BOA, DH.İD. 132/11 (16 April 1913).

94. Genç Osman Geçer, "Bosna Hersek'ten Hilal-i Ahmere maddi yardımlar: Misbah mecmuası orneği (1912–1914)," *TÜBAR* XXXI (2012): 104.

95. See Pardis Minuchehr, *Homeland from Afar: The Iranian Diaspora and the Quest for Modernity (1908–1909)* (the Constitutional Movement Within a Global Perspective), PhD dissertation (Columbia University, 1998); Lale Can, *Spiritual Subjects: Central Asian Pilgrims and the Ottoman Hajj at the End of Empire* (Stanford: Stanford University Press, 2020).

Bibliography

Archival Sources
Arhiv Bosne i Hercegovine (ABiH), Sarajevo
ZMF   Zajedničko ministarstvo finansija
ZV   Zemaljska vlada

BOA (Başbakanlık Osmanlı Arşivi), Prime Ministry Ottoman Archives (now Devlet Arşivleri Başkanlığı Osmanlı Arşivi, Istanbul)
A.MKT.MHM.   Sadaret Mektubi Kalemi Mühimme Kalemi
A.MTZ.BN.   Sadaret Eyalat-ı Mümtaze Kalemi, Bosna
BEO   Bab-ı Ali Evrak Odası
DH.EUM.   Dahiliye Nezareti Emniyet-i Umumiye Müdüriyeti
DH.EUM.EMN.   Dahiliye Nezareti Emniyet Kalemi
DH.KMS.   Dahiliye Nezareti Kalem-i Mahsus Müdüriyeti
DH.MKT.   Dahiliye Nezareti Mektubi Kalemi
HAT   Hatt-ı Hümayun
HR.HMŞ.IŞO.   Hariciye Nezareti Hukuk Müşavirliği, İstişare Odası
HR.SFR.   Hariciye Nezareti Sefaret
HR.SYS.   Hariciye Nezareti Siyasi Kısım Evrakı
HR.TH.   Hariciye Nezareti Tahrirat
HR.TO.   Hariciye Nezareti Tercüme Odası
I.DH.   İrade Dahiliye
I.HUS.   İrade Hususi

I.MMS.	İrade Meclis-i Mahsus
MHD	Muahedenameler
MV.	Meclis-i Vükela Mazbatları
Y.A.HUS.	Yıldız Sadaret Hususi Maruzat Evrakı
Y.A.RES.	Yıldız Sadaret Resmi Maruzat Evrakı
Y.EE.	Yıldız Esas Evraki
Y.KP.	Yıldız Kamil Paşa Evrakı
Y.MTV.	Yıldız Mütenevvi Maruzat Evrakı
Y.PRK.ASK.	Yıldız Perakende Askeri Maruzatı
Y.PRK.AZJ.	Yıldız Perakende Arzuhaller ve Jurnaller
Y.PRK.BŞK.	Yıldız Perakende Mabeyn Başkitabeti Maruzatı
Y.PRK.EŞA.	Yıldız Perakende Elçilik, Şehbenderlik ve Ateşemiliterlik
Y.PRK.HR.	Yıldız Perakende Hariciye Nezareti Maruzatı
Y.PRK.MŞ.	Yıldız Perakende Evraki Meşihat Dairesi Maruzatı
Y.PRK.MYD.	Yıldız Perakende Yaveran ve Maiyet-i Seniyye Erkan-ı Harbiye Dairesi
Y.PRK.TKM.	Yıldız Tahrirat-ı Ecnebiye ve Mabeyn Mütercimliği

Gazi Husrev-begova Biblioteka (GHB), Sarajevo

Papers and Periodicals
Behar (Sarajevo)
Bošnjak (Sarajevo)
Ikdam (Istanbul)
Ittihat ve Terakki (Istanbul)
La Revue d'Orient et de Hongrie (Budapest)
Pester Lloyd (Budapest)
Musavat (Sarajevo)
Sarajevski cvjetnik (Sarajevo)
Sarajevski list (Sarajevo)
Srpska Riječ (Sarajevo)
Tanin (Istanbul)
Vakat (Sarajevo)
Vatan (Sarajevo)

Published Archival Sources
Binark, İsmet, Necati Gültepe, and Necati Aktaş, eds. *Bosna-hersek ile ilgili arşiv belgeleri, 1516–1919*. Ankara: T.C. Başbakanlık, Devlet Arşivleri Genel Müdürlüğü, Osmanlı Arşivi Daire Başkanlığı, 1992.

Duran, Faik Sabri, and Ubeydullah Esat. *Resimli Kitap* 43–48. Istanbul: s.n., 1913.
Izvjestaj o upravi Bosne i Hercegovine. Zagreb: Zajednicko Ministarstvo Financija, 1906.
Sarınay, Yusuf, Mustafa Budak, and H. Y. Ağanoğlu, eds. *Osmanlı belgelerinde Bosna Hersek: Bosna i Hercegovina u osmanskim dokumentima*. İstanbul: T.C. Başbakanlık, Devlet Arşivleri Genel Müdürlüğü, Osmanlı Arşivi Daire Başkanlığı, 2009.
Şimşir, Bilâl N. *Rumeli'den Türk Göçleri: Belgeler / Emigrations Turques Des Balkans: Documents / Turkish Emigrations from the Balkans: Documents*. Ankara: Türk Tarih Kurumu Basımevi, 1989.

Published Primary Sources
Ahmed Cevdet Paşa, and Cavid Baysun. *Tezakir*. Ankara: Türk Tarih Kurumu Basımevi, 1991.
Ali Rüşdü. *Bosna Hersek'in memâlik-i Osmaniyye'den tefrîkiyle Avusturya'ya satmak fikrinde bulunanların vücûb-ı tel'inini nâtık Bosna Hersek ahâlisi nâmına Meb'ûsân ve Ayân-ı Osmanî Meclislerine verilen lâyıhadır*. Dersaadet [Istanbul]: Ruşen Maatbasi, 1324 [1909].
Ali Şadi. *Bosna Hersek yahud Osmanlı'ların Alsas Loren'i*. Dersaadet [Istanbul]: Süha Matbaası, 1327 [1911].
Ali Ulvi. *Avusturya'nın Bosna Hersek'i ilhakına karşı bir müdafaa-ı vatanperverane*. Dersaadet [Istanbul]: Ruşen Matbaası, 1324 [1908].
Asboth, Janos. *An Official Tour Through Bosnia and Herzegovina*. Lon: Swan Sonnenschein, 1890.
Bosnavî, Ömer. *Tarih-i Bosna der zaman-i Hekimzade Ali Paşa*. İstanbul: Süleyman Efendi'nin Matbaası, 1876.
Brenning, Alfred. *Innere Kolonisation*. Leipzig: B. G. Teubner, 1909.
Çelebi, Kınalızade Ali, and Hüseyin Algül. *Ahlâk-i Alâî*. Istanbul: Tercüman, 1974.
Ehli-Islam. *Bezakonja okupacione uprave u Bosni i Hercegovini*. Novi Sad: Srpska štamparija dra. Sv. Miletića, 1901.
Evans, Arthur. *Through Bosnia and the Herzegovina on Foot During the Insurrection*. London: Longmans, 1876.
Hadžić, Osman Nuri. *Muslimansko pitanje u Bosni i Hercegovini*. Zagreb: Tisak Dioničke Tiskare, 1902.
———. "Srpsko-muhamedanska sloga." *Hrvatsko Pravo* 790 (24 June 1898).
Hadžić, Osman Nuri, and Ivan Milićević [Osman-Aziz]. *Bez svrhe: Slika iz života*. Zagreb: Matica hrvatska, 1897.
Heimfelsen, Josef K. *Die Deutschen Kolonien in Bosnien*. Wien: Gerold, 1911.

Hilmi, Ömer. *Ahkâmü'l-evkaf.* İstanbul: Matbaa-yı Amire, 1889.
Koetschet, Josef. *Osman Pascha, Der Letzte Grosse Wesier Bosniens, Und Seine Nachfolger.* Sarajevo: Studnička, 1909.
Ljubušak, Mehmed-Beg Kapetanović. *Budućnost ili napredak Muhamedovaca u Bosni i Hercegovini.* Sarajevo: Spindler & Löschner, 1893.
———. *Što misle muhamedanci u Bosni i Hercegovini.* Sarajevo: Spindler & Löschner, 1886.
Marx, Karl, and Eleanor M. Aveling. *The Eastern Question: A Reprint of Letters Written 1853–1856 Dealing with the Events of the Crimean War.* London: S. Sonnenschein & Co., 1897.
Memorandum nj. preuzvišenom ministru Kallayu predan 19.12.1900 u Sarajevu od predstavnika i zastupnika muslimanskog naroda okupiranih zemalja. Novi Sad: Srpska štamparija dra. Svetozara Miletića, 1901.
Minchin, James G. C. *The Growth of Freedom in the Balkan Peninsula: Notes of Traveler in Montenegro, Bosnia, Servia, Bulgaria and Greece.* London, 1886.
Mehmed Nasrullah, Mehmed Rüşdi, Mehmed Eşref. *Memalik-i Mahruse-i Şahaneye Mahsus Mükemmel ve Mufassal Atlas.* Istanbul: Şirket-i Mürettibiye Matbaası, 1907.
Pfanner, Franz. "Bosnien, ein Land für Ansiedlung." *Weckstimmen für das katholische Volk* 9:11 (1878).
[Pruščak], Hasan Kafı Aq-Hissari. *Usūl El-Hikam Fī Nizām Al-Ālam.* Istanbul, 1868.
Ranke, Leopold von. *The History of Servia, and the Servian Revolution: With a Sketch of the Insurrection in Bosnia; the Slave Provinces of Turkey.* Translated by Mrs. Alexander Kerr. London: Bohn, 1853.
Rida, Muhammad Rashid. "Al hijratu wa hukumu muslimi busna fiha." *Al-Manar* 12 (1909): 410–415.
Schmid, Ferdinand. *Bosnien und Herzegovina: Unter Der Verwaltung Österreich-Ungarns.* Leipzig: Veit, 1914.
Schweiger-Lerchenfeld, Amand. *Bosnien: das Land und seine Bewohner: geschichtlich, geographisch, etnographisch und social-politisch.* Vienna: Verlag von L. C. Zamarski, 1878.
Spencer, Edmund. *Travels in European Turkey: Through Bosnia, Servia, Bulgaria, Macedonia, Thrace, Albania, and Epirus.* London: Hurst and Blackett, 1853.

Secondary Sources
Abou El Fadl, Khaled. "Islamic Law and Muslim Minorities: The Juristic Discourse on Muslim Minorities from Second/Eighth to the Eleventh/Seventeenth Centuries." *Islamic Law and Society* 1:2 (1994): 141–187.

Abu Bakar, Ibrahim bin. *Islamic Modernism in Malaya as Reflected in Hadi's Thought*. PhD dissertation. McGill University, 1992.

Adanır, Fikret, and Suraiya Faroqhi, eds. *The Ottomans and the Balkans: A Discussion of Historiography*. Leiden: Brill, 2002.

Ağanoğlu, H. Yıldırım. *Osmanlı'dan Cumhuriyet'e Balkanlar'ın Makûs Talihi Göç*. Istanbul: Kum Saati, 2001.

Ahmed, Faiz. *Afghanistan Rising: Islamic Law and Statecraft Between the Ottoman and British Empires*. Cambridge, MA: Harvard University Press, 2017.

———. "Contested Subjects: Ottoman and British Jurisdictional Quarrels in Re Afghans and Indian Muslims." *Journal of the Ottoman and Turkish Studies Association* 3:2 (2016): 325–346

Ahmed, Shahab. *What Is Islam? The Importance of Being Islamic*. Princeton: Princeton University Press, 2016.

Akarlı, Engin. "The Tangled Ends of an Empire: Ottoman Encounters with the West and Problems of Westernization—an Overview." *Comparative Studies of South Asia, Africa and the Middle East* 26:3 (2006): 353–366.

Akgündüz, Ahmet. *İslâm hukukunda ve Osmanlı tatbikatında vakıf müessesesi*. Ankara: Türk Tarih Kurumu, 1988.

Aksan, Virginia H. *Ottoman Wars, 1700–1870: An Empire Besieged*. London: Routledge, 2014.

Al-Arnaut, Muhamed Mufaku. "Islam and Muslims in Bosnia 1878–1918: Two Hijras and Two Fatwās." *Journal of Islamic Studies* 5:2 (1994): 242–253.

Alavi, Seema. *Muslim Cosmopolitanism in the Age of Empire*. Cambridge, MA: Harvard University Press, 2015.

Algar, Hamid. *Mīrzā Malkum Khān: A Study in the History of Iranian Modernism*. Berkeley: University of California Press, 1973.

Alić, Dijana, and Maryam Gusheh. "Reconciling National Narratives in Socialist Bosnia and Herzegovina: The Baščaršija Project, 1948–1953." *Journal of the Society of Architectural Historians* 58:1 (1999): 6–25.

Aličić, Ahmed S. "Manuscript *Ahval-i-Bosna* by Muhamed Emin Isević (Early 19th Century)." *Prilozi za orijentalnu filologiju* 50 (2002): 227–264.

———. *Uređenje Bosanskog ejaleta od 1789 do 1878. godine*. Sarajevo: Orijentalni institut, 1983.

Alloul, Houssine, and Roel Markey. "'Please Deny These Manifestly False Reports': Ottoman Diplomats and the Press in Belgium (1850–1914)." *International Journal of Middle East Studies* 48:2 (2016): 267–292.

Altstadt, Audrey. "The Azerbaijani Bourgeoisie and the Cultural-Enlightenment Movement in Baku." In *Transcaucasia, Nationalism, and Social Change*, edited by Ronald Grigor Suny, 199–209. Ann Arbor: University of Michigan Press, 1996.

Amzi-Erdoğdular, Leyla. "Alternative Muslim Modernities: Bosnian Intellectuals in the Ottoman and Habsburg Empires." *Comparative Studies in Society and History* 59:4 (2017): 912–943.

———. "Muslim Migration and Nation-Building in Interwar Yugoslavia and Turkey." In *Borders, Boundaries and Belonging in Post-Ottoman Space in the Interwar Period,* edited by Kate Fleet and Ebru Boyar, 241–265. Leiden: Brill, 2023.

———. "Ottoman Bosnia Herzegovina and Its Muslims." In *Routledge Handbook of Balkan and Southeast European History,* edited by John R. Lampe and Ulf Brunnbauer, 42–49. London: Routledge, 2020.

Anderson, Benedict. *Imagined Communities: Reflections on the Origin and Spread of Nationalism.* London and New York: Verso, 1991.

Argenti, Nicolas, ed. *Post-Ottoman Topologies: The Presence of the Past in the Era of the Nation-State.* New York: Berghahn, 2019.

Arjomand, Said A. "Ideological Revolution in Shi'ism." In *Authority and Political Culture in Shi'ism,* edited by Said Amir Arjomand, 178–209. Albany: State University of New York Press, 1988.

Aščerić-Todd, Ines. *Dervishes and Islam in Bosnia: Sufi Dimensions to the Formation of Bosnian Muslim Society.* Leiden: Brill, 2015.

Aydin, Cemil. *The Idea of the Muslim World: A Global Intellectual History.* Cambridge, MA: Harvard University Press, 2017.

———. *The Politics of Anti-Westernism in Asia: Visions of World Order in Pan-Islamic and Pan-Asian Thought.* New York: Columbia University Press, 2007.

Azapagić, Mehmed Teufik. "Risala o Hidžri." Translated by Osman Lavić. *Anali Gazi Husrev-begove biblioteke* 16-17 (1990): 197–222.

Babuna, Aydin. "The Berlin Treaty, Bosnian Muslims, and Nationalism." In *War and Diplomacy: The Russo-Turkish War of 1877–1878 and the Treaty of Berlin,* edited by M. Hakan Yavuz, 219–220. Salt Lake City: University of Utah Press, 2011.

Bakić-Hayden, Milica. "Nesting Orientalisms: The Case of Former Yugoslavia." *Slavic Review* 54:4 (1995): 917–931.

Baldwin, James E. "Petitioning the Sultan in Ottoman Egypt." *Bulletin of the School of Oriental and African Studies* 75:3 (2012): 499–524.

Balibar, Étienne. *Masses, Classes, Ideas: Studies on Politics and Philosophy Before and After Marx.* New York: Routledge, 1994.

Ballinger, Pamela. *History in Exile: Memory and Identity at the Borders of the Balkans.* Princeton: Princeton University Press, 2003.

Bandžović, Safet. *Iseljavanje Bošnjaka u Tursku.* Sarajevo: Institut za istraživanje zločina protiv čovječnosti i međunarodnog prava, 2006.

———. "Pljevaljski Muftija Šemsekadić u otporu austrougarskoj okupaciji Bosne i Hercegovine i zaposjedanju novopazarskog sandžaka." *Novopazarski Zbornik* (1992): 100–111.

———. "Uzroci muhadžirskih pokreta iz Bosne i Hercegovina 1878–1912." *Almanah-Časopis za pručavanje, prezentaciju i zaštitu kulturno-istorijske baštine Bošnjaka Muslimana* 48/49 (2010): 89–128.

Barkey, Karen. *Empire of Difference: The Ottomans in Comparative Perspective.* New York: Cambridge University Press, 2013.

Barkey, Karen, and Mark von Hagen, eds. *After Empire: Multiethnic Societies and Nation Building: The Soviet Union and the Russian, Ottoman and Habsburg Empires.* Boulder: Westview Press, 1997.

Bauman, Zygmunt. *Modernity and Ambivalence.* Ithaca: Cornell University Press, 1991.

Bećić, Mehmed. "Osmansko tanzimatsko pravo i austrougarski pravni poredak u Bosni i Hercegovini." *Anali Pravnog Fakulteta Univerziteta u Zenici* 12 (2009): 187–201.

———. "Primjena Medželle u postosmanskoj Bosni i Hercegovini." *Godišnjak Pravnog fakulteta u Sarajevu* LVII (2014): 51–65.

Ben-Bassat, Yuval. *Petitioning the Sultan: Protests and Justice in Late Ottoman Palestine, 1865–1908.* London: I. B. Tauris, 2013.

Berkes, Niyazi. *The Development of Secularism in Turkey.* Montreal: McGill University Press, 1964.

Biletić, Sandra. "Dolazak austro-ugarske vojske u Fojnicu 1878. godine: odlomak iz dnevnika fra Marka Kalamuta." *Bosna Franciscana* 51 (2019): 147–168.

Birdal, Murat. *The Political Economy of Ottoman Public Debt: Insolvency and European Financial Control in the Late Nineteenth Century.* London: I. B. Tauris, 2010.

Blumi, Isa. *Foundations of Modernity: Human Agency and the Imperial State.* Hoboken: Taylor & Francis, 2011.

———. "The Great Powers Fixation on Ottoman Albania in the Administration of the Post-Berlin Balkans, 1878–1908." In *Ottoman-Russian War of 1877–1878*, edited by Ömer Turan, 187–196. Ankara: Middle East Technical University Press, 2006.

———. *Reinstating the Ottomans: Alternative Balkan Modernities, 1800–1912.* Basingstoke: Palgrave Macmillan, 2011.

———. *Rethinking the Late Ottoman Empire: A Comparative Social and Political History of Albania and Yemen, 1878–1918.* Istanbul: Isis Press, 2010.

Bogićević, Vojislav. "Emigracija Muslimana Bosne i Hercegovine u Tursku u doba austro-ugarske vladavine 1878–1918." *Historijski zbornik* 1:4/3 (1950).

Boratav, Korkut, A. Gündüz Ökçün, and Şevket Pamuk. "Ottoman Wages and the World-Economy, 1839–1913," *Review* (Fernand Braudel Center) 8:3 (1985): 379–406.

Bougarel, Xavier. "Farewell to the Ottoman Legacy? Islamic Reformism and Revivalism in Inter-War Bosnia-Herzegovina." In *Islam in Inter-War Europe*, edited by Nathalie Clayer and E. Germain, 313–343. New York: Columbia University Press, 2008.

Bourdieu, Pierre. *In Other Words: Essays Towards a Reflexive Sociology*. Stanford: Stanford University Press, 1990.

———. *The Logic of Practice*. Stanford: Stanford University Press, 1990.

Boyar, Ebru. *Ottomans, Turks and the Balkans: Empire Lost, Relations Altered*. London: I. B. Tauris, 2007.

Bracewell, Wendy. "Friends, Lovers, Rivals, Enemies: Blood-Brotherhood on an Early-Modern Balkan Frontier." *Caiete de Antropologie Istorică* 3 (2003): 103–126.

Bračković, Husejn, and Zejnil Fajić. "Mala istorija događaja u Hercegovini." *Prilozi za orijentalnu filologiju* 34 (1984): 163–200.

Brenner, Michael, and Derek J. Penslar, eds. *In Search of Jewish Community: Jewish Identities in Germany and Austria, 1918–1933*. Bloomington: Indiana University Press, 1998.

Brown, L. Carl, ed. *Imperial Legacy: The Ottoman Imprint on the Balkans and the Middle East*. New York: Columbia University Press, 1996.

Brummett, Palmira. *Image and Imperialism in the Ottoman Revolutionary Press, 1908–1911*. Albany: State University of New York Press, 2000.

Buljina, Harun. "Bosnia's 'Young Turks': The Bosnian Muslim Intelligentsia in Its Late Ottoman Context, 1878–1914." In *The Turkish Connection: Global Intellectual Histories of the Late Ottoman Empire and Republican Turkey*, edited by Deniz Kuru and Hazal Papuççular, 27–48. Berlin and Boston: De Gruyter Oldenbourg, 2022.

———. *Empire, Nation, and the Islamic World: Bosnian Muslim Reformists Between the Habsburg and Ottoman Empires, 1901–1914*. PhD dissertation. Columbia University, 2019.

———. "Writing Bosnian in Arabic: The Standardization of the Arebica Script in the Long 19th Century." *Turcica* 54 (2023).

Buturović, Amila, and Irvin C. Schick, eds. *Women in the Ottoman Balkans: Gender, Culture and History*. London: I. B. Tauris, 2007.

Buzov, Snježana. "Ottoman Perceptions of Bosnia as Reflected in the Works of Authors Who Visited or Lived in Bosnia." In *Ottoman Bosnia: A History in Peril*, edited by Markus Koller and Kemal H. Karpat, 83–91. Madison: University of Wisconsin Press, 2004.

Buzpınar, Ş. Tufan. "The Hijaz, Abdülhamid II and Amir Hussein's Secret Dealings with the British, 1877–80." *Middle Eastern Studies* 31:1 (1995): 99–123.

———. "Opposition to the Ottoman Caliphate in the Early Years of Abdülhamid II: 1877–1882." *Die Welt des Islams* 36:1 (1996): 59–89.

Campos, Michelle U. *Ottoman Brothers: Muslims, Christians, and Jews in Early Twentieth-Century Palestine*. Stanford: Stanford University Press, 2010.

Can, Lale. *Spiritual Subjects: Central Asian Pilgrims and the Ottoman Hajj at the End of Empire*. Stanford: Stanford University Press, 2020.

Çelik, Zeynep. *Europe Knows Nothing About the Orient: A Critical Discourse from the East, 1872–1932*. Istanbul: Koç University Press, 2021.

Çetinkaya, Dogan Y. *1908 Osmanlı Boykotu: Bir Toplumsal Hareketin Analizi*. Istanbul: Iletişim, 2004.

Çetinsaya, Gökhan. "The Ottoman View of British Presence in Iraq and the Gulf: The Era of Abdulhamid II." *Middle Eastern Studies* 39:2 (2003): 194–203.

Çidem, Merve. "II. Meşrutiyet'in İlanı Sırasında Kaybedilen Balkan Toprakları ve Olayların Basına Yansıması." *Vakanüvis-Uluslararası Tarih Araştırmaları Dergisi* 3 (2018): 77–97.

Cohen, Julia Phillips. *Becoming Ottomans: Sephardi Jews and Imperial Citizenship in the Modern Era*. New York: Oxford University Press, 2017.

Cole, Laurence, and Daniel L. Unowsky, eds. *The Limits of Loyalty: Imperial Symbolism, Popular Allegiances, and State Patriotism in the Late Habsburg Monarchy*. New York: Berghahn, 2009.

Crews, Robert. "Empire and the Confessional State: Islam and Religious Politics in Nineteenth-Century Russia." *American Historical Review* 108 (2003): 50–83.

———. *For Prophet and Tsar: Islam and Empire in Russia and Central Asia*. Cambridge, MA: Harvard University Press, 2006.

Cvijić, Jovan, and Milorad Vasović. *Govori i članci, I*. Beograd: Srpska akademija nauka i umetnosti, 1987.

Davison, Roderic H. "The Ottoman Boycott of Austrian Goods in 1908–09 as a Diplomatic Question." In *Third Congress on the Social and Economic History of Turkey: Princeton University, 24–26 August 1983*, edited by Heath W. Lowry and Ralph S. Hattox, 1–28. Istanbul: Isis Press, 1990.

———. "Vienna as a Major Ottoman Diplomatic Post in the Nineteenth Century." In *Habsburgisch-osmanische Beziehungen: Relations Habsbourg-Ottomanes: Wien, 26.–30. September 1983: Colloque Sous Le Patronage Du Comité International Des Études Pré-Ottomanes Et Ottomanes*, edited by Andreas Tietze. Wien: Verlag des Verbandes der wissenschaftlichen Gesellschaften Österreichs, 1985.

Deringil, Selim. *Conversion and Apostasy in the Late Ottoman Empire*. Cambridge, UK: Cambridge University Press, 2012.

———. "Legitimacy Structures in the Ottoman State: The Reign of Abdülhamid II (1876–1909)." *International Journal of Middle East Studies* 23 (1991): 345–359.

———. *The Ottomans, the Turks and World Power Politics: A Historical Dictionary of Titles and Terms in the Ottoman Empire*. Piscataway: Gorgias Press, 2010.

———. *The Well-Protected Domains: Ideology and the Legitimation of Power in the Ottoman Empire, 1876–1909*. London: I. B. Tauris, 1999.

Detrez, Raymond. "Reluctance and Determination: The Prelude to the Austro-Hungarian Occupation of Bosnia Herzegovina in 1878." In *Wechselwirkungen: Austria-Hungary, Bosnia-Herzegovina, and the Western Balkans, 1878–1918*, edited by Clemens Ruthner, Diana Reynolds-Cordileone, Ursula Reber, and Raymond Detrez, 21–40. New York: Peter Lang, 2015.

Dizdar, Senada. "Mehmed Šaćir Kurtćehajić: (1844–1872)." *Godišnjak Bošnjačke zajednice kulture »Preporod«* 1 (2014): 314–324.

Dobrača, Kasim. "Mehmed Refik-efendi Hadžiabdić šejhul-islam." *Anali Gazi Husrev-begove biblioteke* V-VI (1978).

Donia, Robert J. "Fin-de-Siècle Sarajevo: Habsburška transformacija grada." *Prilozi* 32 (2003): 149–178.

———. *Islam Under the Double Eagle: The Muslims of Bosnia and Hercegovina, 1878–1914*. Boulder: East European Quarterly, 1981.

———. "The New Masters of Memory: Libraries, Archives and Museums in Postcommunist Bosnia-Herzegovina." In *Archives, Documentation and Institutions of Social Memory: Essays from the Sawyer Seminar*, edited by Francis Blouin and William Rosenberg, 393–401. Ann Arbor: University of Michigan Press, 2007.

———. "The Proximate Colony Bosnia-Herzegovina Under Austro-Hungarian Rule." In *Wechselwirkungen: Austria-Hungary, Bosnia-Herzegovina, and the Western Balkans, 1878–1918*, edited by Clemens Ruthner, Diana Reynolds-Cordileone, Ursula Reber, and Raymond Detrez, 67–68. New York: Peter Lang, 2015.

Durham, Mary Edith. *Twenty Years of Balkan Tangle*. London: G. Allen & Unwin Ltd, 1920.

Elmaci, Mehmet Emin. "1908 Avusturya Boykotunda Liman İşçileri." *Kebikeç* 5 (1997): 155–162.

Elsie, Robert. "The Viennese Scholar Who Almost Became King of Albania: Baron Franz Nopcsa and His Contribution to Albanian Studies." *East European Quarterly* 33:3 (1999): 327–345.

Emgili, Fahriye. *Yeniden Kurulan Hayatlar: Boşnakların Türkiye'ye Göçleri, 1878–1934*. Istanbul: Bilge Kültür Sanat, 2012.

Eren, Ismail. "Turska štampa u Jugoslaviji (1866–1966)." *Prilozi za orijentalnu filologiju* 14–15 (1964–1965): 359–395.

Esenbel, Selçuk. "Japan's Global Claim to Asia and the World of Islam." *American Historical Review* 109:4 (2004): 1140–1170.

Fahmy, Ziad. "Jurisdictional Borderlands: Extraterritoriality and 'Legal Chameleons' in Precolonial Alexandria, 1840–1870." *Comparative Studies in Society and History* 55:2 (2013): 305–329.

Filandra, Šaćir. *Bošnjaci i moderna: Humanistička misao Bošnjaka od polovine XIX do polovine XX stoljeća*. Sarajevo: Bosanski kulturni centar, 1996.

———. *Bošnjačka politika u XX. Stoljeću*. Sarajevo: Sejtarija, 1998.

Filipović, Nedim. *Islamizacija u Bosni i Hercegovini*. Tešanj: Centar za kulturu i obazovanje, 2005.

———. "Ocaklık timars in Bosnia and Herzegovina." *Prilozi za orijentalnu filologiju* 36 (1986): 149–180.

Fortna, Benjamin C. *Imperial Classroom: Islam, the State, and Education in the Late Ottoman Empire*. Oxford: Oxford University Press, 2002.

Franz, Eva Anne. "Catholic Albanian Warriors for the Sultan in Late-Ottoman Kosovo: The Fandi as a Socio-Professional Group and Their Identity Patterns." In *Conflicting Loyalties in the Balkans: The Great Powers, the Ottoman Empire and Nation Building*, edited by Hannes Grandits, Nathalie Clayer, and Robert Pichler, 182–202. London and New York: I. B. Tauris, 2011.

Fuhrmann, Malte. "Vagrants, Prostitutes and Bosnians: Making and Unmaking European Supremancy in Ottoman Southeast Europe." In *Conflicting Loyalties in the Balkans: The Great Powers, the Ottoman Empire and Nation-Building*, edited by Hannes Grandits, Nathalie Clayer, and Robert Pichler, 15–45. London and New York: I. B. Tauris, 2011.

Gašparović, Ratimir. *Bosna i Hercegovina na geografskim kartama od prvih početaka do kraja XIX vijeka*. Sarajevo: Akademija nauka i umjetnosti Bosne i Hercegovine, 1970.

Gavranović, Berislav. *Uspostava redovite katoličke hijerarhije u Bosni i Hercegovini 1881. godine: prilog političkoj historiji Austro-Ugarske Monarhije na Balkanu*. Beograd: Univerzitet u Beogradu, 1935.

Gazić, Lejla. "Ali-Fehmija Džabić kao kritičar klasične arapske poezije." *Prilozi za orijentalnu filologiju* 35 (1985): 29–50.

———. "Destruction of the Institute for Oriental Studies During the Aggression Against Bosnia Herzegovina, 1992–1995." In *Orijentalni Institut u Sarajevu, 1950–2000*, edited by Amir Ljubović and Lejla Gazić, 30–35. Sarajevo: Orijentalni Institut, 2000.

———, ed. *Vakufname iz Bosne i Hercegovine (XV I XVI vijek)*. Sarajevo: Orijentalni Institut u Sarajevu, 1985.

Geçer, Genç Osman. "Bosna Hersek'ten Hilal-i Ahmere maddi yardımlar: Misbah mecmuası orneği (1912–1914)." *TÜBAR* XXXI (2012): 99–110.

Gelez, Philippe. "Vjerska preobraćenja u Bosni i Hercegovini (c.1800–1918)." *Historijska Traganja* 2 (2008): 17–75.

Gelvin, James L., and Nile Green, eds. *Global Muslims in the Age of Steam and Print*. Berkeley: University of California Press, 2014.

Genell, Aimee M. "Autonomous Provinces and the Problem of 'Semi- Sovereignty' in European International Law." *Journal of Balkan and Near Eastern Studies* 18:6 (2016): 533–549.

———. "The Well-Defended Domains: Eurocentric International Law and the Making of the Ottoman Office of Legal Counsel." *Journal of the Ottoman and Turkish Studies Association* 3:2 (2016): 255–275.

Gesink, Indira F. "Islamic Reformation: A History of Madrasa Reform and Legal Change in Egypt." *Comparative Education Review* 50:3 (2006): 325–345.

Gingeras, Ryan. *Eternal Dawn: Turkey in the Age of Atatürk*. New York: Oxford University Press, 2020.

Giomi, Fabio. "Daughters of Two Empires: Muslim Women and Public Writing in Habsburg Bosnia Herzegovina (1878–1918)." *Aspasia* 9 (2015): 1–18.

Gonslaves, Priscilla T. "A Study of the Habsburg Agricultural Programmes in Bosanska Krajina, 1878–1914." *Slavonic and East European Review* 63:3 (1985): 349–371.

Green, Nile. "Rethinking the 'Middle East' After the Oceanic Turn." *Comparative Studies of South Asia, Africa and the Middle East* 34:3 (2014): 556–564.

Grijak, Zoran. *Politicka djelatnost vrhbosanskog nadbiskupa Josipa Stadlera*. Zagreb: Hrvatski institut za povijest, 2001.

Hacisalihoğlu, Mehmet. "Muslim and Orthodox Resistance Against the Berlin Peace Treaty in the Balkans." In *War and Diplomacy: The Russo-Turkish War of 1877–1878 and the Treaty of Berlin*, edited by M. Hakan Yavuz, 125–143. Salt Lake City: University of Utah Press, 2011.

Hadžijahić, Muhamed. *Porijeklo Bosanskih Muslimana*. Sarajevo: Bosna, 1990.

Haj, Samira. *Reconfiguring Islamic Tradition: Reform, Rationality, and Modernity*. Stanford: Stanford University Press, 2009.

Hajdarpasic, Edin. "Frontier Anxieties: Toward a Social History of Muslim-Christian Relations on the Ottoman-Habsburg Border." *Austrian History Yearbook* 51 (2020): 25–38.

———. *Whose Bosnia? Nationalism and Political Imagination in the Balkans, 1840–1914*. Ithaca: Cornell University Press, 2015.

Hallaq, Wael B. *Authority, Continuity and Change in Islamic Law*. Cambridge, UK: Cambridge University Press, 2001.

———. *An Introduction to Islamic Law*. Cambridge, UK: Cambridge University Press, 2009.

Hamed-Troyansky, Vladimir. "Circassian Refugees and the Making of Amman, 1878–1914." *International Journal of Middle East Studies* 49:4 (2017): 605–623.

Hanagan, Michael, and Charles Tilly, eds. *Extending Citizenship, Reconfiguring States*. Lanham: Rowman & Littlefield, 1999.

Hanák, Péter. "Die Parallelaktion von 1898. Fünfzig Jahre ungarische Revolution und fünfzig Jahre Regierungsjubiläum Franz Josephs." In *Der Garten Und Die Werkstatt: Ein Kulturgeschichtlicher Vergleich Wien Und Budapest Um 1900*, 101–115. Wien: Böhlau, 1992.

Handžić, Adem. "O formiranju nekih gradskih naselja u Bosni u XVI stoljeću." *Prilozi za orijentalnu filologiju* 25 (1976): 133–169.

———. "O ulozi derviša u formiranju gradskih naselja u Bosni u XV stoljeću." *Prilozi za orijentalnu filologiju* 31 (1981): 170–178.

———. *Population of Bosnia in the Ottoman Period: A Historical Overview*. Istanbul: Organisation of the Islamic Conference, Research Centre for Islamic History, Art, and Culture, 1994.

———. "Vakuf kao nosilac određenih državnih i društvenih funkcija u Osmanskom carstvu." *Anali Gazi Husrev-begove biblioteke* 9-10 (1983): 113–119.

Hanioğlu, M. Şükrü. *A Brief History of the Late Ottoman Empire*. Princeton: Princeton University Press, 2008.

———. "Garbcılar: Their Attitudes Toward Religion and Their Impact on the Official Ideology of the Turkish Republic." *Studia Islamica* 86 (1997): 133–158.

———. *Preparation for a Revolution: The Young Turks, 1902–1908*. New York: Oxford University Press, 2001.

———. *Young Turks in Opposition*. Oxford: Oxford University Press, 1995.

Hanley, Will. "Papers for Going, Papers for Staying: Identification and Subject Formation in the Eastern Mediterranean." In *A Global Middle East: Mobility, Materiality and Culture in the Modern Age, 1880–1940*, edited by Liat Kozma, Avner Wishnitzer, and Cyrus Schayegh, 177–200. London: I. B. Tauris, 2014.

———. "What Ottoman Nationality Was and Was Not." *Journal of the Ottoman and Turkish Studies Association* 3:2 (2016): 277–298.

Harris, David. *A Diplomatic History of the Balkan Crisis of 1875–1878*. Stanford: Stanford University Press, 1936.

Hasandedić, Hivzija. "Četiri slučaja pokrštavanja Muslimanki u Hercegovini za vrijeme austrougarske uprave." *Glasnik Rijaseta Islamske Zajednice u SFRJ* 54 (1991).

Hauptmann, Ferdo. *Borba Muslimana Bosne i Hercegovine za vjersku vakufsko-*

mearifsku autonomiju. Sarajevo: Arhiv Socijalističke Republike Bosne i Hercegovine, 1967.

———. *Die österreichisch-ungarische Herrschaft in Bosnien und der Herzegowina:* Wirtschaftspolitik Und Wirtschaftsentwicklung, *1878–1918.* Graz: Institut für Geschichte der Universität Graz, Abt. Südosteuropäische Geschichte, 1983.

Healy, Maureen. "Europe on the Sava: Austrian Encounters with "Turks" in Bosnia." *Austrian History Yearbook* 51 (2020): 73–87.

Henig, David. "Crossing the Bosphorus: Connected Histories of 'Other' Muslims in the Post-Imperial Borderlands of Southeast Europe." *Comparative Studies in Society and History* 58:4 (2016): 908–934.

Hobsbawm, Eric. *The Age of Empire, 1875–1914.* London: Weidenfeld and Nicolson, 1987.

Hourani, Albert H. *Arabic Thought in the Liberal Age: 1798–1939.* London: Oxford University Press, 1970.

Humo, Omer. *Sehletul-vusul. grafija i leksika sehletul-vusula.* Mostar: Muzej Hercegovine, 2010.

Humphrey, Caroline. "Loyalty and Disloyalty Along the Russian–Chinese Border." *History and Anthropology* 28:4 (2017): 399–405. [[cont]]

Imamović, Mustafa. *Historija Bošnjaka.* Sarajevo: Preporod, 1996.

———. *Historija države i prava Bosne i Hercegovine.* Sarajevo: Magistrat, 2003.

———. *Pravni položaj i unutrašnjo-politički razvitak Bosne i Hercegovine od 1878. do 1914.* Sarajevo: Bosanski Kulturni Centar, 1997.

Imart, Guy. *Islamic and Slavic Fundamentalisms: Foes or Allies? The Turkestanian Reagent.* Bloomington: Research Institute for Inner Asian Studies, Indiana University, 1987.

Immig, Nicole. "The 'New' Muslim Minorities in Greece: Between Emigration and Political Participation, 1881–1886." *Journal of Muslim Minority Affairs* 29:4 (2009): 511–522.

İnalcık, Halil. "Impact of the Annales School on Ottoman Studies and New Findings (with Discussion)," *Review* (Fernand Braudel Center) 1:3/4 (1978): 69–99.

İnalcık, Halil, and Donald Quataert, eds. *An Economic and Social History of the Ottoman Empire,* vol. 2. Cambridge, UK: Cambridge University Press, 1997.

Ipek, Nedim. *Rumeli'den Anadolu'ya Türk Göçleri, 1877–1890.* Ankara: Türk Tarih Kurumu Basımevi, 1994.

İslamoğlu, Huri. "Property as a Contested Domain: A Reevaluation of the Ottoman Land Code of 1858." In *New Perspectives on Property and Land in the Middle East,* edited by Roger Owen and Martin Bunton, 3–62. Cambridge, MA: Harvard Center for Middle Eastern Studies, 2000.

Islamoğlu-Inan, Huri, and Çağlar Keyder. "Agenda for Ottoman History." In *The Ottoman Empire and the World-Economy*, edited by Huri İslamoğlu-İnan, 58–59. Cambridge, UK: Cambridge University Press, 2004.

Jahić, Adnan. "O imenovanju Dzemaludina Čauševića za reisul-ulemu 1913. godine." *Prilozi* 41 (2012): 59–78.

———. "Usponi i padovi zagonetnog Mostarca—skica za biografiju Šerifa Arnautovića." *Arhivska Praksa* 18 (2015): 455–470.

Jahić, Adnan, and Edi Bokun. "Memorandum Šerifa Arnautovića caru Karlu 1917. godine." *Prilozi* 44 (2015): 145–179.

Janković, Srđan. "Ortografsko usavršavanje naše arabice u štampanim tekstovima." *Prilozi za orijentalnu filologiju* 38 (1988): 9–40.

Jarak, Nikola. *Poljoprivredna politika Austro-Ugarske u Bosni i Hercegovini i zemljoradničko zadrugarstvo*. Sarajevo: Naučno društvo NR Bosne i Hercegovine, 1956.

Judson, Pieter M. *Exclusive Revolutionaries: Liberal Politics, Social Experience, and National Identity in the Austrian Empire, 1848–1914*. Ann Arbor: University of Michigan Press, 1996.

———. *The Habsburg Empire: A New History*. Cambridge, MA: Harvard University Press, 2016.

Juzbašić, Dževad. *Izgradnja željeznica u Bosni i Hercegovini u svjetlu austrougarske politike od okupacije do kraja Kállayeve ere*. Sarajevo: Akademija nauka i umjetnosti Bosne i Hercegovine, 1974.

———. "O iseljavanu iz Bosne i Hercegovine poslije aneksije 1908. godine." In *Migracije i Bosna i Hercegovina: Naučni skup Migracioni procesi i Bosna i Hercegovina od ranog srednjeg vijeka do najnovijih dana–njihov uticaj i posljedice na demografska kretanja i promjene u našoj zemlji, održanog u Sarajevu 26. i 27. oktobra 1989. godine*, edited by Nusret Šehić. Sarajevo: Institut za Istoriju, 1990.

———. *Politika i privreda u Bosni i Hercegovini pod austrougarskom upravom*. Sarajevo: ANUBiH, 2002.

Kalajdžija, Alen. "O klasifikaciji bosanske književnojezičke tradicije." *Anali Gazi Husrev-begove biblioteke* 33 (2012): 277–289.

Kamberović, Husnija. *Begovski zemljišni posjedi u Bosni i Hercegovini od 1878 do 1918. godine*. Sarajevo: Ibn Sina, 2005.

———. "Projugoslavenska struja među muslimanskim političarima 1918. godine." *Historijska traganja* 3 (2009): 91–105.

Kamissek, Christoph, and Jonas Kreienbaum. "An Imperial Cloud? Conceptualising Interimperial Connections and Transimperial Knowledge." *Journal of Modern European History* 14:2 (2016): 164–182.

Kann, Robert A. *The Multinational Empire: Nationalism and National Reform in the Habsburg Monarchy, 1848–1918*, vol. 1. New York: Octagon Books, 1964.

Kapidžić, Hamdija, ed. *Agrarni odnosi u BiH, 1878–1918*. Sarajevo: Arhiv Bosne i Hercegovine, 1969.

———. *Hercegovački ustanak 1882*. Sarajevo: V. Masleša, 1958.

Kara, Ismail. "Turban and Fez: Ulema as Opposition." In *Late Ottoman Society: The Intellectual Legacy*, edited by Elisabeth Özdalga, 160–200. New York: Routledge Curzon, 2005.

Karčić, Fikret. *The Bosniaks and the Challenges of Modernity: Late Ottoman and Hapsburg Times*. Sarajevo: El-Kalem, 1999.

———. *Društveno-pravni aspekt islamskog reformizma: pokret za reformu šerijatskog prava i njegov odjek u Jugoslaviji u prvoj polovini XX vijeka*. Sarajevo: Islamski teološki fakultet, 1990.

———. *Islamske teme i perspektive*. Sarajevo: El-kalem, 2009.

———. "Medjunarodnopravno regulisanje vakufskih pitanja u jugoslovenskim zemljama." *Anali Gazi Husrev-begove biblioteke* IX-X (1983): 141–154.

———. "Pitanje javnopravnog priznanja islama u jugoslovenskim krajevima nakon prestanka osmanlijske vlasti." *Anali Gazi Husrev-begove biblioteke* XI-XII (1985): 113–121.

———. *Šerijatski sudovi u Jugoslaviji, 1918–1941*. Sarajevo: Vrhovno starješinstvo Islamske zajednice u SFRJ, 1986.

———. *Studije o šerijatskom pravu*. Zenica: Bemust, 1997.

Karčić, Fikret, and Mustafa Jahić. "Jedna vazna fetva o pitanju iseljavanja bosanskih Muslimana u vrieme austrougarske uprave." *Prilozi Instituta za Istoriju* 27 (1991): 41–48.

Karčić, Hamza. "Supporting the Caliph's Project: Bosnian Muslims and the Hejaz Railway." *Journal of Muslim Minority Affairs* 34:3 (2014): 282–292.

Karić, Enes. "Aspects of Islamic Discourse in Bosnia-Hercegovina from the Mid-19th Till the End of the 20th Century: A Historical Review." In *Şehrayin. Die Welt der Osmanen, die Osmanen in der Welt; Wahr-nehmungen, Begegnungen und Abgrenzungen*, edited by Yavuz Köse, 285–306. Wiesbaden: Harrassowitz, 2012.

———. "Muḥammad Rašid Riḍā (1865.–1935.) i tematiziranje Bosne i Hercegovine i Balkana u časopisu "Al-Manār" (1898.–1935.)." *Godišnjak Bošnjačke zajednice kulture »Preporod«* 1 (2009): 223–238.

Karić, Dženita. *Bosnian Hajj Literature: Multiple Paths to the Holy*. Edinburgh: Edinburgh University Press, 2022.

Karpat, Kemal H. "Commentary: Muslim Migration: A Response to Aldeeb Abu-Sahlieh." *International Migration Review* 30:1 (1996): 79–89.

———. "The Hijra from Russia and the Balkans: The Process of Self-Definition in the Late Ottoman State." In *Muslim Travelers: Pilgrimage, Migration, and the Religious Imagination,* edited by Dale F. Eickelman and James P. Piscatori. Berkeley: University of California Press, 1990.

———. "The Migration of the Bosnian Muslims to the Ottoman State, 1878–1914: An Account Based on Turkish Sources." In *Ottoman Bosnia: A History in Peril,* edited by Markus Koller and Kemal H. Karpat. Madison: University of Wisconsin Press, 2004.

———. *Ottoman Population, 1830–1914: Demographic and Social Characteristics.* Madison: University of Wisconsin Press, 1985.

———. *The Politicization of Islam: Reconstructing Identity, State, Faith, and Community in the Late Ottoman State.* Oxford: Oxford University Press, 2001.

———. *Studies on Ottoman Social and Political History: Selected Articles and Essays.* Leiden and Boston: Brill, 2002.

———. *The Turks of Bulgaria: The History and Political Fate of a Minority.* Istanbul: Isis Press, 1990.

———. "Yakub Bey's Relations with the Ottoman Sultans: A Reinterpretation." *Cahiers du Monde russe et soviétique* 32:1 (1991): 17–32.

Kasaba, Reşat. *A Moveable Empire: Ottoman Nomads, Migrants & Refugees.* Seattle: University of Washington Press, 2009.

Kasumović, Amila. "Carski osmanski generalni konzulat u Sarajevu (1910–1918)." *Prilozi* 44 (2015): 57–79.

———. "Zemaljska pripadnost stanovnika Bosne i Hercegovine u prvim godinama austrougarske uprave." *Historijska traganja* 6 (2010): 9–34.

Kayaoglu, Turan. *Legal Imperialism: Sovereignty and Extraterritoriality in Japan, the Ottoman Empire, and China.* Cambridge, UK: Cambridge University Press, 2014.

Keddie, Nikki R. *An Islamic Response to Imperialism: Political and Religious Writings of Sayyid Jamāl Ad-Dīn "al-Afghānī."* Berkeley: University of California Press, 1968.

———. "The Pan-Islamic Appeal: Afghani and Abdülhamid II." *Middle Eastern Studies* 3:1 (1966): 46–67.

Kemura, Ibrahim. "Dva patriotska apela bosanskih muslimanskih prvaka iz prvih godina austrougarske okupacije." *Glasnik Vrhovnog islamskog starješinstva u SFRJ* 9–10 (1970): 436–443.

———. *Uloga "Gajreta" u društvenom životu Muslimana Bosne i Hercegovine.* Sarajevo: Veselin Masleša, 1986.

Kerr, Malcolm H. *Islamic Reform: The Political and Legal Theories of Muḥammad 'abduh and Rashīd Riḍā.* Berkeley: University of California Press, 1966.

Khalid, Adeeb. "Pan-Islamism in Practice: The Rhetoric of Muslim Unity and Its Uses." In *Late Ottoman Society: The Intellectual Legacy*, edited by Elisabeth Özdalga, 201–224. London: Routledge Curzon, 2005.

———. *The Politics of Muslim Cultural Reform: Jadidism in Central Asia*. Berkeley: University of California Press, 1999.

Kiel, Machiel. *Studies on the Ottoman Architecture of the Balkans*. Aldershot, Hampshire: Variorum, 1990.

Kırımlı, Hakan. *National Movements and National Identity Among the Crimean Tatars, 1905–1916*. Leiden: Brill, 1996.

Koller, Markus, and Kemal H. Karpat, eds. *Ottoman Bosnia: A History in Peril*. Madison: University of Wisconsin Press, 2004.

Kołodziejczyk, Dariusz. "Khan, Caliph, Tsar and Imperator: The Multiple Identities of the Ottoman Sultan." In *Universal Empire: A Comparative Approach to Imperial Culture and Representation in Eurasian History*, edited by Peter F. Bang and Dariusz Kołodziejczyk, 175–193. Cambridge, UK: Cambridge University Press, 2015.

Korić, Elma. "Bosansko pograničje u vrijeme Dubičkog rata, 1788–1791." *Prilozi za orijentalnu filologiju* 65 (2016): 213–237.

Koskenniemi, Martti. *The Gentle Civilizer of Nations: The Rise and Fall of International Law 1870–1960*. Cambridge, UK: Cambridge University Press, 2010.

Koštić, Mujo. "Državna štamparija i službene i poluslužbene novine u Bosni i Hercegovini od 1866. do 1945. godine." *Novi Muallim* 18 (2004): 96–110.

Kostopoulou, Elektra. "Armed Negotiations: The Institutionalization of the Late Ottoman Locality." *Comparative Studies of South Asia, Africa and the Middle East* 33:3 (2013): 295–309.

Kraljačić, Tomislav. "Iseljavanje muslimana iz Bosne i Hercegovine u Albaniju za vrijeme austrougarske uprave." In *Stanovništvo slovenskog porijekla u Albaniji: zbornik radova sa međunarodnog naučnog skupa održanog u Cetinju 21, 22. i 23. juna 1990*, edited by Jovan R. Bojović. Titograd and Montenegro: Istorijski Institut SR Crne Gore, 1991.

———. *Kalajev režim u Bosni i Hercegovini 1882–1903*. Sarajevo: Veselin Masleša, 1987.

———. "Povratak muslimanskih iseljenika iz Bosne i Hercegovine u toku prvog balkanskog rata." In *Migracije i Bosna i Hercegovina: materijali s naučnog skupa migracioni procesi i Bosna i Hercegovina od ranog srednjeg vijeka do najnovijih dana—njihov uticaj i posljedice na demografska kretanja i promjene u našoj zemlji, održanog u Sarajevu 26. i 27. oktobra 1989. godine*, edited by Nusret Šehić. Sarajevo: Institut za istoriju u Sarajevu, 1990.

———. "Stav srpske vlade prema iseljavanju Muslimana iz Bosne i Hercegovine u posljednjoj deceniji XIX vijeka." *Godišnjak društva istoričara BiH* XXXIX (1988).

Kreševljaković, Hamdija. "Hadži Hafız Džemaludin Hadžijahić." *Glasnik vrhovnog islamskog starješinstva u FNRJ* 8–10 (1955).

———. *Kapetanije u Bosni i Hercegovini*. Sarajevo: Naučno Društvo NR Bosne i Hercegovine, 1954.

———. *Sarajevo u doba okupacije Bosne 1878*. Sarajevo: Naklada piščeva, 1937.

———. *Sarajevo za vrijeme austrougarske uprave (1878–1918)*. Sarajevo: Arhiv grada, 1969.

Kruševac, Todor. *Sarajevo pod austrougarskom upravom 1878–1918*. Sarajevo: Muzej grada, 1960.

———. "Seljački pokret—štrajk u Bosni 1910. godine." *Pregled* 7 (1948): 369–405.

Kujović, Mina. "Muslimanska osnovna i viša djevojačka škola sa produženim tečajem (1894– 1925)—prilog historiji muslimanskog školstva u Bosni i Hercegovini." *Novi Muallim* 41 (2010): 72–79.

Kujraković, Nusret. "*Osvitanje*—prvo udruženje Muslimanki u Bosni i Hercegovini." *Prilozi* 39 (2009): 145–164.

Kurzman, Charles. *Modernist Islam, 1840–1940: A Sourcebook*. Oxford: Oxford University Press, 2002.

Kuş, Ahmet, İbrahim Dıvarcı, and Feyzi Şimşek. *Rumeli'de Osmanlı Mirası: Bosna Hersek–Kosova / Ottoman Heritage in Rumelia: Bosnia Herzegovina—Kosovo*. Istanbul: Nildem Brokerliği, 2010.

Lehfeldt, Werner. *Das Serbokroatische Aljamiado-Schrifttum Der Bosnisch-Hercegovinischen Muslime: Transkriptionsprobleme*. München: R. Trofenik, 1969.

Lieven, Dominic. *Empire: The Russian Empire and Its Rivals*. New Haven: Yale University Press, 2001.

Loizos, Peter. "Ottoman Half-Lives: Long-Term Perspectives on Particular Forced Migrations." *Journal of Refugee Studies* 12:3 (1999): 237–263.

Lory, Bernard. *Le Sort de L'héritage Ottoman en Bulgarie: L'exemple des Villes Bulgares, 1878–1900*. Istanbul: Editions Isis, 1985.

Low, Michael Christopher. *Imperial Mecca: Ottoman Arabia and the Indian Ocean Hajj*. New York: Columbia University Press, 2020.

———. "Unfurling the Flag of Extraterritoriality: Autonomy, Foreign Muslims, and the Capitulations in the Ottoman Hijaz." *Journal of the Ottoman and Turkish Studies Association* 3:2 (2016): 299–323.

Mahmood, Saba. *Politics of Piety: The Islamic Revival and the Feminist Subject*. Princeton: Princeton University Press, 2005.

Mahmutćehajić, Rusmir. "On Ruins and the Place of Memory." *East European Politics and Societies* 25:1 (2011): 153–192.

Makdisi, Ussama. *The Culture of Sectarianism, Community, History and Violence in Nineteenth-Century Ottoman Lebanon.* Berkeley: University of California Press, 2000.

Malcolm, Noel. *Bosnia: A Short History.* New York: New York University Press, 1994.

———. *Kosovo: A Short History.* New York: New York University Press, 1998.

Manasek, Jared. "Protection, Repatriation and Categorization: Refugees and Empire at the End of the Nineteenth Century." *Journal of Refugee Studies* 30:2 (2017): 301–317.

Manjgo, Meho. "O imenovanju hafıza Sulejman-ef. Šarca za reisu-l-ulemu u Bosni i Hercegovini." *Anali Gazi Husrev-begove biblioteke* 48:40 (2019): 123–136.

Mardin, Şerif. *The Genesis of Young Ottoman Thought: A Study in the Modernization of Turkish Political Ideas.* Princeton: Princeton University Press, 1962.

Marriott, J. A. R. *The Eastern Question: An Historical Study in European Diplomacy.* Oxford: Clarendon Press, 1940.

Marsden, Magnus, and David Henig. "Muslim Circulations and Networks in West Asia: Ethnographic Perspectives on Transregional Connectivity." *Journal of Eurasian Studies* 10:1 (2019): 11–21.

Masud, Muhammad Khalid. "The Obligation to Migrate: The Doctrine of Hijra in Islamic Law." In *Muslim Travelers: Pilgrimage, Migration and Religious Imagination,* edited by Dale F. Eickelman and James Piscatori, 29–49. London: Routledge, 1990.

Mazower, Mark. *The Balkans: A Short History.* New York: Modern Library, 2000.

McCarthy, Justin. "Archival Sources Concerning Serb Rebellions in Bosnia 1875–76." In *Ottoman Bosnia: A History in Peril,* edited by Markus Koller and Kemal H. Karpat. Madison: University of Wisconsin Press, 2004.

———. *Death and Exile: The Ethnic Cleansing of Ottoman Muslims, 1821–1922.* Princeton: Darwin Press, 1999.

———. "Ottoman Bosnia, 1800–1878." In *The Muslims of Bosnia-Herzegovina: Their Historical Development from the Middle Ages to the Dissolution of Yugoslavia,* edited by Mark Pinson, 54–83. Cambridge, MA: Harvard University Press, 1994.

Methodieva, Milena B. *Between Empire and Nation: Muslim Reform in the Balkans.* Stanford: Stanford University Press, 2021.

———. "How Turks and Bulgarians Became Ethnic Brothers: History, Propaganda and Political Alliances on the Eve of Young Turk Revolution." *Turkish Historical Review* 5 (2014): 221–262.

———. *Reform, Politics, and Culture Among the Muslims in Bulgaria, 1878–1908.* PhD dissertation. Princeton University, 2010.

Meyer, James H. "Immigration, Return, and the Politics of Citizenship: Russian

Muslims in the Ottoman Empire, 1860–1914." *International Journal of Middle East Studies* 39:1 (2007): 15–32.

———. "Speaking Shari'a to the State: Muslim Protesters, Tsarist Officials, and the Islamic Discourses of Late Imperial Russia." *Kritika* 14:3 (2013): 485–505.

———. *Turks Across Empires: Marketing Muslim Identity in the Russian-Ottoman Borderlands, 1856–1914*. Oxford: Oxford University Press, 2019.

Metcalf, Barbara D. *Islamic Revival in British India: Deoband, 1860–1900*. Princeton: Princeton University Press, 1982,

Mikhail, Alan, and Christine Philliou. "The Ottoman Empire and the Imperial Turn." *Comparative Studies in Society and History* 54:4 (2012): 721–745.

Minawi, Mostafa. "International Law and the Precarity of Ottoman Sovereignty in Africa at the End of the Nineteenth Century." *International History Review* 43:5 (2021): 1098–1121.

———. *The Ottoman Scramble for Africa: Empire and Diplomacy in the Sahara and the Hijaz*. Stanford: Stanford University Press, 2016.

Minuchehr, Pardis. *Homeland from Afar: The Iranian Diaspora and the Quest for Modernity (1908–1909) (the Constitutional Movement Within a Global Perspective)*. PhD dissertation. Columbia University, 1998.

Mirkova, Anna M. "'Population Politics' at the End of Empire: Migration and Sovereignty in Ottoman Eastern Rumelia, 1877—1886." *Comparative Studies in Society and History* 55:4 (2013): 955–985.

Mitchell, Timothy. *Colonising Egypt*. Cambridge and New York: Cambridge University Press, 1988.

Mønnesland, Svein, ed. *Jezik u Bosni i Hercegovini*. Sarajevo: Institut za jezik u Sarajevu, 2005.

Motadel, David, ed. *Islam and the European Empires*. Oxford: Oxford University Press, 2014.

Nakičević, Omer. *Istorijski razvoj institucije Rijaseta*. Sarajevo: Rijaset islamske zajednice u RBiH, 1996.

Neumayer, Christoph, and Erwin A. Schmidl. *The Emperor's Bosniaks: The Bosnian Herzegovinian Troops in the K.u.k. Army History and Uniforms 1878 to 1918*. Vienna: Militaria, 2008.

Nurudinović, Bisera. "Bosanske salname (1866–1878 i 1882–1893)." *Prilozi za orijentalnu filologiju* 10/11 (1960–61): 253–265.

Okey, Robin. *Taming Balkan Nationalism: The Habsburg Civilizing Mission in Bosnia, 1878–1914*. Oxford: Oxford University Press, 2007.

———. "A Trio of Hungarian Balkanists: Béni Kállay, István Burián and Lajos Thallóczy in the Age of High Nationalism." *Slavonic and East European Review* 80: 2 (2002): 234–266.

Özsu, Umut. "The Ottoman Empire, the Origins of Extraterritoriality, and International Legal Theory." In *The Oxford Handbook of the Theory of International Law*, edited by Anne Orford and Florian Hoffman, 123–137. Oxford: Oxford University Press, 2016.

Pahumi, Nevila. "Constructing Difference: American Protestantism, Christian Workers, and Albanian-Greek Relations in Late Ottoman Europe." *Journal of Modern Greek Studies* 36:2 (2018): 293–328.

Palabıyık, Mustafa Serdar. "The Emergence of the Idea of 'International Law' in the Ottoman Empire Before the Treaty of Paris (1856)." *Middle Eastern Studies* 50:2 (2014): 233–251.

Pamuk, Şevket. *The Ottoman Empire and European Capitalism, 1820–1913: Trade, Investment, and Production.* Cambridge, UK: Cambridge University Press, 1987.

Pappé, Ilan. *The Ethnic Cleansing of Palestine.* Oxford: Oneworld, 2007.

Pejanović, Đorđe. *Štamparije u Bosni i Hercegovini, 1529–1951.* Sarajevo: Svjetlost, 1952.

———. *Stanovništvo Bosne i Hercegovine.* Beograd: Naučna knjiga, 1955.

Pelidija, Enes. *Banjalučki boj iz 1737: uzroci i posljedice.* Sarajevo: El-Kalem, 2003.

———. "Dr. Muhamed Hadžijahić—Dostojan nastavljač porodične tradicije." *Znakovi vremena* 10:38 (2007): 10–35.

Petrov, Milen V. "Everyday Forms of Compliance: Subaltern Commentaries on Ottoman Reform, 1864–1868." *Comparative Studies in Society and History* 46 (2004): 730–759.

Pinson, Mark. *The Muslims of Bosnia-Herzegovina: Their Historic Development from the Middle Ages to the Dissolution of Yugoslavia.* Cambridge, MA: Harvard University Press, 1994.

Pinson, Mark, and Roy P. Mottahedeh. *The Muslims of Bosnia-Herzegovina.* Cambridge, MA: Harvard Center for Middle Eastern Studies, 1996.

Pinto, Avram. *Jevreji Sarajeva i Bosne i Hercegovine.* Sarajevo: Veselin Masleša, 1987.

Plunkett, John. *Queen Victoria: First Media Monarch.* Oxford: Oxford University Press, 2003.

Provence, Michael. *The Last Ottoman Generation and the Making of the Modern Middle East.* Cambridge, UK: Cambridge University Press, 2017.

Purivatra, Atif. *Jugoslavenska Muslimanska Organizacija u političkom životu Kraljevine Srba, Hrvata i Slovenaca.* Sarajevo: Bosanski Kulturni Centar, 1999.

Puskar, Samira. *Bosnian Americans of Chicagoland.* Charleston: Arcadia, 2007.

Ra'anan, Uri, Maria Mesner, Keith Armes, and Kate Martin, eds. *State and Nation in Multi-Ethnic Societies: The Breakup of Multinational States*. Manchester and New York: Manchester University Press, 1991.

Rabinow, Paul. *French Modern: Norms and Forms of the Social Environment*. Cambridge, MA: MIT Press, 1989.

Radušić, Edin. "Agrarno pitanje u Bosanskohercegovačkom Saboru 1910–1914." *Prilozi* 34 (2005): 119–154.

Ramadanović, Murat. "Bosanska emigracija u Osmanskom carstvu i sultanov suverenitet u Bosni i Hercegovini." *Znakovi vremena* 9–10 (2000): 318–335.

Rebihić, Nehrudin. "Između orijentalizma i okcidentalizma: Narativi o iseljavanju Bošnjaka u Tursku u bošnjačkoj književnosti prve polovine 20. stoljeća." *Društvene i humanističke studije: časopis Filozofskog fakulteta u Tuzli* 3:12 (2020): 31–58.

Reill, Dominique. "A Mission of Mediation: Dalmatia's Multi-National Regionalism from the 1830s–60s." In *Different Paths to the Nation: Regional and National Identities in Central Europe and Italy, 1830–70*, edited by Laurence Cole, 16–36. Basingstoke: Palgrave Macmillan, 2007.

Rexhepi, Piro. *White Enclosures: Racial Capitalism and Coloniality along the Balkan Route*. Durham and London: Duke University Press, 2023.

Reynolds, Diane. "Kavaljeri, kostimi, umjetnost: kako je Beč doživljavao Bosnu 1878–1900." *Prilozi* 32 (2003): 135–148.

Riedlmayer, András J. "Convivencia Under Fire: Genocide and Book Burning in Bosnia." In *The Holocaust and the Book: Destruction and Preservation*, edited by Jonathan Rose, 266–291. Amherst: University of Massachusetts Press, 2001.

———. "Crimes of War, Crimes of Peace: Destruction of Libraries During and After the Balkan Wars of the 1990s." *Library Trends* 56:1 (2007): 107–132.

Rizvić, Muhsin. *Behar: književnoistorijska monografija*. Sarajevo: Svjetlost, 1971.

———. *Bosansko-muslimanska književnost u doba preporoda (1887–1918)*. Sarajevo: Mešihat islamske zajednice BiH, El-Kalem izdavačka djelatnost, 1990.

Roshwald, Aviel. *Ethnic Nationalism and the Fall of Empires: Central Europe, Russia and the Middle East, 1914–1923*. London: Routledge, 2001.

Ross, Danielle. *Tatar Empire: Kazan's Muslims and the Making of Imperial Russia*. Bloomington: Indiana University Press, 2020.

Rozenblit, Marsha L. "Jewish Ethnicity in a New Nation-State: The Crisis of Identity in the Austrian Republic." In *In Search of Jewish Community: Jewish Identities in Germany and Austria, 1918–1933*, edited by Michael Brenner and Derek J. Penslar. Bloomington and Indianapolis: Indiana University Press, 1998.

Ruthner, Clemens. " 'Naš' mali 'Orijent' jedno postkolonijalno čitanje austrijskih i njemačkih kulturalnih narativa o Bosni i Hercegovini 1878–1918." *Prilozi* 37 (2008): 149–167.

Ruthner, Clemens, Diana Reynolds-Cordileone, Ursula Reber, and Raymond Detrez, eds. *Wechselwirkungen: Austria-Hungary, Bosnia-Herzegovina, and the Western Balkans, 1878–1918*. New York: Peter Lang, 2015.

Ruthner, Clemens, and Tamara Scheer, eds. *Bosnien-Herzegowina und Österreich-Ungarn: Annäherungen an eine Kolonie*. Tübingen: Narr Francke Attempto, 2018.

Šabotić, Izet. "Bosanske muhadžerske enklave u Makedoniji: Nekad i sad." *Glasnik Arhiva i Arhivističkog Udruženja Bosne i Hercegovine* 48 (2018): 131–148.

Said, Edward W. *Orientalism*. New York: Vintage Books, 1978.

Šamić, Midhat. *Francuski putnici u Bosni i Hercegovini u XIX stoljeću (1836–1878) i njihovi utisci o njoj*. Sarajevo: Veselin Masleša, 1981.

———. "Jedna prerada Molijerovih *Skapenovih podvala* u Bosni početkom XX stoljeća." *Radovi Filozofskog fakulteta u Sarajevu* 1 (1963).

Sarıkaya, Yaşar. *Medreseler ve Modernleşme*. Istanbul: İz Yayıncılık, 1997.

Schendel, Willem van. "Geographies of Knowing, Geographies of Ignorance: Jumping Scale in Southeast Asia." *Environment and Planning D: Society and Space* 20 (2002): 647–668.

Schick, Irvin Cemil. "Christian Maidens, Turkish Ravishers: The Sexualization of National Conflict in the Late Ottoman Period." In *Women in the Ottoman Balkans: Gender, Culture and History*, edited by Amila Buturović and Irvin C. Schick, 274–304. London: I. B. Tauris, 2007.

Seferović, Nina. "Kolonija hercegovačkih Muslimana u Kajzeriju u Palestini." *Zbornik radova Etnografskog instituta* 12 (1981).

Šehić, Nusret. *Autonomni pokret Muslimana za vrijeme austrougarske uprave u Bosni I Hercegovini*. Sarajevo: Svjetlost, 1980.

Šehić, Zijad. "Putovanje bosanskohercegovačkih hodočasnika u Meku u doba austrougarske uprave 1878–1918." *Saznanja: Časopis za historiju* 2 (2008): 69–85.

Sekulić, Ana. "From a Legal Proof to a Historical Fact: Trajectories of an Ottoman Document in a Franciscan Monastery, Sixteenth to Twentieth Century." *Journal of the Economic and Social History of the Orient* 62:5–6 (2019): 925–962.

Seton-Watson, Robert W. *The Role of Bosnia in International Politics, 1875–1914*. London: Milford, 1931.

Shaw, Stanford J. "Local Administration in the Tanzimat." In *150. yılında Tanzimat*, edited by Hakki Dursun Yildiz. Ankara: Türk Tarih Kurumu Basımevi, 1992.

Sijerčić, Ejub. *Migracije stanovništva Bosne i Hercegovine*. Sarajevo: Republički zavod za statistiku SR BiH, 1976.

Singer, Amy. *Constructing Ottoman Beneficence: An Imperial Soup Kitchen in Jerusalem*. Albany: State University of New York Press, 2002.
Škapur, Hasan. *Odnos osmanskih vlasti prema Bosanskom ustanku, 1875–1878*. Sarajevo: Centar za osmanističke studije, 2017.
Šljivo, Galib. "Prvi pokušaj bosanskih krajišnika da vrate Cetingrad u sastav bosanskog vilajeta (26. april 1809–14. maj 1810)." *Prilozi* 31 (2002): 111–136.
———. "Sprovodjenje zakona o vojnoj obavezi u banjalučkom i bihaćkom okrugu 1881–1882." In *Naučni Skup 100 godina ustanka u Hercegovini 1882. godine: Sarajevo, 21–22. X 1982*, edited by Hamdija Ćemerlić et al. Sarajevo: Akademija nauka i umjetnosti Bosne i Hercegovine, 1983.
Smiley, Will. *From Slaves to Prisoners of War: The Ottoman Empire, Russia, and International Law*. Oxford: Oxford University Press, 2018.
Sohrabi, Nader. *Revolution and Constitutionalism in the Ottoman Empire and Iran*. New York: Cambridge University Press, 2011.
———. "Reluctant Nationalists, Imperial Nation-State, and Neo-Ottomanism: Turks, Albanians, and the Antinomies of the End of Empire." *Social Science History* 42:4 (2018): 835–870.
Somel, Selçuk A. *The Modernization of Public Education in the Ottoman Empire, 1839–1908: Islamization, Autocracy, and Discipline*. Leiden: Brill, 2001.
Stoler, Ann Laura. *Imperial Debris: On Ruins and Ruination*. Durham: Duke University Press, 2013.
Sugar, Peter F. *Industrialization of Bosnia-Hercegovina: 1878–1918*. Seattle: University of Washington Press, 1963.
Suljkić, Hifzija. "Iseljavanje Muslimana iz Užica u Bosnu 1862. godine." *Glasnik Rijaseta Islamske Zajednice u SFRJ* 54 (1991): 161–179.
Šuško, Dževada. "Bosniaks & Loyalty: Responses to the Conscription Law in Bosnia and Hercegovina 1881/82." *The Hungarian Historical Review* 3:3 (2014): 529–559.
Tanyol, Cahit. *Hoca Kadri Efendi'nin Parlamentosu*. İstanbul: Gendaş, 2003.
Taşbaş, Erdal. *Halifenin Gölgesine Sığınanlar: Göçler ve Muhacirin-i Islamiye Komisyonu*. Ankara: Berikan, 2017.
Tepić, Ibrahim. "Uspostavljanje austrougarske okupacione vlasti u Bosni i Hercegovini u izvjestajima ruskog konzulata u Sarajevu (1879–1880)." *Prilozi instituta za istoriju* 24 (1988).
Todorova, Maria. *Imagining the Balkans*. New York: Oxford University Press, 2009.
Trouillot, Michel-Rolph. *Silencing the Past: Power and the Production of History*. Boston: Beacon Press, 2015.
Tuna, Mustafa. "Madrasa Reform as a Secularizing Process: A View from the Late Russian Empire." *Comparative Studies in Society and History* 53:3 (2011): 540–570.

Turan, Ömer, and Kyle T. Evered. "Jadidism in South-Eastern Europe: The Influence of Ismail Bey Gaspirali Among Bulgarian Turks." *Middle Eastern Studies* 41:4 (2005): 481–502.

Turhan, Fatma Sel. *Ottoman Empire and the Bosnian Uprising: Janissaries, Modernisation and Rebellion in the Nineteenth Century.* London: I. B. Tauris, 2015.

Ünal, Hasan. "Ottoman Policy During the Bulgarian Independence Crisis, 1908–9: Ottoman Empire and Bulgaria at the Outset of the Young Turk Revolution." *Middle Eastern Studies* 34:4 (1998): 135–176.

Unowsky, Daniel L. *The Pomp and Politics of Patriotism: Imperial Celebrations in Habsburg Austria, 1848–1916.* West Lafayette: Purdue University Press, 2005.

Uskufi, Muhamed H., Ahmet Kasumović, and Svein Mønnesland. *Bosansko-turski rječnik.* Tuzla: Općina Tuzla, 2011.

Uzunçarşılı, Ismail Hakkı. *Osmanli devletinin ilmiye teşkilatı.* Ankara: Türk Tarih Kurumu Basimevi, 1988.

———. *Osmanlı Devlet Teşkilatından Kapukulu Ocakları: Acemi Ocağı Ve Yeniçeri OcağI.* Ankara: Türk Tarih Kurumu, 1988.

Volarić, Klara. "Between the Ottoman and Serbian States: Carigradski Glasnik, an Istanbul-based Paper of Ottoman Serbs, 1895–1909." *Hungarian Historical Review* 3:3 (2014): 560–586.

Voll, John O. "Renewal and Reform in Islamic History: Tajdid and Islah." In *Voices of Resurgent Islam,* edited by John L. Esposito, 32–47. New York: Oxford University Press, 1983.

Wallerstein, Immanuel, Hale Decdeli, and Reşat Kasaba. "Incorporation of the Ottoman Empire into the World Economy." In *The Ottoman Empire and the World-Economy,* edited by Huri İslamoğlu-İnan. Cambridge, UK: Cambridge University Press, 2004.

Weber, Eugen. *Peasants into Frenchmen: The Modernization of Rural France 1870–1914.* Stanford: Stanford University Press, 1976.

Weitz, Eric D. "From the Vienna to the Paris System: International Politics and the Entangled Histories of Human Rights, Forced Deportations, and Civilizing Missions." *American Historical Review* 113:5 (2008): 1313–1343.

Werth, Paul W. *The Tsar's Foreign Faiths: Toleration and the Fate of Religious Freedom in Imperial Russia.* New York: Oxford University Press, 2014.

Wolff, Larry. *The Idea of Galicia: History and Fantasy in Habsburg Political Culture.* Stanford: Stanford University Press, 2010.

———. *Inventing Eastern Europe: The Map of Civilization on the Mind of the Enlightenment.* Stanford: Stanford University Press, 1994.

Worringer, Renée. *The Islamic Middle East and Japan: Perceptions, Aspirations, and the Birth of Intra-Asian Modernity.* Princeton: Markus Wiener, 2007.

Wortman, Richard. *Scenarios of Power: Myth and Ceremony in Russian Monarchy*. Princeton: Princeton University Press, 1995.
Yaycioglu, Ali. *Partners of the Empire: The Crisis of the Ottoman Order in the Age of Revolutions*. Stanford: Stanford University Press, 2016.
Yilmaz, Suhnaz, and Ipek K. Yosmaoglu. "Fighting the Specters of the Past: Dilemmas of Ottoman Legacy in the Balkans and the Middle East." *Middle Eastern Studies* 44:5 (2011): 677–693.
Yosmaoglu, Ipek. *Blood Ties: Religion, Violence, and the Politics of Nationhood in Ottoman Macedonia, 1878–1908*. Ithaca: Cornell University Press, 2013.
Younis, Hana. "Brez nikoga u dijaru gurbetu." *Prilozi* 45 (2016): 41–76.
———. "Smrtni slučajevi tokom hadža u Mekku kroz primjere iz građe Vrhovnog šeriatskog suda u Sarajevu u periodu austrougarske uprave." *Anali Gazi Husrev-begove biblioteke* 37 (2016): 197–217.
Zahra, Tara. "Imagined Noncommunities: National Indifference as a Category of Analysis." *Slavic Review* 69:1 (2010): 93–119.
Zaman, Muhammad Qasim. "Religious Education and the Rhetoric of Reform: The Madrasa in British India and Pakistan." *Comparative Studies in Society and History* 41:2 (1999): 294–323.
———. *The Ulama in Contemporary Islam: Custodians of Change*. Princeton: Princeton University Press, 2002.
Zgodić, Esad. *Bosanska politička misao: austrougarsko doba*. Sarajevo: DES, 2003.
———. *Bošnjacko iskustvo politike, osmansko doba*. Sarajevo: Euromedija, 1998.
Zoran-Rosen, Ayelet. "The Emergence of a Bosnian Learned Elite: A Case of Ottoman Imperial Integration." *Journal of Islamic Studies* 30:2 (2019): 176–204.
Zürcher, Erik Jan. *Turkey: A Modern History*. London: I. B. Tauris, 2004.

Index

Figures are indicated by an italic *f* following the page number

Abdülhamid II: caliphate reinvented under, 129; citizenship and, 129; colonialism and, 126–27; competing empires and, 126–27; dethroning of, 67, 126; Hijaz Railway constructed under, 226; hijra and, 97, 100; identity and, 127; image management and, 133; loyalties to, 42; migration and, 67, 78–79; negotiations with Habsburg Monarchy by, 36–37; Pan-Islamism and, 100, 130, 227; petitions to, 145–53, 149*f*; power of, 125–32; protection of non-Ottoman Muslims under, 127–30; public opinion and, 133; reform projects under, 126–27; role of history under, 42; Russo-Ottoman War and, 78
Abdülkerim, Certain, 98–99

Abdullah Efendi, 60
activism, 8–9, 51, 65, 91–94, 144–45, 153–62, 192, 214, 223
Ahmed Cevdet Pasha, 29, 58–59, 119–20, 238n42
Ahmed Şükrü Efendi, 120
Aisha, 85
al-Afghani, Sayyid Jamal al-Din, 130, 203
Ali Rüşdü, 179
Ali Ulvi, 178–79
Aliye, Fatima, 214
allegiances: annexation and composite allegiances, 197–99; Austria-Hungary/Habsburg dynasty and, 7, 10, 12, 17, 42, 45, 109, 183, 192; changing international order affecting, 8, 223; competition for, 42, 48, 108, 109, 119, 129, 134, 138, 139;

307

allegiances (*cont.*)
crisis of, 57; impact of empire on, 15; migration and, 49, 57, 59, 60, 63; negotiating imperial ties and, 141, 142, 143, 154; Ottoman Empire and, 5, 10, 13, 42, 48, 109, 129, 132, 134, 138, 139, 180; scholarship on, 12, 13. *See also* loyalties
Andrássy, Gyula, 33, 35–36
annexation, 169–76, 197–99; autonomy and, 165, 179, 185–86, 190–93, 196–97; Balkan Wars and, 189, 195–96; Berlin Treaty and, 169, 171–73, 175, 178–79; boycott of Austrian goods and, 169–70, 176–77, 179; citizenship and, 73, 177, 181, 191; competing empires and, 116, 139; composite allegiances and, 197–99; education and, 194–95; identity and, 193, 198; Jews and, 199; land policies and, 179, 181, 186–89; legal status of Bosnian Muslims following, 181–82; loyalties and, 191, 193–97; as means to prevent constitution requests, 65; migration and, 65–70, 66*f*, 72–73; *millet* system and, 199; MNO and, 171, 183–85, 190; negotiating imperial ties and, 164; occupation contrasted with, 44–45; Orthodox Christians and, 179–80, 184–86, 188–89; Ottoman ties and, 193–97; party politics and, 184–90; political cartoon of, 174*f*; provincial assembly and, 183–87, 186–87*f*; public proclamation of, 66*f*; reactions to, 172, 176–83; Reis ul-ulema and, 190–92; sovereignty and, 73, 170, 175, 190; Tanzimat reforms and, 186–87; views and debates on migration and, 81, 92, 94, 102; Young Turks Movement and, 2, 65–66, 169, 171, 173–74, 176, 182, 197
Arnautović, Mehmed Šerif, 92, 94–95, 193–96
autonomy, 13, 15; annexation and, 165, 179, 185–86, 190–93, 196–97; *ayans* and, 27–29; Berlin Treaty and, 40, 116, 142; claiming of, 190–93; competing empires and, 115, 117; educational autonomy, 13, 62, 115, 145, 153, 155–65, 179, 190, 194, 208, 220; migration and, 62; MNO and, 162–63, 166–67, 185; modernities and, 204, 208–9; nationalism and, 155, 196; negotiating imperial ties and, 145, 153, 155–65; occupation and, 37–39, 40, 43–44; official recognition of, 164–65; Orthodox Christians and, 117, 158; religious autonomy, 13, 15, 62, 153, 155–65, 179, 198, 220; Tanzimat reforms and, 29–30, 204. *See also* identity; sovereignty
ayans, 27–29
Azapagić, Mehmed Teufik, 90–91, 122, 207

Bakarević, Ibrahim, 53–54
Balkan Wars (1912–1913), 72–74, 79, 95, 102, 137, 182–83, 189, 195–96, 226–27
Bašagić, Ibrahim Beg, 207
Bašagić, Safvet Beg, 213, 219–20, 222
Behar (newspaper), 207, 213–14, 222–25
Berlin Treaty (1878), 1–3; aims of, 1–3;

annexation and, 169, 171–73, 175, 178–79; autonomy and, 40, 116, 142; civilizing mission and, 77–78; competing empires and, 109, 114, 116; demographic shifts resulting from, 78; Jews and, 38–39; migration and, 51, 56, 77–78, 88; nationalism and, 33; negotiating imperial ties and, 142, 150, 157, 161; occupation and, 17, 19–22, 31, 33, 36–38; Orthodox Christians and, 116; pious endowments and, 114; reactions to, 19–20; Russo-Ottoman War and, 126; sovereignty and, 2, 36, 51, 77, 88, 108

Bey, Tursun, 23

Biser (periodical), 213–15, 222, 224–26

Bosnia Herzegovina, Habsburg. *See* Muslims in Habsburg Bosnia Herzegovina

Bosnia Herzegovina or Ottoman Alsace-Lorraine (Şadi), 179

Bosnia under Ottomans. *See* Ottoman Bosnia

Bosnia vilayet map, 128*f*

Bosnian diaspora, 47, 143–44, 147

Bosnianism, 30, 93, 201, 224

Bošnjak (newspaper), 190

Bourdieu, Pierre, 10–11

boycott of Austrian goods, 169–70, 176–77, 179

Brkić, Hamza, 74

(br)othering, 9, 103, 105, 107

Bulgaria: annexation and, 174–76; Balkan Wars and, 79; Berlin Treaty and, 114, 122–23, 205; education in, 218; independence of, 56, 170, 173–74; migration and, 17, 54, 56; modernities and, 205–6, 208; Muslim experience in, 2, 6, 103, 131; pious endowments in, 222; religious rhetoric and symbolism used in, 131; Russo-Ottoman War and, 78; views and debates on migration in, 82, 93, 95–96, 102; Young Turks in, 144, 219

Bulgarian Exarchate, 117, 131

Buljina, Harun, 192

Burián, Istvan, 162, 170

caliphate's ties with the community, 17, 129, 131, 144–46, 157, 161, 163, 165, 167, 226–27

Can, Lale, 129

Catholics and Catholicism, 9, 24, 37, 47, 52, 62–65, 94, 117–18, 151, 155–57, 184–85

Ćatić, Musa Ćazim, 223

Čaušević, Džemaludin, 191–93, 196, 199, 212, 221, 226

centralization reforms, 16, 22, 28–29, 41, 57, 88, 92, 139, 144–45, 154, 200, 205

Charity Commission (İane Komisyonu), 79

Christians. *See* Catholics and Catholicism; Orthodox Christians and Christianity

citizenship, 9–10; annexation and, 73, 177, 181, 191; applications for, 68–69; competing empires and, 129; migration and, 52, 68–69, 72; Tanzimat reforms and, 30

civilizing mission, 13, 39–43, 64, 77–78, 147, 206, 211, 228

colonialism, 40, 64–65, 86–87, 103–4, 126–27, 130–31, 158, 210–11

Committee of Union and Progress (CUP), 70, 72, 102, 144, 173, 176, 179, 219. *See also* Young Turks Movement
competing empires, 108–9, 138–39; annexation and, 116, 139; autonomy and, 115, 117; Berlin Treaty and, 109, 114, 116; citizenship and, 129; consuls and, role of, 132–38; continuities amidst, 109–16; education and, 116, 119, 121, 137; Habsburg organization of Islamic community and, 116–25; hajj and, 112–15, 123–25; identity and, 116; image management and, 133; Jews and, 117, 127; land policies and, 111–15; loyalties and, 121, 138–39; *millet* system and, 116; nationalism and, 116; Orthodox Christians and, 116, 134; Pan-Islamism and, 129–30; pious endowments and, 112–15; power of the sultan-caliph and, 125–32; Şeyhülislam and, 122–23; sovereignty and, 108–9, 125–26, 138; Tanzimat reforms and, 120, 131; treading spheres of influence and, 138–39
confessional groups. *See* Catholics and Catholicism; Jews and Judaism; Muslims in Habsburg Bosnia Herzegovina; Orthodox Christians and Christianity
Congress of Vienna (1815), 126
conscription, 2, 40, 52, 58–62, 61*f*, 75–76, 88–89, 109
Constitutional Revolution (1908), 126
consuls, 6, 51, 109, 132–38, 147, 189
continuities, 3, 5, 8, 12–15, 22, 108–16, 137, 142, 170, 202, 227–29
conversions, 24, 62–65, 155–56, 166

Croatia: annexation and, 189, 198; education in, 151, 204; migration and, 71–72; modernities and, 223; Muslim experience in, 9, 193; nationalism and, 9, 30, 42, 71, 193, 196, 198, 204, 224; plays in, 213
CUP. *See* Committee of Union and Progress
Cvijić, Jovan, 105

Dar al-Harb (Domain of War), 81–92, 107
Dar al-Islam (Domain of Peace), 82–88, 90, 107
Davutoğlu, Ahmet, 1
debates on migration. *See* views and debates on migration
de-Islamization, 2, 4, 106, 116
demographic changes resulting from migration, 17, 38, 50–52, 72–74, 77–79, 87, 89, 93–94, 100–103, 107–8
Đikić, Osman, 223
Donia, Robert, 40
Durham, Edith, 37
Džabić, Ali Fehmi, 65, 136, 155–56, 160–61, 163, 171, 190, 264n41
Džemijetul Hajrije (The Benevolent Society), 71

Eastern Question, 3, 31, 41, 50, 78, 133, 174*f*, 187
education: annexation and, 194–95; autonomy and, 13, 62, 115, 145, 153, 155–65, 179, 190, 194, 208, 220; competing empires and, 116, 119, 121, 137; identity and, 215; modernities and, 201–8, 212, 215–19; negotiating imperial ties and, 150–52,

154–55, 163, 166; occupation and, 43, 205; Orthodox Christians and, 117, 158; pious endowments and, 112, 114, 163; Tanzimat reforms and, 29, 204; views and debates on migration and, 82, 92
Eminagić, Agan, 61*f*

Ferik Veliuddin Pasha, 19–20
Fethi, Ibrahim, 97–98
Firdevs, Ali Beg, 159, 162–63, 171
forum shopping, 51, 129
Franz Joseph I, 20, 33, 110, 155, 164–65, 170, 193
Frasëri, Şemseddin Sami, 210

Gajret (newspaper), 207, 213–14, 225
Gasprinski, Ismail Bey, 93, 203
Gradaščević, Husein Kapetan, 29
Greece, 2, 79, 82, 95–96, 102, 104, 170, 175

Habsburg Bosnia Herzegovina, Muslims in. *See* Muslims in Habsburg Bosnia Herzegovina
Hadžiabdić, Refik, 119
Hadžić, Osman Nuri, 159–60, 216, 222–23
Hadžijahić, Muhamed Emin, 88–90
Hadžiomerović, Mustafa Hilmi, 58, 120
Hafız, Seyyid Ahmed, 34
Hajdarpasic, Edin, 9, 42
Hauptmann, Ferdo, 270n101
Hekimoğlu Ali Pasha, 25
hijra, 81–82, 84–88, 90–91, 93, 95, 107
Hilmi Baba, Bosnalı (Hilmi ibn Huseyn Taşlıcavi Bosnevi), 91–92
Huseyn ibn Ali, 236n5

identity, 11, 229; annexation and, 193, 198; Bosnian identity, 30, 93, 201, 224; competing empires and, 116; education and, 215; imperial identity, 42, 116, 127; migration and, 48; modernities and, 201, 215, 219; nationalism and, 30, 42, 84, 198, 201; Ottomanism and, 127; Pan-Islamism and, 228; views and debates on migration and, 93. *See also* autonomy
Ignatyev, Nikolay Pavlovich, 137–38
imagined communities, 8, 202
imperial continuities, 3, 5, 8, 12–15, 22, 108–16, 137, 142, 170, 202, 227–29
intellectuals and intelligentsia, 7–8, 82, 86–88, 92–93, 107, 143–44, 166, 186, 192, 200–203, 207–29
Ippen, Theodor, 242n108
Iqbal, Muhammad, 209, 211
Islamic Community, 17, 165, 190–92
Islamic Community of Kingdom of Yugoslavia (1918–1941), 165
Islamic reform, 6, 81, 203–5, 219–23
Ittihat ve Terraki (Union and Progress) (newspaper), 100

Jews and Judaism: annexation and, 199; Berlin Treaty and, 38–39; competing empires and, 117, 127; conversion and, 158; demographics and, 117; education and, 117; loyalties and, 12, 199; migration and, 77; *millet* system and, 4–5; negotiating imperial ties and, 158; settlement of, 24, 77–78; sovereignty and, 78

Kadić, Muhamed Enveri, 19–20
Kállay, Benjamin von: attempts to separate Muslims from religious leaders by, 120, 144; Bosnianism promoted by, 30; civilizing mission and, 41; competing empires and, 120, 122; education and, 154; migration and, 77; nationalism and, 154; negotiating imperial ties and, 144, 154–55, 157, 160–62; occupation and, 32
Kapetanović, Jašar-beg, 105
Kapić, Ali Ruždi, 190
Karabeg, Mustafa Sidki, 120
Karatodori Pasha, Aleksandros, 34
Karić, Dženita, 124
Karpat, Kemal, 76
Kemal, Namık, 213–14
Khalid, Adeeb, 217
kiraethana (reading rooms), 220, 221*f*
Küçük Kaynarca Treaty (1774), 26

Land Code (1858), 111
Land Law (1858), 30
land policies: annexation and, 179, 181, 186–89; competing empires and, 111–15; hijra and, 95; migration and, 65, 72–75, 77; modernities and, 209; negotiating imperial ties and, 141, 144, 152, 158; occupation and, 31; Orthodox Christians and, 158, 188–89; Ottoman Bosnia and, 24, 30–31; Tanzimat reforms and, 28–31; views and debates on migration and, 95, 100
Latas, Omer Pasha, 29
Law of Sefer (1859), 30, 111
Ljubušak, Mehmed-Beg Kapetanović, 93, 209–12, 216–17, 219, 222, 224
loyalties, 3, 5–12; annexation and, 191, 193–97; belonging and, 10; competing empires and, 121, 138–39; Jews and, 12; migration and, 16, 51, 57, 73; MNO and, 183, 185–86; modernities and, 211, 224; nationalism and, 8–10, 198; negotiating imperial ties and, 142, 147, 162; nuance of, 10; occupation and, 3, 5–6, 38, 41–42, 48; Reis ul-ulema and, 121; scholarship on, 11–12; views and debates on migration and, 97, 107. *See also* allegiances

Macedonia: annexation and, 175; colonization and, 72, 74; migration and, 56–57, 72, 74, 79; nationalism in, 70, 171; Young Turks Movement and, 72, 173, 182
Marx, Karl, 3
media, 17, 42, 51, 54, 82–83, 92, 129, 169–73, 177–79, 203–5, 210, 212–15
Medžlis-i ulema (council of scholars), 118, 120–21, 160, 164, 190
Mehmed Ali, Kavalalı, 29
Mehmed Fatih II, 23
Mehmed Vehbi Šemsekadić, 21, 65
Merhamet (Compassion) (charitable society), 220–21
Midhat Pasha, 205
migration, 5–7, 49–52, 77–80; annexation and, 65–70, 66*f*, 72–73; autonomy and, 62; Balkan Wars and, 72–74, 79; Berlin Treaty and, 51, 56, 77–78, 88; Bosnian diaspora and, 47, 143–44, 147; causes of, 49–52, 57–62, 65, 75; citizenship and, 52, 68–69, 72; colonization and, 64–65; conscription as motivation

for, 58–62, 61f, 75; conversions and, 62–65; demographic changes resulting from, 17, 38, 50–52, 72–74, 77–79; identity and, 48; instigating of, 70–73; Jews and, 77; land policies and, 65, 72–75, 77, 95, 100; laws banning forced conversions and, 63; loyalties and, 16, 51, 57, 73; nationalism and, 63, 83–84; occupation and, 38–39, 45–47, 52–58; Orthodox Christians and, 52–53, 58, 60, 62–63, 71–72, 78; Ottoman stance toward, 51, 54–56, 59–60, 66–72, 77–80; refugees and, 36, 39, 51, 53–56, 70, 77–79; return migration, 73–77; settlement areas for, 56–57, 71; size of, 75–77, 79; Young Turks Movement and, 65–66, 70. *See also* views and debates on migration

millet system, 4–5, 7, 116, 199, 202

Mitchell, Timothy, 272n3

MNO. *See* Muslim People's Organization

mobilization, 17–18, 153–62, 166–68

modernities, 7, 10–11, 15–16, 200–203, 228–29; associational life and, 219–23; autonomy and, 204, 208–9; Bosnianism and, 7, 15–16, 224; civilizing mission and, 11, 206, 228; colonization and, 210–11; constitution and, 193; continuities and, 228–29; economic thinking and, 222; education and, 201–8, 212, 215–19; European history and, 16, 18; Habsburg modernization, 205–9; identity and, 201, 215, 219; ideologies and, 223–28; Islamic reform and, 203–5, 219–23; land policies and, 209; loyalties and, 211, 224; Muslim modernity, 11, 15, 200, 203; nationalism and, 223–28; Ottoman modernization, 203–5; Pan-Islamism and, 7, 221, 223–25, 227–28; press and, 210, 212–15; print and, 210, 212–15; reformists and, 209–11; Russo-Ottoman War and, 205; Tanzimat reforms and, 203–4, 218, 227; women and, 214–15; yearbooks and, 206–7

Montenegro: annexation and, 197; Balkan Wars and, 79; Berlin Treaty and, 38, 114; border regions awarded to, 4, 37; boycott of Austrian goods and, 177; migration and, 52, 56, 59–60; occupation and, 26–27, 39; Orthodox Christians in, 39; views and debates on migration and, 95, 102; war against Ottoman Empire declared by, 31, 79

Muhacir (newspaper), 100

Muhacirin Komisyonu (Migrants Commission), 79

Muhammad, Prophet, 81, 84–86, 90–91, 113

Muhammad 'Abduh, 208, 225

Mulabdić, Edhem, 215

Musavat (Equality) (newspaper), 71, 164, 190

Muslim loyalties. *See* loyalties

Muslim People's Organization (MNO): annexation and, 171, 183–85, 190; autonomy and, 162–63, 166–67, 185; founding of, 162; loyalties and, 183, 185–86; negotiating imperial ties and, 164, 166–67

Muslim Progressive Party (Muslimanska Napredna Stranka), 171

314 Index

Muslims in Habsburg Bosnia Herzegovina, 1–18; autonomy, 8–12; Berlin Treaty, 1–3; Bosnia Herzegovina lost, 1–2; contributions of volume, 3, 6, 10–16; de-Islamization, 2, 4; Eastern Question, 3–4; European history, 16, 18; identity, 11; loyalties, 8–12; methodological approach of volume, 12–15; migration, 5–7, 10; *millet* system, 5, 7; modernities, 7, 10–11, 16; neo-Ottomanism, 1–2; Orientalism, 3–4; public opinion, 7; response to occupation, 5–6; revisionist literature, 6–7; scholarship, 4, 9–10, 12–14; scope of volume, 15–18; structure of volume, 15–18; studies and sources for volume, 12–15; tracing imperial continuities, 12–15; Young Turks Movement, 6

Mustafa Ali, 24

Muvazene (newspaper), 93, 216

nationalism, 8–9; autonomy and, 155, 196; Berlin Treaty and, 33; (br) othering and, 9, 103, 107; competing empires and, 116; identity and, 30, 42, 84, 198, 201; loyalties and, 8–10, 198; migration and, 63; modernities and, 223–28; occupation and, 42; Orthodox Christians and, 9, 64; Pan-Islamism and, 130, 199; process of nationalization, 8–9, 13, 155, 193, 198; views and debates on migration and, 83–84, 102–7. *See also* Pan-Islamism; Young Turks Movement

Nationality Law (1869), 45–46

negotiating imperial ties, 140–42, 166–68; activism and, 153–62; annexation and, 164; autonomy and, 145, 153, 155–65; Berlin Treaty and, 142, 150, 157, 161; Bosnian diaspora and, 143–44, 147; caliphate and, 162–65; civilizing mission and, 147; colonization and, 158; discourse of silence and, 145; education and, 150–52, 154–55, 163, 166; Jews and, 158; land policies and, 141, 144, 152, 158; loyalties and, 142, 147, 162; MNO and, 164, 166–67; mobilization and, 153–62, 166–68; Orthodox Christians and, 153, 158–59; petitioning the sultan and, 145–53, 149*f*; Reis ul-ulema and, 163–65; Şeyhülislam and, 163–65; sovereignty and, 141–42, 147, 152–53, 163–64, 166–67; transregional constellations and, 142–45; Young Turks Movement and, 144, 160–61, 164

Nigar Hanım, 214

Noradonkyan, Gabriyel, 177

Novi Pazar Sandžak, 4, 36, 56, 67

Nuri, Tırnovalı Osman, 215

Obrenović, Milan, 29, 103

occupation, 1–8, 19–22, 47–48; annexation contrasted with, 44–45; autonomy and, 37–39, 40, 43–44; *ayans* and, 27–29; becoming Habsburg and, 47–48; Berlin Treaty and, 17, 19–22, 31, 33, 36–38; civilizing mission of, 39–43; context prior to, 22–31; education and, 43, 205; expanding Habsburg influence and, 39–47; land policies and, 31; loyalties and, 3, 5–6, 38, 41–42, 48; migration and, 38–39, 45–47, 52–58; Muslim life prior to, 22–31; nationalism and, 42; negotiating mandates and, 32–39; Orientalism and, 32, 43; Orthodox Christians and, 19–20, 47; Ottoman responses to, 19–20, 33–40; provincial subject status in, 45–47; public opinion and, 33–34; resistance to, 5–6, 19–22, 21, 21f, 31, 34–36; sovereignty and, 22, 36–40, 43, 46; Tanzimat reforms and, 27–30, 43

Omanović, Fata, 62

Orientalism, 3–4, 32, 43

Orthodox Christians and Christianity: annexation and, 179–80, 184–86, 188–89; autonomy and, 117, 158; Berlin Treaty and, 116; competing empires and, 116, 134; conversion and, 62; education and, 117, 158; land policies and, 158, 188–89; migration and, 52–53, 58, 60, 62–63, 71–72, 78; *millet* system and, 4–5; nationalism and, 9, 64; negotiating imperial ties and, 153, 158–59; occupation and, 19–20, 47; Patriarch of, 116; settlement of, 24–26; views and debates on migration and, 103, 105

Ottoman Bosnia, 22–31; *ayans* and, 27–29; Bosnianism in, 30; cultural and economic aspects of, 23–25; *devşirme* in, 24; establishment of, 22–23; Janissary corps in, 28; Jews in, 24; land policies in, 24, 30–31; Muslim life in, 22–31; Orthodox Christians in, 24–25, 30; reorganization in, 25; social reforms in, 27–31; sovereignty in, 23; strategic role of, 22–23; Sufi brotherhoods in, 24; Tanzimat reforms in, 28–31; *timar* system in, 24; uprisings in, 29–31

Ottoman Council of Ministers, 55, 66, 77, 96

Ottoman Public Debt Administration, 126

Ottomanism, 1, 127, 193

Pallavicini, Johann von, 177
Pan-Islamism, 6, 107, 129–31, 192, 199, 221, 223–25, 227–28
Pan-Slavism, 6, 57, 63, 84, 133, 136, 138, 196
Paris Treaty (1856), 39
party politics, 167, 170, 184–90
Paşa, Mirliva Hüsnü, 150
Pazarićanin, Osman Beg Ajnić, 67
petitions, 10, 13, 16, 42, 54–55, 96–97, 145–53, 149f. *See also* negotiating imperial ties
Pfanner, Franz, 247n67
pious endowments, 23, 112–15, 119, 136, 154–55, 157, 163–64, 166–67, 185, 191, 207
political mobilization, 17–18, 153–62, 166–68
Pračić, Rifat, 68
print and press, 17, 42, 51, 54, 82–83, 92, 129, 169–73, 177–79, 203–5, 210, 212–15
provincial assembly, 17, 30, 111, 183–87, 186–87f, 191–93, 197, 204
public opinion, 7, 30, 33–35, 64, 132–33, 135, 146, 153, 157–58, 176, 205, 227

Rabinow, Paul, 201
Reform Edict (1856), 28
reforms. *See* Islamic reform; modernities; Tanzimat reforms
refugees, 36, 39, 51, 53–56, 70, 77–79, 83, 87–88, 97, 127, 182–83, 226
Reis ul-ulema, 118, 120–23, 160, 163–65, 185, 190–93, 196, 207
religious communities. *See* Catholics and Catholicism; Jews and Judaism; Muslims in Habsburg Bosnia Herzegovina; Orthodox Christians and Christianity
Rescript of the Rose Chamber (1839), 28
Resul Efendi, 182
Rida, Muhammad Rashid, 16, 81–84, 87, 203
Risala fi al-hijra (Treatise on Migration) (Azapagić), 90–91
Rizvanbegović-Stočević, Mehmed Ali, 143
Russia: annexation and, 170, 172–73; Berlin Treaty and, 38; education in, 217–18; Jews in, 77; migration and, 51–52, 77–78; nationalism in, 8; religious hierarchy in, 119; spheres of influence and, 22; views and debates on migration and, 91, 93, 95, 102
Russo-Ottoman War (1877–1878), 31, 39, 78, 126, 205, 218

Sadrazam Kamil Pasha, 180
Saffet Pasha, 110
Said, Edward, 43
Šarac, Hafız Sulejman, 164, 190–91
Sarajlija, Mustafa, 71
Schmid, Ferdinand, 76
Seferović, Nina, 243n2
Serbia: annexation and, 37, 171–72, 177–78, 198; autonomy and, 104, 178; Balkan Wars and, 79; Berlin Treaty and, 38, 102; boycott of Austrian goods and, 177; Jews in, 39; migration and, 39, 52–54, 56–57; Muslim experience in, 2, 105; nationalism and, 9, 102–6, 159, 185, 204; negotiating imperial ties and, 160; Orientalism and, 255n83; Orthodox Christians in, 60, 188; protest in, 178; views and debates on migration and, 95–96, 98, 102–5, 107, 114; war against Ottoman Empire declared by, 31
Servet-i Fünun (Wealth of knowledge) (newspaper), 169, 213
Şeyhülislam, 95–96, 116, 119–23, 157, 162–65, 190, 194, 208
Sistova Treaty (1791), 26
sovereignty, 5, 8, 11–13, 15–17; annexation and, 73, 170, 175, 190; Berlin Treaty and, 2, 36, 51, 77, 88, 108; competing empires and, 108–9, 125–26, 138; Jews and, 78; migration and, 51–52, 55–56, 58, 67; negotiating imperial ties and, 141–42, 147, 152–53, 163–64, 166–67; occupation and, 22, 36–40, 43, 46; Pan-Islamism and, 107, 129; petitions and, 152–53; views and debates on migration and, 83, 86, 88, 96. *See also* autonomy
Spaho, Fehim, 224
Srpska Riječ (newspaper), 71
Stadler, Archbishop, 62–63
subjecthood, 9, 46, 142
Sulejmanpašić, Rifat Beg, 75
Süleyman Efendi, 181

Tanin (newspaper), 169, 176
Tanzimat reforms, 28–31; annexation and, 186–87; autonomy and, 29–30, 204; citizenship and, 30; competing empires and, 120, 131; education and, 29, 204; establishment of, 28; as foundation for modernization, 29–30; land policies and, 28–31; modernities and, 203–4, 218, 227; occupation and, 27–30, 43; in Ottoman Bosnia, 28–31; Pan-Islamism and, 131
Tarabar, Muhamed Zahirudin, 81–82, 87
Tercüman (newspaper), 64, 93, 177, 225
Teskeredžić, Muharem-Beg, 155
Three Emperors' League, 44
timar system, 24–25, 27
Todorova, Maria, 4, 43
Topal Şerif Osman Pasha, 30, 204
Treaty of Küçük Kaynarca (1774), 26
Turhan Pasha, 173

vakuf, 23, 112–15, 119, 136, 154–55, 157, 163–64, 166–67, 185, 191, 207
Vatan (Homeland) (newspaper), 71, 89, 207, 225
Vienna, Congress of (1815), 126
views and debates on migration, 81–84; annexation and, 81, 92, 94, 102; Balkwan Wars and, 95; colonization and, 86–87, 100, 107; *Dar al-Harb* and, 81–92, 107; *Dar al-Islam* and, 83–88, 90, 107; debates in Bosnia Herzegovina on, 88–95; demographic changes and, 87, 89, 93–94, 100–103, 107–8; education and, 82, 92; hijra as an Islamic concept, 84–88, 90, 107; identity and, 93; imperial diversity and, 106–7; land policies and, 95, 100; loyalties and, 97, 107; nationalism and, 83–84, 102–7; Orthodox Christians and, 103, 105; Ottoman attitudes toward, 95–102, 99*f*; refugees and, 83, 87–88, 97; Serbia and, 102–7; sovereignty and, 83, 86, 88, 96; World War I and, 101–2

Wolff, Larry, 43
women and girls, 62, 95, 112–13, 155–56, 191, 203, 214–15

Yalman, Ahmet Emin, 80
Young Turks Movement: annexation and, 2, 65–66, 169, 171, 173–74, 176, 182, 197; boycott of Austrian goods and, 169; colonization policies of, 70, 72; development of, 173; lack of major cell in Bosnia Herzegovina of, 144; migration and, 65–66, 70, 72; negotiating imperial ties and, 144, 160–61, 164
Yugoslavia, 17, 31, 165

Zvijezda (scholars' association), 180, 220

The authorized representative in the EU for product safety and compliance is:
Mare Nostrum Group
B.V Doelen 72
4831 GR Breda
The Netherlands